Microsoft ®

Windows 2000 Server
Exam 70-215

Copyright - Editions ENI - May 2000
ISBN: 2-7460-0986-2
Original edition: 2-7460-0806-8

ENI Publishing LTD

500 Chiswick High Road
London W4 5RG

Tel. 020 8956 2320
Fax. 020 8956 2321
e-mail: publishing@ediENI.com
http: //www.publishing-eni.com

Editions ENI

BP 32125
44021 NANTES CEDEX 1

Tel. 33.2.51.80.15.15
Fax. 33.2.51.80.15.16
e-mail: editions@ediENI.com
http: //www.editions-eni.com

Collection directed by Joëlle Musset

Preparation for the MCSE exam 70-215
Microsoft Windows 2000 Server

This book is designed to provide effective assistance to a student preparing for the MCSE exam on the Microsoft Windows 2000 operating system.

For optimal assimilation of the topics covered, the book is divided into sixteen chapters, which are structured as follows :

- Statement of **objectives**: a precise enumeration of the skills acquired by a student who has completed the chapter.
- A **theoritical exposé** of the topic: defines the tems and concepts involved and gives an overview of the main themes of the chapter.
- **Practical application** of the theory: shows precisely how to set up the configuration on a machine (screen shots and diagrams).
- **Labs**: grouped together at the end of the book, the labs provide concrete examples of specific parts of the course, which the student works through on his/her computer.
- **Assessment** of skills: each chapter ends with a set of between 10 and 50 questions either directly related to the chapter, or linking the topic in the current chapter to one discussed earlier, prompting the student to make the synthesis (in a separate section, the questions are reiterated along with their answers and relevant comments). There are almost 370 questions on the topics fundamental to master the Windows 2000 Server environment.

Introduction Chapter 1

Installing Windows 2000 Advanced Server Chapter 2

Configuring the system Chapter 3

Administration tools and the MMC Chapter 4

Printer management Chapter 9

Managing disk resources Chapter 10

Configuring disks, partitions and volumes Chapter 11

Labs

Index

Prerequisites for this chapter

☒ Operating systems and networking essentials.

Objectives

At the end of this chapter, you will be able to:

☒ Understand the difference between co-operative and pre-emptive multitasking systems.

☒ Explain what is meant by multithreading, multiprocessing and portability.

☒ Understand the architecture of Windows 2000.

☒ Describe the different Windows 2000 platforms.

Contents

Introduction

A. Overview of Windows 2000 operating systems

Before you start looking at Windows 2000, you must note that this is by no means a completely new operating system. Windows 2000 is an evolved version of the Windows NT 4.0 system that draws on Microsoft's experience in the fields of servers and operating systems. However, Windows 2000 is the biggest server development that Microsoft has undertaken since 1993. This operating system benefits from increased power, increased reliability and increased security. Under Windows 2000, administration is easier. In addition, flexible administration tools that can be fully customized assist these tasks.

In order fully to understand the characteristics of Microsoft operating systems, a few concepts must be defined.

First, this chapter will describe multitasking. It will clearly distinguish between co-operative and pre-emptive multitasking. Next, multithreading will be studied, and this will be followed by multiprocessing. When you examine multiprocessing, you will discover how asymmetric multiprocessing can be used in order to improve fault tolerance

1. Pre-emptive and co-operative multitasking

Multitasking is the ability of an operating system to manage several programs at once. It allocates processor time to each of the programs in turn, so that they can execute. This means that devices and memory must be shared so that the programs can use them. Multitasking can be implemented in two ways: co-operative multitasking and pre-emptive multitasking.

With **co-operative multitasking**, one of the applications that is running on the operating system uses the processor (together with the associated resources). Then, the application frees the processor, and allows the next application in the queue to use it. Each task depends on the others. This means that if a task goes into a loop, or gets blocked, then it will pause all the applications, and it will sometimes even pause the operating system itself. This implementation is used with 16-bit Windows systems.

With **pre-emptive multitasking**, each application uses the processor either for a pre-determined time period, or until another application is given a higher priority than that of the current application. Scheduling and allocation of CPU time for current applications is handled by the operating system without consulting applications that have already run.

Consequently, if an application locks up, it loses its initial processor time and is put to one side, without blocking the system or the other applications. The sharing of the processor and resources (such as printer ports and the keyboard) between applications is managed by the operating system.

2. Multithreading

Multithreading is implemented during the development of a software application, and is managed by the operating system. A thread can be an executable unit, or a part of a program. It can even be the entire program if the application does not offer multithreading.

Multithreading means that several tasks can be carried out "simultaneously", within the same application. With Word for example, when you enter text, the characters are displayed with the required formatting, and any spelling mistakes are corrected at the same time. Furthermore, threads in the same process share the same memory space.

3. Multiprocessing

Multiprocessing is the ability of the operating system to use the processors that are present in the workstation, in order to manage the Windows 2000 system and to run the applications. There are two types of multiprocessing:
- Asymmetric multiprocessing (ASMP): one processor is reserved for the system while the others are used for the applications.
- Symmetric multiprocessing (SMP): execution requests that are made by the operating system and by applications are distributed amongst the different processors. In this case, the system will always have a percentage of free processor time.

The multiprocessing facilities in Windows 2000 are vastly superior to those in NT 4.0. Furthermore, you can now use the task manager so as to link a given process to a given processor.

4. Microsoft Windows 2000 architecture

Windows 2000 is a multitask, multithread 32-bit operating system with SMP architecture.

Windows 2000 is made up of layered operating systems and micro-kernel based client/server systems. The grouping together of these two technologies has allowed two parts of Windows 2000 to be distinguished: **execute (or kernel) mode**, and **user (or application) mode**.

a. Kernel mode

Kernel mode groups together the set of system components that run in this mode. These components are called executive services and have priority in the use of the processor. The kernel plays a key role, as it is responsible for providing the applications with memory, for choosing the processes that must be run at a specific time, and for communicating with the peripherals. The applications depend on the kernel for all their needs. This means that they do not come into direct contact with the peripheral devices, which prevents them from provoking system failure. It must be noted that the Windows 2000 kernel is a development of the Windows NT 4.0 kernel and features improvements such as the handling of several user sessions on the same machine (which allows Windows 2000 to act as a terminal server), and the addition of processor quotas in order to meet the needs of Internet Information Server 5 (such as the ability of controlling the amount of processor time that is granted to each Web site, and the logging of the CPU cycles that are used for each Web query).

Unlike that of Windows NT 4.0, the Windows 2000 kernel supports WDM (*Windows Driver Model*) architecture. This is a new driver model that allows you to use the same drivers on Windows 98 and on Windows 2000. Whilst on Windows NT 4.0 the applications run most of their tasks in user mode, WDM architecture allows these jobs to be transposed into kernel mode, thus allowing them to run quicker. However, in order to take advantage of this feature, applications must be specifically written for this purpose.

Windows 2000 supports EMA (*Enterprise Memory Architecture*), which allows applications to use up to 32 GB of memory. This is a very useful feature for database servers that manage large amounts of data. This is because data can be handled much quicker in RAM than on disk.

☞ *In order to benefit from this architecture, your hardware must support it. In addition, the applications must be developed in a specific way. SQL Server is an example of an application that can use this feature.*

Kernel mode is equipped with a Plug-and-Play module that reduces the time that is required to configure the hardware. In addition, kernel mode offers an energy management module that runs on OnNow/ACPI technology and that reduces the energy that is consumed by the users.

The improvements that have been made to the kernel allow Windows 2000 to operate in cluster mode (two machines that can take over from one another in the case of a problem).

Finally, it must be noted that kernel mode has been developed so as to support any application, whatever the language that is used. To this end, Windows 2000 uses UNICODE, which is a standard that defines a correspondence between bytes and characters. Unlike the ANSI standard that requires an operating system to be developed for each language, UNICODE allows you to use a single source, irrespective of the language that is used. This feature means that you can change the language of the interface without restarting the machine.

b. User mode

Unlike kernel mode, user mode groups together protected sub-systems that underlie user applications. User mode processes do not have direct access to the hardware; they are limited to a memory area that is allocated to them, and they are processed with a low priority level. One of the major developments of Windows 2000 user mode is the presence of Active Directory in the security sub-system.

B. Windows 2000 Server

The Windows 2000 range comprises four platforms:
– Windows 2000 Professional,
– Windows 2000 Server,
– Windows 2000 Advanced Server,
– Windows 2000 Datacenter Server.
Windows 2000 Professional is a workstation product, whilst the three other platforms are Windows 2000 server products. This section describes these different versions, and specifies for each of them, their role in a company and the hardware capacities that are required.

1. Windows 2000 Professional

The purpose of this operating system is progressively to replace Windows 98 and Windows NT 4.0. Windows 2000 Professional combines the simplicity of using Windows 98 with the performance reliability of Windows NT 4.0. In addition, it offers new features that allow you to optimize such aspects as resource access and security in a Windows 2000 domain environment. Furthermore, this operating system offers other features such as plug-and-play, energy options, the new WDM drivers, and the recognition of over 6500 hardware devices.

Introduction

Resource access

Windows 2000 Professional supports the Active Directory client. This provides access to the resources of the directory database (according to the permissions that have been granted). It also provides access to the resources that are contained in a DFS *(Distributed File System)* topology. This allows users to carry out searches in Active Directory in order to find an item such as a printer, a contact, a person or a shared directory, by knowing only one characteristic of the object concerned (such as the name, the location or the telephone number).

Users of portable computers will find it easier to work on documents that are stored on the network. Thanks to **work offline** technology, users can work transparently on their documents via the network in the same way as they would work with local files. Thereby, it is ensured that they will always have an up-to-date version of the document, thanks to a synchronization mechanism that runs upon opening and closing a session. In addition they can use the Networking Connection Wizard in order to set up a secure connection to their company network easily, using a remote connection, or simply by creating a VPN *(Virtual Private Network)* via the Internet. Also, IPP *(Internet Printing Protocol)* allows mobile users to print documents via the Internet on their printers in their offices.

Simplified installation

When you are implementing a network architecture, one of the longest phases is the installation of the workstations. As network administrator, you will save time when then install Windows 2000. You can install a Windows 2000 Professional workstation without leaving your office, thanks to a remote installation service that is supplied with the server versions of Windows 2000. This service is called RIS *(Remote Installation Service)*. Other techniques are also provided in order to reduce the time that you spend in installing workstations. These include the **sysprep.exe** utility, which can be used in order to duplicate the image of a disk on other workstations, using a disk duplication tool from a third-party manufacturer.

Previously, you had to fill in several fields and select several options during the installation process, which meant that you had to stay in front of your computer. The new graphic installation script creation utility allows you to create files that provide responses automatically during the installation process.

File systems

Here again, Windows 2000 is more developed than Windows NT 4.0, as the latter operating system recognizes only FAT16 and NTFS file systems. In addition, Windows 2000 supports the FAT32 file system (that is used by Windows 95 OSR2 and Windows 98 systems).

Furthermore, NTFS has evolved with the version 5.0 that is offered in Windows 2000. The features that are offered with this version include file encryption, disk quota management and distributed link tracking.

Utilities such as Disk Defragmenter, Disk Cleanup and Scandisk allow you to maintain optimal space usage on your disks.

A major development of the backup manager must also be noted. The new backup manager allows you to backup data to different media such as tapes, recordable CD-ROMs, logical disks, ZIP drives and external hard disks. An integrated backup planning utility simplifies the design of a backup plan.

Security

Security is important for all computing networks. Windows 2000 provides a marked improvement in this field. Amongst the numerous security improvements, a major advance concerns file encryption on NTFS 5 volumes. This public key / private key encryption technique means that only by the user who encrypted a document will be allowed to read it. This is done transparently (the document is decrypted automatically without any user intervention). This function is added to the NTFS permissions. However, this feature does not allow you to encrypt documents when you transmit them on the network. The **IPSec** protocol allows you to encrypt all IP traffic within the same LAN, as with a non secure network such as using VPNs on the Internet. It must be noted that the IPSec (*IP Security*) standard was developed by the IETF (*Internet Engineering Task Force*) and allows any system that uses IPSec to communicate thereby ensuring secure IP traffic.

Although versions of Windows NT authenticate using the NTLM protocol, Windows 2000 uses the Kerberos v5 protocol in order to authenticate users. Windows 2000 still supports NTLM protocol for backward compatibility reasons. Thus, a Windows 2000 Workstation that is integrated in a Windows NT4 domain will be authenticated by NTLM. The Kerberos authentication method is quicker and more secure than NTLM. In addition, as it is a standard, a UNIX host can be authenticated by a Windows 2000 domain controller by having an account in Active Directory. Kerberos is also used for authentication across inter-domain trust relationships.

☞ *For more information, see RFC 1510, which describes the Kerberos protocol.*

Minimal configuration
- 166 MHz processor
- 32 MB of RAM (64 MB is recommended).
- 685 MB of disk space. You should allow 1 GB in order to allow for future system development.

It is very important to know the hardware items that make up your computer. These hardware items must be included in the Hardware Compatibility List (HCL), so as to ensure the correct functioning of your system.

If you intend to upgrade your old system (Windows 95/98 or NT Workstation), you can use the command **winnt32.exe /checkupgradeonly**, so as to make a list of the hardware items on your workstation that will not be supported by Windows 2000.

2. Windows 2000 Server

The Windows 2000 Server version offers all the features of Windows 2000 Professional, uses the strong points of Windows NT 4.0 Server, and provides numerous additional features, all of which makes it a formidable enterprise server.

a. Characteristics

Adapting to large networks

Windows 2000 was originally designed to manage very big networks. It meets all administration needs by organizing domains into administrative units. Even for very big networks, a single domain is sufficient. This is because the Windows 2000 directory database allows you to store several million objects (such as user accounts and computer accounts).

Active Directory Service

One of the major new features of Windows 2000 Server is that it manages network objects using a directory. Previously, user accounts, computer accounts and groups were stored in a database called SAM. This database resided on the primary domain controller and a copy was kept on the backup domain controllers. When the primary domain controller was unavailable, users could still open a session on the domain, but the SAM could not be modified without promoting a backup domain controller. In addition, administration was limited by the number of objects that could not exceed 40 000.

The Active Directory database is duplicated on all the Windows 2000 domain controllers, each of which has a read/write copy. This feature enhances fault tolerance. This approach simplifies administration and ensures the development capacity of the system. The total cost of ownership (TCO) is very competitive. This is because the group strategies belong to Active Directory, which limits the time that is required in order to configure each client machine concerning distribution of applications and to set up user working environments. An additional strong point of active directory is that it uses a set of standard protocols. This makes it compatible with any other system. These protocols include the Domain Name System (DNS) and the LDAP protocol for database access.

Administrative tools

Although a number of administration tools are provided as standard, Windows 2000 offers Microsoft Management Console (MMC), which allows you to customize and to create several consoles so as to meet your administration needs. Thereby, you have all the tools that you require.

Enhancing network services

Apart from the supplementary services that are available with Windows 2000, such as the index service, the certificate service, the remote installation service (RIS) and the remote storage service, some services have been markedly improved. For example the DDNS (*Dynamic DNS*) that authorizes DNS and DHCP clients to register with a DNS server automatically. Again the TCO is reduced in this case. This is because the administrator no longer need be concerned by the update of the DNS database, as this item develops according to the clients. Integrating DNS zones into Active Directory provides fault tolerance and load sharing.

The DHCP service is also optimized so as to help clients to register with the DNS server. The class extensions allow you to attribute configurations according to criteria such as that of belonging to a class. You can also create super-extensions and multicast extensions.

Internet services have also been improved thanks to the Windows 2000 kernel, which supports processor quotas and the different supplementary features such as IPP (*Internet Printing Protocol*), which allows you to print via the Internet, and the reservation of bandwidth for Web sites.

Introduction

Remote network access

Increasingly, companies need to access remote networks via, telephone lines, the Internet, X25 networks, Frame Relay networks, ATM or ISDN. These requirements are met by standard versions of Windows 2000. These provide a very effective, remote access service that allows you act as remote access server and VPN *(Virtual Private Network)* server. The security is ensured on the IP transit level, in the tunnel that is created by PPTP or L2TP protocols, and on authentication level.

Backup

The backup utility that is supplied with Windows 2000 is now comparable to tools that are supplied by specialists in this field. Using a graphic calendar, you can program all types of backup.

A major advantage of this utility is that it allows you to make a full backup of your system and to restore a server without losing information. Active Directory objects can be restored also.

Network monitor

The network monitor is derived from that which is delivered with SMS. It allows you to capture frames that are being transmitted on the network. You can do this by filtering them, either according to specific protocols, or according to specific machines or according to specific contents. This is an essential tool that allows you to understand and to analyze your network. It will help you to solve problems in many situations.

Windows 2000 a veritable router

In addition to the implementation of RIP v2, the routing features of Windows 2000 have been enhanced by the use of OSPF *(Open Shortest Path First)*, which is a widely used, link state routing protocol. RIP is used with smaller networks. whilst OSPF is more suitable for large networks.

Terminal Services

The features of Windows NT 4 Terminal Edition are offered by the Windows 2000 Server versions in the form of a service. This service provides a Windows 2000 desktop to users who have machines that are not powerful, and that do not support 32-bit applications. The desktop along with the applications that are run by the user in the terminal server session, are run entirely on the server. In addition, administrators can install Terminal Server services with the sole objective of remotely administering servers.

b. Minimal configuration

– 166 MHz processor
– 64 MB of RAM (128 MB is recommended).
– 685 MB of disk space. You should allow 1 GB in order to allow for future system development.

It is very important to know the hardware items that make up your computer. These hardware items must be included in the Hardware Compatibility List (HCL), so as to ensure the correct functioning of your system.

3. Windows 2000 Advanced Server

The Windows 2000 Advanced Server version offers the same features as the Server version. In addition, Advanced Server allows you to organize several servers into a cluster configuration. The advantage of this feature is that users can access services 24 hours a day, as, if one server fails, the other server in the cluster will take over automatically. Similarly, if an application fails, you can start it on the other server. In addition to fault tolerance features, organizing machines into a cluster configuration allows you to spread the workload for network services such as Web services.

This Windows 2000 version is more suitable than the Server version, for the processing of large volumes of information (for example, for databases, transactions or for decision aids). This capacity is provided by the EMA (*Enterprise Memory Architecture*), which allows Windows 2000 to manage up to 8 GB of RAM on Intel.

SMP features allow Windows 2000 Advanced Server to run on 8 processors.

4. Windows 2000 Datacenter Server

Windows 2000 Datacenter Server is characterized by the SMP, which can be configured so as to allow a Windows 2000 server to manage up to 32 processors. This version can manage up to 64 GB of RAM on Intel systems.

Of course, the Datacenter Server version offers all the features that are supported by Windows 2000 Server, along with the cluster configuration and the workload distribution features.

Prerequisites for this chapter

☒ Knowledge of the main components of a computer: memory, hard disk, processor, file systems, files and directories.

☒ Experience of the micro-computing environment: device configuration options.

☒ Knowledge of IDE and SCSI peripherals.

☒ Knowledge of an operating system.

Objectives

At the end of this chapter, you will be able to:

☒ Describe the information that you need in order to install Windows 2000: role of the HCL, system and boot partitions, FAT16-FAT32 and NTFS file systems, licensing mode and required hardware configuration.

☒ Install Windows 2000 by different methods: using a CD-ROM and using the network.

☒ Use switches associated with the commands winnt.exe and winnt32.exe.

☒ Use **setup manager** in order to create answer files for installations without interactive delays.

☒ Use **sysprep.exe** in order to prepare the disk so as to create an image of it.

☒ Join a domain.

☒ Troubleshoot installation problems.

Installing Windows 2000 Advanced Server

Contents

A. Required configuration

1. Minimal hardware requirements

You can install Microsoft Windows 2000 Advanced Server in different ways. Whichever method you choose, you must carry out a series of tasks that is called the « **pre-installation** ». If you carry out these tasks you will save a lot of time.

First you must check that the hardware that will be used is referenced in the hardware compatibility list (HCL) that is supplied by Microsoft. In fact, a hardware item that in not included in this list could make the operating system malfunction, and cause you to lose time in diagnosing the problem. You can find a copy of this HCL (**HCL.txt**) on the Windows 2000 CD-ROM, in the **support** directory.

Alternatively, it is available on the Internet at the address http://www.microsoft.com/hwtest/hcl.

Amongst the pre-installation tasks, it is useful to list certain information such as the choice of licensing mode, how your disks are partitioned, the choice of file systems and the role that your server plays (stand-alone or member server).

<u>Minimal configuration required for the installation</u>
<u>of Microsoft Windows 2000 - Server versions:</u>

- Processor: Pentium 166 MHZ.
- 64 MB of RAM (128 MB is recommended) for Intel type computers.
- 1.2 GB of disk space for the system partition (2 GB is recommended so as to accommodate future system evolution).
- Standard VGA graphic card
- Network adapter.
- Keyboard, mouse or other pointer peripheral.
- CD-ROM drive, floppy-disk drive (optional).

2. Knowledge of hardware components

Although Windows 2000 automatically detects and configures your peripherals when it is installed, it is useful to know these components.

Type of card	Required Information
Video	reference and bus width (at least VGA)
Network	IRQ, I/O address, type of connector (e.g. BNC, TP or AUI), DMA (if used)
SCSI controller	model, bus width, IRQ
Mouse	Type, port (COM1, COM2, bus or PS/2)
Sound	IRQ, I/O address, DMA
External modem	port used (e.g. COM1 or COM2.)
Internal modem	mod, port used or IRQ and I/O address (for non-standard configurations)

IRQ occupation table > hardware IRQs:

IRQ 0 System clock

IRQ 1 Keyboard

IRQ 2 Redirected towards IRQ 8 to IRQ 15, sometimes useable

IRQ 3 Serial port COM2

IRQ 4 Serial port COM1

IRQ 5 Parallel port LPT2: often available

IRQ 6 Floppy-disk controller

IRQ 7 Parallel port LPT1:

IRQ 8 Real time clock

IRQ 9 Available

IRQ 10 Available

IRQ 11 Available, unless SCSI

IRQ 12 Available

IRQ 13 Math coprocessor; available if the processor is a 486 SX

IRQ 14 IDE disk controller

IRQ 15 Second E-IDE disk controller; sometimes available

3. Memory address configuration

It is also important to be well aware of the input/output addresses that are available when you install a PC device. This is because an address conflict with another hardware item would prevent the system from running correctly.

Here is the list of input/output ports that are most commonly used:

I/O Addresses	Devices that generally use this address interval
1F0-1F8	Hard disk controller
2F8-2FF	Second serial port
278-27F	Second parallel port
378-37F	First parallel port
3B0-3DF	VGA, SVGA
3F0-3F7	Floppy-disk controller
3F8-3FF	First serial port
280-340	Useable for a new device (e.g. a network interface card at 300-31F)

Troubleshooting

In order to view the settings of the complete set of devices, along with any conflict problems, you can use the **Computer Management** utility, after you have installed Windows 2000. In order to start this utility, right-click the **My Computer** icon and then select **Manage**.

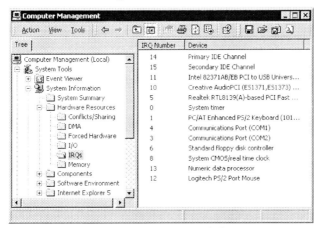

By expanding **System Information**, and then **Hardware Resources**, you will find all the necessary information such as the list of IRQs that are used, and the memory addresses that are used. It must be noted that the **Conflicts/Sharing** sub-directory indicates any conflicts between devices.

B. Installing

During the installation phase, you can modify your partitioning scheme and carry out certain operations on your disks (delete and create partitions). Use this feature simply to configure the partition on which you want to install the system. Subsequently, you can use the **Disk Manager** utility that is supplied with Windows 2000 in order to configure your other partitions or disks.

It is strongly recommended that you install your system on a 2-GB partition in order to allow for the future development of your system. If you do not allow enough space for the system partition, you might have to re-install your server because you lack space (possible causes include evolution of the swap file and the installation of applications that store information on the system partition).

1. Disk partitioning scheme

During the installation phase, you can modify your partitioning scheme and carry out certain operations on your hard disks. This is necessary in order to specify the partitions on which Windows 2000 must be installed.

You can install the preloader, (Windows 2000 boot sector) and the loader, **NTLDR**, on the first partition (the **system partition**), and you can install the rest of the files on a separate partition (the **boot partition**).

On an Intel platform, the system partition is the primary (active) partition. The boot partition, which contains the Windows 2000 kernel (**NTOSKRNL.EXE**), can be a logical drive on an extended partition.

The system partition does not need a great deal of space. In most cases, 10 MB is ample. This partition can remain in FAT, so that it will support a multiple boot and simplify troubleshooting in the event of any startup problems.

The essential files that are contained on this partition can be duplicated onto a boot diskette. This will provide not only a copy of these files, but also a backup diskette that you can use in the event of a simple system boot problem.

In the most critical cases, the full set of four backup diskettes provide access to the Windows 2000 system in order to carry out repair work, for instance.

The boot partition, which contains system files such as the Windows 2000 kernel, must have at least 1.2 GB of space This will allow for future system developments such as the inclusion of numerous high-volume DLLs into the system32 subdirectory of the installation directory. In addition, you must not forget to allow space for the swap file and a possible spool file.

This partition will be converted to NTFS for obvious security reasons.

Alternatively, you can install Windows 2000 completely on a single partition. In this case the system partition and the boot partition will be the same.

2. Choosing a file system

Windows 2000 supports FAT, FAT32 and NTFS file systems.

a. NTFS file system

NTFS (*NT File system*) 5.0 is recommended file system for Windows 2000. It enhances security by allowing security control at directory and file level. It manages disk and file compression. In addition, it allows users to control the disks by applying quotas and providing data encryption.

If you wish to configure your server as domain controller, you must have at least one partition that is formatted in NTFS in order to store the shared system volume.

b. FAT/FAT32 file system

If you want still to be able to start up your old operating system, such as MS-DOS, Windows 95 or Windows 98, then you must keep a file system that is recognized by the systems that make up the multiple boot. FAT and FAT32 do not provide security control at file and directory level. The FAT file system does not support partitions larger than 2 GB. FAT32 is a development of FAT that overcomes this limitation.

☞ *You can convert a disk from FAT/FAT32 format to NTFS format without losing data. However, it must be noted that this operation is irreversible. You can make this conversion using the following command:*
   CONVERT 'drive' : /FS:NTFS

☞ *If you wish to convert from NTFS to another file system, you must back up your data and format the partition for the desired file system. You can then restore your data.*

With Windows 2000 you must choose NTFS in the following circumstances:
- Windows 2000 is the only operating system that is installed.
- You wish to install file and print services for Macintosh.
- You would like to have local security control (this is strongly recommended!).
- You would like efficiently to manage large partitions (of over 500 MB).
- An audit of the file system is required.
- You want to manage compression individually.
- You want to keep permission equivalences when you migrate Novell files to Windows.
- You wish to manage disk quotas.
- You wish to encrypt your data (EFS).
- You wish to mount volumes in empty directories.

– You wish to implement remote storage.
– You wish to install Active Directory.

If you decide to use NTFS 5.0, it is advisable to convert your file system during the installation process. This is because permissions are applied for certain specific groups in specific directories in the file system tree. If you convert later using the **convert** command, then irreversible local **Full Control** permissions will be granted to the **Everyone** group.

3. Licensing mode

During the installation phase, you will be asked to choose the licensing mode. You can choose between the **per server licensing mode** and the **per seat licensing mode**.

Per server licensing

The **SMB** (Server Message Block) server service, which is based on the NetBIOS protocol, introduces this idea of Microsoft license. The license applies to a given computer that sets up one or more simultaneous connections. Thus, one computer counts as one license, even if several connections are set up on the server.

Consequently, the number of **per server licenses** that is required for a specific server corresponds to the **maximum number of different clients** that could connect to this server at the same time.

☞ *When the maximum number of connections is reached, an error message appears and new connections are refused. In this case a message is recoded in the Event Viewer.*

☞ *You can alter the number of per server licenses using the Control panel - Licensing.*

Per seat licensing

In this licensing mode, the seat, or the specific client is subject to a license. This license corresponds to a **right of connection**, it does not correspond to the right to add specific software in order to allow system interconnection. In this case, the servers have no particular restriction concerning the maximum number of concurrent connections, provided that each client has a recognized seat.

☞ *You can convert from per server licensing mode to per seat licensing mode at any time using the Control Panel - Licensing. However, this action is irreversible.*

4. Domain planning

During the installation, you must choose whether your Windows 2000 server will be integrated into a domain or into a workgroup.

A domain is a logical configuration in which all the network resources are administered by domain controllers. Sharing, resource security and configuration of the workstations are centralized; the administrator manages security, resources and network user accounts.

The workgroup or peer-to-peer network, logically groups together a few users. Its application implies that each user of a computer that is situated in the workgroup is responsible for his/her own data (including sharing, backup, and access restrictions). This also means that each user manages his/her own user account database. Consequently, each user that wants to access each of the machines in the workgroup must be declared in each of the account databases. In summary, the workgroup model is applicable in a network that contains a small number of users and for which security is not a major concern.

A computer that belongs to a peer-to-peer network can join a domain and a computer that belongs to a domain can join a peer-to-peer network.

If you want to join a domain during the installation, you must know a certain number of parameters:

- The name of the domain (DNS) you wish to join.
- In order to join a domain, a computer must have a unique computer account on the domain. If this computer account was not created before installing Windows 2000, you can create it during the installation. In order to be able to do this, you must know the account name and password, for an account that has enough rights so as to be able to include a computer in the domain.
- A server that acts as domain controller and a server on which the DNS service is installed and configured.

In order to join a workgroup, you need enter only the name of the workgroup you wish to join.

☞ If you include your Windows 2000 server in a domain, it will become a **member server**. If you include your Windows 2000 server in a workgroup, it will become a **stand-alone server**.

☞ During the installation of Windows 2000 Server, you can make your server a member server or a stand-alone server. If you want your server to act as domain controller, then you must install Active Directory after you have installed Windows 2000 Server.

5. Installing using a CD-ROM

You can run the Windows 2000 installation program on a
CD-ROM in several ways:
- Either, you have a Microsoft operating system; in which
  case you need only insert the CD-ROM in the CD-ROM
  drive and then run the installation program, **setup.exe.**
- Or, your BIOS will start up on the CD-ROM, which will start
  the Windows 2000 installation program, automatically.
- Or, you create a set of installation diskettes. You can do
  this by running the Makeboot.exe program using the
  command **makeboot a**. This command is situated in the
  bootdisk directory of the CD-ROM. Then, start up the
  computer using these diskettes.

If you run the setup.exe program using an operating system,
here are the steps that you must follow:

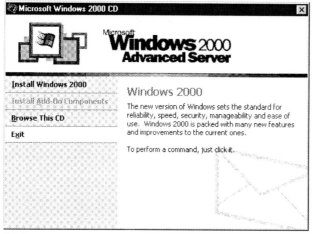

Click **Install Windows 2000**.

You then have the choice of upgrading your current system
(cf. Chapter 15 - Upgrading a network to Windows 2000), or
of installing a new copy of Windows 2000. Select **Install a
new copy of Windows 2000 (Clean Install)**.

Following this screen, you can select a number of options such as the language that you want to use, whether you wish to use accessibility options, and even the location of the Windows 2000 files and the name of the installation folder (winnt by default). In order to access these last two options, click **Advanced Options**:

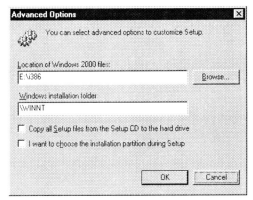

Then, you will be able to upgrade your file system to NTFS 5.0. You are strongly advised to do this during the installation of Windows 2000 for security reasons, and also so as to optimize the file system (unless you would like a multiple boot involving another operating system that does not support NTFS, such as Windows 95/98 or MS-DOS).

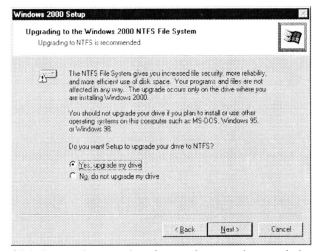

Click the **Next** button twice after you have made your choice.

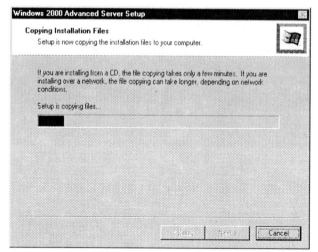

The installation program then copies the installation files onto your computer before it reboots in order to continue the installation in text mode.

a. In text mode

Here are the different steps in the text mode:
- The setup program copies a minimal version of Windows 2000 into memory.
- If you have *SCSI (Small Computer System Interface)* or *RAID (Redundant Array of Independent Disks)* peripherals that are not listed in the HCL, then press the F6 key at the beginning of text mode so as to load their drivers.
- Then, either choose the installation partition, or possibly create it.
- At this stage, you must select the file system onto which the operating system will be installed.
- Then indicate the name of the installation directory (this is \WINNT by default).

☞ *If you are installing by running the **setup.exe** program from the operating system then the text mode part will not ask you to select the file system and the installation directory. This is because these two steps will already have been carried out.*

At this stage your computer will reboot for the second time.

b. In graphic mode

Collecting information

During the graphic part of the installation you must specify the following items:
– Regional settings.
– Name and the organization that holds the license.
– Licensing mode (per seat or per server).
– Computer name (which must be unique on the network) along with the password of the local administrator account.

The components that you want to install:

• Certificate Services that allows you to create certificates security authentication using public keys.

• Cluster Service that allows servers to run in clusters.

• Internet Information Service (IIS).

• Management and Monitoring Tools.

• Message Queuing Services.

• Indexing Service, which allows you to find text that is contained in files.

• Script Debugger.

• Networking Service (DHCP-WINS-DNS...).

• Other Network File and Print Services that group together file services for Macintosh, and print services for Macintosh and Unix.

• Remote Installation Service, which allows you remotely to implement Windows 2000 Professional workstations.

• Remote Storage, which allows you to store to magnetic tape, data that is seldom used.

• Terminal Services for terminal emulation.

☞ *It must be noted that IIS and the script debugger are installed by default.*

After you have selected the services, you are asked to adjust the date and time before installation of the network management.

Installing the network management

This essential part of the Windows 2000 installation begins with the detection of the network interface card. When you have configured your network driver, Windows 2000 tries to find a DHCP (*Dynamic Host Configuration Protocol*) server on your network in order automatically to provide you with an IP address. If no DHCP server is available, an IP address that is situated in the network range 169.254.0.0/16 is automatically attributed. This is done so that you will be able to boot your computer without an error message appearing, and so that you will be able to communicate with the hosts that have an address in the same range.

The installation program then asks you whether you wish to install network components automatically or whether you wish to customize their installation. If you choose a typical installation then the following components will be installed:

- Client for Microsoft networks; which allows your computer to access network resources.
- File and Printer sharing for Microsoft networks; which allows other computers to access your computer.
- TCP/IP as DHCP client.

If you choose a custom installation then you can choose other components. For example, you can specify a static IP configuration, or you can add new communications protocols or other services.

The following step allows you to choose whether you want to join a workgroup or a domain.

The components that you have chosen are then installed.

When this step is finished, the installation program copies bitmap type files, applies the configuration that you defined previously, and saves the configuration onto the local hard disk. Then any temporary files that were used during the Windows 2000 installation are deleted before the computer is restarted one last time in order to complete the installation.

6. Installing from the network

This method is more efficient if you want to install Windows 2000 on several computers. In order to start this method you need to copy the contents of the i386 directory from the CD-ROM to a network share.

Then, you need install only a minimum network management version on the destination machine (for example, network client 3.0 on MSDOS) so that you will be able to connect to this resource and start the installation using the **WINNT.EXE** command. In addition, you can use the **WINNT32.EXE** command if you are installing Windows 2000 from a 32-bit Microsoft operating system. These commands will create a temporary directory called **Win_nt.~ls** and will copy the Windows 2000 installation files into this temporary directory.

☞ *If you are installing from an MSDOS client, run the **smartdrv** program before running the **winnt.exe** command in order to accelerate the installation process.*

a. Installing program switches

The programs WINNT and WINNT32 provide command line parameters that allow you to customize Windows 2000 installation:

```
WINNT [/s[:sourcepath]]
[/t[:temporary_drive]]
[/u[:answer_file]] [/udf:id[,UDF_file]]
[/r:folder] [/r[x]:folder] [/e:command]
[/a]
```

`/s[:sourcepath]`	Specify the location of the Windows 2000 source files. This must be a full path in the format x:\[path] or \\server\share [\path]
`/t[:]temporary_drive`	Specifies the drive that must contain the temporary installation files, and install Windows 2000 on this drive. If you do not specify a drive, the installation program will choose the partition that has the most free space.
`/u[:answer_file]`	Automatic operation that uses an optional script. This type of installation requires the switch /s.
`/r:folder`	Allows you to install an additional directory.
`/rx:folder`	Allows you to copy an additional directory.
`/e:command`	Runs a command before the final phase of program installation.
`/a`	Installs accessibility options.

Here are the switches for the **winnt32.exe** command:

`/copydir:directory`	Creates an additional directory.
`/cmd:com-mand`	Runs a command before the final phase of program installation.
`/debug[level][:file]`	Creates a debugging file. By default the file c:\winnt32.log is created at level 2.
`/s:sourcepath`	Specifies the location of the Windows 2000 installation source files. In order to copy these files simultaneously from different sources, use the switch /s for each source.

/syspart: disk	Copies the startup files on a hard disk and marks it as active. When you have run this command you can install the disk on another computer, for example. When you start up this computer, the program will start at the next step. You must use the switch /tempdrive with /syspart.
/tempdrive	Specifies a drive for installation.
/unattended [number of seconds] [:answer file]	Carries out an automatic installation. The answer file provides the information that you must provide during the installation. You can specify the number of seconds between the moment when the system finishes copying the files and system re-boot. You can set this number of seconds simply, if you are upgrading to Windows 2000.
/udf:id, udf_file	Indicates that the identifier (id) that is used by the installation program in order to specify a uniqueness database file (UDF) will modify an answer file. The /UDF parameter replaces the values that are in the answer file with those that are contained in the UDF file. The identifier (id) determines the values of the UDF file that will be used.

☞ *Use the /**makelocalsource** switch if you are installing from a CD-ROM, so as to make a local copy of the installation files. This is particularly useful if you need to add components that are required by the source files. Then, you no longer need the CD-ROM.*

b. Creating an answer file

You can automate the installation of Windows 2000 so that you will not have to respond to all the steps of the installation sequences that are in text and in graphic mode. In order to do this, you must create an answer file (or unattended file), which is a file that provides responses to the installation program.

Setup Manager is a graphic utility that allows you to create answer files and UDF files. This utility is part of the Windows 2000 Resource Kit.

When you have installed the Resource Kit, start the Setup Manager Wizard.

Then, click **Next**.

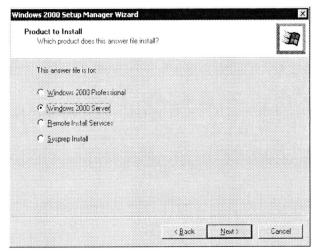

The first option **Create a new answer file**, allows you to create an unattended answer file.

You must select the destination system for this answer file. It must be noted that you can create an answer file for RIS types of installation (remote installation of Windows 2000 Professional), and for Sysprep, which will be covered later on in this chapter.

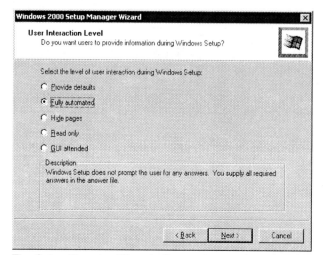

The Setup Manager Wizard offers various options that differ in their levels of interactivity with the installation program. For example, the last option **GUI attended,** allows you to create an answer file for the text mode part.

Then, enter the name of your company.

The next step asks you to enter the license number of your server product, followed by your chosen licensing mode (per seat or per server).

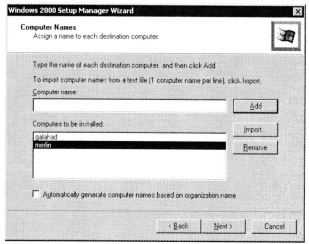

In this step, you must specify the names of the destination computers. If you have a text file that contains this list of names, you can import it by clicking the **Import** button. You file must list one name per line (otherwise, incorrect lines will be omitted).

If you prefer that the system generates names for your computers automatically, then you must activate the **Automatically generate computer names based on organization name** check box.

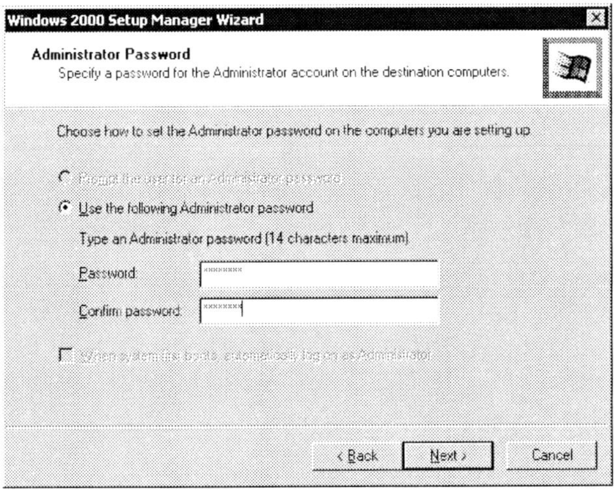

Specify the password of the computer's local administrator. For security reasons, you should never enter an empty password. The longer you make your password, the more difficult it will be to guess. In addition, if you combine uppercase and lowercase letters and numbers, it will be that much more difficult to "crack".

The Setup Manager Wizard then takes you step by step through graphic windows that are similar to those shown above in order to allow you to specify all the fields that will be required during the installation process (such as display resolutions, settings of network components, whether you want to join a domain or a workgroup and the time zone). When you have completed these steps the following screen will appear, which indicates that you have now created a basic unattended file. If you wish to include specific options in this file, then select **Yes, edit the additional settings**.

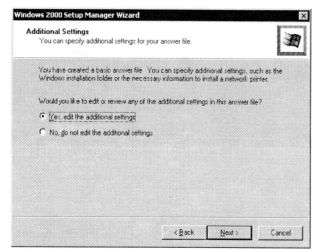

You will then be able to specify telephony options, the different languages you wish to install, the name of the destination directory (winnt by default), connection to network printers and a command that must be run upon opening the first session.

When you have specified all the options, you must indicate the method with which you want to use this unattended file.

If you select the **No, this answer file will be used to install from a CD** option, then the following step will allow you to specify the location and the name of the file. If you will be installing, starting from the CD-ROM, place this file on a floppy disk and call it **winnt.sif**. The winnt.exe program will search automatically for this file on the floppy disk when you start from the CD-ROM.

On the other hand, if you select **Yes, create or modify a distribution folder**, then not only will you be able to do as this option suggests, but also you will be able:

– to add mass storage devices to your automatic installation.
– possibly to replace the Hardware Abstraction Layer (HAL) so as to improve the portability of the system by isolating the hardware differences.
– run a command at the end of the unattended installation.
– change the logos that appear during the installation program.
– copy additional files or directories to the destination computer.
– copy the distribution files (in the case of the creation of a new distribution directory), either from the CD-ROM or from another path.

The result may be as follows:

```
;SetupMgrTag
[Unattended]
    UnattendMode=FullUnattended
    OemPreinstall=No

[GuiUnattended]
    AdminPassword=PassWord123
    TimeZone=110

[UserData]
    ProductID=000000-000000-000000-000000-000001
    FullName="ENI "
    OrgName=Service

[Display]
    BitsPerPel=32
    Xresolution=800
    YResolution=600
    Vrefresh=72

[LicenseFilePrintData]
    AutoMode=PerSeat

[TapiLocation]

[RegionalSettings]

[MassStorageDrivers]

[OEMBootFiles]

[OEM_Ads]

[SetupMgr]
    ComputerName0=gallahad
    ComputerName1=lancelot

[Identification]
    JoinWorkgroup=WORKGROUP

[Networking]
    InstallDefaultComponents=Yes
```

☞ *You can use an answer file so as to promote your member or stand-alone server to domain controller, after the server has been installed. In order to do this you must indicate the command* **dcpromo** **/answer: answer_file** *just after the installation. The dcpromo answer file must contain all the information that is required in order to install Active Directory.*

Some parameters must be unique on the network such as the name of the computer. In order to accommodate this constraint, when you create an unattend.txt file, you can create also, a udf file so as to specify the parameters that must change from one computer to another. When you use Setup Manager, it will automatically create this udf file, associate it with the unattend.txt file, and include in it all the parameters that must be unique. In addition, Setup Manager will create a .bat file and include the command line that will be required in order to start these customized installations. Here is an example of the unattend.udf file:

```
;SetupMgrTag

[UniqueIds]
    lancelot=UserData
    gallahad=UserData

[lancelot:UserData]
   ComputerName=lancelot

[gallahad:UserData]
    ComputerName=gallahad
```

Here is the syntax that is required in order to run this type of custom installation:

```
Winnt32.exe /u:unattend.txt /
udf:gallahad,unattend.udf
```

7. Using disk duplication

In order to install Windows 2000 on a large number of machines, the most efficient technique would be that of disk duplication. This method consists of creating a disk image of a computer on which Windows 2000 has been installed and configured, and then restoring it onto the destination machines. The utility that is used to implement this disk duplication is called **sysprep.exe**.

The following sequence must be followed:
- Install and configure Windows 2000 on a computer that is called the reference computer.
- Install the applications on this computer. Do not forget to copy the custom user parameters in the default user profile. In order to do this, right-click **My Computer** and then select **Properties**. Under the **User Profiles** tab, select the profile that you want to use for the software installation and then click the **Copy To** button.

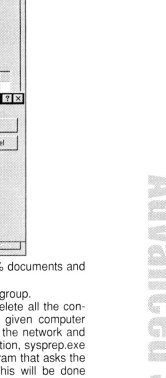

Under **Copy profile to**, enter %systemdrive% documents and settings\default user.

Under **Permitted to use**, select the **Everyone** group.

- Run the **sysprep.exe** utility in order to delete all the configuration settings that are specific to a given computer (computer name that must be unique on the network and SID the unique security identifier). In addition, sysprep.exe will install the part of the installation program that asks the user to enter a new computer name. This will be done after the image has been restored on the destination computer, once this computer has been restarted. So that this will be carried out automatically without user intervention, you can create an answer file **sysprep.inf** using the Setup Manager Wizard. This file must be located in the **sysprep** directory, on the system partition along with the files **sysprep.exe** and **setupcl.exe**.

Sysprep will be run after your computer has been restarted. Log on as administrator and then run the following command:

Drive:\sysprep\sysprep.exe –switches

The switches are as follows:

`-quiet`   Runs sysprep.exe without displaying messages on the screen.

`-pnp`   Forces plug and play to detect and install on the destination computers, hardware items that may be different from those on the reference computer.

-reboot Forces the destination computers to reboot after installation of the image.

-nosidgen Runs sysprep.exe without generating a unique security identifier. Use this switch if you are not duplicating the hard disk on which you are running sysprep.exe.

☞ *Important note: sysprep.exe does not support Windows 2000 Professional or Windows 2000 Server as stand-alone server.*

☞ *Important note: you can install the images only on computers that have the same mass storage device driver and the same hardware abstraction layer (HCL) as the reference computer.*

Once the disk has been prepared, the image is ready to be created using a disk duplication utility of a third-party vendor.

8. Promoting a stand-alone server to member server

At any time, you can **migrate** your stand-alone server from the workgroup to which it belongs, to a domain so that it will become a member server.

In order to do this right-click the **My Computer** icon and select the **Properties** option.

Under the **Network Identification** tab, click the **Properties** button.

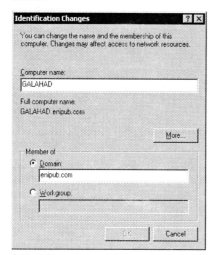

Select **Domain** and then enter the name of the domain that you wish to join.

In order to include a stand-alone server in a Windows 2000 domain, you must create a computer account in the domain concerned. There are two ways of doing this:

- From the server, by specifying a domain user account of a domain into which a computer account can be created.

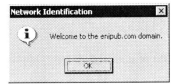

- From a domain controller using the **Active Directory Users and Computers** utility.

The 'Welcome to the domain' window then appears:

![Network Identification dialog box — Welcome to the enipub.com domain. OK]

The next time that you log on, you will be able to choose between using a user account that is declared in the domain and using an account that is local to your computer.

![Log On to Windows dialog — Microsoft Windows 2000 Advanced Server, Built on NT Technology. User name: Andrew. Password: ******. Log on to: GALAHAD (this computer) / ENIPUB / GALAHAD (this computer). Options <<]

9. Resolving installation problems

You may possibly encounter some problems when you are installing. Here are the problems that are the most commonly met:

- Hardware not recognized: check that your components are present in the HCL.
- Antivirus is activated in the bios: deactivate virus detection by the bios.
- No network interface card is installed: install a virtual network interface card, in order to have connections and a good configuration.
- Cannot join a domain: check the network adapter settings, the name of the domain, the protocol that is used and possibly its addressing. Also, check that a computer account has been created in the domain.
- Not enough disk space: use the installation program so as to delete the partition and then to recreate it with a suitable size.
- CD-ROM is not supported: change the CD-ROM drive or install via the network.

Labs

To be absolutely sure that you have assimilated this chapter, work through the corresponding labs. These are set out from page 615 to page 621.

☒ Pre-requisites for installing Windows 2000.

☒ Installing and configuring the MS DOS 3.0 network client.

☒ Connecting to the distribution files shared directory of Windows 2000 Professional workstation.

☒ Configuring the Windows 2000 installation.

☒ Creating an answer file for automized installation of a Windows 2000 Professional workstation.

☒ Preparing a disk in order to create an image for replication.

Assessing your skills

Try the following questions if you think you know this chapter well enough.

Required configuration for Windows 2000

1   What must you always check before you start installing Windows 2000?
....
....

2   How much RAM do you need in order to install Windows 2000 for the server versions (Server, Advanced Server and Datacenter Server) on an Intel platform?
....
....
....

3   How much disk space do you need for the system partition?
....
....

4   What is the difference between a system partition and a boot partition?
....
....
....
....
....
....
....

Choice of file systems

5   Which file systems are supported by Windows 2000?
....
....
....
....

6   Data security is a key item in the implementation of your server. Which file system will you choose for your disks?
....
....
....

7 How would you convert a partition from FAT to NTFS after the installation process, without the risk of losing data on the partition you wish to convert? ❏

....

8 Which conditions must you take into account when you convert a partition to NTFS, during and after the installation process? ❏

....
....
....
....
....

Licensing mode

9 The MERLIN server has been configured to support 10 simultaneous connections in per server licensing mode. From his/her workstation a user is using the following connections: ❏

F:\\MERLIN\RFC
G:\\MERLIN\DATA
H:\\MERLIN\APPLIS
I:\\ARTHUR\CONTRACT

For this licensing mode, how many more connections can be made to MERLIN, given that only this workstation is connected at present? ❏

....

10 A user is connected to the same shared directory from three different machines. How many licenses are being used for the connection of this user? ❏

....
....
....

11 How many per server licenses do you need if you have three servers and 50 clients? ❏

....
....
....
....

Server roles in a domain

12 What is the difference between a stand-alone server and a member server? ❏

....
....
....
....

13 What is the difference between a domain and a workgroup? ☐
....
....
....
....

14 Which parameters do you need to know, and which conditions must be met so that you can join a domain? ☐
....
....
....
....
....
....
....
....
....

15 Which information do you need to know in order to join a workgroup? ☐
....
....
....
....

16 What is the difference between a domain controller and a member or stand-alone server? ☐
....
....
....
....

17 What do a member/stand-alone server and a domain controller have in common? ☐
....
....
....
....
....

Installing

18 Can you make a new installation of Windows 2000 using the WINNT32.EXE program? ☐
....
....
....
....
....

Installing Windows 2000 Advanced Server

19 What are the different methods of installing Windows 2000?   ❑

....
....
....
....
....
....
....

20 Which utility must you use before starting a disk   ❑
duplication, so as to create an image that must be duplicated
on different machines?

....

21 Which program must you use in order to create answer   ❑
files that will allow you to carry out automatic (unattended)
installations?

....
....
....
....
....

22 How can you convert your stand-alone server to a   ❑
member server?

....
....

Troubleshooting installation problems

23 What must you do if an IDE CD-ROM drive is not   ❑
detected when you locally install Windows 2000 using boot
diskettes?

....
....

24 During the installation process using the WINNT32.EXE   ❑
command, the files are copied to an NTFS partition set.
Upon the first startup, a message indicates that all the files
are absent or damaged. What could be the cause of this
problem?

....
....
....

25 During the installation process, you tried to join the domain DOMAIN1.COM, without success, even though you have entered your name and password several times in order to make sure that your input is correct. You are using the administrator account that is local to your workstation and you have checked that you are using the same network protocol as that used by the domain controller server. The domain controller is on line during the installation process, as is a DNS server. What is causing this problem?

....
....
....

26 During the installation, your SCSI CD-ROM drive has not been recognized. What must you do?

....
....
....

Results

Check your answers on pages 50 to 54. Count one point for each correct answer.

Number of points | /26 |

For this chapter you need to have scored at least 20 out of 26.

Look at the list of key points that follows. Pick out the ones with which you have had difficulty and work through them again in this chapter before moving on to the next.

Key points of the chapter

☐ Required configuration for Windows 2000.

☐ Choice of file systems.

☐ Licensing mode.

☐ Server roles in a domain.

☐ Installing.

☐ Troubleshooting installation problems.

Solutions

Required configuration for Windows 2000

1   What must you always check before start installing Windows 2000?

Check that the hardware items that make up the central server are included in the hardware compatibility list (HCL).

2   How much RAM do you need in order to install Windows 2000 for the server versions (Server, Advanced Server and Datacenter Server) on an Intel platform?

The minimum RAM required is 64 MB. The recommended amount of RAM is 128 MB for an Intel platform.

3   How much disk space do you need for the system partition?

1.2 GB of disk space is required for the system partition (2 GB is recommended in order to allow for future system development).

4   What is the difference between a system partition and a boot partition?

When you install Windows 2000, you create a system partition and a boot partition. The system partition is that which contains all the files that are required for system startup (NTLDR, boot.ini, ntdetect.com). This partition must be active. The boot partition contains the directory of Windows 2000 installation files along with the system kernel (NTOS-KERNEL.EXE). This is %systemroot%, which generally corresponds to the c:\winnt path. The same partition can fulfill both of these roles.

Choice of file systems

5   Which file systems are supported by Windows 2000?

Windows 2000 recognizes FAT16, FAT32 and NTFS file systems.

6   Data security is a key item in the implementation of your server. Which file system will you choose for your disks?

NTFS is the only file system that ensures the security of your local data. In addition, NTFS allows you to encrypt your data using an encryption key.

7 How would you convert a partition from FAT to NTFS after the installation process, without the risk of losing data on the partition you wish to convert?

Use the command convert drive-letter /FS :NTFS.

8 Which conditions must you take into account when you convert a partition to NTFS, during and after the installation process?

You must ensure that Windows 2000 has not been installed as part of a multiple boot with another operating system that does not recognize NTFS (such as Windows 95/98, MS DOS and Windows 3.1). If this is the case, then these other operating systems will not be able to read the information that is contained on these partitions. If you convert the system partition to NTFS, then you will no longer be able to boot on the operating systems that do not support NTFS.

Licensing mode

9 The MERLIN server has been configured to support 10 simultaneous connections in per server licensing mode. From his/her workstation a user is using the following connections:

F:\\MERLIN\RFC
G:\\MERLIN\DATA
H:\\MERLIN\APPLIS
I:\\ARTHUR\CONTRACT

For this licensing mode, how many more connections can be made to MERLIN, given that only this workstation is connected at present?

Only one connection has been used. Consequently, 9 connections remain.

10 A user is connected to the same shared directory from three different machines. How many licenses are being used for the connection of this user?

The licenses are counted according to the number of different client computers. Consequently, three connections are used in order to connect this single user.

11 How many per server licenses do you need if you have three servers and 50 clients?

If you want all your clients to be able to access all your servers simultaneously, then you need 50 licenses per server, which makes 150 licenses. In this case it will be more judicious to by 50 per seat licenses.

Server roles in a domain

12 What is the difference between a stand-alone server and a member server?

A stand-alone server works in a workgroup, whilst a member server is included in a domain.

13 What is the difference between a domain and a workgroup?

A domain and a workgroup are both logical configurations. The difference between them is that, in a workgroup, each computer runs in peer-to-peer mode. This model is used in small networks that contain no more than 10 machines and that do not require centralized administration. No server is required and each machine manages its own security, its own resource access and its own accounts database. With a domain, network resources are administrated by domain controllers. If a user wishes to access network resources, then he/she must be authenticated by a domain controller. With this logical structure security and resource management is handled by one or more administrators.

14 Which parameters do you need to know, and which conditions must be met so that you can join a domain?

You must know the name of the domain you wish to join. A domain controller must be present in the domain, as must a DNS server. You also need a computer account in the domain. You can create this during the installation, if you know either the name and password of an account that has the right to add workstations to the domain, or those of an administrator that you will probably have created.

15 Which information do you need to know in order to join a workgroup?

You need to know only the name of the workgroup that you wish to join.

16 What is the difference between a domain controller and a member or stand-alone server?

A domain controller has a directory database that groups together all the network objects of the domain. Thus, the domain controller can validate logons to the domain. Member servers and stand-alone servers have only a database of accounts that are, local to the machine, and independent from the domain.

17 What do a member/stand-alone server and a domain controller have in common?

Windows 2000 supplies the services in both cases.

Installing

18 Can you make a new installation of Windows 2000 using the WINNT32.EXE program?

Yes. On a 32-bit system, you can run the winnt32.exe command.

19 What are the different methods of installing Windows 2000?

You can install Windows 2000 by connecting to a network share, to which the contents of the I386 directory have been copied. You must run either the WINNT.EXE command or the WINNT32.EXE command according to the system you are using. You can install from the CD-ROM, either by booting on this device provided that your BIOS allows you to do so, or by starting up using the 4 installation diskettes. Alternatively, you can run setup.exe from the CD-ROM, if you already have a Microsoft operating system. Disk duplication is also a means of remotely installing Windows 2000.

20 Which utility must you use before starting a disk duplication, so as to create an image that must be duplicated on different machines?

*You must use **sysprep.exe** in order to delete all the settings that are specific to each particular computer.*

21 Which program must you use in order to create answer files that will allow you to carry out automatic (unattended) installations?

Setup Manager, from the Windows 2000 resource kit, provides a graphic wizard that allows you to create answer files. You can use these answer files, not only for unattended installation, but also so as to install using the RIS service or by disk duplication.

22 How can you convert your stand-alone server to a member server?

You can do this, either during the installation process by including your server in a domain, or after installation by using the Network Identification tab of My Computer properties.

Troubleshooting installation problems

23 What must you do if an IDE CD-ROM drive is not detected when you locally install Windows 2000 using boot diskettes?

In order to start Windows 2000 installation on MSDOS with the MSCDEX.EXE driver, you must access the CD-ROM using WINNT.EXE, rather than using the boot diskettes, which will not be able to detect the CD-ROM drive.

24 During the installation process using the WINNT32.EXE command, the files are copied to an NTFS partition set. Upon the first startup, a message indicates that all the files are absent or damaged. What could be the cause of this problem?

Partition sets were implemented only with the first Windows NT system. When the system restarts with a new registry, the disk scheme is viewed differently. The new system can no longer access partitions that are managed as sets or with fault tolerance.

25 During the installation process, you tried to join the domain DOMAIN1.COM, without success, even though you have entered your name and password several times in order to make sure that your input is correct. You are using the administrator account that is local to your workstation and you have checked that you are using the same network protocol as that used by the domain controller server. The domain controller is on line during the installation process, as is a DNS server. What is causing this problem?

In order to create a computer account in a domain, you must use an account that has the right to add workstations to the domain. However, in this case, administrator account that is local to the workstation is being used, which does not have this right.

26 During the installation, your SCSI CD-ROM drive has not been recognized. What must you do?

Install CD-ROM driver that is supplied by the manufacturer, by pressing the F6 *key at the beginning of the installation process.*

Prerequisites for this chapter

☒ Knowledge of a Microsoft graphic environment.
☒ Networking essentials: configuring a network interface card, connection components used.
☒ Essential knowledge of PC hardware and software components.

Objectives

At the end of this chapter, you will be able to:
☒ Understand the registry database on Windows 2000.
☒ Understand the concepts of keys, subkeys, hives and value entries.
☒ Identify hives and understand the roles that they play.
☒ Use Control Panel in order to configure the system.
☒ Configure the display.
☒ Add/remove programs.
☒ Add/remove/troubleshoot devices.
☒ Manage driver signature options.
☒ Create hardware profiles.
☒ Configure a service.
☒ Optimize the paging file.
☒ Diagnose and solve hardware problems.
☒ Understand network protocol configuration parameters.
☒ Configure TCP/IP.
☒ Apply TCP/IP filtering.
☒ Disable NetBIOS.
☒ Install NetBEUI, DLC and AppleTalk.
☒ Configure Nwlink.
☒ Configure Windows 2000 Server as a router.
☒ Understand the different types of routing protocols.
☒ Optimize links.

Contents

Configuring the system

You can access most of the Windows 2000 settings using the **Control Panel**. Other settings can be accessed in the registry.

You can access **Control Panel** either via **My Computer** or using the **Start** menu. The Control Panel is represented by the ⊞ ControlPanel icon, and contains a set of modules that concern the different parts of the operating system.

You can access some of these modules by other shortcuts (for example, you can access the **Display** module by right-clicking the desktop, and then selecting the **Properties** option).

All the **Control Panel** modules provide a secure, user-friendly graphic interface. On the other hand, handling settings via the registry is very basic; one erroneous operation can put the operating system out of action. The tool that you can use in order to edit the Windows 2000 configuration registry is described below.

A. Registry

1. Overview

The registry files are the equivalents of the configuration files that were used with Windows 3.x, such as WIN.INI and SYSTEM.INI. As from Windows 95/98, Windows NT 4.00 and Windows 2000, the configuration of the system, the programs and the user's environment is recorded in the registry. In order to edit this registry, you must use the standard tool that is delivered with Windows 2000: the **Registry Editor**.

Registry Editor

This tool is not provided in the form of an icon in the **Administrative Tools** group. In order to start it, you must run REGEDT32.EXE.

☞ *In most cases however, you can modify the registry without using the Registry Editor. You can configure the system via the user interface. In particular, you can use Control Panel.*

However, some configuration settings can be modified only using the Registry Editor. These include the following operations:
- Locking the numeric keyboard before logon (so as to enter the password),
- Customizing the desktop before logon (so as to display the logo of the company, for example),
- Configuring TCP protocol (size of emission/reception windows),

- Activating the WINS proxy agent,
- Generating an error log for the PPP protocol.

Group policies provide another means of modifying a machine's registry. This registry contains the configuration of the local machine (software and hardware) along with the profile that is implemented by the user upon logon.

The Registry Editor provides a structured view of the complete configuration of a machine. Consequently, there is a separate registry for each computer that is installed.

This registry contains all the system parameters:
- Kernel components,
- Device drivers,
- Installed applications,
- User profiles,
- Profiles of available hardware,
- Database of system users (local to a workstation or to a member/stand-alone server).

The registry has a tree structure. There are **trees** and **subtrees**.

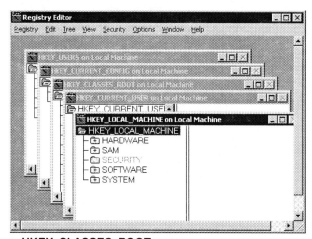

- **HKEY_CLASSES_ROOT**
  is the subtree that is located in HKEY_LOCAL_MACHINE/Software/Classes. This subtree manages file-class association data and OLE (Object Linking and Embedding).
- **HKEY_CURRENT_CONFIG**
  is part of the HKEY_LOCAL_MACHINE subtree: HKEY_LOCAL_MACHINE\System\CurrentControlSet\Hardware Profiles\xxx\. This subtree contains settings that are specific to the current hardware profile.
- **HKEY_CURRENT_USER**
  points to HKEY_USERS/SID (Security IDentifier).
- **HKEY_LOCAL_MACHINE.**
- **HKEY_USERS.**

This subtree corresponds to the two previous subtrees, HKEY_LOCAL_MACHINE and HKEY_USERS. These subtrees will now be described. As its name suggests, HKEY_USERS contains configuration settings that relate to the user environment, whilst HKEY_LOCAL_MACHINE contains configuration data that relate to, devices, the operating system, system security and the accounts database.

Each subtree is made up of a set of **hives** (for example: the HKEY_LOCAL_MACHINE subtree contains the SAM, SECURITY, SOFTWARE and SYSTEM hives). Each hive is made up of a set of **keys** and **subkeys**. These keys and subkeys contain **value entries** that accomodate the intermediate information of the structure.

The registry then, is made up of a set of files, which include *hives*. The other items that allow the registry to be built are the user profiles that are stored in the **NTUSER.DAT** files. These files are located in **\%systemdrive%\Documents and settings\user_name\.**

The hives allow the **HKEY_LOCAL_MACHINE** subtree to be built.

These files are stored in **\%systemroot%\ System32\ Config**. This directory contains files without name extensions (for example **sam.**). It also contains **.log** files (for example **sam.log**), which allow logging of the modifications that are made to each hive.

These hives are as follows:

SAM

This hive contains the computer's accounts database: *Security Account Manager*.
In the case of a Windows 2000 Professional workstation and a member server, this database is local to the machine.
Associated files: **sam., sam.log**

Security

This hive is extremely important as it contains the Local Security Authority, or LSA. The LSA authorizes, or forbids, a user to **Log on locally** or to **Access this computer from the network**.
Associated files: **security., security.log**

Software

Associated files: **software., software.log**

System

The **system** hive contains information on the devices and the services that are installed. This is the only hive that is duplicated in **system.alt** (backup file).
Associated files: **system., system.alt, system.log**

☞ *It must be noted that the HARDWARE subkey is not a hive! It is a volatile key (a key that is stored in volatile memory). It is made up from hardware information that is detected upon system boot by **NTDETECT.COM**.*

The value entries can have different data types:
REG_DWORD
    a numeric value on four bytes.
REG_SZ
    a text string, REGister String Zero (a string of characters that is terminated with a 0 in C language).
REG_MULTI_SZ
    a set of text strings.
REG_BINARY
    binary data.
REG_EXPAND_SZ
    similar to REG_SZ except that you can include variables such as %SYSTEMROOT% and %USERNAME%.

2. Registry Editors of Windows 95 and of Windows 2000/NT

There are two Registry Editors on Windows 2000. Regedt32.exe is the registry editor for Windows NT and for Windows 2000, and regedit.exe, the registry editor for Windows 95, is also supplied with Windows 2000. The advantages of regedit.exe will be discussed later on in this chapter.

☞ *It must be noted that, although the Windows 95 and the Windows NT/2000 registries are not 100 % compatible, it useful to use regedit.exe in certain cases. These cases will be discussed later on in this chapter.*

☞ ***Regedit.exe*** *of Windows 95 must not be confused with **regedit.exe** of Windows 3.11! This can easily be done, especially as they have the same name and use the same icon! However, they do not offer the same features. The utility that was supplied with Windows 3.11 was the OLE (Object Linking and Embedding) registration editor. It functioned with **WIN.INI,** and with the **REG.DAT** files for each application that concerned OLE.*

Registry editor for Windows 2000 : regedt32.exe

Regedt32 features are suited to Windows 2000. It allows remote administration.

In the menu bar:

– The **Registry** menu provides access to the local register (**Open Local**) and to a remote computer (**Select Computer**). In addition, this menu allows you to print a subtree, and to save it as a text file.

– You can use the **Edit** menu in order to add a key or a value. You can display the value of each key according to its format, for example: binary, decimal or string.

– The **Security** menu allows you to apply permissions on keys and hives. It also allows you to audit the access to the different parts of the registry and to define the ownership of these various parts.

– The **Options** menu allows you to access the registry in **Read Only Mode** so that you can go through the registry without making any changes. It must be noted that this mode does not apply to the administrator, who can modify the registry even in read only mode!

☞ *Never change the access permissions for the registry unless you are sure that you know what you are doing! You might prevent certain services from accessing certain keys, and thereby create a problem that is difficult to identify.*

Modifying a registry using the Windows 2000 registry editor

In order to modify a value in the registry:

➢ Select the subtree, followed by the key that contains the value you wish to modify.

➢ Double-click the value in the right-hand pane and then modify it.

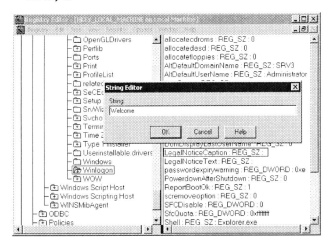

In order to add a value:

➢ Select the appropriate key and choose the **Add Value** option from the **Edit** menu.

➢ Specify the name of the value, respecting the case, and then indicate the data type that must be associated with it.

➢ Enter the data.

Registry editor for Windows 95 : regedit.exe

This registry editor is often used on Windows 2000 because it offers advanced search features. Unlike **regedt32**, which allows you to search only on keys and subkeys, the Windows 95 editor allows you to search at the level of values and their contents.

However, it does not have the same editing capabilities and you are even recommended not to use it for these purposes. In addition, it does not offer a **Read Only Mode**, nor does it provide a **Security** menu so as to specify permissions.

☞ *It must be noted once again, that some of the registry parts that are offered by regedit.exe do not exist on Windows 2000: Notably, this is the case with the **HKEY_DYN_DATA** subtree.*

B. Configuring devices

1. Display

Several tabs are provided:

Display

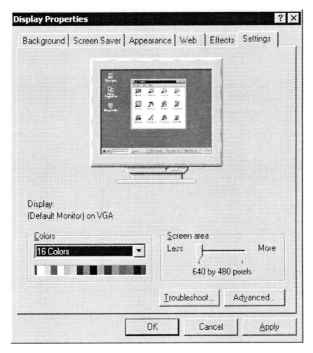

Background

This tab offers images and wallpapers that you can use as a screen background. By clicking the **Browse** button, you can add your own pictures for use as wallpapers.

Screen Saver

This tab offers a variety of screen savers. These programs move an image around the screen so as to protect the phosphorous layer being damaged by prolonged display of a fixed image. You can parameter most of the screen savers and you can protect them with passwords.

This tab also allows you to manage the power supply.

Appearance

This tab allows you to customize the colors of such items as menu fonts, title bars and dialog boxes.

Web

This tab allows you to display images or HTML files as wallpapers.

Effects

This tab allows you to modify the icons that are on your desktop and to apply visual effects to them (such as smoothing the edges of fonts).

Settings

This tab allows you to adjust the number of colors and the resolution of the screen.

Windows 2000 allows you to connect up to ten monitors on the same computer in order to extend its display capabilities. One of the advantages that are offered by this feature is to allow a user to work on several applications at the same time, by moving from screen to screen. In order to use this feature, you must use PCI (*Peripheral Component Interconnect*) or AGP (*Accelerated Graphics Port*) type graphic cards. Consult the HCL so as to find out the list of graphic cards that support this feature. Then add the AGP or PCI graphic cards in free slots, connect up your different screen monitors and restart your computer. Windows 2000 automatically detects the new peripherals and installs the drivers. Then, go into the display properties and select **Extend my desktop on these screens**.

2. Add/Remove Programs

This module allows you to install, to remove and to modify programs. If you decide to diffuse applications using the publication technique, users will be able to consult the published applications with a view to installing them using this module.

Add/Remove
Programs

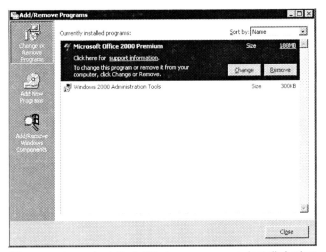

After you have installed Windows, you can install further services such as DHCP server service, DNS server service, network analysis tools, print services for UNIX, games and accessories. In order to install such services click the **Add/Remove Windows Components** button.

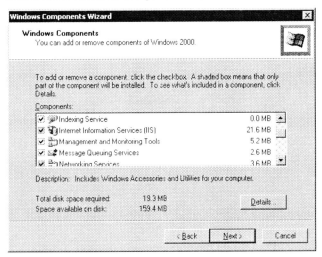

3. Keyboard

This module allows you to configure the settings of your keyboard such as the character repeat delay and rate, the input language and the driver that is used.

Keyboard

In addition to this graphic interface, you can use the registry in order to specify whether or not the numeric keyboard must be active during logon. By default, the numeric keyboard is deactivated before logon and activated during logon. In order to change these settings you can use the registry editor so as to modify the **InitialKeyboardIndicators** value.

InitialKeyboardIndicators=0: numeric keyboard deactivated
InitialKeyboardIndicators=2: numeric keyboard activated

In order to change the keyboard status after logon, modify this value in **HKEY_CURRENT_USER\Control Panel \Keyboard**. In order to change the keyboard status before logon, modify this value in **HKEY_USER\ .DEFAULT\ Control Panel\Keyboard**.

4. Add/Remove Hardware

Windows 2000 supports the Plug and Play feature by automatically installing the drivers of devices that offer the Plug and Play feature. The feature means that you can physically connect a new device and then let Windows automatically sort out its configuration (IRQ...). The advantage of this feature is that you no longer have to worry about this set up, which allows you to avoid all sorts of conflict problems.

Add/Remove
Hardware

If you have devices that are not Plug and Play, use the **Add/Remove Hardware** program so as to install, remove, disconnect or troubleshoot these devices.

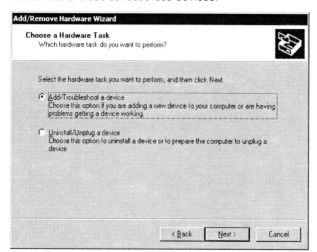

If you select **Add/Troubleshoot a device**, Windows 2000 looks for new Plug and Play devices. If no Plug and Play device is detected then you can install one by selecting **Add a new device**.

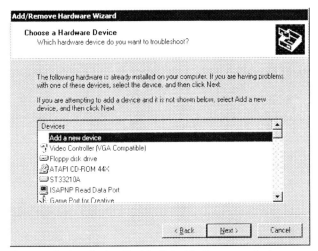

If you select a device that is listed in the pane that appears under **Devices**, and then click **Next**, Windows 2000 will indicate the status of this device.

5. Date/Time

This module allows you to adjust the date, the time and the time zone.

Date/Time

6. Printers

This module allows you to add and remove printers. This feature will be described in more detail in Chapter 9 of this book.

Printers

7. Power Options

This module allows you to reduce the energy consumption of your computer by specifying that the monitor and/or the hard disks must be turned off automatically after a specified idle time. You can use these options provided that your hardware supports them.

Power Options

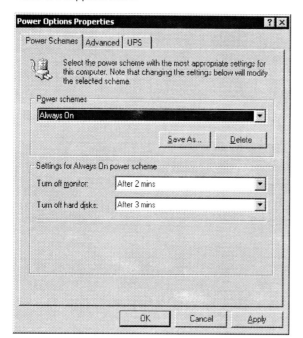

8. System

This module allows you to access a certain number of tabs that concern system properties.

System

a. Network Identification tab

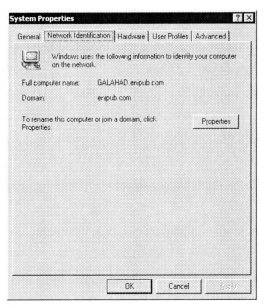

Under this tab you can join a domain or a workgroup. You can even change the name of your computer provided that your computer is not a domain controller.

b. Hardware tab

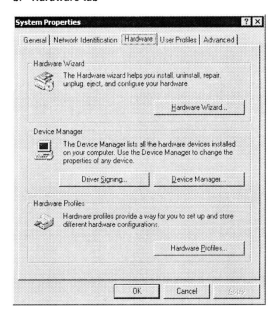

The **Hardware Wizard** allows you to start up the Add/Remove Hardware module.

Under **Device Manager**, the **Driver Signing** button allows you to specify a security level that must be met when new drivers are installed.

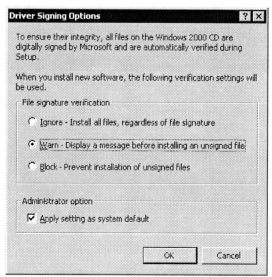

Most system failures are caused by badly written device drivers. Microsoft guarantees that all drivers that are signed by them are compatible with the Windows 2000 environment. However, some drivers have not received this signature because their manufacturers decided that this was not necessary. In order to promote the stability of your system, you can forbid the installation of drivers that have not been signed.

☞ *Windows 2000 Datacenter version does not authorize the installation of drivers that have not been signed.*

The **Device Manager** allows you to view the status of your devices. It also allows you to uninstall them, to disable them and to view their properties. An alternative way of accessing **Device Manager** is to right-click **My Computer** and then to select **Manage**.

The **Hardware Profiles** button allows you to create different startup configurations. For example, if you use a portable computer, you could create two hardware profiles: one in which the network adapter is disabled, and the other in which the network interface card is enabled.

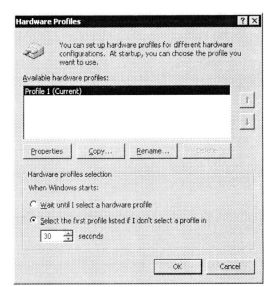

By default, only one hardware profile is created. This hardware profile is called **Profile 1**, and it contains the current hardware configuration. In order to create a second hardware profile, click **Copy**.

☞ *A configuration name cannot contain extended characters.*

When you have created your alternative hardware profile, all you need do is to start up your machine on the profile that you wish to configure and then start up **Device Manager**.

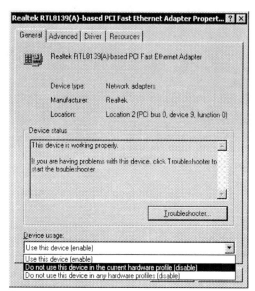

Select the device that you want to deactivate for the current hardware profile. Then, in the drop-down list that appears under **Device usage**, select **Do not use this device in the current hardware profile (disable)**.

c. Advanced tab - Performance Options

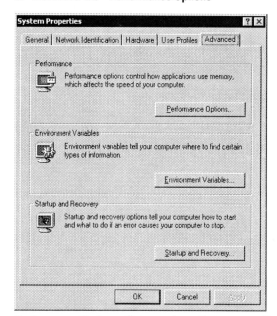

Performance Options allow you to optimize execution priority for applications and services that run in the background.

The application that is running on the foreground is that for which the title bar appears in dark blue (if you are using standard colors). This is the application with which the user is currently working. Select **Applications** in order to define a priority level that is higher than that of the background application. If you select **Background services**, then all the applications will have the same priority.

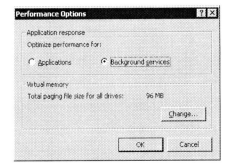

☞ *By default, Windows 2000 Server privileges the applications that run in the background (this improves the performance of network services). On the other hand, Windows 2000 Professional privileges the applications that run in the foreground.*

Configuring the paging file

In order to modify the size or the location of the paging (swap) file, click the **Change** button in the **Performance Options** dialog box.

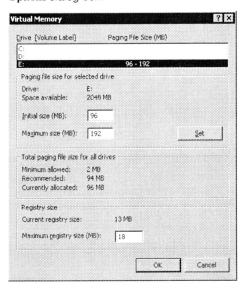

By default, the paging file is located in the root of the partition that contains system files. Its name is **pagefile.sys**. You can resize this file so as to optimize the functioning of the system. In addition, you can move the file so as to optimize read/write access to the disk. In order to do this, select the drive on which you wish to place your paging file, and define the **Initial size (MB)** and the **Maximum size (MB)** in the corresponding text boxes. Then click **Set** so as to fix these values.

Sizing the paging file

For both Windows 2000 Server and Professional, by default, the initial size of the paging file is based on the following relationship:

Pagefile.sys = size of the computer's RAM + 50%

☞ *If there is not enough free disk space on the system partition, then the partition that contains the most free disk space is used.*

The size of the paging file will never fall below its initial size. It will increase according to its needs but it will never exceed its maximum size. The performance of your system will deteriorate if certain applications need to swap to disk. The minimum size of a paging file is 2 MB.

☞ *When you restart your computer, Windows 2000 resizes your paging file to its initial size.*

☞ *In order to view information concerning the paging file, select* **Folder Options** *in the* **Tools** *menu of Windows Explorer. Then click the* **View** *tab and deactivate the* **Hide protected operating system file** *option.*

Optimizing the paging file

If your system has several hard disks, it might be a good idea to place a paging file on each of them. This can be particularly useful if your disk controller handles simultaneous read/writes. When there are several paging files, the virtual memory manager balances the load between these different files.

As part of the optimization process, it is helpful to separate the hard disks according to types of activity. For example, it is useful to create a paging file on a different partition from that which contains the system files. However, if the size of your paging file on the system partition is less than that of the RAM on your system, then Windows 2000 will not be able to create a debugging information file in the event of an error.

In any case, in order to avoid slowing down the system, you must ensure that the minimum size of the paging file is always adequate. If this is not the case then the paging file will grow up to the maximum size that was specified, to the detriment of the overall performance of the machine.

In addition, it must be noted that you can define the size of the registry. As soon as the size of the registry comes close to the maximum size, you must increase this maximum size. Otherwise, you might lose configuration information.

In terms of performance, you can also configure your server according to its role. For example, according to whether it is a distributed applications server (SQL server, for instance), or whether it is a file and print server, and so forth.

In order to do this, display the properties for your connection and then select **File and Printer Sharing for Microsoft Networks**. Click the **Properties** button and then choose from the following options:

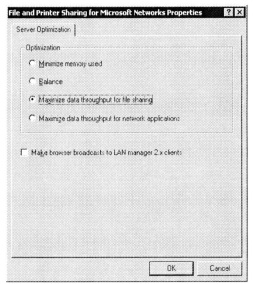

- **Minimize memory used**: choose this option in order to optimize your server, if it supports a small number of client connections (for example in a workgroup).
- **Balance**: choose this option in order to optimize your server if it acts as a file and print server, and if it executes other services.
- **Maximize data throughput for file sharing**: choose this option in order to optimize your server if it acts solely as a file and print server.
- **Maximize data throughput for network applications**: choose this option in order to optimize your server if it acts as an applications server (for example, SQL server, or Exchange Server).

d. Advanced tab - Environment Variables

Environment variables contain information that is used by the system, for example the **TEMP** variable, which specifies where temporary files are stored.

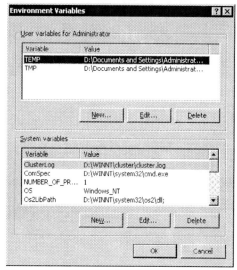

There are two types of environment variable:
- user variables,
- system variables.

The user variables that are defined vary according to the user concerned. Users can add, modify and delete user environment variables.

System variables do not apply to an individual user, they apply to the whole system. Consequently, they apply irrespective of the user who is logged on. Only administrators can modify system variables.

e. Advanced tab - Startup and Recovery

This dialog box allows you to specify the default options that must be configured upon startup. It also allows you to specify what the system must do in the event of a fatal error.

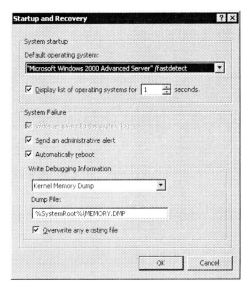

Under **System startup** you can specify the system that must be booted by default (this is the option that is highlighted in the startup menu). In addition, you can indicate for how long the startup menu must be displayed.

In reality, this graphic tool modifies the **boot.ini** file, which contains startup options.

The following options are used in order to define the actions of the system in the event of a fatal error:

– Write an event to the system log
– Send an administrative alert so that a recipient will receive a message concerning the problem.
– Reboot, copying the contents of volatile memory to a file, which is called **memory.dmp** by default. This file will help the Microsoft technical support to diagnose the causes of this error. In fact, when a failure occurs, the contents of volatile memory are written to the paging file, which is then copied to the memory.dmp file upon the next startup. A new paging file is then created.

9. Services

Users of **Windows NT 4.0** will be used to carrying out operations on services via the **Services** icon of the Control Panel.

With Windows 2000, in order to access the services you must select **Administrative Tools** followed by **Computer Management** (alternatively you can right-click **My Computer** and then select **Manage**).

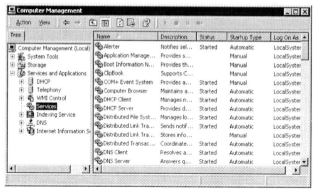

The **Computer Management** console allows you to handle the services of any computer on the network. For this purpose, select **Computer Management (Local)** and then click **Action - Connect to another computer**.

You can carry out different tasks on a service by right-clicking it.

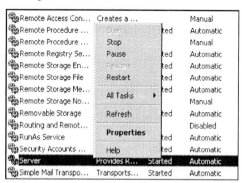

- The **Stop** option allows you to stop the service. If other services depend on this service then they will be stopped too. However, if the service that you want to stop depends on other services, then these other services will not be stopped.
- The **Pause** option stops the service without stopping any of the services that depend on it.
- The **Restart** option allows you to restart the service along with all its dependencies.

In order to view the dependencies of a particular service, right-click the service concerned and select **Properties**. Then, select the **Dependencies** tab.

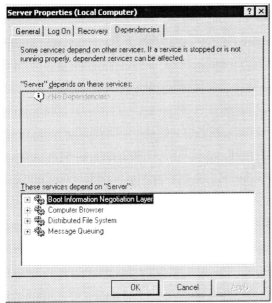

– The **General** tab allows you to change the name and the description that is displayed in the **Computer Management** program. It also allows you to select the type of startup (automatic, manual or disabled). In addition it allows you to start, stop, pause or resume the service.
– The **Log On** tab allows you to specify the user account with which the server must start up. In addition, you can enable or disable the service for specific hardware profiles.
– The **Recovery** tab allows you to define the action that must be taken if the service fails. You can choose from the options: **Take No Action**, **Restart the Service**, **Run a File** and **Reboot the Computer**. You can define different actions according to whether it is the first failure, the second failure, or a subsequent failure of the service. A fail count is provided that you can re-initialize automatically after a specified number of days.

10. Scanners and Cameras

This program provides a wizard in order to allow you to add scanners or digital cameras.

Scanners and
Cameras

11. Mouse

You can customize the use of the mouse. For example, you can adjust the double-click speed, modify the mouse pointer, or specify whether it must be right-handed or left-handed (thus inverting the button roles). You can even configure your mouse so that you can open documents by a single click.

Mouse

12. Modems

If no modem (MOdulator DEModulator) is detected by Windows 2000, then you can add one manually using the **Phone and Modem Options** program. In addition, you can declare a **Null Modem** cable in order to link two computers together via their serial ports.

Phone and
Modem ...

In order to add a modem, click the **Modems** tab and then click the **Add** button.

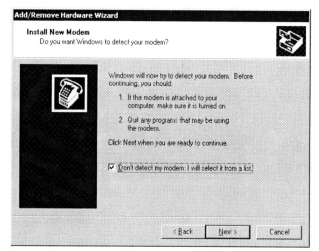

If you do not want Windows 2000 to try to detect your modem automatically, then activate the **Don't detect my modem; I will select it from a list** check box. Then, you need only select the manufacturer and the model of your modem. If your modem does not appear in the list, and your vendor has supplied you with the driver that is compatible with your operating system, then you can click the **Have Disk** button. When you have selected the modem, indicate the port on which it is connected so as to complete the installation. After your modem has been installed you can modify its properties at any time.

In addition, this program allows you to configure your usage settings. For example, if you have a telephone card or if you must dial a number so as to obtain an outside line.

In order to set up these options, select the **Dialing Rules** tab and then click the **New** button. Alternatively, if you wish to modify an existing configuration, then click the **Edit** button.

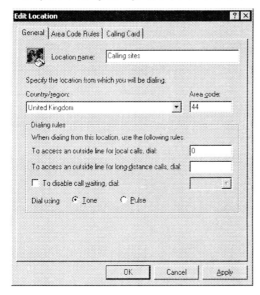

13. Troubleshooting hardware problems

If one of your devices is malfunctioning, you can go into the Control Panel, open the configuration icon of the device that is causing the problem, and then click the **Troubleshoot** button (for most devices this button is under the **Hardware** tab). The online help will then guide you step by step in an attempt to diagnose the cause of the problem, and thereby to help you to solve it.

In addition you can use the **Device Manager** program in order to monitor the status of your devices.

An icon with a red cross on it indicates that the corresponding device is disabled.

An icon that is marked with a black exclamation point on a yellow background indicates, either that the device concerned is badly configured, or that a driver has not been installed for this device.

14. Configuring network interface cards

If your network interface card is not automatically detected and installed by Windows 2000, then you must use the **Add/Remove Hardware** program from the **Control Panel** in order to install it.

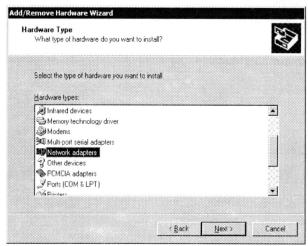

Windows 2000 will then automatically configure your network card.

There are two ways of viewing the properties of your card:

– Right-click **My Network Places** and select **Properties**. Then, right-click **Local Area Connection** and again select **Properties**.

– Alternatively, go into Control Panel and double-click the **Network and Dial-up Connections** icon. Then, right-click **Local Area Connection** and select **Properties**.

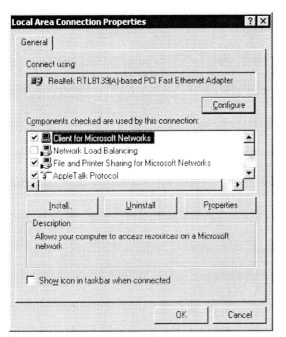

If you activate the **Show icon in taskbar when connected** check box, then you will be able to double-click the 📇 icon in order to display the connection status of your local area network.

If you click the **Disable** button, then you will disable your network interface card. In order to re-activate the network connection back, select the properties of My Network Places and double-click the grayed-out **Local Area Connection** icon. Alternatively, you can right-click this grayed-out icon and then select **Enable**.

Coming back to the **Local Area Connection Properties** dialog box, The **General** tab shows the card by which the network connection has been made, along with all the items that are used by this connection. These items must include a communications protocol. By clicking the **Configure** button, you can view the properties of your network interface card.

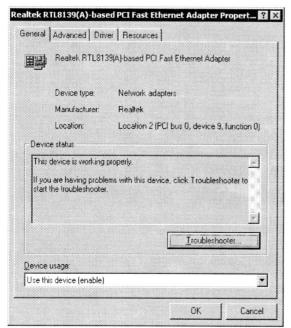

- The **General** tab allows you to enable or to disable this device with respect to the different hardware profiles. It also allows you to run the **Troubleshooter** program, which is useful if you have a problem with your network interface card.
- The **Advanced** tab provides access to settings that you can configure for the card. The settings that are proposed will depend on the card concerned.

- The **Driver** tab provides information on the driver that is used by the card (concerning the files that correspond to the driver). This tab also allows you to uninstall or to update this driver.
- The **Resources** tab allows you to view the resource settings that are used by your card (such as the IRQ and input/output address).

C. Choosing a protocol

Windows 2000 manages several protocols. Each of them has its peculiarities and its fields of application.

This section will describe the cases in which you must use one protocol rather than another.

TCP/IP (Transmission Control Protocol/Internet Protocol)

The Internet is based on this protocol. It is a routable protocol and handles extended networks. It requires an explicit addressing scheme.

Transport compatible Nwlink IPX/SPX/NetBIOS

This is an NDIS 5.0 version of the Novell IPX/SPX *(Internetwork Packet eXchange/Sequenced Packet eXchange)* protocol.

NWLink allows communication between MS-DOS, OS/2, Windows and Windows 2000 computers, by means of RPCs *(Remote Procedure Calls)*, of Windows sockets or by Novell NetBIOS IPX/SPX. IPX is a routable protocol. IPX addressing is implemented dynamically on the clients.

NetBEUI (NetBIOS Extended User Interface)

This protocol is used on Lan Manager, Lan Server, Windows 95 and Windows for Workgroups systems. This is a fast and efficient protocol that is usable only on small LANs. It is not a routable protocol and is based on broadcasting. However, it has the advantage that it does not need configuring.

DLC (Data Link Control)

This protocol provides access to SNA systems and to certain network print devices.

AppleTalk

This protocol allows a Windows 2000 server that runs services for Macintosh, to communicate with Macintosh clients. This is also a routable protocol.

Configuring the system

D. Configuring TCP/IP

1. TCP/IP settings

a. Internet services

TCP/IP offers services:
- at application level,
- at network level.

Interconnection services at application level

The user perceives TCP/IP as a set of programs that offer services that use the network for different purposes. Here are the main application services:
- electronic mail
- file transfer
- remote connections

Interconnection services at network level

Programmers who develop applications using TCP/IP have a different perspective from that of the users. Programmers use different interconnection services:

Packet delivery service in connectionless mode

This service underlies all the other services. The data packets are transmitted from one machine to other, and each machine is identified by an address.

At this level, the packets are routed independently from each other. Also, there is no guarantee of a reliable delivery, and neither is there any guarantee that the packets will arrive in the correct order.

Reliable transport service

Network applications require error-free communications. This is achieved notably thanks to techniques of automatic recovery in the event of errors.

The reliable transport service manages these sorts of problems. It allows an application to set up a connection with another application that runs on another machine, just as if there was a direct and permanent connection.

b. The advantages of TCP/IP

Even though many other protocols provide identical services to those offered by TCP/IP, the set of TCP/IP standards offer a number of advantages:

Independence from the network technology

TCP/IP is independent of any hardware or manufacturer. It can run with a wide range of technologies. It uses a transmission unit, called a DATAGRAM, which specifies how the information must be transmitted on a given type of network.

Universal connectivity

Each machine that is connected via TCP/IP is assigned a unique address, and each pair of machines can communicate with each other. The intermediate nodes use addresses that are contained in the DATAGRAMS in order to decide how the packets must be routed.

End to end acknowledgement

TCP/IP ensures direct acknowledgement between the source machine and the destination machine, even if the machines are not connected on the same physical network.

Standardized application protocols

Apart from transport protocols, TCP/IP includes various application protocols. In particular, these application protocols concern the mail service, file transfer (FTP, TFTP) and remote login (rlogin).

Programmers who develop applications are often able to use existing programs, which provide the services that they need.

c. Internet addressing

An Internet address is called an *IP address*. It uniquely identifies the machine, and also the network in which the machine is situated. This feature allows efficient routing of information. This address is encoded on 32 bits, and is used for all communications with the machine.

Each address is made up of a network identifier and a machine identifier. A first set of bits corresponds to the network, and a second set of bits corresponds to the machine. Under no circumstances, must the bits in either the machine part, or the bits in the network part, be either all set to one, or all set to zero.

IP address classes

The IP address class of an address can be determined from the most significant bits in the address. Only the first three address classes can be used for machine addresses.

Class A

Class A addresses correspond to networks that contain more than 2^{24} machines. 7 bits are used for the address of the network, and 24 bits are used for the address of the machine.

```
0          8         16         24         31
┌─┬─────────┬─────────────────────────────────┐
│0│Network ID│           Machine ID            │
└─┴─────────┴─────────────────────────────────┘
```

☞ *The value of the first byte is between 1 and 126 (inclusive).*

Class B

This class corresponds to networks in which the number of machines varies from 2 to 2^{16}-2. 16 bits are available for the number of the machine, and 14 bits are available for the number of the network.

```
0          8         16         24         31
┌─┬─┬───────────────┬───────────────────────┐
│1│0│   Network ID  │       Machine ID       │
└─┴─┴───────────────┴───────────────────────┘
```

☞ *The value of the first byte is between 128 and 191 inclusive.*

Class C

21 bits are used for the number of the network, and 8 bits are used for the number of the machine. Consequently, you can use this class for small networks that contain from 1 to 2^8-2 (254) machines.

```
0          8         16         24         31
┌─┬─┬─┬─────────────────────┬───────────────┐
│1│1│0│      Network ID      │   Machine ID  │
└─┴─┴─┴─────────────────────┴───────────────┘
```

☞ *The value of the first byte is between 192 and 223 (inclusive).*

☞ *A router is a machine that has several addresses. Therefore it cannot have a unique address. Consequently, it must have as many addresses as it has accesses to different networks. One IP address identifies one access to the network, and not one machine on the network.*

Class D

A multicast address can be attributed to a host, in addition to its unique address. This technique allows several peripherals to be identified simultaneously (so that they can receive a multimedia emission, for example).

☞ *The value of the first byte is between 224 and 239 (inclusive).*

Network address and broadcast address

An address in which the machine number is equal to zero is used to refer to the network itself. Consequently, a machine cannot have an address in which all the bits of the machine number are reset to zero.

If all the bits of an address that correspond to the machine number are set to one, then it is a broadcast address. A broadcast address references all the machines in the network.

☞ *On some UNIX systems, an address with all its bits reset to zero is used to signify a broadcast from the host.*

Local broadcast address

An address in which all the bits are set to one, corresponds to a local broadcast address that is intended for all the machines in the network in which the machine that is emitting the address is located. In this case, the emitting machine does not need to know its own network address.

Network address completely reset to zero

If a machine does not yet know its network number, it can send a message in which the network number is zero. In this case the destination of the message will be interpreted as being the current network. The workstations that respond to the request will return a network address that is completely formed. This will allow the emitter to know the address of its network.

Drawbacks of Internet addressing

One drawback of Internet addressing is that if a machine is moved from one network to another then its address must be modified accordingly.

Another difficulty of Internet addressing is that, if a class C addressing scheme is used, and the number of machines subsequently exceeds 254, then a class B scheme must be used and the network address must be modified accordingly. Typically, this can be a problem for a portable computer.

The most important drawback of IP addressing is that the path that is followed depends on the network number, which is contained in the address.

☞ *In the event of failure of one of the networks, a machine that has several addresses might be accessible through one address, and not through another.*

Dotted decimal notation

IP addresses are composed of four decimal integers that are separated by dots when they are intended for users or for programmers. For example: 128.10.2.30.

Local loopback address

The local loopback address is equal to 127.0.0.1. This address is used for inter-process communications on the local machine. A local broadcast address in which the network number is equal to 127 is never emitted on the network.

NIC (Network Information Center)

All the IP addresses are allocated by a central organization that is called the NIC. This is done in order to guarantee the uniqueness of the network part. However, an organization that is assigned a network number can choose its own machine numbers.

A network number is assigned only when an organization wishes to connect to the Internet. On the other hand, if an organization decides to operate autonomously, it is free to choose whatever network number it considers to be appropriate.

2. IP configuration

IP Address

It is essential that you do not choose the IP address of a LAN arbitrarily. Such an approach could have undesirable effects for you, and for others, and in any case would not allow you to work on the network.

Subnet mask

In order to understand the role of the subnet mask, you must write it in binary (for this purpose you can use the Windows 2000 Calculator in scientific view!). The purpose is precisely to identify the bits that encode the IP network number, from amongst the bits that are used to encode the host number. A bit that is set to '1' in the subnet mask signifies that the corresponding bit in the IP address is part of the network number. On the other hand, a '0' in the subnet mask designates a bit that is used in the IP address so as to encode part of a host number.

For example, suppose you have an IP address of 192.142.1.15 that is associated with a subnet mask of 255.255.255.0. In binary, this IP address is 11000000.10001110.00000001.00001111 whilst the subnet mask in binary is 11111111.11111111.11111111. 00000000. By carrying out a LOGICAL AND between the address and the subnet mask you determine the IP address of the network. With a LOGICAL AND, the association of two **1**s produces **1**, and the association of two **0**s, or of one **1** and one **0**, produces **0**. The result in binary is 11000000.10001110.00000001.00000000, which equals 192.142.1.0 in decimal.

Default gateway

The default gateway is the IP address of the router interface that allows you to leave the LAN. Without this indication, a network peripheral cannot communicate beyond a router, and the information could not leave the LAN.

☞ *A Windows 2000 computer that has two network interface cards can act as a router for a given protocol (IP, IPX or AppleTalk). Windows 3.11 can also act as an IP router.*

3. Automatic configuration

For the automatic configuration of TCP/IP protocol, the network must contain a server that will that will distribute IP configurations to clients that request them. This type of server is called a DHCP (*Dynamic Hosts Configuration Protocol*) server. A DHCP server must have a static IP configuration. Windows 2000 Server can perform this function.

In order to transform your computers into DHCP clients you must:

– Right-click **My Network Places** and then select **Properties**.
– Right-click **Local Area Connection** and then select **Properties.**
– Under the **General** tab, select **Internet Protocol (TCP/IP)** and then click the **Properties** button.

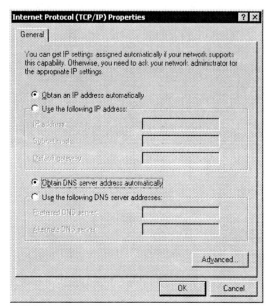

- Select **Obtain an IP address automatically**.
- Then, you can choose automatically to obtain the address of the DNS server for which your machine is a client via the DHCP server. Alternatively, you can choose to enter this address manually.

The DHCP server can supply many items of information, including the following:
- IP address (compulsory)
- Subnet mask (compulsory)
- Default gateway(s)
- The IP address of one or more DNS servers
- The IP address of one or more WINS servers
- Node type (the resolution mode of netBIOS names)
- Domain name

4. Manual configuration

For the client computers in your network, it is useful to use DHCP protocol in order to distribute IP configurations. This technique avoids any duplication of addresses. In addition, this approach simplifies and speeds up the administration.

However, your servers require a fixed addressing scheme. This is particularly important if services such as DNS, DHCP and WINS run on these servers.

In order to configure the IP addresses of your servers manually, check to ensure that the addresses that are used by your servers do not correspond to addresses that could be allocated by a DHCP server.

The **Advanced** button allows you to complete this IP configuration.

- The **IP Settings** tab allows you to add one or more IP addresses for the same interface, along with several gateway addresses.

Configuring the system

☞ *Important note: if you specify several gateway addresses for an interface, the first will always be used if it is accessible. For example, if you attempt to contact a host that is not on your sub-network, then the query will be directed to the first default gateway. If this gateway knows the destination host (from its routing table), then it will forward the packet. Otherwise, it will return a message stating that the host is inaccessible, even though it might be accessible via another gateway. These other gateways will be used only if the first gateway is physically inaccessible.*

☞ *A **metric** is associated with each network interface. This value is integrated into the routing table of the computer. It indicates the cost of reaching a given network. If, in a routing table, a network is accessible via two separate interfaces, then the interface that has the smaller metric will be used.*

- The **DNS** tab allows you to specify the IP addresses for supplementary DNS servers, with a view to providing fault tolerance. A DNS name server allows you to resolve host names into IP addresses (for example: ping merlin, or ping merlin.enipub.com)
- The **WINS** tab allows you to specify a list of the WINS servers that will be used for resolving NetBIOS names (for example: net view \\merlin). This tab also allows you to disable netBIOS. By default, NetBIOS is enabled on TCP/IP. If you disable NetBIOS, you will no longer be able to us My Network Places in order to display the list of servers that are available on your network.

Example:

With

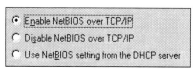

the result is as follows:

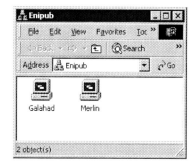

With

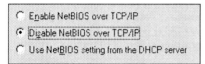

the result is as follows:

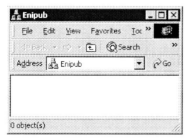

– The **Options** tab allows you to filter IP packets.

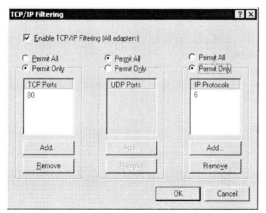

In this example, the filtering is enabled. Only Web queries (TCP port number 80) will be accepted. In addition, only TCP protocol will be authorized (port number 6 in an IP packet is that used for TCP transport protocol; whilst port number 17 is that used for UDP).

In order to test the filtering, you can run an ftp command to a server (SRV3 in the example below) on which the filtering is enabled:

```
D:\>ftp srv3
> ftp: connect :Connection refused
ftp> dir
Not connected.
ftp>
```

The ftp application runs on ports TCP 20 and 21, whereas the filter specifies that packets will be allowed through only if the TCP port number is 80.

If you disable this filter:

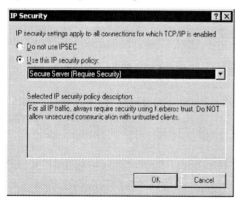

```
E:\WINNT\System32\cmd.exe                        _ □ ×

E:\>ftp galahad
Connected to galahad.enipub.com.
220 GALAHAD Microsoft FTP Service (Version 5.0).
User (galahad.enipub.com:(none)): administrator
331 Password required for administrator.
Password:
230-Welcome to the Galahad FTP server
230 User administrator logged in.
ftp> dir
200 PORT command successful.
150 Opening ASCII mode data connection for /bin/ls.
03-31-00  03:17PM       <DIR>          RFC
03-31-00  03:17PM       <DIR>          Utilities
03-31-00  03:12PM       <DIR>          White papers
226 Transfer complete.
ftp: 147 bytes received in 0.01Seconds 14.70Kbytes/sec.
ftp> quit
221  See you later

E:\>
E:\>
E:\>
```

Again in the **Options** tab, you can disable IP security.

In order to make IP traffic secure, Microsoft has included the IPSec (*IP Security*) standard in the Windows 2000 products. IPSec is an industry standard that was produced by the IETF (*Internet Engineering Task Force*) so as to ensure the security of IP traffic. By default, it is disabled. This topic will be covered further in Chapter 12, which deals with security.

5. IP Routing

A Windows 2000 server can act as a router. In order to enable it to do this it must be equipped with at least two network interface cards. You can install and configure a second adapter in exactly the same way as for the first adapter.

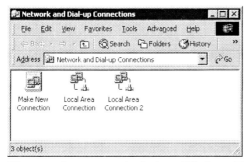

When you have several adapters, Windows 2000 represents each by a separate **Local Area Connection** icon. You can rename these icons if you wish to make them more explicit.

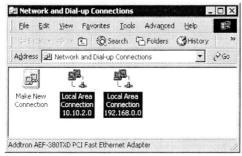

In order to enable the routing between these two networks:

➢ In **Administrative Tools** select **Routing and Remote Access**. The first time that you run this program, you must configure your server.

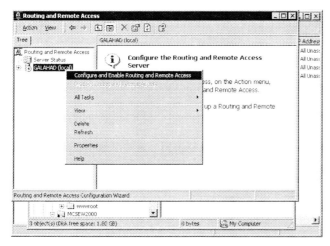

➢ Right-click the icon that represents your server, and then select **Configure and Enable Routing and Remote Access**.

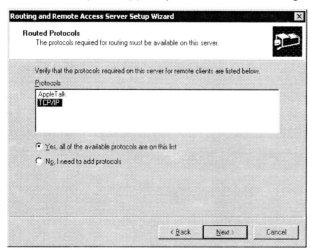

In order to make your server a router, select **Network router**. Then select the protocol(s) that you wish to use for routing.

The routable protocols that are installed on your server appear in this list.

When Windows 2000 has all the information it needs, it starts the Routing and Remote Access service.

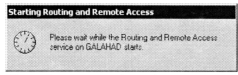

When these steps have been completed, your Windows 2000 server will act as a router.

You can consult its routing table by running the **route print** command in a command prompt. Alternatively, using the **Routing and Remote Access** program, right-click **Static Routes** and then select **Show IP Routing Table**.

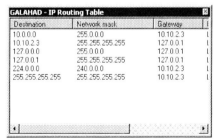

You can add static routes, simply by right-clicking **Static Routes** and then selecting **New Static Route**.

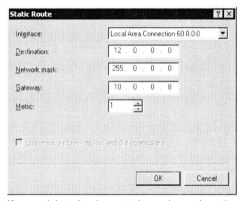

If you wish to implement dynamic routing, then you must use the **Routing and Remote Access** program. This type of routing allows routers automatically to exchange their routing table without intervention of the administrator. In order to implement dynamic routing, you must use a routing protocol that will transport routing tables between routers that use the same routing protocol.

There are two types of routing protocol:
– Distance vector routing protocols (for example: RIP).
– Link state routing protocols (for example: OSPF).

Windows 2000 allows you to implement both types of protocol with RIP and OSPF.

a. Distance vector routing protocol

RIP uses the number of hops as a metric. The best route is considered to be that which crosses the least number of routers. Windows 2000 implements version 2 of RIP. This version sends multicasts routing tables, unlike version 1 that broadcasts them (in addition, RIP v2 sends routing tables only when necessary, whereas RIP v1 sends its routing information every 30 seconds). RIP version 2 supports subnetting, whereas RIP v1 allows only network addresses that belong to a class (A, B or C).

The RIP routing protocol is easy to implement and can be used for small networks. As soon as the metric of a route exceeds 15 hops, RIP considers that the route is not reliable and it deletes the route from its routing table. This is done so as to avoid looping.

For example, suppose you have three routers that exchange their routing tables via RIP.

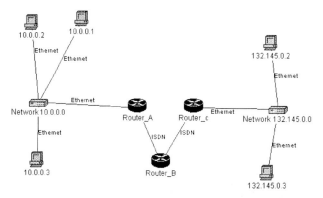

Router_A sends its routing table to Router_B. Router_B then updates its own table with the information from Router_A. This means that Router_B knows of the network 10.0.0.0 with a metric of 1. Suppose that the network 10.0.0.0 breaks down. Just before this breakdown, the routers converged, which means that they all have updated routing tables. At the moment of the failure, Router_C was not yet aware that network 10.0.0.0 was inaccessible. Router_C's routing table tells it that network 10.0.0.0 is accessible via Router_B with a metric of 2. Following this network problem, Router_A stops routing on its interface that leads towards network 10.0.0.0. However, Router_B sends its routing table to Router_A, indicating a route in order to access network 10.0.0.0 with a metric of 1. Consequently, Router_A updates its routing table with the new information: network 10.0.0.0 is accessible via Router_B with a metric of 2. Router_C receives the information again, and updates its routing table, and so forth.

Thereby, a looping situation occurs. It is for this reason that RIP considers a network to be inaccessible when it has a metric that is greater than 15. But what happens when the network contains more than 15 routers? This is why RIP is useful particularly for small networks.

☞ *Windows 2000 supports RIP for IP and for IPX. RIP IPX is the only routing protocol supported by Windows 2000 that is IPX/SPX compatible.*

☞ *RIP version 1 is described in RFC 1058 and RIP version 2 is described in RFC 1723.*

b. Link state routing protocol

Link state routing protocols use routing tables that operate with an SPF (*Short Path First*) algorithm. The routing tables of these routers can be compared to a geographical map. The routers know all the routes that lead to the destination network. Thus, if they can no longer send the packets via the best route, they are able to find an alternative route in an intelligent way. Unlike distance vector protocols that usually communicate only with their neighbors, this type of routing protocol sends information to all the routers on the network.

☞ *OSPF is described in RFC 1583.*

c. Implementation

In order to implement a routing protocol, use the **Routing and Remote Access** program and then right-click **General**.

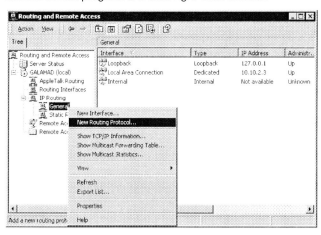

E. Configuring IPX/SPX

On a Windows 2000 machine you can install the Microsoft version of the IPX/SPX protocol.
Go into the properties of your network connection and click the **Install** button.

Select **Protocol** and then click **Add**.

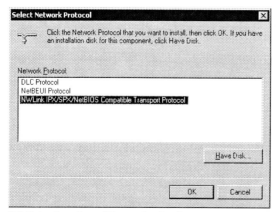

NWlink is the Microsoft implementation of IPX/SPX (*Internetwork Packet eXchange/Sequence Packet eXchange*). It is also the NetBIOS protocol that is used in Novell networks. It is used in networks in which Windows computers communicate with Novell computers.
If your want your Novell clients to be able to access resources that are situated on a Windows 2000 server, then you must install File and Print Services for Netware.
So as to ensure that these services will function correctly, you must specify the frame type that is used by the Novell machines, and then specify the IPX number manually.

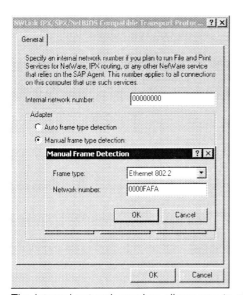

The internal network number allows you to simulate an IPX network number for applications that run on the Microsoft network. By default, this virtual network number is set to 00000000. You must indicate a virtual network number manually if you install File and Print Services for Netware with several frame types running on the same network interface card. Similarly, you must also do this if you use these services with several network adapters. Finally a third case that requires you to configure this internal network number is when your applications use the SAP *(Service Advertising Protocol)* protocol. SAP allows Novell servers to indicate the roles that they play on the network. For example, a server that sends SAP messages that are identified by the number 4, indicates that it is a file server. Similarly, the number 7 specifies a print server. SAP messages are broadcasted.

The IPX/SPX protocol can run with various frame formats. For this reason, when you install NWlink it is important that you configure the frame types that are used by the Novell network. If the Windows 2000 server acts as a router, it can route between networks that are based on different frame types. By default, Windows 2000 automatically detects the frame type that is used.

Each network that runs on IPX/SPX has a unique network number. All computers that are located on the same segment must have the same network number. An IPX address has the format *network_number.mac_address_of _card*. This address has a length of 80 bits (32 bits for the network number and 48 bits for the MAC address). In order to find out information such as the network number and the frame type, on a Windows 2000 computer enter **ipxroute config** in the command prompt.

```
<C> Copyright 1985-1999 Microsoft Corp.

D:\Documents and Settings\Administrator>cd ..

D:\Documents and Settings>cd ..

D:\>ipxroute config

NWLink IPX Routing and Source Routing Control Program v2.00


Num   Name                    Network    Node           Frame
===============================================================
0.    Internal                8ae17dfe   000000000001   [None ]
1.    IpxLoopbackAdapter      8ae17dfe   000000000002   [802.2]
2.    Local Area Connection 60. 00000000 004033d24db7   [802.2]
3.    NDISWANIPX              00000000   f24b20524153   [EthII] -

Legend
======
- down wan line

D:\>
```

IPX and the registry

You can use the registry editor in order to set up the frame type by adding two values:
– NetworkNumber, which indicates the network number
– PktType, which indicates the frame type
PktType has REG_MULIT_SZ type values. These values are 0 for Ethernet_II, 1 for Ethernet_802.2, 2 for Ethernet_802.3, 3 for SNAP, 4 for ARCnet and FF for automatic detection.
These values must be added under:
HKEY_LOCAL_MACHINE\SYSTEM\CurrentControlSet\Services\Nwlnk ipx\Parameters\Adapters*your_network_adapter*

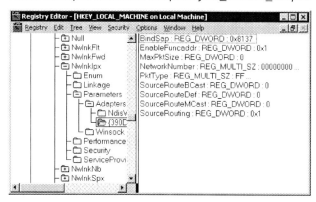

F. Installing NetBEUI

The NetBEUI (*NetBIOS Extended User Interface*) protocol is easy to use because it has an addressing scheme. It is used on small networks. It is not routable, which means that it does not cross routers (unless the routers are configured so that they will let broadcasts through). Lan Manager, Lan Server and Windows systems use this protocol.

In order to install NetBEUI, go into the properties of the network connection, and click **Install**. Then click **Protocol** followed by **Add**, and select **NetBEUI Protocol**. All the machines on the same physical network that have this protocol can communicate with each other.

☞ *Do not confuse NetBEUI and NetBIOS. NetBEUI is a transport protocol that runs on layer 4 of the OSI model. NetBIOS runs on layer 5 of the OSI model (the session layer). NetBIOS can use NetBEUI, as it can use TCP.*

G. Installing DLC protocol

DLC (*Data Link Control*) provides access to SNA systems and to certain network print devices. You can install DLC in the same way as you would install the other protocols.

H. Installing AppleTalk

This protocol allows a Windows 2000 machine that runs Services for Macintosh to communicate with MAC clients. This is a routable protocol. AppleTalk addresses are 24 bits in length (16 bits for the network part and 8 bits for the host part).

I. Optimizing bindings

When you install several protocols on a computer that is equipped with one or more network interface cards, then bindings are set up between the protocols, the services and the network adapters. On the same network interface card, several communications protocols can be bound together (TCP, NetBEUI and NWlink), and these protocols can be bound to several services.

The order of these bindings affects the performance of your servers. For example, if you install NetBEUI and TCP/IP on your Windows 2000 server that uses two network adapters, then might want one of your network segments to run only on TCP/IP, whilst another segment runs only NetBEUI. It may be useful to change the order of these bindings.

This is because, when you initialize a communication, the system tries first to communicate using the protocol that is positioned at the top of the bindings list. If this protocol proves to be unsuitable, then it will silently use the second protocol on the list, and so forth. In this case, it might be useful to delete a protocol binding on a card (for example, on a segment that uses TCP/IP, you could disable NetBEUI).

Similarly, if your server needs several communication protocols, then you should position at the top of the list, the protocol that the applications use most frequently. This will improve the performance of your server.

☞ *If you need only one protocol, do not install all the protocols on the basis that you may need them at some time in the future. By limiting yourself to those protocols that you really need, you will improve the performance of your machine. You can always install other protocols, as and when you need them.*

You can modify the status of your bindings as follows:

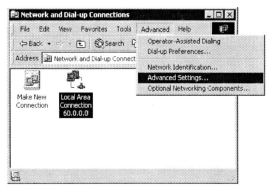

Select **Advanced Settings**.

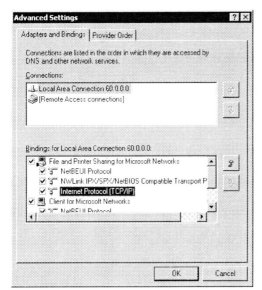

In order to change the order of your bindings, click the protocol concerned and then use the buttons ⬆ and ⬇.
In order to disable a protocol, deactivate the check box for the protocol that you do not want to use on the connection.

Labs

To be absolutely sure that you have assimilated this chapter, work through the corresponding labs. These are set out from page 622 to page 630.

☒ Exploring the registry.

☒ Driver signing option.

☒ Hardware profiles.

☒ Updating device drivers and troubleshooting hardware problems.

☒ Managing services and processes.

☒ Optimizing system performance.

☒ Configuring TCP/IP.

☒ Installing and viewing IPX/SPX settings.

☒ IP Routing.

Assessing your skills

Try the following questions if you think you know this chapter well enough.

Registry

1 How can you modify the registry? ❑
....
....

2 From which files is the registry built? ❑
....
....
....
....

3 What is a hive? ❑
....
....
....

4 What is the role of the SAM hive? ❑
....
....

5 What is the role of %systemroot%\system32\config\ ❑
system.alt?
....

6 What is the purpose of the .LOG files that are located in ❑
the **config** subdirectory?
....
....
....

7 What is the HARDWARE key? ❑
....
....

8 Which subtree stores the associations between files and ❑
OLE information? Which hive stores this information?
....
....

9 What are the subtrees HKEY_CURRENT_USER and ❑
HKEY_CURRENT_CONFIG?
....
....
....

10 Is it possible to modify the registry of a remote machine? ❑
....

11 Who is HKEY_CURRENT_USER? ❑
....

12 Which hive contains the LSA? ❑
....

13 What is a value? ❑
....
....

14 What is the name of the Windows 95 registry editor? ❑
....

15 Which registry editor allows you to carry out advanced ❑
searches?
....

16 Which registry editor provides a read only mode? ❑
....

17 You have not converted to NTFS, your partition that ❑
contains system files. However, you want to use the
regedt32.exe **Security** menu. Is this possible?

....
....
....
....

18 Using the **Security** menu of the Windows 2000 registry ❑
editor, you have decided to protect yourself by deleting all
the permissions except for those for the administrator. What
could be the consequences of this action?

....
....
....

Configuring the environment

19 How can you change the properties of your display? ❑
....
....
....

20 You wish to add the DHCP service on your server. How ❑
will you achieve this?
....
....
....

Configuring the system

21 Using the **Keyboard** icon of the **Control Panel**, you are unable to activate the numeric keyboard before logon. How will you solve this problem?

....

....

....

22 You wish to equip your Windows 2000 with a sound card that does not have a plug-and-play feature. Which program allows you to carry out this operation?

....

....

23 You wish to change the name of your server using the **Network Identification** tab of the **System Properties** dialog box. However, the **Properties** button is grayed out. What might be causing this problem?

....

....

System performance

24 In order to promote the stability of your system, you do not want any unsigned driver to be installed on your Windows 2000 server. How can ensure that unsigned drivers cannot be installed?

....

....

....

25 You want to be sure that network services are privileged with respect to foreground applications on your Windows 2000 server. How can you check this?

....

....

....

26 What is the default size of a paging file?

....

27 What is the name of the paging file?

....

28 What is the role of the paging file?

....

....

....

29 Can you have several paging files on the same disk?

....

....

30 How can you optimize your system by the location of your paging files?

....
....

31 Your Windows 2000 server system has two hard disks, each of which has a capacity of 2 GB, organized into two partitions of 1 GB. The system files are on the first disk and the performance of the machine is inadequate. On which partition of which disk must you locate the paging file in order to improve the performance?

....

32 Which utility allows you to work on services?

....
....

33 Is it possible to work on the services of a remote computer?

....
....

34 How can you find out if a service depends on another service?

....

35 Is it possible to restart a service along with its dependencies?

....
....

Configuring the network environment

36 Which communication protocols are standard supplies with Windows 2000?

....
....

37 What is NWLink?

....
....

38 As a client, you work with TCP/IP more than you work with NetBEUI. However, you need both protocols. How can you optimize your system given that you share resources, mainly with clients who use NetBEUI, but also by a few clients who use TCP/IP?

....
....
....

39 Which items of information are essential in order to carry out an IP configuration?

....

....

40 Which two methods allow you to configure clients with the TCP/IP protocol?

....

....

41 One of your servers has a network interface that is connected to the Internet, and another of your servers is connected to a LAN. You use NetBIOS name resolution on the LAN, but you wish to disable the listening for NetBIOS datagrams on the interface that is connected to the Internet. How will you achieve this?

....

....

....

42 Your Windows 2000 server has two network interface cards. You want it to act as a router. What must you do in order to route packets from one subnetwork to the other subnetwork?

....

....

43 What does dynamic routing mean?

....

....

....

44 Which routing protocols does Windows 2000 support?

....

....

....

45 How must you configure the TCP/IP settings of client machines so as to enable them to access a different subnetwork from the one in which they are located?

....

....

....

46 What is a routable protocol?

....

....

....

47 Is NetBEUI a routable protocol? Is TCP/IP a routable protocol?

....

....

48 What are the format and the size of an IPX/SPX address? ☐

....
....
....

49 On how many bits is an AppleTalk address defined? ☐

....
....

Results

Check your answers on pages 113 to 118. Count one point for each correct answer.

Number of points | /49 |

For this chapter you need to have scored at least 37 out of 49.

Look at the list of key points that follows. Pick out the ones with which you have had difficulty and work through them again in this chapter before moving on to the next.

Key points of the chapter

☐ Registry.

☐ Configuring the environment.

☐ System performance.

☐ Configuring the network environment.

Solutions

Registry

1   How can you modify the registry?

You can do this, either using the Control Panel, or using the registry editor, or using group policies.

2   From which files is the registry built?

*The files that are contained in **%systemroot%\system 32\config** are used so as to build the hives that make up part of its structure (HKEY_LOCAL_MACHINE). In addition, the **NTUSER.DAT** user profile files that are contained in **%systemdrive%\documents and settings\ user_name** are used. Finally, the **HARDWARE** volatile key is built by NTDETECT. COM upon startup of the machine.*

3 What is a hive?

*A hive is a part of the registry. It corresponds physically to a file. These files are stored in **%systemroot%\system32\config**.*

4 What is the role of the SAM hive?

The SAM hive is the part of the registry that contains the account database that is local to the machine.

5 What is the role of %systemroot%\system32\config\system.alt?

This is a copy of the SYSTEM hive.

6 What is the purpose of the .LOG files that are located in the **config** subdirectory?

These are log files of the modifications that have been made to the respective hives. In the event of a problem, they allow incident free recovery, and thereby, they avoid any inconsistencies in the registry.

7 What is the HARDWARE key?

This is a volatile key that is built up by NTDETECT.COM upon machine startup.

8 Which subtree stores the associations between files and OLE information, and in which hive?

The HKEY_CLASSES_ROOT subtree stores this information in HKEY_LOCAL_MACHINE\software\classes.

9 What are the subtrees HKEY_CURRENT_USER and HKEY_CURRENT_CONFIG?

HKEY_CURRENT_USER corresponds to HKEY_USERS \SID of the current user.
HKEY_CURRENT_CONFIG is
HKEY_LOCAL_MACHINE\System\CurrentControlSet\ Hardware Profiles\profile number.

10 Is it possible to modify the registry of a remote machine?

Yes, provided that you have enough rights.

11 Who is HKEY_CURRENT_USER?

This is the user that is currently logged on.

12 Which hive contains the LSA?

The Local Security Authority corresponds to the Security hive.

13 What is a value?

This is an item of information that is stored at hive level in the registry structure. This value has a name, a type and a content.

14 What is the name of the Windows 95 registry editor?

Regedit.exe.

15 Which registry editor allows you to carry out advanced searches?

The Windows 95 editor, regedit.exe.

16 Which registry editor provides a read only mode?

The Windows 2000 editor, regedt32.exe.

17 You have not converted to NTFS, your partition that contains system files. However, you want to use the regedt32.exe **Security** menu. Is this possible?

Registry keys must not be confused with NTFS folders. There is no link between NTFS and permissions that are associated with objects that are neither folders nor files. Consequently, the answer is yes.

18 Using the **Security** menu of the Windows 2000 registry editor, you have decided to protect yourself by deleting all the permissions except for those for the administrator. What could be the consequences of this action?

Some Windows 2000 services may no longer have enough rights in order to access the registry. It would be very difficult to diagnose the problem.

Configuring the environment

19 How can you change the properties of your display?

*By using the **Display** program of **Control Panel**. Alternatively, you can right-click the desktop and select **Properties**.*

20 You wish to add the DHCP service on your server. How will you achieve this?

*Use **Add/Remove Programs** from **Control Panel**. Then click the **Add/Remove Windows Components** button.*

21 Using the **Keyboard** icon of the **Control Panel**, you are unable to activate the numeric keyboard before logon. How will you solve this problem?

Using the registry editor, change the InitialKeyboard Indicators value to 2. This value is located under HKEY_USER\.DEFAULT\ Control Panel\Keyboard.

22 You wish to equip your Windows 2000 with a sound card that does not have a plug-and-play feature. Which program allows you to carry out this operation?

*The **Add/Remove Hardware** program of **Control Panel**.*

23 You wish to change the name of your server using the **Network Identification** tab of the **System Properties** dialog box. However, the **Properties** button is grayed out. What might be causing this problem?

This machine is certainly a Windows 2000 domain controller. In this case you cannot change the name of the server.

System performance

24 In order to promote the stability of your system, you do not want any unsigned driver to be installed on your Windows 2000 server. How can ensure that unsigned drivers cannot be installed?

Using Control Panel, double-click the System icon and click the Hardware tab. Then click the Driver Signing button and select the Block - Prevent installation of unsigned files option.

25 You want to be sure that network services are privileged with respect to foreground applications on your Windows 2000 server. How can you check this?

Using the System icon of Control Panel. Click the Advanced tab followed by the Performance Option button. Check that the Background services option is selected.

26 What is the default size of a paging file?

RAM+50%.

27 What is the name of the paging file?

Pagefile.sys.

28 What is the role of the paging file?

The paging file allows the system to free volatile memory so that it will be available for applications that need it. The system does this by transferring information from the RAM to the paging file on disk.

29 Can you have several paging files on the same disk?

Yes, provided that they are placed on separate partitions: each paging file must be located in the root of the partition.

30 How can you optimize your system by the location of your paging files?

By creating one paging file per physical disk. The system will then balance the load automatically.

31 Your Windows 2000 server system has two hard disks, each of which has a capacity of 2 GB, organized into two partitions of 1 GB. The system files are on the first disk. However, the performance of the machine is inadequate. On which partition of which disk must you locate the paging file in order to improve the performance?

On one of the partitions that is located on the second disk.

32 Which utility allows you to work on services?

In *Administrative Tools*, you can use either the *Services* program, or the *Computer Management* program.

33 Is it possible to work on the services of a remote computer?

Yes, by right-clicking *Computer Management (Local)* in the *Computer Management* program, and then selecting *Connect to another computer*.

34 How can you find out if a service depends on another service?

By selecting the *Dependencies* tab in the properties of the service.

35 Is it possible to restart a service along with its dependencies?

Yes, when a service is restarted, the system restarts all its dependencies also.

Configuring the network environment

36 Which communication protocols are standard supplies with Windows 2000?

TCP/IP, NetBEUI, NWLink, Apple Talk and DLC.

37 What is NWLink?

This is the NDIS version of IPX/SPX.

38 As a client, you work with TCP/IP more than you work with NetBEUI. However, you need both protocols. How can you optimize your system given that you share resources, mainly with clients who use NetBEUI, but also by a few clients who use TCP/IP?

At server service level, place NetBEUI at the top of the list followed by TCP/IP. At workstation service level, place TCP/IP at the top of the list followed by NetBEUI. You can carry out these operations using the *Adapters and Bindings* tab, of the *Advanced Settings*, of *Network and Dial-up Connections*.

39 Which items of information are essential in order to carry out an IP configuration?

An IP configuration requires, at least, an IP address and a subnet mask.

40 Which two methods allow you to configure clients with the TCP/IP protocol?

You can either do this manually, or you can do it dynamically using a DHCP server.

Configuring the system

41 One of your servers has a network interface that is connected to the Internet, and another of your servers is connected to a LAN. You use NetBIOS name resolution on the LAN, but you wish to disable the listening for NetBIOS datagrams on the interface that is connected to the Internet. How will you achieve this?

*In the **Internet Protocol (TCP/IP) Properties** dialog box, click the **Advanced** button followed by the **WINS** tab, and then select **Disable NetBIOS over TCP/IP**.*

42 Your Windows 2000 server has two network interface cards. You want it to act as a router. What must you do in order to route packets from one subnetwork to the other subnetwork?

*Configure the server as a router using the **Routing and Remote Access** program in the Administrative Tools.*

43 What does dynamic routing mean?

Dynamic routing allows routers dynamically to exchange their routing tables using a routing protocol.

44 Which routing protocols does Windows 2000 support?

Windows 2000 supports RIPv2 as a distance vector routing protocol, and OSPF as a link state routing protocol.

45 How must you configure the TCP/IP settings of client machines so as to enable them to access a different subnetwork from the one in which they are located?

Client machines must have either a gateway address in their IP configuration, or a static route in their routing table.

46 What is a routable protocol?

A routable protocol is a protocol that uses addresses that can be interpreted by a router in order to forward the packet to its destination. TCP/IP, IPX/SPX and Apple Talk are examples of routable protocols.

47 Is NetBEUI a routable protocol? Is TCP/IP a routable protocol?

NetBEUI is not a routable protocol. TCP/IP is a routable protocol.

48 What are the format and the size of an IPX/SPX address?

An IPX address has the format: network_number .mac_address_of_the_card. This address has a length of 80 bits (48 bits are used for the MAC address of the card, and 32 bits are used for the network number).

49 On how many bits is an AppleTalk address defined?

An AppleTalk address is defined on 24 bits: 14 bits are used for the network part and 8 bits are used for the machine part.

Prerequisites for this chapter

☒ General knowledge of administration tools.

☒ General knowledge of the Windows 2000 environment.

Objectives

At the end of this chapter, you will be able to:

☒ Install administration tools on a workstation or on a stand-alone/member server.

☒ Customize administration tools.

☒ Distinguish between a snap-in component and an extension.

☒ Save consoles in different modes.

Contents

Administration tools and the MMC

A. Installing administration tools

Computers that run Windows 2000 must be administered using the MMC (*Microsoft Management Console*). When you install Windows 2000, a series of consoles are created that allow you to manage your machine. On a domain controller, further MMCs are provided that allow you to manage network services.

You can install the administration tools on your member or stand-alone server, or on your Windows 2000 Professional workstation.

For this purpose, go into **Control Panel**, and double-click **Add/Remove Programs**. Select **Add New Programs**, then click the **CD or Floppy** button. Go into the I386 directory of the Windows 2000 Advanced Server CD-ROM, and install Adminpak.msi.

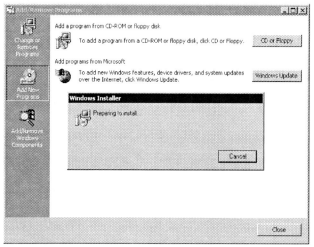

Windows Installer then installs the administration tools on your computer. It adds these tools into the **Start - Administrative Tools** menu.

Before:

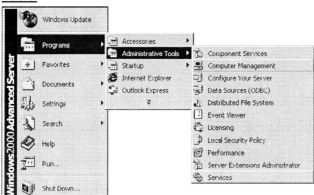

After:

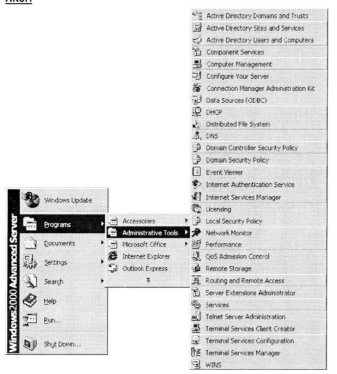

In order to uninstall these tools, use **Add/Remove Programs** in Control Panel.

Then select **Windows 2000 Administration Tools**, and click the **Remove** button.

B. Customizing administration tools

Even though Windows 2000 offers a full range of tools, you might find it useful to create your own console. For example, suppose that all that you want to do is to manage DNS and DHCP. In this case you could design an MMC that contains only those components that will help you to manage DNS and DHCP. You could even include in your console, the component that will allow you to manage the services. This would allow you to stop and to restart your DNS and DHCP services, as and when you need to do so.

A customized console is a file that has an .MSC name extension. Into this file, you can add snap-in components. A snap-in is an application management component.

In order to create a customized MMC, run the mmc.exe program.

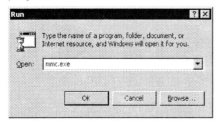

A blank console appears, into which you can add snap-in components (**Add/Remove Snap-in**):

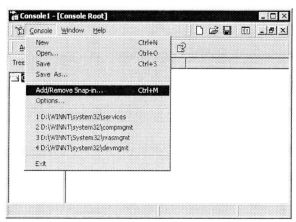

After clicking the **Add** button, you can select the snap-ins that you want to add to your console:

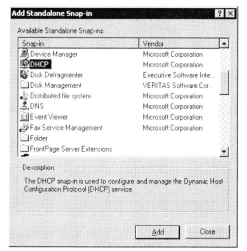

When you have created your console, you must save it so that you will be able to re-use it. You can create as many MMCs as you like. In addition, you can add as many snap-ins as you like into each console.

☞ *If user profiles have been implemented, then you must place this MMC in your own profile in order to be able to use it from any machine in the network.*

☞ *In this way, you can create customized consoles so that you can delegate certain administrative tasks to other users. These customized consoles can be sent by e-mail for example.*

Terminology:

As an example, take the following MMC:

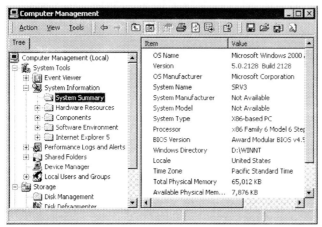

- This section deals with the Snap-ins for **Computer Management**.
- A snap-in can have one or more **extensions**. In the example above, the snap-in **Computer Management** has extensions that include **Event Viewer** and **Device Manager**. An extension is a snap-in that is attached to a parent snap-in. Some snap-ins can be both snap-ins and extensions. This is the case for Event Viewer.

When you create your own MMC, you can use an extension as a snap-in for the console that you are designing. In order to do this, run an MMC, and then add a snap-in.

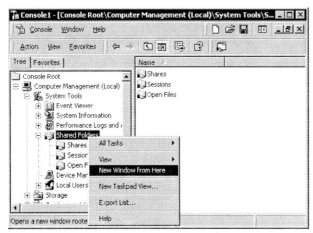

Right-click the extension that you want to use as a snap-in for your console, and select **New Window from Here**. Then, all you have to do is to save your console.

You may wish to add a snap-in and then remove a few of its extensions. You can do this when you add the snap-in, by clicking the **Extensions** tab.

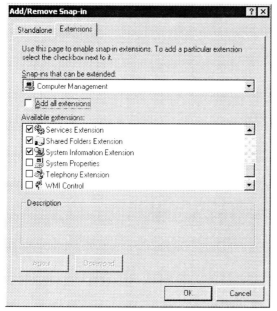

Deactivate the check boxes for the extensions that you do not want to display.

If you create customized consoles in order to provide them to users whose administrative roles are limited, then you can design your consoles, either so that the users will be able to modify them, or so that they will not be able to modify them.

By default, a console is created in **Author mode**. This means that you allow full access to all the features of the MMC. Consequently, the users will be able, to add or to remove snap-ins, to create windows, to display all parts of the console tree, and to save all their modifications.

In order to change the mode, open the **Console** menu and then select **Options**.

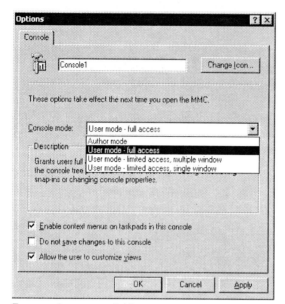

Four modes are available:
- **Author mode**: allows users to modify the console (for example to add/remove snap-ins, to modify extensions and to create new windows).
- **User mode - full access**: allows users to explore the console, to create new windows and to open new windows. However, it does not allow users to add or to remove snap-ins, nor does it allow them to save the console.
- **User mode - limited access, multiple window**: allows users to display several windows in the console, but it does not allow them to create other windows. In this mode, users can neither add snap-ins, nor remove them.
- **User mode - limited access, single window**: this mode is similar to the previous one, except that users are not allowed to open several windows.

There is a difference between displaying a new window, and creating a window:
- In order to display a new window, right-click in its own window, the snap-in that you want to display, and then select **New Window from Here**.

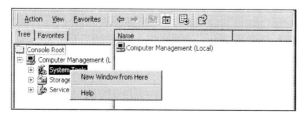

– In order to create a new window, right-click **Console Root**, and then select **New Window from Here**.

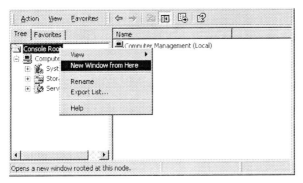

Second logon

When you log on with a user name, you have the privileges of this user in order to run applications. Windows 2000 allows you to use a **second logon** so that you can run certain applications.

In order to do this, right-click the application that you wish to run with different privileges, and then select **Run as** (with some applications, you must press the ⬚Shift key before you right-click).

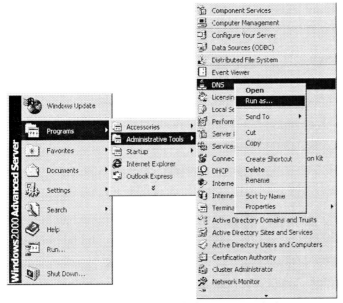

Then, enter the user name and the password that are associated with the account concerned, along with the domain in which the account is situated.

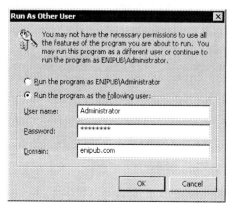

When you use this option, you will receive a new access token that is valid only for the application concerned. The other applications will continue to run with the privileges of the first logon.

In addition, you can access this feature using a **command prompt**, or using the **Run** utility. In these cases the command is as follows:

Runas /user :domain\user_name program

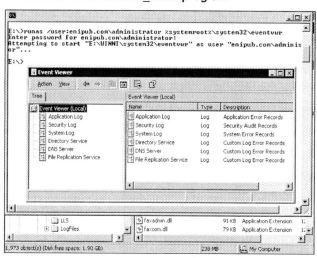

☞ *The administration tools are located in the directory %systemroot%\system32.*

A simple way of organizing your programs that are situated in the **Start** - **Programs** - **Administrative Tools** menu is to go into Control Panel and then double-click the **Administrative Tools** icon.

You can administer a Windows 2000 server remotely using the terminal emulation services (terminal service). These features will be covered in Chapter 14.

Labs

To be absolutely sure that you have assimilated this chapter, work through the corresponding labs. These are set out from page 631 to page 632.

☒ Installing administrative tools.

☒ Customizing administrative tools.

☒ Second logon.

Assessing your skills

When you feel happy with your level of knowledge on this chapter, answer the following questions.

Administration tools

1 Which program must you use in order to install administration tools on your Windows 2000 Professional machine?

....
....

2 What must you use in order to administer Windows 2000?

....
....

3 What does MMC mean?

....
....
....

4 What are the advantages of administration consoles?

....
....
....
....

5 How can you create a customized MMC?

....
....

6 What is the name of the components that you add to an MMC?

....
....
....
....

7 What are the different modes in which you can save a console?

....
....
....
....
....
....
....

8 What is the safest way of carrying out an operation on a client machine that needs administrator privileges?

....
....
....
....
....
....
....

9 Where are the administration tools stored?

....

10 How can you uninstall the administration tools on a client machine?

....
....

11 How can you run an application with a different privilege level than that of your logon?

....
....
....

Results

Check your answers on pages 131 to 132. Count one point for each correct answer.

Number of points | /11 |

For this chapter you need to have scored at least 8 out of 11. Look at the list of key points that follows. Pick out the ones with which you have had difficulty and work through them again in this chapter before moving on to the next.

Key points of the chapter

☐   Administration tools.

Solutions

Administration tools

1   Which program must you use in order to install administration tools on your Windows 2000 Professional machine?

*You must use **Adminpack.msi**, which is located in the I386 directory of the Windows 2000 server CD-ROM.*

2   What must you use in order to administer Windows 2000?

Using consoles (MMC).

3   What does MMC mean?

Microsoft Management Console.

4   What are the advantages of administration consoles?

Using MMC, you can customize your administration tools so that you have a single interface for all the programs that you need in order to carry out administrative tasks.

5   How can you create a customized MMC?

*Run the **MMC.EXE** program, either using a command prompt, or using the Start - Run menu.*

6   What is the name of the components that you add to an MMC?

*In order to create a customized console, you must create a new MMC into which you can add **snap-ins**. Each snap-in can be an extension structure.*

7   What are the different modes in which you can save a console?

There are four modes in which you can save your consoles (author mode and three user modes). Author mode allows you to carry out all possible tasks in an MMC, such as adding or removing snap-ins. The different user modes offer different levels of restriction concerning console modification.

8 What is the safest way of carrying out an operation on a client machine that needs administrator privileges?

Rather than closing your current user session, in order to log on as administrator on the client machine, it is preferable to use the second logon feature. This feature allows you to use the permissions of another user account, solely for the application that you run in this mode.

9 Where are the administration tools stored?

In the %systemroot%\system32 directory.

10 How can you uninstall the administration tools on a client machine?

Using the Add/Remove Programs icon of Control Panel.

11 How can you run an application with a different privilege level than that of your logon?

*By executing the **runas** command from a command prompt. Alternatively, you can right-click the application that you wish to run and then select Run as.*

Prerequisites for this chapter

☒ General knowledge of using Windows 2000 (such as adding services and handling consoles).

☒ Essential knowledge of name resolution in an IP environment.

Objectives

At the end of this chapter, you will be able to:

☒ Describe the operating principle of a DNS service.

☒ Define the system components of Internet names.

☒ Install and configure the DNS service on Windows 2000.

☒ Configure the DNS server so that it will accept dynamic registrations.

☒ Understand the transfer zone mechanism.

☒ Create subdomains.

☒ Troubleshoot a DNS server.

☒ Configure DNS clients.

Contents

A. TCP/IP and Internet protocols

1. Introduction

The TCP/IP family was developed by an American state organization, the DoD (*Department of Defense*). It comprises around a hundred protocols, and defines a model with four network layers. TCP/IP appeared in the early 70s, ten years before the OSI model.

This is one of the most popular communication and application protocols. It is used to connect together heterogeneous systems, independently of the physical layer.

TCP (*Transfer Control Protocol*) is a transport protocol. It ensures a reliable service, which is connection oriented for a stream of bytes.

In contrast to TCP, UDP (*User Datagram Protocol*) is a connectionless transport protocol. It is very fast, but it is not very reliable.

☞ *UDP is used on the Internet in order to transport live sound on certain radio sites. In these cases, the data that is transferred does not require the transmission to be perfect.*

IP (*Internet Protocol*), provides a packet delivery system that is connectionless and unreliable. It manages logical addresses that decompose the identifier of each node into a logical network number, and a peripheral number. This logical address has a length of 4 bytes (with IP version 4).

☞ *IP v.6 protocol, or IP Next Generation, is currently being developed. It will be compatible with IP v.4, but it will require that all the TCP/IP protocols are rewritten. The IP address will be extended to 16 bytes. The Windows 2000, DNS server service allows you to add IPv6 hosts.*

One of the keys to the success of the Internet protocols is that the model proposed is independent of the physical layer.

2. History

In 1970, Stanford University developed ARPANET (*Advanced Research Project Agency NETWork*) and the TCP/IP architecture. The DoD financed this work, and the physical media were based essentially on packet communication.

In 1993, the DARPA (*Defense Advanced Research Project Agency*), who had standardized the principal TCP/IP modules, made the use of TCP/IP obligatory for all the machines that were connected to ARPANET.

ARPANET developed from a small packet switching network on point-to-point telephone links, into an immense hybrid network called the **Internet**.

☞ *Today, ARPANET is the part of the Internet that is used by the DoD for research and development.*

The integration of Internet protocols into BSD (*Berkeley Software Distribution*) Unix, and the free diffusion of this operating system to universities, largely contributed to the success of this protocol suite.

The protocols continue to evolve thanks to the *Internet Activity Board*, and to the readily accessible RFC (*Request For Comment*) standardization documents.

3. The Internet protocol suite and the OSI model

It must be remembered that the TCP/IP model appeared ten years before the OSI model, which was heavily inspired by certain TCP/IP protocols. However, it is useful to compare the OSI model, which has seven layers, with the Internet protocols, which operate on four layers:

OSI model	*TCP/IP model*				
5-6-7	Application	Telnet	ftp	dns	snmp
4	Transport	TCP		UDP	
3	Internet	ARP	IP	ICMP	
1-2	Network Interface	Ethernet	Token Ring	Others	

a. User application services

A certain number of services and applications are based on the TCP/IP protocol stack.

TELNET is a terminal emulation protocol. A session is set up between a workstation (telnet client) and a remote machine (telnet server). All communication that is entered on the client is transmitted to the telnet server, where it is executed. The echo of the remote process is returned to the workstation, which reads the command report. Consequently, telnet must know the commands of the remote operating system.

FTP *(File Transfer Protocol)* uses a reliable mode and runs on TCP. The big advantage of FTP is that you can use it between different operating systems that are based on heterogeneous file systems. After the connection has been set up (when the name and the password have been accepted), the ftp client sees the directory of the user who logged onto the ftp server, in addition to the client's own local working directory.

☞ *On the Internet, there are many ftp sites that allow anyone to download files (this is done using the ftp guest user, which is called **anonymous**, and which has no password).*

Using the special FTP commands, you can copy files from one directory to another (according to the permissions that you have on each system).

☞ *Internet operators now offer connections to ftp sites in graphic mode. Such interfaces allow you to download files by a simple click, without knowing any special commands.*

TFTP or *Trivial FTP*, allows you to download information rapidly, but it does not guarantee its integrity. It is unreliable because it uses UDP protocol, rather than TCP.

RIP *(Routing Internet Protocol)* is a dynamic routing protocol. One of its fundamental roles concerns the exchange of routing information between routers, so that each of them is able to use the network list in order to propose a *better* route (in this context, a "better" route is one that crosses fewer routers).

☞ *Routed is a version of RIP that is implemented on UNIX 4.2 BSD.*

SMTP is a simple transfer protocol that is used for electronic mail (*Simple Mail Transfer Protocol*). It uses UDP and IP. It does not provide a user interface.

NFS or *Network File System* was developed by SUN around 1985. It is a distributed file system that runs in a heterogeneous environment (application layer). It allows users of different computers and operating systems to access a remote file system without the need to learn any specific new commands.

DNS is short for *Domain Name System*. Rather than trying to remember the IP address of a machine, it is simpler to work with names. At first, these names were aliases that were stored locally. Then, they were available to everyone from a centralized file (/etc/hosts on Unix). Progressively, a distributed hierarchical database management system was set up that associates each IP address with one or more names. Today, the Internet uses such a database. At the root of this world-level domain tree, there are 13 DNS servers. These servers are strategically placed and they know the DNS servers that are situated on the next level down, which manage all types of organization along with the country suffixes. This approach allows you to define DNS servers at different levels of the domain tree.

For example, *www.dev.microsoft.com* corresponds to a machine, which is called www, and which is in the *dev* (development) subdomain, of the *microsoft* domain, of the *com* (commercial) type of organization.

There is nothing to stop Microsoft from managing one DNS server in the *microsoft.com* domain, and another in the *dev.microsoft.com* subdomain.

WINS, or *Windows Internet Name Service*, is a (NetBIOS) windows name service that runs in internetwork (internetwork must not be confused with the Internet, and similarly, WINS must not be confused with DNS). The products that are based on the NetBIOS layer (including those of Microsoft) handle high-level identifiers that are called **NetBIOS names** (for example, workstation names). These names must be short (from 8 to 15 characters), and they must be unique on the internetwork concerned. The major drawback with this approach is that it does not allow a hierarchical structure. Internetwork functioning is possible because NetBIOS uses IP, which is a routable protocol.

☞ *In fact, NetBIOS was originally intended for LANs. It found a specific machine by sending a broadcast packet to all the workstations (in order to find out the physical address that is associated with a name). The problem with this approach is that generally a broadcast does not cross a router.*

The purpose of WINS therefore, is to **manage a centralized database** on a WINS server that **associates a NetBIOS name with an IP address**. This **dynamic** database is built up by all the name registration requests that are made by the (WINS) clients. First, these clients register their names and addresses with the server. Then, the other clients query the server.

A client communicates with its server by specifying the server's IP address. The client can either register itself, or it can request the resolution of a name into an IP address.

DHCP or *Dynamic Host Configuration Protocol* is a protocol that automatically configures TCP/IP options for clients, in a NetBIOS environment.

This protocol allows you dynamically to attribute, an IP address, and a subnet mask. In addition, it even allows you to attribute such items as the IP address of a DNS server, and a default gateway IP address (the IP address of a router that allows you to go out of your LAN).

This protocol is very useful, especially for portable machines that must change the network in which they run, and consequently their IP network number.

SNMP or *Simple Network Management Protocol*, uses UDP and allows you remotely to administer both hardware and software. On the one hand, the SNMP agents must provide information, or respond to queries from an administration manager or platform (for example, HPOV, HP Open View on HP-UX). In this way, the SNMP manager collects large amounts of information from routers, switches, bridges and specific applications. In addition, it provides statistical information and sends commands to devices in order remotely to manage events.

Locally, the SNMP agents run on certain, selected layers of the OSI model, and store the information in databases that are called MIB (*Management Information Base*).

4. Resolving names

Applications that are developed on Windows 2000 can work directly with TCP/IP sockets, in the same way as Telnet and FTP applications do. Other applications use communications that are based on NetBIOS. This technique frees these applications from the underlying protocol:

Applications using the NetBIOS layer		Applications using the protocol directly
NetBIOS Interface		WinSockets
NetBEUIprotocol	IPX protocol	TCP/IP protocol

Applications that are based on NetBIOS communicate using machine names such as GALAHAD, MERLIN and EXCALIBUR, for example.

On the other hand, Windows Sockets applications use Internet names or host names. In both cases, the objective is to use convivial names that are easy to remember, in an environment where only IP addresses can be used to identify the computers!

a. NetBIOS names

Resolution methods

Suppose that you want to access a computer that is located on the other side of a router, by specifying its NetBIOS name. For this purpose, you may wish to use the command **NET VIEW \\computer**, for example.

By default, a broadcast will be used in order to resolve a NetBIOS name into an IP address. Consequently, as the broadcast will not get past the router, the **NET VIEW** command will generate **Error 53**, so as to indicate that the name was not found.

In order to solve this problem, you can use an LMHOSTS (Lan Manager HOSTS) static mapping file. Alternatively, you can use a service that implements registration requests, in addition to name resolution requests: Windows Internet Name Services (WINS).

Using LMHOSTS

First you must rename the LMHOSTS.SAM (sample) file, in order to remove the name extension.

(Remember that this on Windows NT and Windows 2000 machines, this file is located, in the \winnt\system32 \drivers\etc directory, and that on Windows 95 machines it is situated in the \win95 directory).

Your next step is to edit this file so that it contains the following information:

```
# start of LMHOST file
#
10.0.0.1            merlin

# do not forget at least one new line
# after the line: 10.0.0.1          merlin
```

You will now be able to use commands that call NetBIOS:

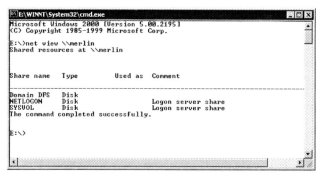

If you know that an entry in the LMHOSTS file will be used frequently then you can add the #PRE command (in uppercase characters) at the end of the line. This will cause this entry to be placed in the memory cache. In this way, not only will you avoid failure of the broadcast, but you will also avoid needless analysis of the LMHOSTS file. The entry will

be loaded into the memory cache, either upon initialization, or following the command **nbtstat -R**.
The LMHOSTS file will then look like this:

```
# start of LMHOST file
#
10.0.0.1              merlin   #PRE

# do not forget at least one new line
# after the line: 10.0.0.1        merlin
```

b. Internet names

Here again you have the problem of resolving host names into IP addresses. Whilst the NetBIOS world offers the WINS and the LMHOSTS solutions, Internet offers two similar solutions: use of the HOSTS file, or use of a DNS server.

Using the HOSTS file

This file is located in the \WINNT\system32\drivers\etc directory on Windows NT and Windows 2000 machines, and in the \WINDOWS directory on Windows 95 machines. It is compatible with the UNIX format, and is made up of a series of lines that have the following structure:

```
IP_address Host_name alias
```

Here is an example of the HOSTS file on the GALAHAD machine that allows you to contact the MERLIN machine that is located on another network:

```
# start of the HOSTS file on the GALLAHAD machine
#
127.0.0.1              localhost
10.0.0.1               merlin   merlin.ediENI.com
#
# end of HOSTS file
```

You can now use the PING command, or the TELNET command using, either the simple name, or the FQDN *(Fully Qualified Domain Name)*, rather than the IP address:

```
E:\WINNT\System32\cmd.exe                                    _ □ ×

E:\>ping merlin

Pinging merlin.enipub.com [10.10.2.1] with 32 bytes of data:

Reply from 10.10.2.1: bytes=32 time<10ms TTL=128
Reply from 10.10.2.1: bytes=32 time<10ms TTL=128
Reply from 10.10.2.1: bytes=32 time<10ms TTL=128
Reply from 10.10.2.1: bytes=32 time<10ms TTL=128

Ping statistics for 10.10.2.1:
    Packets: Sent = 4, Received = 4, Lost = 0 (0% loss),
Approximate round trip times in milli-seconds:
    Minimum = 0ms, Maximum = 0ms, Average = 0ms

E:\>ping merlin.enipub.com

Pinging merlin.enipub.com [10.10.2.1] with 32 bytes of data:

Reply from 10.10.2.1: bytes=32 time<10ms TTL=128
Reply from 10.10.2.1: bytes=32 time<10ms TTL=128
Reply from 10.10.2.1: bytes=32 time<10ms TTL=128
Reply from 10.10.2.1: bytes=32 time<10ms TTL=128

Ping statistics for 10.10.2.1:
    Packets: Sent = 4, Received = 4, Lost = 0 (0% loss),
Approximate round trip times in milli-seconds:
    Minimum = 0ms, Maximum = 0ms, Average = 0ms

E:\>
```

B. Domain Name System

1. General definition

TCP/IP utilities, such as Telnet or FTP, can communicate using the IP address of the remote machine. Alternatively, they can use the name of the remote machine, which is different from the NetBIOS name that is used on Windows hosts. It is easier for a user to refer to the "MERLIN" machine, rather than to the 132.147.160.1 IP address!

Because of its size, the Internet network cannot use only simple names in order to refer to all the machines that it contains. As with all big organizations, it was decided to divide the network into different areas, each of which corresponds either to a geographical entity, or to a function, or to a type of activity. Each "department" can then be subdivided itself, so as to form a tree structure, with manager that is responsible for managing the set of names that are used within the structure.

In the context of TCP/IP interconnections, the mechanism that is used to manage these sets of names is called **Domain Name System** or **DNS**.

The TCP/IP DNS system uses the following domains:

Name	Signification
COM	Commercial enterprise
EDU	Educational establishments
GOV	Government establishments
MIL	Military organizations
NET	Major network sites
ORG	Other organizations
ARPA	Arpanet domains
INT	International organizations
Country Code	Each country

Originally, the Internet existed only in the USA and the domain names had suffixes that indicated the type of organization. The network has since been extended to all countries, and there is now a domain per country. Consequently, the sites with name suffixes that indicate a type of organization are principally located in the USA; whilst for sites outside of the USA with a country suffix, the type of organization is not repeated. Thus, the tree structure is based on the type of organization and on the geographical location.

Examples:

The ANDROMEDA server in the training department of the ENI commercial organization in the UK could have the following name:

```
andromeda.training.eni.uk
```

For a server called SUPPORT that is situated in the Microsoft organization in the USA, the DNS name would be:

```
Support.Microsoft.com
```

☞ *The DNS is case insensitive.*

Here is an example tree structure:

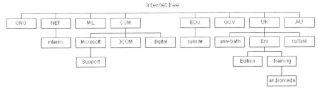

In practice, however, this tree structure is very simplified and there are an extremely large number of domains, already on the third level!

When you access a machine, you can use a relative name, as in the following command:

```
FTP andromeda
```

Alternatively, you can use the FQDN (*Fully Qualified Domain Name*), which is an absolute reference:

```
FTP andromeda.training.eni.uk
```

2. Windows 2000 and the DNS

Windows 2000 uses the DNS standard for its domain names. For example, your Windows 2000 domain could be called ENI.UK.

Consequently, you must use the DNS service in a network that contains Windows 2000 domains. In addition, the DNS system is used in order to resolve host names into IP addresses, and to locate network services that run in the domain. For example, when you open a session on a Windows 2000 domain, you query your DNS server in order to obtain the list of domain controllers that are can authenticate your logon.

Before you can promote a member or stand-alone server to a domain controller (by installing Active Directory), you must have access to a DNS server.

3. Implementing a DNS server

The version of the DNS service that is provided by Microsoft for Windows 2000 offers a number of advantages over the versions of this service that can be found on a UNIX system, or even on a Windows NT 4 server.

A DNS server has a database in which host names are associated with IP addresses. With most DNS servers, this association is done manually. The Windows 2000 DNS allows registrations to be made automatically, either by the client itself, or by a DHCP server in the case where the client receives its IP configuration via such a server. In addition to saving administration time, the huge advantage that is offered by this approach is that the DNS database is always up-to-date.

The Windows 2000 DNS supports **SRV** type records. These records are used when a client needs to find a server that plays a specific role. Consequently, in addition to its host name, each machine registers the list of roles that it plays. For example, a client that wishes to search in Active Directory must first locate an LDAP server via the DNS server.

The DNS service has also been improved with respect to its zone transfer method. This will be covered later on in this chapter. In addition, the DNS service can be integrated into Active Directory.

The DNS service can be installed as follows:

➢ Open Control Panel, and double-click the **Add/Remove Programs** icon.

➢ Click the **Add/Remove Windows Components** button, followed by the **Components** button. Then select the **Networking Services** component, and click the **Details** button.

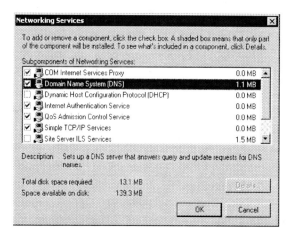

➢ Activate the **Domain Name System (DNS)** check box, and then click the **OK** button.

➢ Click the **Next** button in order to start installing the service (you must provide the Windows 2000 installation source files).

☞ *When the DNS service is installed, a registry key is added under HKLM\System\CurrentControlSet\Services\DNS. In addition, a DNS directory, which contains the DNS database, is added under %systemroot% system32.*

When you have installed DNS, the first thing you must do is to create a zone over which the server will have authority. In order to do this, start the DNS utility from the Administrative Tools menu, and then right-click the server name.

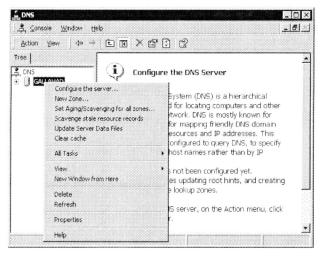

➢ Either, you can select **Configure the server**, in which case a wizard will guide you step by step, through the creation of your zones

➢ Or, you can select **New Zone**.

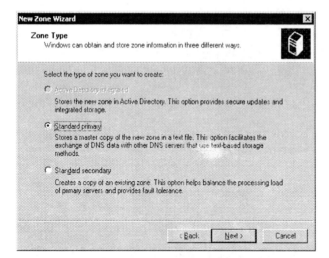

> First, you must create the primary zone. A secondary zone supplies the server with a copy of the primary zone. It provides fault tolerance, and it allows you to spread the workload.

> Select **Standard primary**, and then click **Next**.

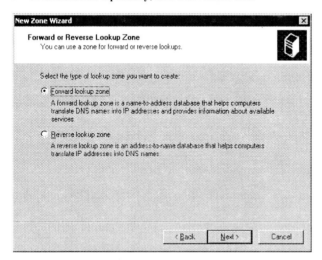

> You must select the type of zone that you wish to create: You can choose a forward lookup zone, which allows you to resolve host names into IP addresses. Alternatively, you can choose a reverse lookup zone, which is used in certain applications in order to resolve IP addresses into host names (for example, NFS and Nslookup use this technique).

➢ Select **Forward lookup zone**, and then click the **Next** button.

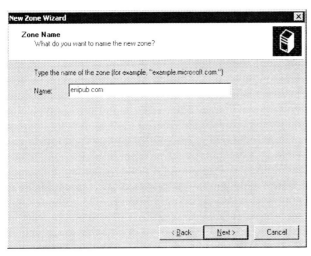

➢ Enter the name you want to give to the zone that you wish to manage, and then click **Next**.

➢ The system automatically creates a zone file with a name that is based on that of the zone, as follows: ***zone_name.dns***. You can either modify this name, or you can click **Next** so as to accept it.

➢ Click **Finish** in order to accept the creation of your zone.

The DNS window then shows the zone along with the default records:

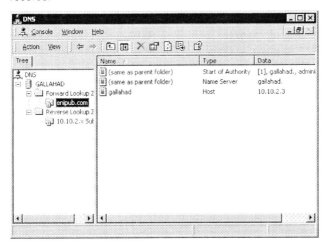

When you have created the forward lookup zone, you can also create the reverse lookup zone. In order to do this, right-click **Reverse Lookup Zone** in the DNS window, and then select **New Zone**.

➢ Select **Standard primary** and then click **Next**.

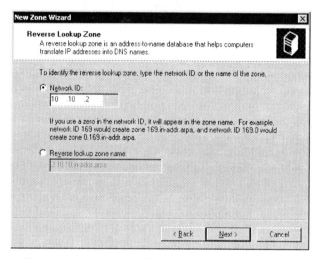

➢ Enter the network address that corresponds to the reverse lookup zone. Windows 2000 then automatically creates the corresponding zone file with the name: **network_address_in_reverse_order.in-addr.arpa**

➢ Click **Next**, twice, and then click **Finish** in order to complete the operation.

4. Configuring DNS zones

a. Zone types

When you configure your DNS server, you can choose from three types of zone:
- Standard primary,
- Standard secondary,
- Active Directory-integrated.

These zones contain records that are associated with the namespace of the zone, in order to resolve the queries that come from the DNS clients.

Standard primary

The server that is configured as the primary server must have this type of zone. This is the primary copy of the zone database (which, in fact, is a text file). The zone can be administered from the server on which this zone file resides.

Standard secondary

This is a copy of the standard primary zone. This copy is in read-only mode. The purpose of such a zone is to provide fault tolerance with respect to the standard primary zone. If clients can no longer access the standard primary zone, then the standard secondary zone can be used. In addition, this type of zone allows you to spread the workload. Clients that send queries to a name server have the IP addresses of the servers to which they can make such requests. You can stipulate that certain users must first send their requests to the server that manages the secondary zone, and that other servers must first query the server that manages the primary zone. You can apply this technique because the secondary zone is a copy of the primary zone, and therefore both of these zone files contain the same information. However, any modifications must always be made to the primary zone.

Active Directory-integrated

This zone file is stored in the Active Directory.

☞ *The standard primary zone files and the standard secondary zone files are stored on the servers that accommodate them, in the tree %systemroot %\system32\dns. With an Active Directory-integrated zone, there is no zone file on the server. The zone file is located in the Active Directory.*

You can change the type of zone at any time. This can be useful if you manage a primary zone and a secondary zone, for example. If the primary zone server breaks-down, then the secondary zone can respond to client queries. However, no modification can be made to the zone file because it is in read-only mode. In this case, it might be useful to convert the secondary zone into a primary zone.

In order to do this, right-click the zone that you want to convert, and then select **Properties**.

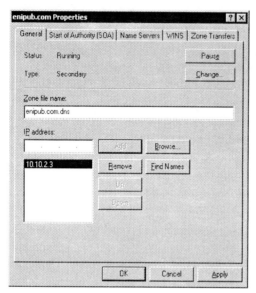

Click the **Change** button in order to display the following dialog box:

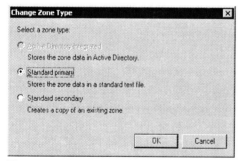

The **Active Directory-integrated** option appears grayed-out in this dialog box unless the zone that you wish to convert is located on a domain controller.

If you change a primary zone into an Active Directory-integrated zone, then the file that is located under **%systemroot%\system32\dns** is copied into the Active Directory before it is deleted from the disk. Following this operation, this zone file is considered as an Active Directory object. The zone information is then duplicated onto all the domain controllers, in the same way as user accounts are copied. In this case, all the domain controllers on which the DNS service has been install can act as DNS servers. In addition, all the DNS servers are primary servers, and zone modifications can be carried out on any of them.

b. Dynamic updating

The Windows 2000 DNS service offers a dynamic update feature that automatically modifies zone files. This feature reduces the administrator's maintenance workload.

☞ *The implementation of Dynamic DNS is defined in RFC 2136. Secure dynamic update is defined in RFC 2137.*

➢ Open the **DNS** console, right-click the zone name and then click **Properties.**

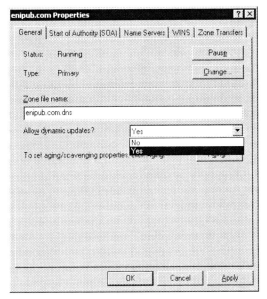

➢ Open the **Allow dynamic updates?** drop down list and then select **Yes.**

If you are managing an Active Directory-integrated zone, then you will also have the **Only secure updates** option. This option allows the DNS server to accept dynamic updates only from servers and clients who are authorized to send dynamic updates. The objective of this option is to prevent non-authorized users from modifying a zone. This feature also allows you to specify the users who are authorized to modify the zones.

☞ *During IP configuration of DHCP clients, the Windows 2000 DHCP server service can automatically supply the DNS with the necessary information so that it can update its zone. Chapter 13 of this book, which covers the DHCP, describes how you can implement this technique.*

c. Zone Transfer

When a network contains a master name server (which provides the source of primary zone information) and one or more secondary name servers (each of which has a copy of the primary zone), then a process that is called **zone transfer** takes place between these servers. Most DNS servers, including that of Windows NT 4, support **AXFR** zone transfer, whereas Windows 2000 supports **AXFR** or **IXFR** zone transfer.

AXFR is also known as full zone transfer. All the zone information is duplicated from the master name sever onto all the secondary name servers.

On the other hand, IXFR transfers only that information that has been modified. IXFR is also known as incremental zone transfer.

This zone transfer process takes place as soon as the master name server sends a notification to its secondary name servers. Zone transfer also occurs upon startup of a secondary server, or upon startup of the DNS server service, or when the refresh interval expires, or when the SOA *(Start Of Authority)* serial number is incremented.

You can modify some of the settings that define when a zone transfer must take place.

➢ Open the **DNS** console, right-click the zone name, and then select **Properties**.

➢ Select the **Start of Authority (SOA)** tab.

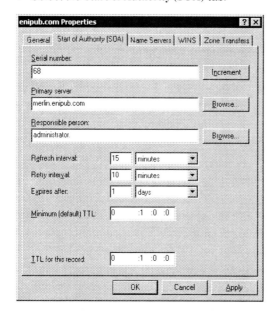

Serial number

This number indicates whether any zone modifications have taken place. It is incremented automatically when a modification is made.

Refresh interval

This item allows you to define the time interval between successive requests for zone transfers that are made from a secondary name server to its primary name server.

Retry interval

This item allows you to define the time that must elapse before a secondary name server that was not able to contact its master name server, tries again to contact its master name server in order to obtain a zone transfer.

Expires after

If this time interval elapses before the secondary name server manages to contact its master name server, then the secondary name server will stop responding to client queries.

In order to force a zone transfer, right-click the secondary zone and then select **Transfer from master**.

In order to adjust the zone transfer settings, right-click the primary zone, and then select **Properties**. Select the **Zone Transfers** tab.

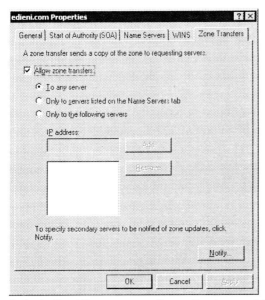

Activate the **Allow zone transfers** option box and then select the option that indicates where you want to transfer this zone.

5. Creating records manually

In addition to supporting dynamic updates, the Windows 2000 DNS server allows you manually to create new records.

In order to create a new record, right-click the zone concerned. From amongst all the available records, you can then choose, a new host or a new alias.

– **New Host**: this type of record allows you to map a host name to an IP address for clients that cannot register automatically.

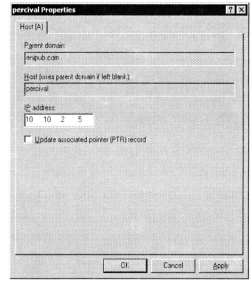

Enter the host name of the client, along with its IP address. Notice the **Update associated pointer (PTR) record** option. If you create a reverse lookup zone, this option allows you to record the client in it.

– **New Alias**: this type of record allows you to create an alias for a host name.

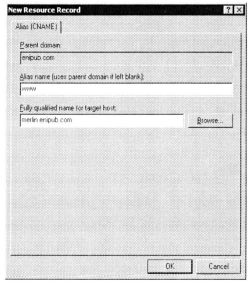

The example that is given above will allow you to use http://www.enipub.com instead of http://merlin.enipub.com.

6. Creating subdomains

You can create subdomains in order to organize your namespace. If you wish to include several domains in your Windows 2000 network, then you must create several DNS zones. These zones can belong to a contiguous namespace. For example, the enipub.com zone can contain a subdomain that is called training.enipub.com. The objective of organizing the zone in this way is to allow the administrators of the training service to manage their own zone.

In order to do this, you must create the primary enipub.com zone on one server, and the primary training.enipub.com zone on another server.

If you do not carry out any further actions, then the DNS client users of the enipub.com server will be able to resolve all the names of the enipub.com zone, but they will not be able to resolve the names of the training.enipub.com zone. Similarly, client users of the DNS server that manage the DNS training.enipub.com zone, will be able to resolve the names of this zone, but will not be able to resolve the names of the enipub.com zone. However, you may want everyone to be able to resolve all the names, irrespective of the zone to which they belong.

Here are the actions that you must carry out on the DNS server that manages the enipub.com zone, so as to implement two-way communication between both DNS domains:

➢ Right-click the zone name, and then click **New Delegation**.

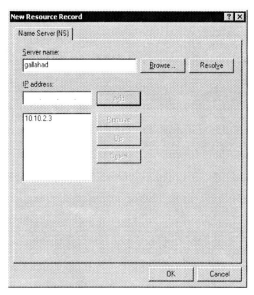

> Enter the name of a delegated domain, and then click **Next**.

> Click the **Add** button in order to indicate the server to which must be sent the queries that refer to the training.enipub.com zone.

> Click the **OK** button followed by the **Next** button. Then click the **Finish** button in order to complete the operation.

At this stage, clients of the DNS server that manages the enipub.com zone will be able to resolve queries for the training.enipub.com zone.

However, the clients of the DNS server that manages the training.enipub.com zone will still not be able to resolve queries for the enipub.com domain.
In order to allow them to do so, carry out the following operations on the server that manages the training.enipub.com zone:

➤ Open the **DNS** console. Right-click the server name and then select **Properties**. Then, select the **Forwarders** tab.

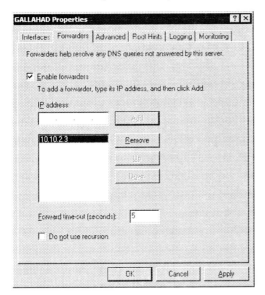

➤ Activate the **Enable forwarders** check box, and then enter the IP address of the parent server (in the example above, this is the IP address of the server that manages the enipub.com zone). The objective of this operation is to forward all the queries that cannot be resolved by the server that manages the training.enipub.com zone, to the server for which the IP address is indicated as the redirector (in the example above, this is the server that manages the enipub.com zone).

7. Testing the DNS server

As you must have a DNS server in a Windows 2000 domain, it is judicious to make sure that the Windows 2000 domain functions correctly, before you consider implementing Active Directory.
You can check that your Windows 2000 domain runs correctly in several ways:

➤ Open the DNS console. Right-click the name of the server that you want to test, and select **Properties**. Then, select the **Monitoring** tab.

> You can test recursive queries along with simple (or iterative) queries.

With a recursive query, a request always receives a response (a negative response when a resolution fails, or a positive response is returned when at least one resolution is possible). A query cannot be forwarded to another server in order to carry out the resolution that was requested.

So as to test this type of query, Windows 2000 uses DNS Resolver (its own client) in order to contact the DNS server (itself). However, the client query is recursive and requests resolution of a server name record type, for a DNS root server. This approach allows you to test the forwarding operation in addition to zone delegations.

An iterative query returns to a client, a response that contains, either the IP address of the desired host, or, failing this, the IP address of another DNS server that could resolve the query.

In order to test this sort of query, Windows 2000 uses its DNS client so as to contact the DNS server (itself).

Alternatively, you can test a DNS server using the **Nslookup** utility. You can use this utility either interactively, or non-interactively. Here is the syntax for this utility in non-interactive mode:

```
Nslookup -option computer_to_find -
dns_server_to_be_used
```

```
E:\WINNT\System32\cmd.exe                              _ □ ×
E:\>nslookup galahad merlin
Server:  merlin.enipub.com
Address:  10.10.2.1

Name:    galahad.enipub.com
Address:  10.10.2.3

E:\>
```

Nslookup also allows you to check the existence of SRV records from any TCP/IP client. The example below allows you to check the existence of an ldap server:

```
Microsoft Windows 2000 [Version 5.00.2128]
(C) Copyright 1985-1999 Microsoft Corp.

C:\>nslookup
Default Server:  merlin.enipub.com
Address:  10.10.2.1

> set type=srv
> _ldap._tcp.eni.fr
Server:  merlin.enipub.com
Address:  10.10.2.1

_ldap._tcp.enipub.com    SRV service location:
          priority     = 0
          weight       = 100
          port         = 389
          svr hostname = merlin.enipub.com
merlin.enipub.com    internet address = 10.10.2.1
>
```

This example indicates that the merlin.enipub.com server, which has an IP address of 10.10.2.1, is the LDAP server.

In addition, you can use all the TCP/IP utilities, such as **ping** and **tracert**, specifying the domain name of the host that you wish to reach, so as to check that the DNS server resolves the name properly.

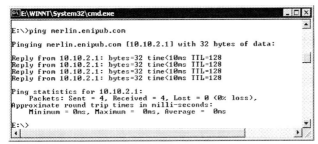

In the DNS console, the **Logging** tab of the **DNS Server Properties** dialog box allows you to create the log file dns.log (under %systemroot%\system32\DNS), in which you can specify the types of record that you wish to analyze.

8. Configuring the clients

In order to be able to use the services that are offered by a DNS server, a machine must be a client of the DNS server.

a. Configuring the Windows 2000 DNS client

➢ Right-click **My Network Places**, then click **Properties**.

➢ Right-click **Local Area Connection**, then click **Properties**.

➢ Display the TCP/IP properties.

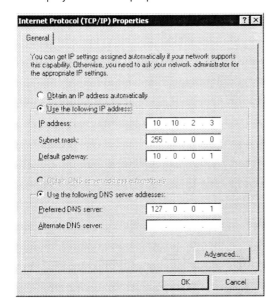

Enter the IP address of your DNS server. If you have a secondary DNS server, then you can add its address in order to provide fault tolerance.

☞ *There is no correlation between the concept of master and secondary DNS servers, and that of preferred and alternate DNS servers. In order to spread the workload, you might find it useful to define the master DNS server as the preferred DNS server for one set of users, and then to reverse the roles for a second set of users.*

You can define more than two DNS servers using the **Advanced** button.

b. Configuring the Windows NT DNS client

➤ Display **Network Neighborhood - Properties**.

➤ Select the **Protocols** tab and display the **Properties** of the **TCP/IP Protocol**.

➤ Select the **DNS** tab and click the **Add** button so as to enter the address(es) of the DNS server(s) that you wish to use.

☞ *As with all TCP/IP parameters (such as WINS addresses), the DNS servers that are indicated statically have priority over those that are provided by DHCP.*

c. Configuring the Windows 98 DNS client

➤ Display **Network Neighborhood - Properties**.

➤ Double-click the TCP/IP protocol that corresponds to the network adapter. Then, select the **DNS Configuration** tab and enter the server address.

➤ Click **Add**.

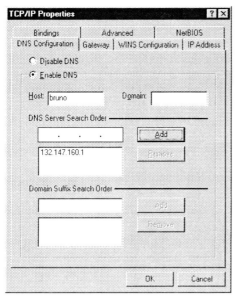

The DNS server address is then placed in the **DNS Server Search Order** list.

Labs

To be absolutely sure that you have assimilated this chapter, work through the corresponding labs. These are set out from page 633 to page 635.

☒ Installing the DNS service.

☒ Configuring the DNS service.

Assessing your skills

Try the following questions if you think you know this chapter well enough.

TCP/IP

1   Which transport layer protocol is connection oriented?   ☐

....

2   How many bytes are there in an IP address?   ☐

....

3   Which protocol is used for terminal emulation?   ☐

....

4 Which transfer protocol is fast? ❑
....

5 Which protocol allows you to administer remotely? ❑
....

6 What is the purpose of a dynamic routing protocol? ❑
....
....
....

Resolving names into IP addresses

7 Which service allows you to resolve the www.enipub.com ❑
name into an IP address?
....

8 Which file allows you to resolve Internet names? Where ❑
is it stored on Windows 2000?
....
....

9 Which file allows you to resolve NetBIOS names? Where ❑
is it stored on Windows 2000?
....
....

10 Your Windows 2000 network uses only the TCP/IP ❑
protocol. There are no WINS servers on your LAN, but you
want to connect to a shared resource on the other side of a
router. How can you do this as quickly as possible?
....
....
....

DNS

11 What is the role of the DNS service? ❑
....
....

12 How can you configure a Windows 2000 server so that it ❑
will act as a DNS server?
....
....

13 How can you configure a Windows 2000 client so that it ❑
will become a DNS client?
....

14 Can a DNS server be its own client? ❑
....

15 Can a machine be a DNS server and a DHCP client? ❑
....
....
....

16 Can a machine be a DNS server and a WINS client? ❑
....

17 Is the DNS database updated statically or dynamically? ❑
....
....
....
....

18 What is the difference between a recursive query and an ❑
iterative query?
....
....
....
....

19 Which peculiarities of the DNS service that is provided ❑
with Windows 2000, simplify its administration and help
clients to find specific servers on the network?
....
....
....
....
....

20 What are the different zone types that are supported by ❑
DNS on Windows 2000?
....
....
....

21 What is the difference between a forward lookup zone ❑
and a reverse lookup zone?
....
....
....
....

22 Where is the zone information stored for an Active ❑
Directory-integrated zone?
....
....

23 Where is the zone information stored for a standard ❑
primary zone or for a standard secondary zone?
....
....

24 What is the purpose of zone transfer?

....
....
....
....

25 How does Windows 2000 support zone transfer?

....
....
....

26 Why is it useful to create DNS subdomains?

....
....
....

27 What are the different methods that you can use in order to check that your DNS server is functioning correctly?

....
....
....
....

28 Who can be a DNS client?

....

Results

Check your answers on pages 165 to 167. Count one point for each correct answer.

Number of points | /28 |

For this chapter you need to have scored at least 21 out of 28.

Look at the list of key points that follows. Pick out the ones with which you have had difficulty and work through them again in this chapter before moving on to the next.

Key points of the chapter

☐ TCP/IP.

☐ Resolving names into IP addresses.

☐ DNS.

Solutions

TCP/IP

1   Which transport layer protocol is connection oriented?
TCP.

2   How many bytes are there in an IP address?
4 bytes (32 bits).

3   Which protocol is used for terminal emulation?
Telnet.

4   Which transfer protocol is fast?
TFTP is fast because it uses UDP. However, it is less reliable than FTP.

5   Which protocol allows you to administer remotely?
Simple Network Management Protocol (SNMP).

6   What is the purpose of a dynamic routing protocol?
Unlike static routing, dynamic routing allows routers automatically to exchange their routing tables using a routing protocol.

Resolving names into IP addresses

7   Which service allows you to resolve the www.enipub.com name into an IP address?
Domain Name System (DNS).

8   Which file allows you to resolve Internet names? Where is it stored on Windows 2000?
The hosts file that is situated in the directory %systemroot%\ system32\Drivers\etc\.

9   Which file allows you to resolve NetBIOS names? Where is it stored on Windows 2000?
The hosts file that is situated in the directory %systemroot %\system32\Drivers\etc\.

10   Your Windows 2000 network uses only the TCP/IP protocol. There are no WINS servers on your LAN, but you want to connect to a shared resource on the other side of a router. How can you do this as quickly as possible?
*When you connect to the resource, rather than using the NetBIOS name of the server, you must use its IP address directly. For example, you can use the command **Net use f:** **132.145.0.1\\W2k**.*

DNS

11 What is the role of the DNS service?

The DNS service allows you to resolve the (Internet) host name into an IP address.

12 How can you configure a Windows 2000 server so that it will act as a DNS server?

*You must add the DNS service using the **Add/Remove Programs** icon from **Control Panel**.*

13 How can you configure a Windows 2000 client so that it will become a DNS client?

By going into TCP/IP properties.

14 Can a DNS server be its own client?

Yes.

15 Can a machine be a DNS server and a DHCP client?

A DNS server must have a static IP configuration, because DNS clients query the DNS server using the server's IP address, which they find out from their TCP/IP configuration.

16 Can a machine be a DNS server and a WINS client?

Yes.

17 Is the DNS database updated statically or dynamically?

With most DNS servers, the host name/IP address correspondence database is updated manually. The Windows 2000 DNS service, which is also known as DDNS (Dynamic DNS), supports dynamic updating of DNS clients.

18 What is the difference between a recursive query and an iterative query?

A recursive query always receives a definite response, whereas with an iterative query the response can be either the IP address of the host that was requested, or the address of another DNS server that could resolve the query.

19 Which peculiarities of the DNS service that is provided with Windows 2000, simplify its administration and help clients to find specific servers on the network?

The Windows 2000 DDNS allows you dynamically to update clients and to record SRV resources. This latter peculiarity allows clients to locate servers that play certain roles, such as that of a domain controller, or that of an LDAP server.

20 What are the different zone types that are supported by DNS on Windows 2000?

With the Windows 2000 DNS service, you can configure standard primary zones, standard secondary zones and Active Directory-integrated zones.

21 What is the difference between a forward lookup zone and a reverse lookup zone?

Forward lookup zones allow you to resolve host names into IP addresses. Reverse lookup zones allow you to resolve IP addresses into host names.

22 Where is the zone information stored for an Active Directory-integrated zone?

This information is stored as an object in Active Directory.

23 Where is the zone information stored for a standard primary zone or for a standard secondary zone?

This information is stored on a DNS server disk in the directory %systemroot%\system32\dns.

24 What is the purpose of zone transfer?

Zone transfer allows you to transmit the DNS database from the server that runs the standard primary zone to the server(s) that run standard secondary zone(s).

25 How does Windows 2000 support zone transfer?

Windows 2000 supports incremental zone transfer (IXFR). IXFR allows you to transfer only the zone modifications, unlike AXFR, which transfers the whole zone. Windows versions prior to Windows 2000 offer only AXFR transfer.

26 Why is it useful to create DNS subdomains?

They allow you to organize the namespace of your Windows 2000 domain. In addition, they allow you to delegate zone authority to another name server.

27 What are the different methods that you can use in order to check that your DNS server is functioning correctly?

*You can go into the DNS console and use the Monitoring tab of your DNS server's Properties dialog box. Alternatively, you can use either the TCP/IP **nslookup** utility, or any of the other TCP/IP commands (such as **ping**, **telnet** and **tracert**) that refer to an FQDN name (for example: ping merlin.enipub.com).*

28 Who can be a DNS client?

Any client that uses TCP/IP.

Prerequisites for this chapter

☒ Knowledge of DDNS.

☒ Knowledge of the IP world.

☒ General knowledge of network services.

☒ Network administration essentials.

Objectives

At the end of this chapter, you will be able to:

☒ Describe Active Directory.

☒ Install Active Directory.

☒ Create the logical structure of Active Directory.

☒ Add domain contollers into existing domains and into new domains.

☒ Choose between a mixed domain and a native domain.

☒ Define the special roles that are played by certain domain controllers.

☒ Change the servers that play these roles.

☒ Define Active Directory replication.

☒ Create the physical structure of Active Directory.

☒ Generate replication traffic between sites.

☒ Uninstall Active Directory from a Windows 2000 domain controller.

Active Directory

Contents

A. Overview

Active Directory is probably the biggest advance that Microsoft has made since the first server versions. It is a directory database that groups together all the database objects. As soon as you have a domain that is running on Windows 2000, Active Directory is your working tool. This directory database simplifies the administration of your system, and it offers a high fault tolerance as it is a distributed database.

Active Directory uses a set of standard protocols, which makes this database a network component that all applications can use. For example, Exchange 2000 can use distribution groups that are created in Active Directory so as to send messages to the users of these groups. Provided that they written for the purpose, all applications can benefit from the advantages that are offered by Active Directory.

Active Directory supports the following standard protocols:
- **TCP/IP**: network protocol.
- **DNS**: the Windows 2000 domain namespace is based on this service.
- **DHCP**: this IP configuration distribution protocol allows you to provide IP addressing to clients who request it. In addition it allows you to provide the DNS with information concerning distributed addresses.
- **NTP**: Network Time Protocol. All Windows 2000 machines must be synchronized because the Kerberos authentication message is based on a time-stamped access ticket.
- **LDAP**: this protocol provides access to Active Directory. When you search in Active Directory, you use an LDAP server first.
- **LDIF**: allows you to synchronize Active Directory (*Ldap Data Interchange Format*)
- **Kerberos version 5**: allows logon authentication.
- **X509 v3 certificates**: allows certificate authentication (this is used with EFS in order to encrypt folders or files, for example).

Whereas the Windows NT 4 accounts database can contain 40 000 objects per domain, the Windows 2000 directory database can contain several million objects. This provides a development potential to meet all requirements. Fault tolerance is ensured provided that you have at least two domain controllers in your domain. In fact, as Active Directory is a distributed directory database, all the domain controllers have the same information. This is made possible by a replication technique that is known as **Multi-master**. It means that a client can consult any domain controller in order to carry out a search in Active Directory. This ensures spreading of the workload.

B. Terminology

1. Logical structure

The logical structure of the Active Directory database is made up of forests, of trees, of domains, and also of organizational units.

Here is an example of a forest in which there are two trees, each of which is composed of three domains.

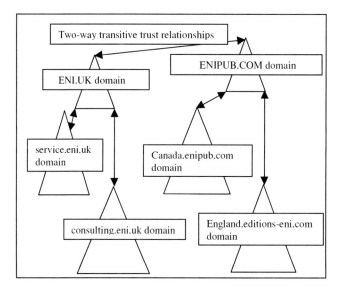

The first tree is composed of the domains eni.uk, service.eni.uk and consulting.eni.uk. The second tree is composed of the domains enipub.com, Canada.enipub.com and England.enipub.com.

This set of two trees makes up a forest.

The domains in a forest are linked together by two-way transitive trust relationships. In the example above, the consulting.eni.uk domain trusts the eni.uk domain, which in turn trusts the enipub.com domain. Therefore, the consulting.eni.uk domain trusts the enipub.com domain. These relationships are created automatically when the forest is confugured.

Thus, a tree is a set of domains that share a contiguous namespace.

In each domain, the network objects are organized into *organizational units* (a network object can be an item such as a user account, a computer account or a printer). The organizational units (OUs) make up a logical hierachical structure that meets an administrative need. Network objects that are included in the OUs will be subject to the rules that are defined in these OUs.

You can delegate the administration of each OU. In this way, you can spread the administrative tasks amongst several administrators. Thus, you can delegate the total control of an OU, or alternatively, you can grant only the permission to carry out certain specific tasks (such as creating new OUs, or changing account passwords for users of an OU).

Thanks to this feature, in order to delegate the administration of a Windows 2000 domain, you do not have to create several domains and then appoint administrators for each domain. All you have to do is to create a set of OUs in the domain. Different people will then be able to manage each of the OUs.

2. Objects

In the Active Directory, an object can be an item such as a user account, a printer, a computer account, a published shared folder or a group.

Each object is made up of a set of attributes, that represent the object. For example, the attributes of the user object could include a first-name, a surname, a login name, a telephone and a web page, whilst those of a printer could include a name, a location and a description.

Some of the attributes of an object are obligatory (for example, a user surname), whilst others are optional (for example a user's telephone number).

All these attributes are defined in the schema. You can modify the schema yourself, so as to add new attributes for the objects. Applications can also modify the schema. For example, you may wish to add to the user object, an attribute that contains the badge number. The schema is present on all domain controllers and it is treated as an object of the Active Directory.

All the objects that have the same type have the same attributes. However, each of these objects must have different attribute values.

A set of objects that have the same attributes is called a class. For example, when you create a user, you create an object in the **User** class. When you create this object you will not modify the schema. You will modify the schema, only when you create, either new classes, or new attributes.

In order to modify the schema, you must use the **Active Directory Schema** snap-in.

☞ *You must remember that when you modify the schema, you can affect the state of your network. You must have a thorough understanding of the schema before you modify it.*

☞ *Adding attributes to the schema is irreversible. You cannot remove an attribute from a schema, once you have created it.*

The Directory Service uses several naming conventions.

- **Relative Distinguished Name**: this is the full name of an attribute of an object.

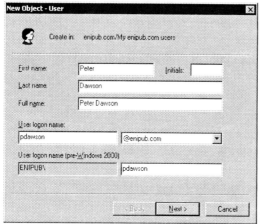

In the example above, the relative distinguished name is Peter Dawson.

- **User Principal Name**: this is a user's login name followed by the name of the domain in which the object is located. In the example above, this name could be **pdawson@enipub.com**.

- **Distinguished Name**: every Active Directory object has a distinguished name that allows you to locate it within a domain or within an OU. In the example above, the distinguished name of the user Peter Dawson is as follows: DC=com, DC=enipub, OU=my users of enipub.com, CN=Peter Dawson. This means that the user for whom the relative distinguished name is Peter Dawson is located in the « my users of enipub.com » OU, which is in the enipub.com domain (CN stands for *Common Name*, DC stands for *Domain Component*, and OU stands for *Organizational Unit*).

The **ADSI Edit** snap-in allows you to modify the schema.
Each object has a unique number called the GUID (*Globally Unique IDentifier*). This number never changes, even if you rename the object (if you change its relative distinguished name), or change the location of the object (if you change its distinguished name).

☞ *As you cannot have two objects in the same OU that have the same relative distinguished name, you cannot have two objects that have the same distinguished name.*

C. Installing

You can install Active Directory on a Windows 2000 member or stand-alone server. When the directory database has been installed, your server will become a domain controller.
Active Directory will be a database file called **NTDS.DIT** that is located under %systemroot%\ntds, by default. You can choose another path when you install Active Directory.
In order to install Active Directory you need an NTFS partition so as to store the shared system directory (SYSVOL). This is because the replication of directory database modifications is managed according to sequential version numbers that are supported by the NTFS system.

☞ *Active Directory is a Jet Blue aka ESE database.*

In order to install Active Directory, you must run the **DCPROMO.EXE** command. The accounts database (SAM) that is on your server will be copied into the directory database before it is removed from your computer. Consequently, you will not lose accounts information when you migrate your Windows NT domain controllers to Windows 2000. If you run the **dcpromo** command on a Windows 2000 domain controller, then you will downgrade your controller to a member or stand-alone server. In this case you will obtain a clean SAM database.

In order to install Active Directory, you need a computer that is running one of the three server versions of Windows 2000 (Server, Advanced Server or Datacenter Server), a partition that is formatted in NTFS, the TCP/IP protocol, and a DNS that has been installed and configured.

☞ *If the DNS service is not installed when you run dcpromo, then the Active Directory installation process will offer to install and configure it. You must have a DNS service that supports dynamic records and resource (SRV) type records.*

Before you start installing Active Directory, you must understand exactly the role of your server in the Active Directory logical structure. When you install the Windows 2000 directory database, the system will ask you whether your server must be included into an existing domain, or whether you wish to create a new domain. If you wish to create a new domain you must know whether your new domain must be included in an existing domain tree, or whether you wish to create a new domain tree. Finally, if you wish to create a new domain tree, you must know whether your new tree must be included in an existing forest, or whether you wish to create a new forest.

The flow chart below summarizes this decision chain:

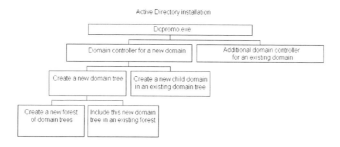

Here are the steps that you must follow in order to install Active Directory:

➢ Open, either a command prompt, or the **Run** menu.

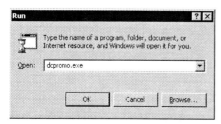

➢ Enter **dcpromo.exe** so as to start the Active Directory Installation Wizard.

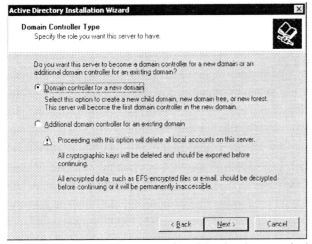

– In most cases, you are strongly advised to have a single domain. Before Windows 2000, it was useful to create several domains, either for administrative reasons, or when the limit of 40 000 objects was reached. With Windows 2000, as you can delegate administration, and create several million objects, it may well be preferable to work with a single domain.

However, it may be useful to create several domains in the following cases:

– You wish to reduce replication traffic. The Active Directory information that circulates between domains is that which is brought to the global catalog server.
– You wish to apply very different policies in different domains.
– You company is merging with another company and you want to maintain a separation between the data of the two companies.
– You wish to update several Windows NT domains: although several Windows NT domains can be merged into one, you consider it to be useful to carry on working with several domains.

1. Creating a new, or root, domain

The first time that you install Active Directory, you will create a new (root) domain in a new forest. In order to do this, here are the steps that you must follow after you have started dcpromo:

➢ Select **Domain controler for a new domain**, and click the **Next** button.

➢ Select **Create a new domain tree**, and click the **Next** button.

➢ Select **Create a new forest of domain trees**, and click the **Next** button.

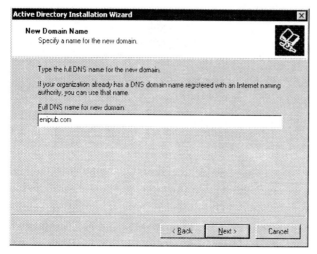

➢ Enter the DNS name of your domain, and click the **Next** button.

➢ Then, enter the NetBIOS name of your domain. By default, Windows 2000 suggests that you keep the same name as the DNS name. Computers that runs a pre-Windows 2000 operating system will be able to use this name.

➢ Click the **Next** button.

➢ Indicate the path in which you want to store Active Directory information. By default, the directory %systemroot%\NTDS is suggested so as to store the database and the log. These items can be stored on a FAT partition or on an NTFS partition.

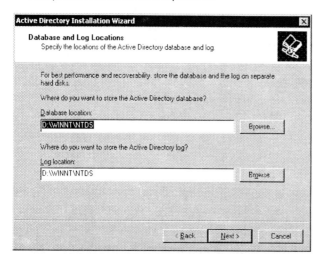

In order to optimize the performance of your server, you may wish to place the database and the log on separate disks.

➢ Click the **Next** button.

➢ Enter the path for the **Shared System Volume** (Sysvol). This folder must be located on an NTFS partition. It includes group policy definitions, scripts, and replication information.

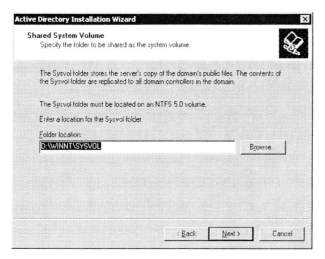

➢ Click the **Next** button.

Windows 2000 tries to detect a DNS server that has the domain name that you have just indicated. This DNS must support dynamic updates. If there is no DNS server that is configured in order to manage your zone, then the Active Directory Installtion Wizard offers to install and to configure the DNS service.

➢ Select **Permissions compatible only with Windows 2000 servers**.

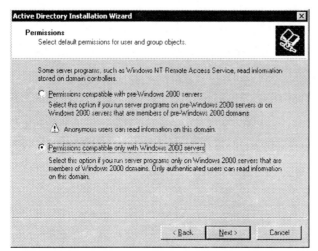

If you select the **Permissions compatible with pre-Windows 2000 servers** option, then the Everyone group will have permission to read all the attributes of all the Active Directory objects. This option is used in the case where you have upgraded a Windows NT 4 server to Windows 2000, with the RAS service installed. When you promote your server to Windows 2000 domain controller, you must choose this option so that you can continue to use the RAS service.

In order to run, the Windows NT 4 RAS service uses a system logon account with a logon name and an empty password. Windows 2000 does not allow NULL sessions to read Active Directory attributes.

➢ Click the **Next** button.

➢ Enter a password for the directory services restore mode Administrator, and then confirm it. When you start the system in Active Directory restore mode, you start Windows 2000 without loading the directory database so that you can restore it from a backup copy. In order to do this, you must log on as the Administrator with the password that you indicate in the dialog box below.

> Click the **Next** button.

Before you click the **Next** button so as to start the installation of Active Directory, check that you agree with all the actions that will be carried out.

Then, the installation of Active Directory can begin:

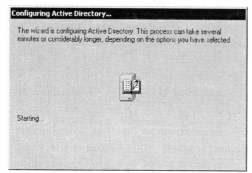

When the installation has finished, the following dialog box appears:

➢ Click **Finish**. Windows 2000 then offers to restart the computer in order allow the modifications to take effect.

➢ Click the **Restart Now** button.

When you have restarted your computer, you will be able to log on to your domain.

2. Adding a domain controller to an existing domain

Once you have created a domain, you can add new domain controllers to it. You are strongly recommended to have at least two domain controllers in order to ensure fault tolerance and so as to spread the workload.

Here are the steps that you must follow in order to add a new domain controller:

➢ Run dcpromo.exe.

➢ Select **Additional domain controller for an existing domain**.

➢ Indicate the domain, and the user name and passwork of an account that has enough rights in order to add a domain controller.

➢ Then, indicate the DNS name of the domain for which your server must be a controller.

➢ Enter the path for the directory database and for the log.

➢ Enter the path for the shared system volume.

➢ Indicate the password for the administrator account in order to carry out a possible future restart in restore mode.

➢ The replication of the Active Directory database then begins:

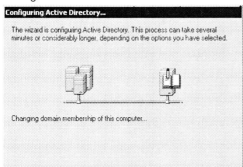

Configuring Active Directory...

The wizard is configuring Active Directory. This process can take several minutes or considerably longer, depending on the options you have selected.

Changing domain membership of this computer...

➢ Restart your computer when the operation is completed.

3. Adding a child domain

You can create a child domain, once you have created a root domain.

For example, if you have a domain that is called enipub.com, then you can create a child domain that is called service.eni.com. These two domains will make up a tree.

➢ Run dcpromo.exe.

➢ Select **Domain controller for a new domain**.

➤ Select **Create a new child domain in an existing domain tree**.

➤ Indicate the user name, password and domain for an account that is a member of the company's administrators group. This group is situated in the root domain and it grants its members the right to modify the forest.

➤ Then indicate the DNS name of the parent domain for which your domain will be a child domain, along with the name of your child domain.

➤ Indicate the NetBIOS name of your new subdomain.

➤ Enter the path for the directory database and for the log.

➤ Enter the path for the shared system volume.

➤ Specify whether on not you use services that run on Windows NT systems.

4. Adding a tree into an existing forest

When you add a tree into an existing forest you can create a new contiguous namespace. For example, suppose that your company has merged with another company that has a DNS domain that is registered on the Internet. Your company wants to keep its namespace, which is also registered. In this case it will be useful to create a new tree in the forest.

➤ Run dcpromo.exe.

➤ Select **Domain controller for a new domain**.

➤ Select **Create a new domain tree**.

➤ Select **Place this new domain tree in an existing forest**.

➤ Indicate the user name, password and domain for an account that is a member of the company's administrators group that exists in the root domain.

➤ Indicate the DNS name for the new domain.

➤ Indicate the NetBIOS name for your new domain.

➤ Enter the path for the directory database and for the log.

➤ Enter the path for the shared system volume.

➤ Specify whether on not you use services that run on Windows NT systems.

5. Choosing a domain mode

When you install a domain, it is configured in **mixed mode** by default. This mode allows both domain controllers that on Windows 2000 and those that run on Windows NT, to operate together in a Windows 2000 domain. This is very useful when you are upgrading your servers to Windows 2000. Once the migration has been successfully completed (after you have checked that you still have all items such as your user accounts and your groups), you can convert your domain to **native mode**. Some Active Directory features are exclusive to this mode. Native mode allows you to nest groups within other groups, and it allows you to create universal groups.

In order to switch to native mode, open the **Active Directory Users and Computers** console. Right-click the name of your domain and then select **Properties**.

➢ Click the **Change Mode** button. The dialog box then appears as follows:

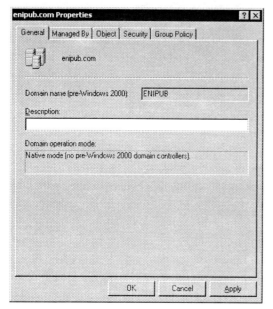

☞ *Converting from mixed mode to native mode is irreversible. When you have done this you can no longer return to mixed mode.*

D. Roles of domain controllers

1. Operations masters

In a Windows 2000 domain, all the domain controllers are identical. The directory database is duplicated and distributed on each domain controller. This is therefore a multiple master replication. However, certain actions cannot be carried out in multiple master mode. Because of this certain domain controllers play very specific roles. These domain controllers are known as operations masters and they run in *Flexible Single Master Operation (FSMO)* mode.
There are five FSMO roles:
– Schema master,
– Infrastructure master,
– Principal Domain Controller (PDC) emulator,
– Domain naming master,
– Relative Identifier (RID) master.
Some of these roles must be unique in the forest, such as the schema master and the domain naming master.

In each domain of a forest, there can be only one RID master, and there can be only one PDC emulator.

In addition, each domain must have an infrastructure master. The schema master implements the modifications that are made to the directory schema.

The domain naming master controls the addition and the removal of domains in the forest.

The first domain controller that is installed in the forest plays these two roles.

The RID master is responsible for distributing RID pools to all the domain controllers that request them (domain controllers request new RID pools when they have used up their stock of RID pools). When a domain controller creates an object, it assigns a unique security identifier (SID) to this object. This SID is composed of a unique domain SID, followed by a RID that is unique for each object in the domain.

The PDC emulator is unique in a domain. It acts as PDC for Windows NT clients. This FSMO manages password changes and replicates updates to secondary domain controllers in the case where the Windows 2000 domain is in mixed mode where both Windows 2000 domain controllers and Windows NT secondary domain controllers are present in the domain.

In native mode, when a domain controller changes a password, it sends the information immediately to the domain controller that is acting as PDC emulator. When a logon fails because of an incorrect password, the domain controller that tried to validate the logon will send the request to the PDC emulator before it refuses the logon.

The infrastructure master is responsible for the consistency of information concerning Active Directory object names with respect to their SIDs. When an account is renamed, a certain amount of time may elapse before the information is updated in all the domains in the forest. The infrastructure master then, maintains the relationship between the names of users, or of groups, and their membership of the groups to which they belong.

You can find out which roles are played by a domain controller.

In order to find out which domain controller plays the domain naming master role, open the **Active Directory Domains and Trusts** console. Then right-click **Active Directory Domains and Trusts** within this console, and select **Operations Master**.

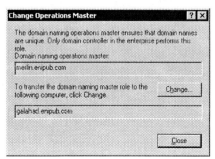

In order to transfer this role to another server, carry out the operation shown above on the domain controller that must become the domain naming master, and then click the **Change** button.

In order to find out which domain controller is playing the role of an operations master that is specific to a domain, open the **Active Directory Users and Computers** console. Then right-click **Active Directory Users and Computers** within this console, and select **Operations Master**.

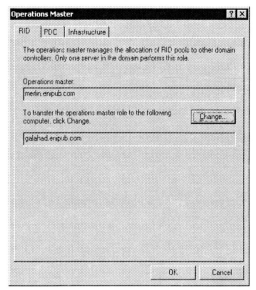

In order to transfer to another server, the role of PDC emulator, that of RID master, or that of infrastructure master display the dialog box shown above on the server that must play the role concerned. Then click the **Change** button.

Finally, in order to find out which server is acting as schema manager, or to transfer it to another server, open an MMC and add the **Active Directory Schema** snap-in. Then, right-click **Active Directory Schema** and select **Operations Master**.

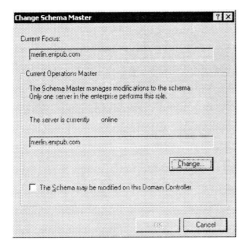

> If the **Active Directory Schema** snap-in is not available when you try to add it, then you must install the **adminpack. msi** administration tools that are situated in the i386 directory of the CD-ROM Windows 2000.

2. Global catalog server

A global catalog server is a domain controller with a catalog that references the attributes that are used most by all the Active Directory objects.

The Active Directory database is divided into three partitions, or naming contexts: the schema naming context, the configuration naming context and the domain naming context. Only schema and configuration information can be replicated between domains. As the information that concerns the objects of a domain are not replicated to the other domains in the forest, the global catalog server is used for searching at forest level. If you are looking for an object in the forest, you can ask a global catalog server that will be able to answer your query.

The global catalog is the only source of information on the objects that are replicated between domains. Because of this, it is useful to have at least one global server catalog per domain. The global catalog servers keep a copy of the catalog of each of the other domains. By default, only one global catalog server is created on the first server in the forest in which Active Directory was installed. You can add new global catalog servers as follows:

➢ Open the **Active Directory Sites and Services** console.

➢ Expand **Sites**, followed by the name of the site containing the server that must become the global catalog server. By default, there is only one site, which is called Default-First-Site-Name.

> Then, expand the **Servers** folder, followed by the server concerned. Right-click the **NTDS Settings** icon and select **Properties**.

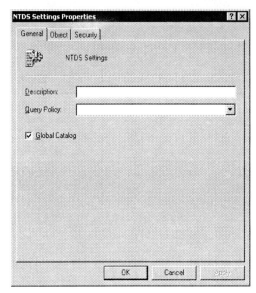

> Activate the **Global Catalog** check box.

In addition to allowing you to search in a forest, global catalog servers are useful during the logon process. When a logon is made, the server that receives the request consults a global catalog server in order to obtain information concerning membership of universal groups so that it can create an access token. If the global catalog server is not available, then the user will not be able to logon locally. However, members of the administrators group will still be able to log on to the domain.

☞ *It is advisable to have a global catalog server on either end of slow links.*

E. Replication

1. Overview

The replication process provides all domain controllers with an up-to-date directory database. When an administrator or a user alters the Active Directory, then the modified Active Directory must be replicated on all the domain controllers. This replication takes place in multiple master mode because all domain controllers have equal status. No master is in charge of the replication process.

Within a domain, all the attributes and objects of Active Directory are replicated on all the domain controllers. This process generates a certain amount of network traffic. You can control this traffic across slow links. In order to do this, you must create **sites**, which are independent of logical structures of the domains. A site is a set of one or more subnets. There are two types of replication:
- intra-site replication,
- inter-site replication.

Intra-site replication updates the directory database within a site. Consequently, this process takes place between domain controllers over fast links.

Inter-site replication involves network traffic between sites, and consequently, over slow links.

Within a site, replication is generated automatically between domain controllers using KCCs (*Knowledge Consistency Checkers*). On the other hand, inter-site replication must be set up manually.

When you install the first domain controller in a forest, then a site that is called **Default-First-Site-Name** is created automatically, by default. This site contains all the subnets, and when you create a domain controller, it will also belong to this site.

☞ *You can rename the **Default-First-Site-Name** site.*

2. Creating sites and subnets

You can create sites and subnets using the **Active Directory Sites and Services** console.

➢ Right-click the **Sites** folder, and then select **New Site**.

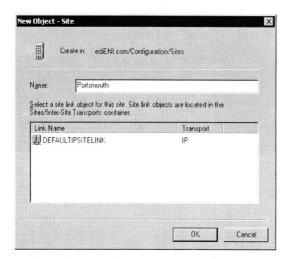

> Enter the name that you want to give to your site, and select the link that you wish to use in order to replicate. Then click the **OK** button.

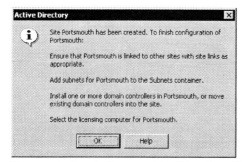

Your next step is to associate this site with one or more subnets:

> Right-click the **Subnets** folder and then select **New Subnet**.

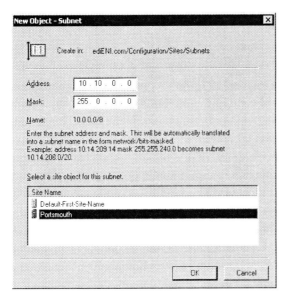

➢ Enter the network address along with that of the mask, and select the site with which the subnet must be associated.

Once you have associated the subnet with the site, when you install a domain controller with an address that corresponds to that of the subnet, then the new domain controller will be added automatically to the site concerned, and not to the **Default-First-Site-Name** site.

On the other hand, if you create sites and subnets after you have installed all the domain controllers, then you must move them into the sites to which they belong. You can carry out this operation as follows:

➢ Open the **Active Directory Sites and Services** console.

➢ Expand the **Sites** folder, followed by the **Default-First-Site-Name** folder.

➢ Then, expand the **Servers** folder and right-click the server that you wish to move.

➢ Select **Move**.

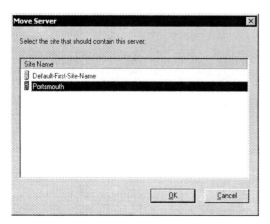

> Select the site to which you want to move the server, and then click the **OK** button.

Repeat this process for all the servers that you want to move.

3. Intra-site and inter-site transport

a. Intra-site replication

Replication within a site is carried out using RPC (*Remote Procedures Call*), which runs on IP. It provides a relatively quick information transaction and is therefore suitable for intra-site replication. When you modify Active Directory on a domain controller, the domain controller will wait five minutes before sending a notification message to the other domain controllers on the same site. Of course, the domain controller is able to record further modifications during this time. When the domain controllers find out about the notification, they copy the modifications from the domain controller that sent them the message. If no notification is received for six hours, then the domain controllers start the replication process with their partners so as to ensure that no information has been forgotten. However, certain important information is replicated automatically without waiting five minutes. This information includes the modification of such items as the LSA, an account policy, and a user password policy.

With an intra-site replication, replication traffic is not compressed, so as to reduce the workload on the domain controllers.

The KCC organizes the replication amongst all the domain controllers on your site.

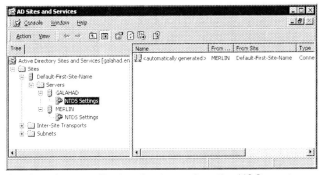

If a domain controller breaks down, then the KCC creates a new replication loop so as to implement a complete replication on the site. Three objects are required in order to make up this loop:

– Server object ⊟ GALAHAD

Each domain controller has a server object that is independent of the computer account that is created in Active Directory. This object is used to generate the replication.

– NTDS Settings object 🛱 NTDS Settings

This object contains all the connections that are generated either by the KCC, or by you, for Active Directory replication.

– Connection object 🛱 GALAHAD

This is the direction in which the information is replicated. This is a one-way connection.

Even though KCC generates a replication loop automatically, you can add **connection objects** so that a specific domain controller will replicate directly with another domain controller. In order to do this, go into the **Active Directory Sites and Services** console and expand the tree down to the **NTDS Settings** object that belongs to the domain controller for which you want to add a new connection. Right-click this object and select **New Active Directory Connection**. Select the domain controller and click **OK**. Then, enter a name for the connection object, and click **OK**.

☞ *You can use the network monitor in order to analyse the traffic concerning the RPC replication. As RPC chooses its uses a dynamic port number, it is difficult to create filters so as to observe only the replication data. However, you can use the registry so as to force the RPC calls to use a static port number. In order to do this, you must add a REG_DWORD value type under HKEY_LOCAL_MACHINE\SYSTEM\CurrentControlSet\ Services\NTDS\parameters. Then you can use this value in order to fix the port number.*

Active Directory

☞ *The Replication Monitor (REPLMON) utility from the resource kit allows you to display the topology of the replication using a graphic interface.*

b. Inter-site replication

With inter-site replication, you can choose between RPC and SMTP (*Simple Mail Transfer Protocol*) protocols. However, you can use SMTP only for inter-site replication between different domain controllers. The traffic that runs over slow links is compressed by 10 to 15% in order to improve the throughput. However, the domain controllers use more CPU time so as to compress and to decompress the data. Unlike intra-site replication, there are no special provisions for the replication of urgent information such as passwords, for example.

When you create a site, you also create a link for the site. By default, a single link is created. This link is called Defaultipsitelink. You can create new links in order to link several sites together, if you do not wish to use the Defaultipsitelink link for this purpose.

You can create a new link as follows:

➢ Go into the **Active Directory Sites and Services** console.

➢ Expand the **Sites** folder, followed by the **Inter-Site Transports** folder. Then, right-click the **IP** folder, if you wish to create a link that uses RPC. Alternatively, right-click the **SMTP** folder, if you wish to create a link that uses SMTP.

➢ Select **New Site Link**.

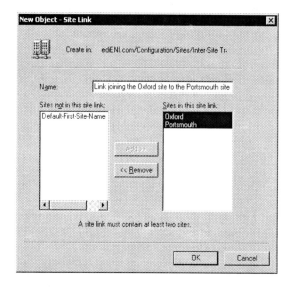

➤ Enter a name for you link, and then select the sites that you wish to link together. Then, click the **OK** button in order to confirm the operation.

In order to set up the transit on this link, right-click it and then select **Properties**.

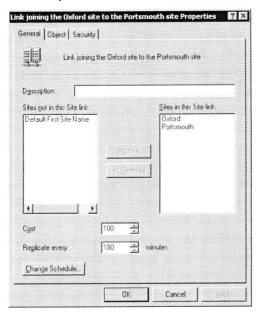

➤ You must define the following items:
- A cost: the smallest cost must be chosen in the case of several links connecting the same sites.
- A replication frequency: If you choose a higher value for this item (in minutes), then the slow link will be used less, but the replication waiting time will be longer.
- A schedule: by clicking the **Change Schedule** button, you can indicate the periods in which the replication can take place on the slow link.

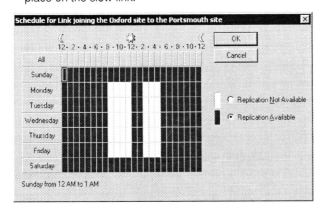

Active Directory

The links between sites are transitive. Suppose that you have three sites, the first called Portsmouth, the second called Oxford and the third called Dover. If you create a link that joins Portsmouth to Oxford, and a link that joins Portsmouth to Dover, then replication will also take place between Dover and Oxford.

If your network has limited routing, then it may be useful to create a site link bridge, and to disable the implicit transitivity between the links. In order to do this, go into the **Active Directory Sites and Services** console, and expand **Sites**, followed by **Inter-Site Transports**. Then, right-click either the IP protocol, or the SMTP protocol, and select **Properties**.

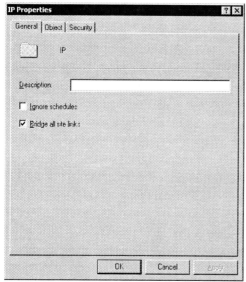

Then, deactivate the **Bridge all site links** check box.

In order to create a site link bridge between the Oxford site and the Dover site, if the network does not route via the Portsmouth site, then right-click the protocol that is used for the link bridge (either IP or SMTP). Then select **New Site Link Bridge**.

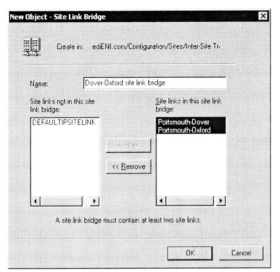

Give a name to your site link bridge, and then indicate the sites that must be linked together. Click **OK** so as to complete the operation.

In this case, the cost of the site link bridge is the sum of the site link costs (in the example above, the cost will be the sum of the cost of the Portsmouth-Oxford link, and that of the Portsmouth-Dover link).

With inter-site replication, a server is in charge of replicating the information, together with another server on the remote site. These servers are called bridgeheads. By default, the KCC must define which domain controller is the bridgehead server. However, you can choose to designate the server that will play this role, yourself. In order to do this, right-click the name of the server concerned in the **Active Directory Sites and Services** console, and then select **Properties**.

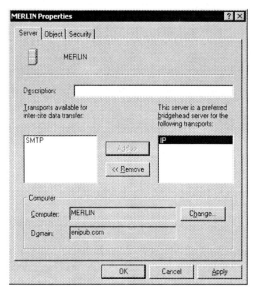

Then select the transport protocol (RPC (IP) or SMTP) for which the server will be the bridgehead.

c. Manual replication

You can force replication between domain controllers at any time.

➢ Go into the **Active Directory Sites and Services** console, and expand **Sites**, followed by the site to which you wish to replicate.

➢ Then, expand the server that must replicate the information and click **NTDS Settings**.

➢ Right-click the connection that you wish to use in order to replicate.

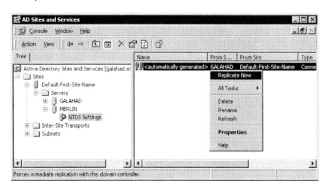

➢ Select **Replicate Now**.

You must remember that the connection objects replicate only one way. If you want to replicate in both directions, then you must carry out the same operation on the other domain controller.

F. Uninstalling

In order to uninstall Active Directory on your server, run the **dcpromo.exe** command a second time. If you wish to uninstall Active Directory on a domain controller that is acting as global catalog server, make sure that you have another server that is playing this role in the forest, unless you want to delete the domain completely.

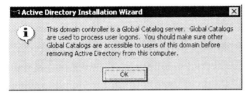

> Click **OK**.

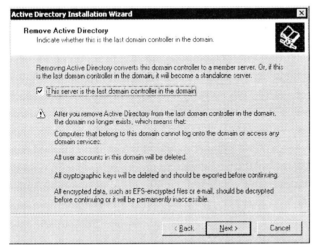

If the server concerned is the last domain controller in the domain, then activate the **This server is the last domain controller in the domain** check box. In this case, all the user accounts and the computer accounts that are in the domain will be deleted, and no one will be able to logon to the domain any more because the domain will no longer exist.

> Click the **Next** button.

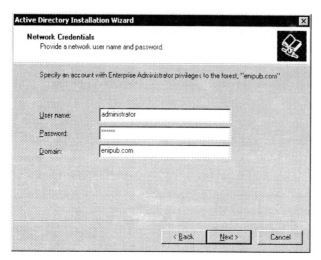

> ➢ Enter the details of an account that is a member of the company's **Administrators** group, if you must delete the domain.

> ➢ Click the **Next** button.

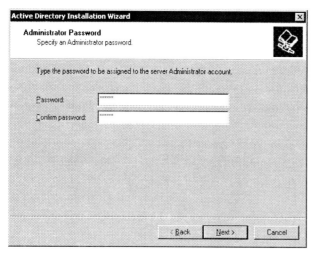

> ➢ Enter the password for the account of the local machine administrator. Then click the **Next** button.

> ➢ In the **Summary** dialog box, once again click **Next**.

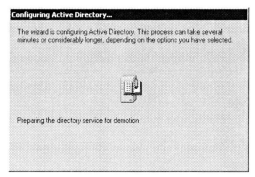

When the uninstall process is completed, restart the server.

Labs

To be absolutely sure that you have assimilated this chapter, work through the corresponding labs. These are set out from page 636 to page 640.

☒ Installing Active Directory.

☒ Changing a domain from mixed mode to native mode.

☒ Adding a global catalog server.

☒ Creating a new site.

☒ Uninstalling Active Directory.

Assessing your skills

Try the following questions if you think you know this chapter well enough.

Active Directory

1 What is the name of the Windows 2000 directory database? □

....

2 What is the role of the Windows 2000 directory database? □

....
....
....

3 What role does the DNS protocol play in Active Directory?

....

....

....

4 What role does the LDAP protocol play in Active Directory?

....

....

....

5 What role does the SNTP protocol play in Active Directory?

....

....

....

6 What is the principal authentication protocol on Windows 2000?

....

7 What is a tree?

....

....

....

8 What is a forest?

....

....

....

9 Which type of trust relationship is implemented between Windows 2000 domains that are in the same forest?

....

....

....

10 What does « multiple master replication » mean?

....

....

....

....

11 What is the role of an organizational unit (OU)?

....

....

....

12 What is an object?

....

....

....

13 What is an attribute? ☐
....
....
....

14 Can several different objects have the same attributes? ☐
....
....
....

15 Where are attributes defined? ☐
....

16 Can you add new attributes for a given class? ☐
....

17 Can you add new classes?
....

18 Alan Price is a user account that has been created in an ☐
OU that is called user, in the company.uk domain. What is
the full name of this object?
....

Installing

19 Which command can you use in order to install Active ☐
Directory on a Windows 2000 server?
....

20 What is the name of the Active Directory database file? ☐
Where is it stored by default?
....
....
....

21 Which items do you need in order to install Active ☐
Directory?
....
....
....
....

22 What is the name of the shared system directory? ☐
....

23 What is the role of the shared system directory? ☐
....
....
....

24 What is the name of the first domain that is created in a ☐
forest?
....
....

Active Directory

25 You have just migrated your Windows NT domain controllers to Windows 2000. The migration was successful and you do not intend using a pre-Windows 2000 domain controller in your domain. What must you do in order to take advantage of all the features of Active Directory?

....

....

Domain controllers

26 What do you call domain controllers that play specific roles in the forest or in the domain?

....

....

....

27 What are the five specific roles that domain controllers can play?

....

....

....

....

28 Which roles must be unique within a forest?

....

....

....

29 Which roles must be unique within a domain?

....

....

....

30 Can you transfer roles from one domain controller to another?

....

....

....

....

31 You want to delete a domain controller that is playing the role of global catalog server. In this case, what must you ensure before you uninstall Active Directory?

....

....

....

32 What is the purpose of a global catalog server?

....

....

....

33 Can you have several global catalog servers in the same forest? Can you have several global catalog servers in the same domain?

....
....
....
....

34 The users of your domain complain that they can no longer log on to the domain. This problem occurred after you disconnected a domain controller in order to transform it into a member server. However, you have checked that you could log on to the domain with your administrator account. What might be causing the problem?

....
....
....
....

Replication

35 Which items allow you to control replication traffic across slow links?

....

36 What are the two types of replication?

....
....
....

37 Which information is replicated within a domain?

....
....
....

38 Which information is replicated between different domains?

....
....
....

39 What is the name of the site that is created by default when you install the first domain controller in a forest?

....
....
....
....

Active Directory

40 How is replication managed in a site?

....
....
....
....

41 Which transport protocols can you use for inter-site replication? Which transport protocols can you use for intra-site replication?

....
....
....
....

42 How much time must elapse before modifications that have been made to the directory database will be replicated between domain controllers on the same site?

....
....
....
....

43 Is there any type of information that will be replicated without this time lapse?

....
....
....
....

44 What is the role of a site link?

....
....
....

45 What is the name of the site link that is created by default when you install Active Directory?

....
....

46 What is the role of a site link bridge?

....
....
....
....

47 Which settings can you define for a link, which will allow you to manage the traffic across the link?

....
....
....

48 Which console is used in order to create sites, subnets and links?

....

49 Which three objects do you need in order to replicate? ❑
....
....
....

50 Can you force replication between domain controllers? ❑
....
....
....
....

Results

Check your answers on pages 209 to 215. Count one point for each correct answer.

Number of points   │   /50   │
For this chapter you need to have scored at least 38 out of 50.
Look at the list of key points that follows. Pick out the ones with which you have had difficulty and work through them again in this chapter before moving on to the next.

Key points of the chapter

☐ Active Directory.

☐ Installing.

☐ Domain controllers.

☐ Replication.

Solutions

Active Directory

1   What is the name of the Windows 2000 directory database?

Active Directory.

2   What is the role of the Windows 2000 directory database?

The Active Directory database groups together all the network objects in order to organize, and to simplify, administrative tasks.

3   What role does the DNS protocol play in Active Directory?

This protocol is used in order to resolve host names into IP addresses, and to search resources on the network. In addition, DNS supplies the namespace for Windows 2000 domains.

4   What role does the LDAP protocol play in Active Directory?

LDAP allows you to look for objects in Active Directory.

5   What role does the SNTP protocol play in Active Directory?

SNTP allows you to synchronize the clocks of the computers in a domain.

6   What is the principal authentication protocol on Windows 2000?

Kerberos v5.

7   What is a tree?

A tree is a set of domains that has a contiguous namespace.

8   What is a forest?

A forest is a set of one or more trees that are linked together by two-way, transitives trust relationships.

9   Which type of trust relationship is implemented between Windows 2000 domains that are in the same forest?

Two-way, transitives trust relationships

10   What does "multiple master replication" mean?

Multiple master replication means that, if modifications are made to the directory database on a domain controller, then the domain controller can replicate the modifications to the other domain controllers without any of them being in charge of the replication process.

11   What is the role of organizational units (OUs)?

OUs allow you to organize network objects in order to simplify their administration.

12   What is an object?

An object can be an item such as a user account, a computer account, a printer that is included in Active Directory, or a group.

13   What is an attribute?

An attribute is a characteristic of a class of objects. For example, the "telephone number" attribute is specific to the user object class.

14   Can several different objects have the same attributes?

Yes, all the objects that are in the same object class have the same attributes.

15   Where are attributes defined?

In the schema.

16   Can you add new attributes for a given class?

Yes, you can do this by modifying the schema.

17   Can you add new classes?

Yes, you can do this by modifying the schema.

18   Alan Price is a user account that has been created in an OU that is called user, in the company.uk domain. What is the full name of this object?

DC=uk, DC=company, OU=user, CN=Alan Price.

Installing

19   Which command can you use in order to install Active Directory on a Windows 2000 server?

Dcpromo.exe.

20   What is the name of the Active Directory database file? Where is it stored by default?

The Active Directory database file is called Ntds.dit. It is stored in the directory %systemroot%\ntds

21   Which items do you need in order to install Active Directory?

You must have, an NTFS partition in order to store the shared system volume, a member or stand-alone server that runs the TCP/IP protocol, and a DNS server that supports dynamic updates and SRV type resources.

22   What is the name of the shared system directory?

Sysvol.

23   What is the role of the shared system directory?

It contains group policy definintions, scripts and replication information.

24   What is the name of the first domain that is created in a forest?

Root domain.

25   You have just migrated your Windows NT domain controllers to Windows 2000. The migration was successful and you do not intend using a pre-Windows 2000 domain controller in your domain. What must you do in order to take advantage of all the features of Active Directory?

You must transform your domain from mixed mode to native mode.

Domain controllers

26 What do you call domain controllers that play specific roles in the forest or in the domain?

They are called operations masters that run in FSMO (Flexible Single Master Operation) mode.

27 What are the five specific roles that domain controllers can play?

- *Schema master*
- *Infrastructure master*
- *PDC emulator*
- *Domain naming master*
- *Relative identifier master*

28 Which roles must be unique within a forest?

- *Schema master*
- *Domain naming master*

29 Which roles must be unique within a domain?

- *PDC emulator*
- *Infrastructure master*
- *Relative identifier master*

30 Can you transfer roles from one domain controller to another?

Yes. In order to do this, go into Active Directory Users and Computers on the domain controller that must play the role in question. Right-click the name of your domain, and then select Operations Masters. Under the tab that concerns the role that your server must play, click the Change button. This method can be used in order to transfer those roles that are unique on a domain. For the other two roles, you must use the Active Directory Schema snap-in in order to transfer the schema master role, and you must use the Active Directory Domains and Trusts in order to transfer the domain naming master role.

31 You want to delete a domain controller that is playing the role of global catalog server. In this case, what must you ensure before you uninstall Active Directory?

You must ensure that there is another global catalog server in the forest. Otherwise, the users will no longer be able to log on.

32 What is the purpose of a global catalog server?

This type of server is used to make searches at forest level, and also to control the logon process.

33 Can you have several global catalog servers in the same forest? Can you have several global catalog servers in the same domain?

You can have as many global catalog servers as you like in a domain, or in a forest. However, the more global catalog servers that you have, the more traffic there will be between them. A suitable compromise may be to have one global catalog server in a domain, and one on each site that contains workstations.

34 The users of your domain complain that they can no longer log on to the domain. This problem occurred after you disconnected a domain controller in order to transform it into a member server. However, you have checked that you could log on to the domain with your administrator account. What might be causing the problem?

The probable cause of this problem is that the domain controller that was deleted was certainly the only global catalog server in the forest. Although administrators do not need the global catalog server in order to log on to the domain, ordinary users cannot log on without it.

Replication

35 Which items allow you to control replication traffic across slow links?

Sites.

36 What are the two types of replication?

Intra-site replication, which replicates Active Directory modifications within the same site, and inter-site replication, which replicates Active Directory modifications between sites.

37 Which information is replicated within a domain?

The information that is replicated within a domain concerns the schema naming context, the configuration naming context and the domain naming context. These naming contexts, or partitions, contain domain objects and attributes.

38 Which information is replicated between different domains?

Only information that concerns the schema naming context, and the configuration naming context, are replicated between different domains.

39 What is the name of the site that is created by default when you install the first domain controller in a forest?

The Default-First-Site-Name site is created when you install Active Directory. It contains all the subnets. Consequently, all newly-created servers will join this site, until you create new sites and associate them with new subnets.

40 How is replication managed in a site?

Within a site, connection objects are created by the KCC in order to create a replication loop that implements complete replication of Active Directory on all the domain controllers on the site. This loop is created automatically, and it is modified dynamically upon any changes in the network topology.

41 Which transport protocols can you use for inter-site replication? Which transport protocols can you use for intra-site replication?

With inter-site replication, you can use either RPC protocol, or SMTP protocol, provided that the domain controllers concerned do not belong to the same domain. With intra-site replication, RPC protocol must be used.

42 How much time must elapse before modifications that have been made to the directory database will be replicated between domain controllers on the same site?

By default, when a domain controller modifies Active Directory, it must wait 5 minutes before notifying its replication partners. If a domain controller has not received any notification after 6 hours, it starts the replication process so as to be sure that it has not "missed" any modifications.

43 Is there any type of information that will be replicated without this time lapse?

Yes, such information is called urgent information. This information comprises modifications to passwords, modifications to the LSA and mofications to account policies or to password policies. This "urgent" classification applies only to intra-site replication processes.

44 What is the role of a site link?

A site link allows you to link together several sites so that the domain controllers on these sites will be able to replicate the directory database at set times.

45 What is the name of the site link that is created by default when you install Active Directory?

DefaultIpSiteLink.

46 What is the role of a site link bridge?

A site link bridge allows you to link together at least two sites in a network that is not fully routed (for example, suppose that site A and site C are both connected to site B by a link. However, replication must also be made between site A and site C. In the case where the network does not route via site B, then a site link bridge will allow you to replicate Active Directory information between site A and site C).

47 Which settings can you define for a link, which will allow you to manage the traffic across the link?

You can define a cost, a schedule, and a replication frequency within the timetable that is defined for the link.

48 Which console is used in order to create sites, subnets and links?

Active Directory Sites and Services.

49 Which three objects do you need in order to replicate?

You must have a server object. This server object must have a child object that is called NTDS Settings. The NTDS Settings object groups together all the connection objects that allow replication with another domain controller.

50 Can you force replication between domain controllers

*Yes. In order to do this, go into the **Active Directory Sites and Services** console. Right-click the connection object that corresponds to the server with which you want to replicate. Then select **Replicate Now**. If two domain controllers are not direct replication partners, then you can make two domain controllers direct replication partners by adding a connection object under the NTDS Settings object.*

Active Directory

Prerequisites for this chapter

☒ Knowledge of console management.

☒ To have read Chapter 6 on Active Directory.

Objectives

At the end of this chapter, you will be able to:

☒ Define the advantages and the role of group policies.

☒ Define the components that are required by group policies.

☒ Create/delete policies.

☒ Apply policies to containers.

☒ Set up group policies.

☒ Optimize the implementation of group policies.

☒ Configure the users' environnement.

☒ Know the order in which group policies must be applied.

☒ Use group policy inheritance and propagation.

☒ Use permissions on policies.

☒ Deploy applications using group policies.

☒ Apply service packs using group policies.

☒ Update applications using group policies.

☒ Delete applications using group policies.

Group policies

Contents

A. Overview

A group policy is a set of parameters that you can apply to users, to groups of users and to computers. You can define group policies at site level, at domain level or at organizational unit (OU) level. When a group policy applies to such a container, it applies to all the network objects that the container holds.

Group policies allow you, to restrict the capabilities of user's desktops, to apply account and password policies, to deploy applications, to set up security options, to run scripts, to implement audits, and to change user rights.

In summary, group policies provide an administration tool that allows you to reduce the Total Cost of Ownership (TCO) by managing the working status of users.

Group policies are implemented in the form of Active Directory objects. These are known as GPOs (*Group Policy Objects*). A GPO is made up of two parts that are stored in different locations:

– GPC (*Group Policy Container*) is an Active Directory object that contains the attributes of the GPO. In order to view the GPC in Active Directory, go into the **Active Directory Users and Computers** console. Then, open the **View** menu and select **Advanced Features** in order to display the **System** folder.

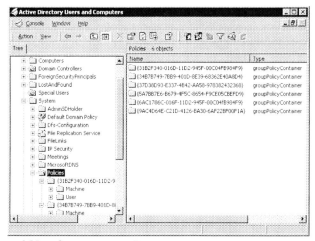

– GPT (*Group Policy Template*) is stored in the **sysvol** directory and contains a template of settings that can be applied to a GPO.

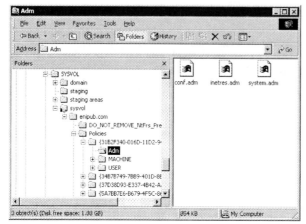

Consequently, when you create a group policy, you will create an Active Directory object that is linked to a container (an OU, a site or a domain). You can link the same GPO to several containers, and you can link several GPOs to the same container.

B. Managing GPOs

As you can apply a group policy to a site, to a domain, or directly to an OU, you must use two different consoles:
- **Active Directory Sites and Services**: in order to apply GPOs at site level.
- **Active Directory Users and Computers**: in order to apply GPOs at domain level, or at OU level.

1. Creating a GPO

You can create a group policy as follows:

➤ Open, either the **Active Directory Sites and Services** console,

Active Directory Sites and Services

or the **Active Directory Users and Computers** console:

Active Directory Users and Computers

from the **Administrative Tools** menu.

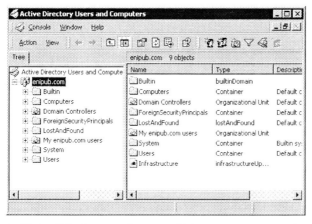

➤ Right-click the container to which you want to apply a policy:

– Either, a domain:  enipub.com

– Or an OU: My enipub.com users

You can apply GPOs only to organizational units, which are indicated by an icon. You cannot apply GPOs to containers that are indicated by an icon. In fact you can apply group policies to any of the OU that you create, or to any of the OUs that have already been created, which correspond to the domain controllers.

➤ Select **Properties** and then select the **Group Policy** tab.

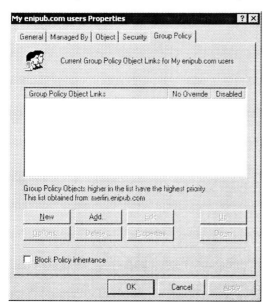

If you carry out such an operation on the domain or on the OU that contains the domain controllers, you must view a default policy in the GPO list.

➤ In order to create a new policy, click the **New** button.

A new policy appears that has the name **New Group Policy Object**, by default. You can rename this policy in order to call it something that is more meaningful. As you can apply several GPOs to the same container, it is better to give your policy a name that represents the action that is provided by the policy so that you will be able to find it quickly.

2. Adding a GPO

You can link a container to a GPO that already exists, by right-clicking the container, and then selecting **Properties**. Select the **Group Policy** tab, and then click the **Add** button.

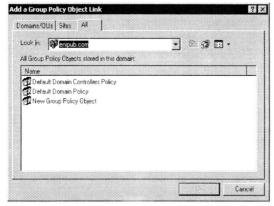

– The **All** tab allows you to view all the GPOs, irrespective of the containers to which the GPOs are linked.
– The **Domains/OUs** tab lists GPOs according to the location to which they are applied.
– The **Sites** tab lists the GPOs that are applied at site level.

➤ Select the policy that you wish to apply to the container and then click the **OK** button.

☞ *You may find it useful to create your GPOs in a container that you have designed specially for this purpose, and then deactivate your GPOs for this container. When you have done this you will be able to use the Add button in order to link the policies to the required containers.*

3. Deleting a GPO

A policy that is applied to a container is merely a link to the GPC. Consequently, when you delete a policy, you can choose to delete only the link (**Remove the link from the list**), or you can choose to delete the link and the GPO (**Remove the link and delete the Group Policy Object permanently**).

➢ In order to delete a group policy, select it and then click the **Delete** button.

C. Group policy settings

When you have added your GPO, click the **Edit** button. The list of settings that you can modify appears in the **Group Policy** window.

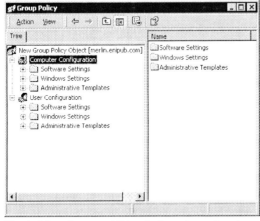

The left-hand pane of this window shows two tree structures: one concerns computer settings, and the other concerns user settings.

Here are the different types of policy that you can implement:

– **Software Settings**: allow you to publish, or to attribute, programs. This type of policy is available in both of the tree structures. This item allows you to deploy programs, either for users or for computers.

- **Administrative Templates**: allow you to set up the user environment (in order to define the level of access to the Control Panel and to the **Start** menu, to enable or disable offline folders, or to define disk quotas).
- **Scripts**: allow you to run scripts, either when users log on or log off (under **Windows Settings** in the User Configuration), or during shutdown or startup of a computer (under **Windows Settings** in the Computer Configuration).
- **Security Settings**: allow you to define the security that you want to apply (including user rights, accounts and passwords policy, and IPSec security).
- **Folder Redirection**: allows you to set up directory redirection.

When a user logs on, the GPOs are consulted so as to find out which settings must be applied, either to the user, or to the computer on which the user is logging on. In order to speed up the logon process, you can deactivate any user or computer settings that are not used.

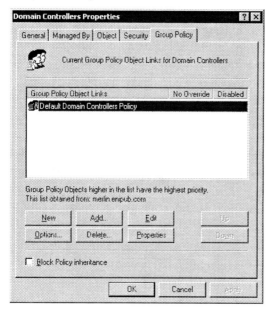

> Select the policy concerned and then click the **Properties** button.

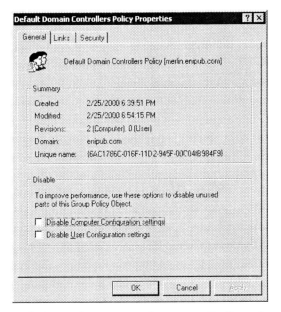

> ➤ Activate the **Disable Computer Configuration settings** check box, if only the user components are used in the policy. Activate the **Disable User Configuration settings** if only the computer components are used in the policy.

D. User environment

When a user logs on, Windows 2000 consults the **SYSVOL** folder for the domain controller so as to find a policy file that is called **Registry.pol**. Two registry.pol files are present in the GPT for each GPO: one of these files contains computer settings, and the other contains user settings.
In order to control user environments, you must use mainly the **Administrative Templates**. These contain registry database values that will be modified locally on the machine on which the user logs on. You can use a graphic interface in order to modify these values. When you apply group policies that concern user settings, you modify **HKEY_ CURRENT_USER** and when you apply computer settings you modify **HKEY_LOCAL_ MACHINE**.

The values that you can set include the following:
– Windows components; for example you can set Windows Installer, Internet Explorer, and Windows Explorer (these values can be applied to users and to computers).
– System; these include disk quotas, and logon settings (these values can be applied to users and to computers).

- Network; (these values can be applied to users and to computers).
- Printers (these values can be applied to computers).
- Control Panel (these values can be applied to users).
- Desktop (these values can be applied to users).
- Start menu & Taskbar (these values can be applied to users).

In order to apply a setting in a policy, double-click the policy concerned.

Then, select one of the following options:

- **Not Configured**: When you select this option, Windows 2000 will ignore this setting and will not modify the corresponding registry database value.
- **Enabled**: When you select this option, Windows 2000 will apply this setting, and the value will be added to the **Registry.pol** file.
- **Disabled**: When you select this option, Windows 2000 will not apply this setting, and the value will be added to the **Registry.pol** file.

In addition to selecting one of these three options, you must add values, for some settings.

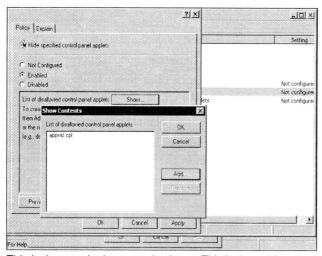

This is the case in the example above. This is the setting that is called **Hide specified control panel applets**. This setting is activated (**Enabled**). By clicking the **Show** button, you can list the applets concerned: appwiz.cpl is the **Add/Remove Programs** icon (the **.cpl** filename extension is used for control panel applets). Alternatively, you can enter the name of the icon.

E. Applying GPOs

1. Order of application

When you start up your machine, the settings that have been defined for the computer will be applied, along with the startup scripts.

Then, when the user logs on, the user settings are applied followed by the logon scripts. By default, the logon scripts must finish executing within ten minutes.

Once these policies have been applied, they are refreshed every 90 minutes. By this means, the current policies will always be applied to computers and to users, even if they do no disconnect.

On domain controllers and on member servers, these policies are refreshed every 5 minutes.

☞ *You can modify these values for the policies in Administrative Templates - System - Group Policy.*

- Policies can be applied at different levels. First, the policies that are defined at site level are applied, then, those that are defined at domain level are applied, and finally, those that are defined at OU level are applied. The policies will be accumulated, as long as they do not conflict with each other. In the event of a conflict, then the policy that is nearest to the user will be applied (for example, the policy that is defined at OU level).

- If several policies have been defined for the same container, then the policies will be read in the list order, from bottom to top. Consequently, in the event of any conflict, the policy that is situated at the top of the list will be applied. Of course, if there is no conflict, then the policy settings will be cumulated.

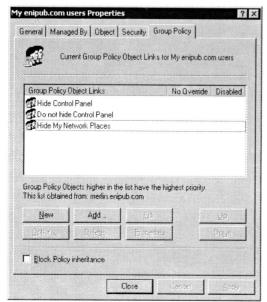

In the example above, if the policy names represent the policy contents, then, for the users of this container, Control Panel and My Network Places will be hidden.

You can change the list position of a policy using the **Up** and **Down** buttons.

2. Inheriting

By default, policies are inherited from parent containers. For example if no policy has been defined for the users of an OU, then settings may be applied that have been defined at site level, at domain level, or even at the level of an OU that is a parent of the container. If you do not want a container to inherit policies that have been defined for containers that are higher in the tree (for parent containers), then you can block the inheritance at the level of the (target) container concerned.

➢ Right-click the container concerned and then select **Properties**. Select the **Group Policy** tab.

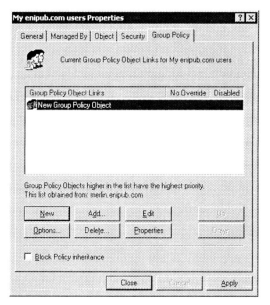

➢ Activate the **Block Policy inheritance** check box.

If you activate this check box, then only the policies that apply to the container will be applied to the objects that are in the container. This rule will apply, except in the case where the **No Override** option has been set for the parent container. This option allows an administrator to force the application of a policy, either in the event of a conflict, or even if the **Block Policy inheritance** option has been set for a child container.

In order to set the **No Override** option for a GPO:

➢ Right-click the container, select **Properties** and then select the **Group Policy** tab.

➢ Select the GPO concerned and then click the **Options** button.

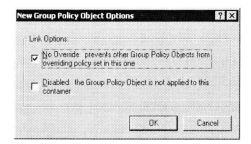

➢ Activate the **No Override…** check box.

It must be noted that this dialog box also allows you to disable a policy for a container.

3. Permissions

In order that a policy can be applied to the users of a container, then these users must have at least, **Read** and **Apply Group Policy** permissions.

➢ Select the policy that must be applied, click the **Properties** button, and then select the **Security** icon.

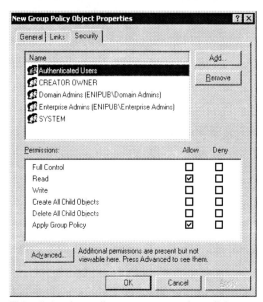

This dialog box allows you to apply policies to a group of users. It also allows you to remove a user from the policy.
By default, policies are not applied to administrators.

F. Deploying applications

1. Publication and attribution

Group policies allow you to distribute applications and service packs to users and to computers. Intellimirror provides this feature.
Applications deployment runs on Windows Installer technology. This service runs on each Windows 2000 computer (it can also run on other operating systems such as Windows NT). It allows you to install and to maintain applications. You can use this service in order to install new application components as and when your users need them. This service can also replace missing files or repair corrupt files. It can do this automatically without user intervention by taking the required files from the installation sources.

Before an application can be deployed, it must be in the form of a **package** that can be interpreted by Windows Installer. Such a package is made up of an installation file that has an .MSI filename extension, together with other files that are required in order to install the product.

☞ *This installation method will become increasingly common. Some application development products already offer such packages.*

Using group policies, you can deploy applications as follows:

➢ Create a share that can be accessed by the users concerned. This share must contain the source of the product in MSI format.

➢ Create a new policy, either at site level, or at domain level, or at OU level.

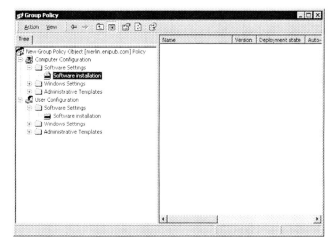

➢ If you want to deploy the programs to computers irrespective of the people that will use it, right-click **Software installation**, under **Computer Configuration**. Alternatively, If you want to deploy the programs to users irrespective of the computers that they will use, right-click **Software installation**, under **User Configuration**.

➢ Select **New**, followed by **Package**.

➢ Select the MSI file of the package that you wish to deploy.

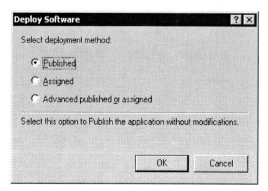

➤ You must choose one of three options:

Published

When you publish an application, the users will be able to install the program with the **Add/Remove Programs** icon from the Control Panel. Alternatively, a user can double-click the file with a name extension that is associated with the published program in order automatically to install the program without using the **Add/Remove Programs** icon. This option is available only in the group policies for user settings.

Assigned

When an application is assigned, a shortcut is added in the **Start** menu. In order automatically to install this application, the user must either select this shortcut, or double-click the document with a name extension that is associated with the published program. If you assign an application to computers, rather than to users, then the application will be automatically installed on the computers concerned.

Advanced published or assigned

This option allows you to customize the installation of the products concerned.

Published applications appear with the ⬛ icon, whereas assigned applications appear with the ⬛ icon.

You can modify the application settings by double-clicking the package concerned in the **Group Policy** window.

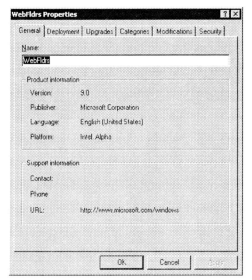

You can set up the deployment using six tabs:
- **General**: this tab shows product information, along with the deployment name.
- **Deployment**: this tab allows you to define how the application must be deployed (either published or assigned). In addition, you can specify, whether or not the application must be installed when the user double-clicks a file with the name extension that is associated with the program, whether or not a published application package must be displayed in the **Add/Remove Programs**, and whether or not the application must be uninstalled if the user is no longer associated with the container in which the policy has been placed.
- **Upgrades**: this tab allows you to create application upgrade packages (for new versions, or for service packs).
- **Categories**: this tab allows you to arrange published applications in the **Add/Remove Programs** applet, into categories that you create.
- **Modifications**: this tab allows you to customize your packages.
- **Security**: this tab allows you to apply permissions.

Before you can arrange published applications into categories, you must first create the categories concerned. You can do this by right-clicking **Software Installation**, selecting **Properties**, and then selecting the **Categories** tab.

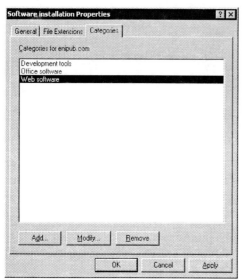

Click the **Add** button so as to define the name of a new category.

Here is the **Add/Remove Programs** screen that the users will see before the applications are published:

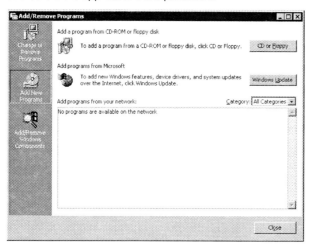

Here is the **Add/Remove Programs** screen that the users will see after the applications have been published:

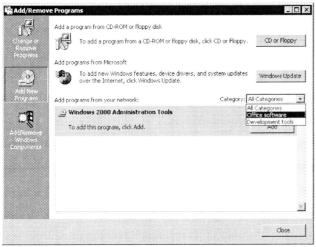

In order to install the application, a user need only click the **Add** button.

2. Upgrades and service packs

Once your application has been either published or assigned, you can upgrade it (with the latest version of the product), or you can apply any service packs concerned.
You can upgrade the version of a program as follows:

➢ Add the new version of the program to the group policy as a new package.

➢ Right-click your new package and select **Properties**. Select the **Upgrades** tab and then click the **Add** button.

➢ Select the package that must be upgraded, then indicate whether you want to uninstall the existing package and then install the upgrade package, or whether you wish to upgrade over the existing package.

➢ If you want to force the upgrade when the user next uses the application, then enable the **Required upgrade for existing packages** option. Alternatively, you must disable this option if you prefer to allow the user to choose when the upgrade must be carried out.

You can add a service pack to a program as follows:

➢ Place the service pack files in MSI format in the directory that contains the software distribution files.

➢ Right-click the package for which you want to apply the service pack.

> Select **All Tasks**, followed by **Redeploy application**.

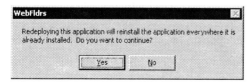

> Click **Yes** in order to confirm the redeployment.

You can add remove a program as follows:

> Right-click the package that you wish to remove.

> Select **All Tasks**, followed by **Remove**.

You then have two options:
- You can force the program removal. In this case, the application will be uninstalled upon the next computer startup, or upon the next user logon.
- Alternatively, you can prevent any fresh installations of the software, whilst allowing users who have installed the program to continue to work with it.

☞ *You can deploy applications that are not originally in MSI format by creating an MSI package for the program concerned. In order to do this, you must use the **WinINSTALL** tool that is included on the Windows 2000 CD-ROM.*

Labs

To be absolutely sure that you have assimilated this chapter, work through the corresponding labs. These are set out from page 641 to page 646.

☒ Managing user environment.

☒ Deploying applications using group policies.

Assessing your skills

Try the following questions if you think you know this chapter well enough.

Structure

1 What is a GPO? ☐
....
....
....

2 What is a GPC? ☐
....

3 Where are GPCs stored? ☐
....

4 What is a GPT? ☐
....
....
....

5 Where are GPTs stored? ☐
....

Managing group policies

6 Which consoles allow you to apply GPOs? ☐
....
....
....

7 To which items can you apply group policies? ☐
....
....

Group policies

8   You have created a relatively complex group policy, and
you have applied it to an OU that you called Accounting. You
want to apply the same policy to an OU that is called
Finance. What is the quickest way of doing this?

....
....
....
....

9   You applied a GPO to an OU, but now you no longer
want to apply this GPO to this OU. However, you do not
want to delete this GPO because it is associated with several
other OUs. What must you do?

....
....
....
....
....

10   You are the administrator of an organizational unit that is
called Department. This OU contains two child OUs that are
called Sales and Accounting. You have delegated the
administrative tasks for these two child OUs to two separate
administrators. However, you want to apply the policy that
you have defined to all the objects of these two OUs. How
can you ensure this?

....
....
....

11   As the administrator of an OU, you want to apply your
own group policies to the objects in your container. You do
not want your container to inherit the group policies of a
parent container. What will you do so as to achieve these
objectives?

....
....

Optimizing

12   You have created a group policy in order to restrict
access to the Control Panel for the users in your domain. In
order to achieve this objective, you created a GPO, and you
associated it with all the users in the domain. How can you
optimize the application of this policy?

....
....
....
....
....

13 In order to clarify your administrative organization, you have created two group policies, which you have applied to the same OU. The first group policy is called « **Prevent access to My Network Places** », and the second group policy is called « **Prevent access to the Control Panel** ». These names describe the roles of the respective policies. How can you optimize your policies in order to speed up the logon process?

....
....
....

Applying group policies

14 In which order must group policies by applied?

....

15 If you define for the same container, several GPOs that have conflicting settings, which policy will be applied for these conflicting settings?

....
....

16 How much time must elapse before group policies are refreshed on domain controllers and member servers? How much time must elapse before group policies are refreshed on workstations?

....
....
....
....

17 If several policies are applied on the same container, which polices will be effectively applied?

....
....
....
....
....
....

18 What is the role of the **Block Policy inheritance** option?

....
....

19 What is the role of the **No Override** option?

....
....
....
....
....

20 You are the administrator of your OU and you apply a policy for which you specify the **Block Policy inheritance** option. However, some settings in your policy are not applied to the objects in your container. What might be the cause of this problem?

....
....
....
....

21 You want to apply a group policy to an OU that contains all the users in you domain. However, this group policy must not be applied to some of these users. You do not want to create an OU especially for these users, as other policies are applied to the OU in which they are situated. What will you do to achieve your objectives?

....
....
....
....
....
....
....
....

Deploying applications

22 What are the different methods that you can use in order to deploy applications?

....
....

23 On what condition can you deploy an application using group policies?

....

24 What is the role of Windows Installer?

....
....
....
....
....

25 When you publish applications, you want to organize them according to their functions. Is it possible to do this?

....
....

26 How can users consult applications that have been published?

....
....
....

27 You want to upgrade an application that has been published or attributed to users. How can you do this?

....

....

....

....

Results

Check your answers on pages 241 to 245. Count one point for each correct answer.

Number of points [/27]

For this chapter you need to have scored at least 20 out of 27.

Look at the list of key points that follows. Pick out the ones with which you have had difficulty and work through them again in this chapter before moving on to the next.

Key points of the chapter

☐ Structure.

☐ Managing group policies.

☐ Optimizing.

☐ Applying group policies.

☐ Deploying applications.

Solutions

Structure

1 What is a GPO?

A GPO (Group Policy Object) comprises a set of parameters that are applicable to users, to groups of users or to computers.

2 What is a GPC?

A GPC (Group Policy Container) represents the attributes of the GPO.

3 Where are GPCs stored?

GPCs are stored as objects in Active Directory.

4 What is a GPT?

A GPT (Group Policy Template) is a folder that represents a framework of settings that are applicable to a GPO.

5 Where are GPTs stored?

GPTs are stored in the SYSVOL directory.

Managing group policies

6 Which consoles allow you to apply GPOs?

You can apply GPOs using the Active Directory Sites and Services console, or the Active Directory Users and Computers console.

7 To which items can you apply group policies?

You can apply group policies to a site, to a domain and/or to organizational units.

8 You have created a relatively complex group policy, and you have applied it to an OU that you called Accounting. You want to apply the same policy to an OU that is called Finance. What is the quickest way of doing this?

Right-click the Finance 'OU, select Properties and activate the Group Policy tab. Then click the Add button so as to select the policy that is located in the Accounting OU.

9 You applied a GPO to an OU, but now you no longer want to apply this GPO to this OU. However, you do not want to delete this GPO because it is associated with several other OUs. What must you do?

You can deactivate the policy by clicking the Options button, under the Group Policy tab. Alternatively you can select the policy concerned, click the Delete button and activate the Remove the link from the list option.

10 You are the administrator of an organizational unit that is called Department. This OU contains two child OUs that are called Sales and Accounting. You have delegated the administrative tasks for these two child OUs to two separate administrators. However, you want to apply the policy that you have defined to all the objects of these two OUs. How can you ensure this?

You must apply the GPO to the parent OU, which is called Department. Then, you must click the Options button, and activate the No Override link option.

11 As the administrator of an OU, you want to apply your own group policies to the objects in your container. You do not want your container to inherit the group policies of a parent container. What will you do so as to achieve these objectives?

By activating the Block Policy inheritance check box that is situated under the Group Policy tab.

Optimizing

12   You have created a group policy in order to restrict access to the Control Panel for the users in your domain. In order to achieve this objective, you created a GPO, and you associated it with all the users in the domain. How can you optimize the application of this policy?

By deactivating the computer configuration settings in the policy, as the parameters that are defined in the GPO apply only to the users. If you do this then the logins will be speeded up, as the computer settings will no longer be read Select the policy concerned, and click the Properties button under the Group Policy tab.

13   In order to clarify your administrative organization, you have created two group policies, which you have applied to the same OU. The first group policy is called **Prevent access to My Network Places**, and the second group policy is called **Prevent access to the Control Panel**. These names describe the roles of the respective policies. How can you optimize your policies in order to speed up the logon process?

By creating a single group policy in which you prevent access to My Network Places and to Control Panel.

Applying group policies

14   In which order must group policies by applied?

Site, then domain, followed by OU.

15   If you define for the same container, several GPOs that have conflicting settings, which policy will be applied for these conflicting settings?

The policy that will be applied is that which is situated at the top of the policy list.

16   How much time must elapse before group policies are refreshed on domain controllers and member servers? How much time must elapse before group policies are refreshed on workstations?

On domain controllers and member servers, group policies are refreshed every 5 minutes. On workstations, group policies are refreshed every 90 minutes.

17   If several policies are applied on the same container, which polices will be effectively applied?

All the policies will be applied, provided that they have not been deactivated. All settings that do not conflict with other settings will be applied. In the event of conflict between settings, the settings that will be applied are those that are included in the highest policies in the list.

Group policies

18 What is the role of the **Block Policy inheritance** option?

This option allows you to stipulate that the system must not apply policies that are included in parent containers.

19 What is the role of the **No Override** option?

This option allows you to force the application of a policy to all the objects that are located in the OU, and to all the objects that are situated in child OUs, irrespective of the policy settings that are located in the child OUs. The No Override option takes priority over the Block Policy inheritance option.

20 You are the administrator of your OU and you apply a policy for which you specify the **Block Policy inheritance** option. However, some settings in your policy are not applied to the objects in your container. What might be the cause of this problem?

A group policy has probably been defined for a parent OU with the No Override option, and this policy probably has settings that conflict with your policy.

21 You want to apply a group policy to an OU that contains all the users in you domain. However, this group policy must not be applied to some of these users. You do not want to create an OU especially for these users, as other policies are applied to the OU in which they are situated. What will you do to achieve your objectives?

In order that a policy can be applied, users or computers must have Read and Apply Group Policy permissions. Therefore, you must remove the Apply Group Policy permission for the users for whom the policy must not apply. In order to do this, select the policy concerned, click the Properties button, and modify the permissions under the Security tab.

Deploying applications

22 What are the different methods that you can use in order to deploy applications?

Publication and attribution.

23 On what condition can you deploy an application using group policies?

The application must be in MSI format.

24 What is the role of Windows Installer?

Windows Installer is a service that allows you to deploy and to maintain applications. Windows Installer is able to install new application components without user intervention. It can also repair damaged files, or replace missing files.

25 When you publish applications, you want to organize them according to their functions. Is it possible to do this?

Yes. You can do this by creating categories, and by organizing the applications into these categories.

26 How can users consult applications that have been published?

*Go into **Control Panel**, double-click the **Add/Remove Programs** icon, and click the **Add New Programs** button.*

27 You want to upgrade an application that has been published or attributed to users. How can you do this?

*Add a group policy that contains the new version of the program. Go into the properties of this new package, activate the **Upgrades** tab and add the package that will be upgraded by this new package.*

.

Prerequisites for this chapter

☒ Knowledge of the Windows 2000 environment.

Objectives

At the end of this chapter, you will be able to:

☒ Create user accounts that can be used for logging on locally and for logging on to the domain.

☒ Describe the predefined accounts.

☒ Describe the account settings and the personal settings for a user account.

☒ Modify a user account.

☒ Reset passwords.

☒ Add a user to a group.

☒ Create local, global and universal groups.

☒ Described the predefined groups.

☒ Carry out a search in Active Directory.

☒ Move an account from one OU to another OU.

☒ Define group scopes and group types.

☒ Implement user profiles and home directories.

Contents

User and group management

You can administer user accounts and groups using two different consoles:
- **Active Directory Users and Computers** in order to manage the domain.
- **Computer Management** in order to manage the accounts and the local groups of a member server, of a stand-alone server or of a Professional workstation.

A. Managing a local computer

1. Users

A local user account is an account that can be used in order to log on locally to a computer. With this type of account, you can access only the local resources of a machine.

These accounts are stored in the accounts database of the local computer. This is the SAM database, which is stored under the directory %systemroot%\system32\config. These account databases are present only on workstations, and on member and stand-alone servers. On a domain controller accounts and groups are stored in Active Directory.

If a user who is logged on locally wishes to access resources that are situated on another computer, then the user must have an account on the other machine.

a. Predefined accounts

When you install Windows 2000, two user accounts are created:
- the Administrator account, and
- the guest account.

Administrator

The administrator has the maximum power on a machine. The administrator manages the system configuration, which includes the following tasks:
- managing security policy,
- managing user accounts and group accounts,
- managing the software configuration of the operating system,
- creating folders and installing files on the hard disks,
- installing and configuring printers,
- administrating the sharing of file and printer ressources,
- logical and physical organisation of data on the disks (including formatting, and partitioning),
- backing up and restoring data.

You cannot delete the Administrator account, but you can rename it.

☞ *You are recommended to rename the Administrator account because it is more difficult to find the password of an account when you do not know its name.*

☞ *In addition, it is useful not to display the name of the last user who logged on to a machine. You can do this by adding the value DontDisplayLastUserName: REG_SZ: 1 in the registry location: HKEY_LOCAL_MACHINE\SOFTWARE\ MICROSOFT\Windows NT\current Version\Winlogon\.*

Guest

As the name indicates, this account is intended for occasional users, or for inexperienced users. For security reasons, the *Guest* user has a minimum amount of rights on the system.

☞ *By default, this account is disabled, and does not have a password. When you enable this account, you introduce a major weak point into the security system.*

b. Creating a user account

You can create a local user account using the **Local Users and Groups** folder of the **Computer Management** console.

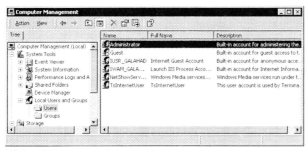

Right-click **Users** and then select **New User.**

User name

> This is the name that must be entered by the user in order to log on to the machine. This field is obligatory and must not exceed 20 characters.

Full name

> This is the user's full name. It is used for administrative reasons.

Description

> This field allows you to specify such details as the user's position in the company, and the user's geographical location.

Password and **Confirm password**

> The administrator can assign a password to the user.

User must change password at next logon

> If you enable this option, then the user must choose a password when he/she logs on for the first time. Then, the user will no longer have to choose a password on subsequent logons, and will be able to use the password that he/she entered upon the first logon. This option allows the administrator to let the user choose his/her own password. However, in this case the administrator will have no unilateral means of finding out a user's password.

User cannot change password

> This option is useful so as to fix certain passwords, such as that of the guest user and those of accounts that are user by several people. This option helps the administrator to manage user passwords.

Password never expires

> You must use this option if you do not want the password to expire. This option can be useful with an account that is used by an application or by a service.

Account is disabled
> You must enable this option if you do not want anyone to use an account (for example, when a user goes on holiday). When you disable an account a cross appears on the icon (🖳).

☞ *If you select the User must change password at next logon option, then the User cannot change password option, and the Password never expires option, are grayed out.*

c. Modifying a user account

Once you have created a local account, then it appears in the **Computer Management** console, in the user list under the **Users** folder

You can modify the characteristics that you have defined for a user, later. In order to do this, select the user concerned and then press the ⌧Enter⌧ key. Alternatively, you can open the **Action** menu and select **Properties**.

It must be noted that this dialog box contains a new option that is grayed out: **Account is disabled**. This option will become available if you define an account policy that indicates that the account must be locked out after a specified number of failed logon attempts.

The User Properties dialog box offers a number of additional tabs:
- The **Member Of** tab indicates the groups of which the user is a member. If you wish to include the user in a new group, then click the **Add** button and select the desired group.
- The **Profile** tab allows you to specify the path of the user's profile. This topic will be covered in greater detail later on in this chapter.
- The **Dial-in** tab allows you to specify how this account must be used via remote network access or via VPN *(Virtual Private Networking)*.

When you rename a user account you do not lose all the information that is associated with the account (such as group memberships and permissions). In fact, when you handle a user account, you use the login name of the user. However, Windows 2000 associates this name with a security identification number (SID). This number is unique, and has the following format:

S-1-5-21-527237240-2111687655-1957994488-500

When you rename an account you will modify the login name; on the other hand the SID never changes. When you grant permissions to a user account, then these permissions are attributed to the SID that is associated with the account. If you delete an account, and then recreate the account with the same name, then you will have created a new account that is associated to a new SID. Because of this, you will not recover the permissions that had been granted to the previous account.

If you wish to rename, or to delete an account, then you can either right-click the account concerned, or you can use the **Action** menu.

d. Modifying a password

With Windows NT 4.0, you could change the password that is associated with a user account by modifying the properties of the account. With Windows 2000 however, you must right-click the account concerned and then select the **Set Password** option (alternatively, you can use the **Action** menu).

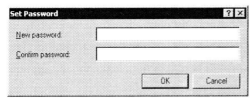

You cannot modify a password via the properties of the account so as to enable the administration of this item to be delegated. With the Windows 2000 approach, you can grant to users, or to groups of users, the sole power of changing their passwords, without allowing them to change any other characteristics of their accounts.

☞ *An administrator cannot find out a user's password.*

2. Groups

a. Introduction

Groups allow you to simplify user administration. A group contains a set of user accounts that have the same administrative needs. Thus, rather than granting permissions to each user individually, an administrator can simply grant the permissions to a group.

The permissions and rights that are assigned to a group apply to all the users who are members of the group.

☞ *A user can be a member of several groups.*

In the local accounts database of a member/stand-alone server, or of a workstation, only one type of group can be created: a local group. Local groups are represented by the 🔣 icon.

b. Creating a group

You can create a group by right-clicking the **Groups** folder in the **Computer Management** console, and then selecting **New Group** (alternatively you can select the **Groups** folder and then use the **Action** menu).

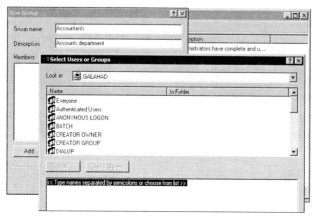

Give the group a meaningful name, and possibly a description, and then click the **Add** button. You can choose, to include users, either from the local accounts database, or from a domain.

c. Predefined groups

On member/stand-alone servers, and on Windows 2000 Professional workstations, a number of groups are predefined during the installation of Windows 2000.

These groups have rights that allow them to carry out a certain number of tasks on the local machine, such as making backups, and administering resources.

These predefined groups are as follows:

– **Administrators**: the members of this group can carry out all the computer's administrative tasks. By default, the only member of this group is the administrator account. When you include a workstation, or a stand-alone server, in a domain, then the global administrators group of the domain is included automatically, in the local administrators group of your computer. This is done so that the domain administrators can manage all the machines that are in their domain.

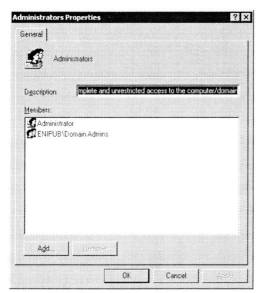

Thus, in the example above, the Administrators group of the ENIPUB domain have been included in the local Administrators group of the member server. Thanks to this approach, the domain administrator can administer this computer in the same way as the local machine administrator.

- **Guests**: as the name indicates, this group is used for occasional access. For security reasons, the users of this group are granted only a minimum number of system rights. By default, the **Guest** account is automatically included in this group.
- **Backup Operators**: the members of this group can use the Windows 2000 Backup utility in order to backup and to restore data.
- **Users**: all the user accounts that you create are included in this group. They can carry out only the tasks that you specify and have access only to those resources for which you have granted permissions. When your workstation, or your server joins a domain, the users group of the domain is automatically included in the users group of your machine.
- **Power Users**: the members of this group can share resources, and they can create and modify user accounts from the computer's local accounts database. Thereby, they can carry out certain administrative tasks without being in total control of the machine.

In addition to these groups, every computer that runs Windows 2000 has system groups. You cannot modify the membership of these groups, which reflect the status of your system at a given time.

- **Everyone** group: this group includes all users: those you have created, the guest account, and all the users of the other domains. It must be noted that, when you share a resource, this group has Full Control permission.
- **Authenticated Users** group: this group includes all users that have a user account and a password for the local machine, or for Active Directory. It is preferable to grant permissions to this group, rather than granting them to the Everyone group.
- **Creator Owner** group: every user that has taken possession of a resource is a member of this group, for the resource concerned. The owner of a resource has full powers on this resource.
- **Network** group: this group includes all users that access a resource via the network.
- **Interactive** group : this group contains all the users who are logged on locally (in the case where you use Terminal Services, this group contains all the users who are logged on to the Terminal Server).

B. Managing a domain

Every person who uses the network must have a user account in order to log on to the domain and thereby have access to the network resources. These user accounts are created in the Windows 2000 directory database.

When a user logs on to the domain, the logon information is sent to the domain controller, which compares it with the information that is contained in the Active Directory database. When the logon has been validated, the user can access all the network resources for which he/she has the permission to access.

When you promote a Windows 2000 server to domain controller (by installing Active Directory), the group and user information that is contained in the SAM database are migrated to the Active Directory database.

1. Managing domain users

a. Predefined accounts

When you install Windows 2000, two user accounts are created:
- the Administrator account, and
- the guest account.

Administrator

The administrator has the maximum power on a machine. The administrator manages the system configuration, which includes the following tasks:
- managing security policies,
- managing user accounts and group accounts,
- managing the software configuration of the operating system,
- creating folders and installing files on the hard disks,
- installing and configuring printers,
- administrating the sharing of file and printer ressources,
- logical and physical organisation of data on the disks (including formatting, and partitioning),
- backing up and restoring data.

You cannot delete the Administrator account, but you can rename it.

☞ *You are recommended to rename the Administrator account because it is more difficult to find the password of an account when you do not know its name.*

☞ *In addition, it is useful not to display the name of the last user who logged on to a machine. You can use group policies for this purpose.*

Guest

As the name indicates, this account is intended for occasional users, or for inexperienced users. For security reasons, the Guest user has a minimum amount of rights on the system.

By default, this account is disabled, and does not have a password. You can rename this account. When you enable this account, you introduce a major weak point into the security system.

b. Creating a user account

Before you start creating users, you might find it useful to define a naming convention that will allow you to identify each user, and above all, that will allow you to ensure that each logon name is unique in the domain. For example, one possible naming convention could be to use the first letter of the user's first name, followed by the users surname. If this rule leads to a duplication of logon names, one way of solving the problem could be to add the second letter of the first name. For example, suppose you have one user who is called Peter Jenkins and another user who is called Paul Jenkins. Then, you could define their login names as **pejenkins** and **pajenkins**, respectively.

In order to create domain user accounts, you must use the **Active Directory Users and Computers** console.

You must create this user object in a container. In order to do this, right-click the organizational unit in which you want to create the account, and then select **New** followed by **User** (alternatively, you can use the **Action** menu).

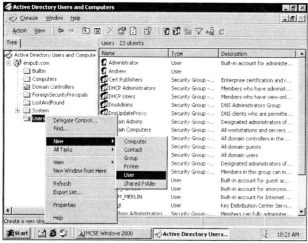

The **New Object - User** dialog box appears:

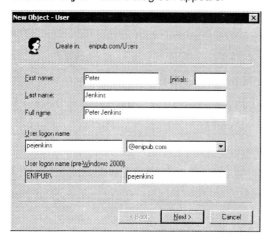

First name

> This field is obligatory. It allows you to enter the user's first name.

Last name
The user's surname is also obligatory.
Full name
This name must be unique on the organizational unit in which you are creating the user account.
User logon name
The user will enter this name so that it can be authenticated by the domain controller. This name must be unique in the domain, and must be in conformity with your naming convention. It must be noted that this logon name is followed by the name of the domain in which you are creating the user. In the example above, the user will be able to log on as pejenkins@enipub.com.
User logon name (pre-Windows 2000)
Users who work with a pre-Windows 2000 version must log on with this name. This name must not exceed 20 characters.
When you have completed these fields, click **Next**.

Password and **Confirm password**
The administrator can provide a password for the user.
User must change password at next logon
If you enable this option, then the user must choose a password when he/she logs on for the first time. Then, the user will no longer have to choose a password on subsequent logons, and will be able to use the password that he/she entered upon the first logon. This option allows the administrator to let the user choose his/her own password. However, in this case the administrator will have no unilateral means of finding out a user's password.

User cannot change password

This option is useful so as to fix certain passwords, such as that of the guest user and those of accounts that are user by several people. This option helps the administrator to manage user passwords.

Password never expires

You must use this option if you do not want the password to expire. This option can be useful with an account that is used by an application or by a service.

Account is disabled

You must enable this option if you do not want anyone to use an account (for example, when a user goes on holiday). When you disable an account a cross appears on the icon.

☞ *If the predefined OUs do not suit your needs, select the name of your domain in the Active Directory Users and Computers console, and then open the Action menu and select New followed by Organizational Unit.*

☞ *When you create an object it is replicated automatically on all the other domain controllers.*

c. User account properties

Personal properties

Personal properties are the attributes of the user. This information includes such items as the users geographical address, and the user's telephone numbers. This information is stored in the Windows 2000 directory database so that users will be able to find it very easily.

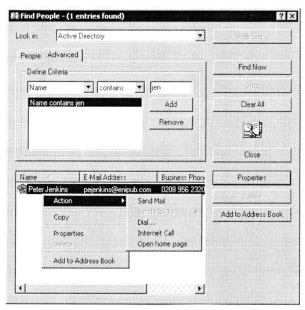

This information allows you to find a user very easily.

You can look for a user in two ways:

- Open the **Start – Search – For People** menu, and then select **Active Directory** in the **Look in** drop-down list box.

user and group management

When you have found your contact, you can carry out a certain number of actions. For example, you can send the user an electronic mail message, you can open the user's web page, or you can view the user's properties in order to find out his/her geographical address.

- Alternatively, using the **Active Directory Users and Computers** console you can open the **Action** menu and then select **All Tasks** followed by **Find**. This method allows you to carry out searches according to more advanced criteria.

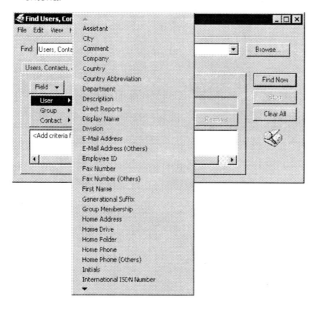

Account properties

Unlike personal properties, account properties do not supply information on the user. They supply information concerning the running of the account (including items such as time period restrictions, and account expiry).

In order to view or to enter account properties, double-click the user concerned and select the **Account** tab.

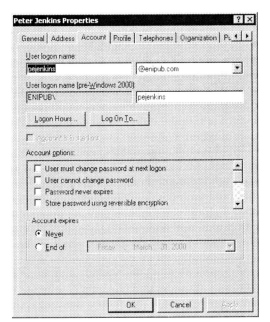

Under **Account options** you can modify the settings that were specified when the account was created. These settings include the following:

– Password never expires,
– User must change password at next logon,
– User cannot change password,
– Account is disabled.

In addition, the following options are also available:

Smart card is required for interactive logon
Windows 2000 allows you to request authentication using a smartcard, provided that your system is equipped with a card reader.

Account is sensitive and cannot be delegated
This option ensures that control of this account will not be delegated.

Account is trusted for delegation
This option allows the user to delegate administrative tasks to other users.

Store password using reversible encryption
You must use this option if there are any users in the Windows 2000 network who work with Apple computers.

Do not require Kerberos preauthentification
You must use this option if the user account uses another version of the Kerberos protocol.

Use DES encryption types for this account
You must enable this check box if you use DES (*Data Encryption Standard*) encryption. DES supports encryption methods such as IPSec, and MPPE.

Account expiry

You can set an account expiry date (this may be useful in the case where you know that a user will leave the company on a fixed date, for example on June 5th, 2000). You can set an expiry date as follows:

Under **Account expires** select the **End of** option, and open the list box so as to display the calendar. Then select the date on which you want the account to expire.

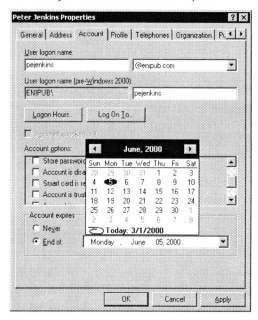

Time period restrictions

For security reasons, you may want to define the time periods during which a user will be allowed to log on. In order to do this, select the **Logon Hours** button.

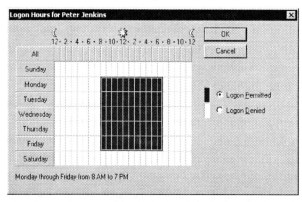

Select the desired logon hours, and then enable either the **Logon Permitted** or the **Logon Denied** option button according to your requirements.

Access restrictions

You can restrict the access of the user to certain, specified machines. In order to do this, click the **Log On To** button, and then add the names of the computers onto which the user must be allowed to log.

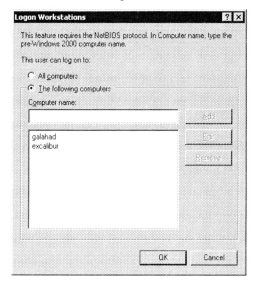

d. Copying user accounts

If you must create a large number of user accounts with the same characteristics, you may find it quicker to create a template account that includes all the common characteristics, and then to copy it.

When you copy an account, the following settings are maintained:

– Logon Hours.
– The following account options:
  User must change password at next logon,
  User cannot change password,
  Password never expires,
  Account is disabled.
– Access restrictions (Log On To).
– Account expiry date.
– Profile options and the home directory (for these settings you must use the %username% variable).
– Group membership.

In order to copy an account, right-click the account concerned, and then select **Copy**.

e. Modifying an account

Resetting a password

If a user forgets his/her password, then you must reset it (after first verifying the user's identity). You can reset a password by right-clicking the user's account, and then selecting **Reset Password**.

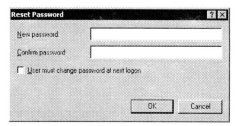

Moving a user object

As the organizational unit tree structure is not fixed, you can move a user account (or any other object) from one OU to another OU. In order to do this, right-click the account that you want to move, and then select **Move**.

Select the OU to which you want to move the user object, and then click **OK**.

You can move objects from an OU in a domain, to another OU in another domain by using the **MOVETREE** command from the Windows 2000 resource kit.

2. Managing groups

a. Group Types

As has been discussed earlier on in this chapter, groups help you to manage user accounts so that you can allow them to access resources. Thereby, groups allow you to simplify administrative tasks.

Active Directory has introduced a number of group features that were not avaiable with Windows NT 4.0.

There are two types of group:

- Security groups, which are used in order to manage the resources of one or more domains.
- Distribution groups, which can be used, for example, to send electronic mail messages to all the users in such groups. These groups cannot be used for security purposes. Applications such as Exchange 2000 work with the Windows 2000 directory database, and can therefore use distribution groups.

☞ *Although you can use security groups as you would use distribution groups, you are strongly recommended not to do so, as some applications are able to read only distribution groups. In addition, when a user logs on, Windows 2000 creates an access token that contains the list of all the security groups to which the user belongs. If you use security groups for distribution purposes, you may slow down the logon process.*

Each of these group types has a scope that specifies the people who can belong to them (user accounts, group accounts or computer accounts) along with the extent to which they can be applied.

There are three types of group scope:

- **Domain local**: allows you to apply permissions.
- **Global**: allows you to organize user accounts.
- **Universal**: allows you to group together users that come from any domain, and to grant them permissions in any domain.

The contents of these groups will differ according to whether the domain configuration is in native mode, or in mixed mode.

A mixed mode domain allows Windows NT 4.0 domain controllers to operate in a Windows 2000 domain.

When you have upgraded all pre-Windows 2000 domain controllers, then you can switch to native mode. When you have switched to native mode, you will be able to use universal groups, and you will be able to nest groups inside other groups (for example, a global group can be a member of another global group in native mode).

☞ *After you have installed your Windows 2000 domain controllers, your domain will be in mixed mode. Switching to native mode is irreversible. In order to switch to native mode, go into your domain properties in the* **Active Directory Users and Computers** *console.*

In mixed mode:
- A **domain local** group can contain users and global groups that come from any domain.
- A **global** group contains users that come from the same domain as that of the global group.
- **Universal** groups do not exist in mixed mode.

In native mode:
- A **domain local** group can contain user accounts, global groups, and universal groups that come from any domain in the forest. It can also contain domain local accounts that come from its own domain.
- A **global** group can contain user accounts and global groups from the same domain.
- A **universal** group can contain user accounts, global groups and universal groups from any domain in the forest.

Domain local groups can obtain permissions on the domain in which it is located.

Global groups and universal groups can obtain permissions on all the domains in the forest.

b. Creating groups

In order to create these groups, go into the **Active Directory Users and Computers** console.

➤ Select the OU in which you want to create your group.

➤ Open the **Action** menu, and select **New** followed by **Group**.

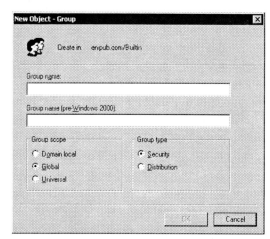

➢ Select the **Group type** (**Security** or **Distribution**) along with the **Group scope** (**Domain local**, **Global** or **Universal**).

➢ Give a meaningful name to the group.

It must be noted that you can specify a different name with which this group may be used on a pre-Windows 2000 machine.

When you have created your group, you can double-click it, in order to edit its properties:

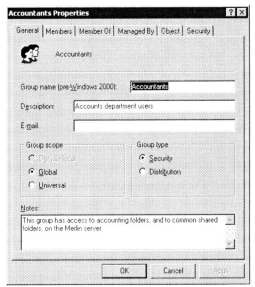

If the domain is in native mode, then you will be able to modify the **Group type** at any time. You can also modify the **Group scope**:

– You can change from a global group to a universal group provided that your global group in not a member of another group. This is because, a global group cannot contain a universal group.

– You can change from a domain local group to a universal group provided that your domain local group does not contain any other domain local groups. This is because, a universal group cannot contain a domain local group.

The **Members** tab allows you to view, to add, or to remove, user accounts or computer accounts in this group. An alternative way of adding a user to a group, is to display the properties of the user concerned, and then to use the **Member Of** tab in this dialog box.

The **Member Of** tab allows you to display the list of the groups to which your group belongs. This tab also allows you to insert your group into another group.

The **Managed By** tab allows you to specify the person or the group that must manage your group. For example, a user can view this tab in order to find out the telephone number of the person who is responsible for this group, so as to contact this person if any problem occurs.

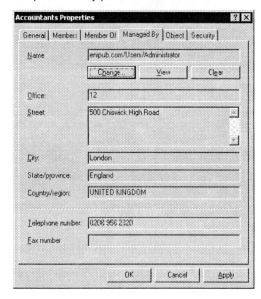

c. Carrying out actions on a group

Finding a group using Active Directory

If you have many different groups that are in different OUs, then you might find it useful to search for a group using Active Directory so that you can administer it.

➢ Open the **Active Directory Users and Computers** console, open the **Action** menu, and select **Find**.

➢ Enter the name of the group that you seek and then click **Find Now**.

➢ Then, when your group has been found, you can double-click it, or right-click it, in order to administer it.

Deleting a group

When you delete a group, you do not delete the accounts that are members of the group.

The rights and the permissions that are associated with this group are deleted. When you create a group, a security identifier (SID) is associated with it. This SID is unique and cannot be re-used. Consequently, if you delete a group, and then create a group with the same name, then a new SID will be associated with this group. The permissions of the former group will not be applied to the new group.

In order to delete a group, right-click it and then select **Delete**. Alternatively, you can use the **Action** menu.

Renaming a group

When you rename a group, you will change the name of the group, but the SID that is associated with the group will stay the same. The members of this group are retained, and they can carry on using the resources for which the group has permissions.

d. Strategies for using groups

A domain local group can have permissions only on the domain in which it is located. Consequently, whenever possible you must try to organize users into global groups, and then include these global groups (which can come from any domain in the forest) into domain local groups.

Then, you can assign permissions for resources to the domain local groups, and these permissions will automatically apply to the member users of the global groups.

e. Predefined groups

Remember that all the computers that run Windows 2000 have a certain number of predefined groups, which are created when Windows 2000 is installed.

Predefined global groups

Domain Guests

The **Guest** user account is automatically included in this group. In addition, this global group is itself automatically included in the **Guests** domain local group.

Domain Users

All the user accounts that you create are included in this group. These accounts can carry out only those tasks that you specify and have access only to those resources for which you grant permissions. These accounts are automatically included in the **Users** domain local group.

Domain Admins

The Administrator account belongs to this group, which itself is included in the **Administrators** domain local group. In fact, the Administrator user account has no particular rights as a user account. The Administrator obtains its rights by being a member of this global group, which itself belongs to the **Administrators** domain local group.

Enterprise Admins

The members of this group have administrator rights on the whole network (they are not limited to the domain).

Predefined domain local groups

Account Operators

The members of this group can administer user accounts and groups (they can add, remove and modify these items). However, they cannot touch the Administrator account, nor can they touch the accounts the accounts of the other members of the **Account Operators** group.

Server Operators

The members of this group can share resources, and they can back up and restore data on the domain controllers.

Print Operators

The members of this group can manage the network printers of the domain controllers.

Administrators

The members of this group can administer the domain controllers, along with any machine that is included in the domain. By default, the **Domain Admins** global group and the Administrator account belong to the **Administrators** domain local group.

Guests

This group includes the **Domain Guests** global group and the **Guest** user account. Members of the **Guests** domain local group have few rights.

Backup Operators

The members of this group can backup and restore on all of the domain controllers.

Users

This group includes the **Domain Users** global group. You can use this group in order to apply rights and permissions to everybody that has an account in the domain.

By default, the different operator groups do not have members. You can include user accounts in these groups in order to assign specific rights to your users.

If a user must carry out backup operations, then it is better to include this user in the Backup Operators group, rather than in the Administrators group. In order to control security, it is preferable to limit a user's rights to those functions that the user must carry out.

It must be remembered that, in addition to these groups, every computer that runs Windows 2000 has system groups. You cannot modify the membership of these groups, which reflect the status of your system at a given time.

- **Everyone** group: this group includes all users: those you have created, the guest account, and all the users of the other domains. It must be noted that, when you share a resource, this group has **Full Control** permission.
- **Authenticated Users** group: this group includes all users that have a user account and a password for the local machine, or for Active Directory. It is preferable to grant permissions to this group, rather than granting them to the **Everyone** group.
- **Creator Owner** group: every user that has taken possession of a resource is a member of this group, for the resource concerned. The owner of a resource has full powers on this resource.
- **Network** group: this group includes all users that access a resource via the network.
- **Interactive** group: this group contains all the users who are logged on locally (in the case where you use Terminal Services, this group contains all the users who are logged on to the Terminal Server).

3. User profiles and home directories

a. User profiles

Local user profiles

A local user profile is a file that is stored locally in a folder that bears the user's logon name. This folder is stored in the **Documents and settings** directory. When no roaming profile exists for a user on a server, a new folder is created locally with the name of the user, and with the contents of the **Default user** profile. The user environment is then built up by adding the information that is contained in the **All users** folder. All modifications that are made by the user are saved in the new user profile. The initial **Default user** profile is unchanged. If the user has the same account name in order to log on locally and to log on to the domain, then two separate folders are created. Notably, this is the case for the administrator:

Administrator   Administrator, enipub

The user's environment is contained in each of these folders. The profile file is called **ntuser.dat**.
The profile provides the user's environment (including such items as screen background colours, and customized Start menu) each time that the user logs on.

Roaming user profiles

With local profiles, the user will go into his/her environment only if the user logs on to the machine on which his/her environment has been configured.
In many networks, users move from machine to machine. It is useful then, for the user to be able to go into his/her environment on whatever machine to which the user logs on. This can be achieved by configuring roaming profiles.
When a user logs on, Windows 2000 automatically downloads the user's profile. However, before it does this, Windows 2000 compares the user's profile with that which is on the machine on to which the user is logging. This approach allows Windows 2000 to download only the differences between the two profiles, so as to speed up the logon process.

Roaming personal profiles

Here are the steps that you must follow in order to create a roaming profile:

➢ Open the **Active Directory Users and Computers** console, and double-click the user for whom you wish to create a roaming profile.

➢ In the user's **Properties** dialog box, select the **Profile** tab and input the path that leads to the user profile (before doing this you must have created a shared directory on the server concerned, in which the profiles can be placed).

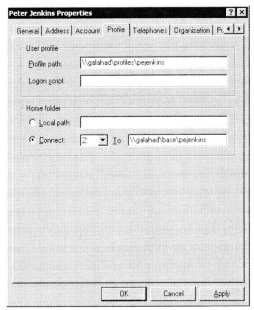

The path that leads to a profile must have a UNC name (\\server name\share\).

If you use the %username% variable, then a directory will be automatically created with the name of the logon account. This approach is especially useful if you have to create a large number of user accounts. In this case, you could create a template account, in which you use this variable so as to specify the path that leads to each user. Windows 2000 will replace this variable with the logon name of the user.

Every user who logs on has a listed profile, as in the example below:

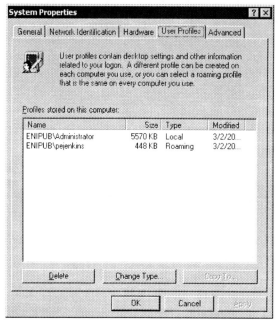

In order to access this dialog box, go into Control Panel and open the system icon. Then, select the **User Profiles** tab.

This dialog box allows you to copy a user profile to another user profile, replacing the contents of the latter. In order to do this, click the **Copy To** button, so as to display the following dialog box:

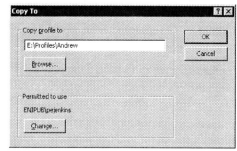

Input the path to which you want to copy this profile. Then, indicate as necessary who must be allowed to use this profile (under **Permitted to use**).

In order to define the profile type, click the **Change Type** button under the **User Profiles** tab.

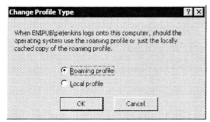

The profiles are saved upon log-off. If several users are logged on with the same user account, and therefore with the same profile, then the profile that will be saved is that of the last user to log-off.

Mandatory roaming profiles

If you use the same profile for all your users, then you must create a mandatory roaming profile. This type of profile is compulsory for the user, and is in read-only mode. In fact, if a user modifies his/her profile, then this profile will not be saved upon log-off.

This approach is very useful when there are several users who must have a common desktop (for example, with the same shortcuts that lead to the same applications, and the same reference letters so as to connect to network devices).

In order to transform a roaming profile into a mandatory roaming profile, rename the ntuser.dat file as **ntuser.man** (with 'man' as in mandatory).

The following example creates a mandatory roaming profile that is stored on a server called Galahad.

➢ Log on with the account that must be used as a template.

➢ Organize the user environment so that it will be suitable for the users concerned. For example, you may wish to add network connections, or to modify the **Start** menu by adding shortcuts onto the desktop.

➢ When you have finished configuring the desktop, log off so as to save the profile.

➢ Then, log on as the administrator, and create the shared directory in which you will save the profile. For example, create a profiles directory, and then share it, using the same name as the share name. Then, create another directory, and save the common profile. You could call the directory "common", for example

➢ Go into the Control Panel, open the **System** icon, and select the **User Profiles** tab.

➢ Select your template profile, and then click **Copy To**, so as to save it in the "common" directory.

➢ In order to do this, input the path that leads to the shared directory, and then authorize the **Everyone** group to use this profile.

➢ In order to make the profile mandatory, rename the **ntuser.dat** file as **ntuser.man**, in the directory into which you have just copied the profile (using Windows Explorer, display the file name extensions so that you will not confuse the two ntuser files!).

➢ Open the **Active Directory Users and Computers** console and specify the path that leads to the profile for the users concerned.

➢ In the properties dialog boxes for the users that must use this profile, select the **Profile** tab, and enter the path that leads to the profile: \\galahad\profiles\common.

➢ Finally, log on with the account of the user to whom you have applied the profile, in order to verify that the operation was carried out successfully.

You are strongly recomended to place roaming profiles on a computer that does not act as a domain controller. This approach will speed up logons, as it will allow the resources of the domain controller to be used solely for the logon process.

b. Home directory

The home directory of a user, is the user's reception folder. It can be either a local path, or a network path. If you use a network path for this purpose, then you can save your data in your home directory, irrespective of the machine on to which you are logged. In addition, this technique eases backup operations.

If you use an NTFS partition in order to accomodate the home directories, then you can use the %username% variable so as to create a user's home directory automatically, according to the user's logon name. In addition, the user will have access to his/her home directory. The NTFS Full Control permissions will be assigned automatically to the user, and to the administrator.

Under the **Profile** tab of the user properties:

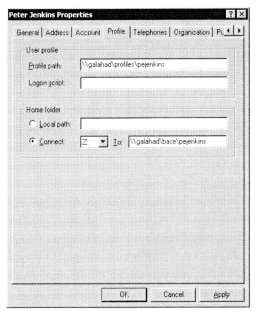

This example creates on the Galahad server, a directory called "base" that is shared with full control permissions for the **Everyone** group. The %username% variable ensures that the user's home directory will be created automatically in the "base" directory. Thereby, if the "base" directory was created on an NTFS partition, then, apart from the administrator, only the user will have access to his/her own home directory.

☞ *The home directories on Windows 2000 have improved with respect to those on Windows NT 4.0. With Windows NT, when you explore the disk that is associated with your home directory, you view the list of all the home directories of all the users, even though you do not have the permissions to access them. This approach is inconvenient when there are a lot of users. With Windows 2000, the drive letter that is associated with the home directory, references directly the home directory.*

Labs

To be absolutely sure that you have assimilated this chapter, work through the corresponding labs. These are set out from page 647 to page 653.

☒ Managing user accounts in Active Directory.

☒ Managing groups.

☒ Personal roaming user profiles.

☒ Mandatory user profiles.

☒ Implementing a user home directory.

Assessing your skills

Try the following questions if you think you know this chapter well enough.

Managing users

1 Which console must you use in order to create local accounts on a Windows 2000 member/stand-alone server or on Windows 2000 Workstation?

....

....

....

2 Which console must you use in order to manage the network resources of your domain?

....

3 What is the best way of temporarily preventing the use of an account, in order to minimize risks at security level?

....

4 Which accounts are predefined on a Windows 2000 machine?

....

....

5 You want to allow your users to choose their passwords for themselves. How will you create their user accounts in order to do this?

....

....

6 For a user's account, can you select the **User must change password at next logon** option, and the **User cannot change password** option, at the same time? ☐
....
....

7 A user cannot log on because he/she has forgotten his/her password. You want to delete the user's password in order to assign a new one. You edit the properties of the user's account, but find that you cannot change the user's password. What must you do in order to solve this problem? ☐
....
....

8 When you edit the properties of a user account you notice that the **Account is locked out** option is grayed-out. What must you do in order to lock out the user's account? ☐
....
....
....
....
....
....

9 What is the difference between the personal properties of a user account and the account properties? ☐
....
....
....
....
....
....

Managing groups

10 A group of users have inadvertently deleted the group to which they belong, and they can no longer access the resources of a folder. You create a new group with the same name as the group that was deleted. However the group users are still unable to access the folder. What might be the cause of this problem? ☐
....
....
....
....

11 Can you create a global group on a workstation? ☐
....
....

12 Which two types of group are available in native mode? Which two types of group are available in mixed mode? ☐
....

13 Which group scopes are available in native mode? Which group scopes are available in mixed mode?
....
....
....

14 What can a domain local group contain in mixed mode?
....
....

15 What can a domain local group contain in native mode?
....
....
....

16 What can a global group contain in mixed mode?
....

17 What can a global group contain in native mode?
....
....

18 What can a universal group contain in mixed mode?
....

19 What can a universal group contain in native mode?
....
....
....

20 Can you change the scope of a group in mixed mode?
....

21 Can you change the scope of a group in native mode?
....
....
....
....
....

22 You are the administrator of a company that has several thousand objects in the Active Directory account database. You want to make some modifications to a group that is called RAS. You cannot remember in which OU you created this group. How can you quickly find this group?
....
....

23 What is the role of the predefined group that is called Account Operators?
....
....

24 Which group scope allows you to organize users in a domain? ❏
....

25 Which computers store local and global groups? ❏
....
....
....
....

Profiles

26 Where are local profiles stored on a Windows 2000 machine? ❏
....

27 A user regularly changes workstations within a domain. ❏ What will happen if you do not configure a roaming profile for this user? How can you ensure that the user will be able to work in his/her environment on each computer without implementing a roaming profile?
....
....
....

28 How do you create a mandatory roaming profile? ❏
....
....

29 Is it possible to create a local roaming profile? ❏
....

30 Can you create a non-mandatory roaming profile for a ❏ group? What will be the consequences of such an action?
....
....
....

31 You have configured mandatory roaming profiles in a ❏ domain. However, the server that stores these profiles is unavailable. Will the users concerned be able to log on to the domain? If so, in which case?
....
....
....
....

32 How can you quickly create home directories for around ❏ a hundred accounts?
....
....
....
....
....

User and group management

Results

Check your answers on pages 284 to 288. Count one point for each correct answer.

Number of points | /32 |

For this chapter you need to have scored at least 24 out of 32.

Look at the list of key points that follows. Pick out the ones with which you have had difficulty and work through them again in this chapter before moving on to the next.

Key points of the chapter

☐ Managing users.

☐ Managing groups.

☐ Profiles.

Solutions

Managing users

1   Which console must you use in order to create local accounts on a Windows 2000 member/stand-alone server or on Windows 2000 Workstation?

You must use the Computer Management console. You can access this console via the Administrative Tools menu. Alternatively, you can right-click the My Computer icon.

2   Which console must you use in order to manage the network resources of your domain?

You must use the Active Directory Users and Computers console.

3   What is the best way of temporarily preventing the use of an account, in order to minimize risks at security level?

You must deactivate the account.

4   Which accounts are predefined on a Windows 2000 machine?

The Administrator account and the Guest account are predefined on a Windows 2000 machine. By default, the Guest account is disabled.

5 You want to allow your users to choose their passwords for themselves. How will you create their user accounts in order to do this?

*You must enable the **User must change password at next logon** option.*

6 For a user's account, can you select the **User must change password at next logon** option, and the **User cannot change password** option, at the same time?

No, these two options are incompatible with each other, and Windows 2000 prevents this inconsistency.

7 A user cannot log on because he/she has forgotten his/her password. You want to delete the user's password in order to assign a new one. You edit the properties of the user's account, but find that you cannot change the user's password. What must you do in order to solve this problem?

*You must right-click the user account, and then select the **Reset Password** option.*

8 When you edit the properties of a user account you notice that the **Account is locked out** option is grayed-out. What must you do in order to lock out the user's account?

You cannot lock out an account manually. The system carries out this action when you have an account policy so that an account will be locked out after X unsucessful logon attempts. You can only disable the account in order to ensure that it will not be used.

9 What is the difference between the personal properties of a user account and the account properties?

The personal properties of an account are a set of attributes that contain information about a user such as the user's telephone number and address. Account properties are a set of options that allow you to define the behaviour of the account (for example they allow you to define time restrictions, and when the account will expire).

Managing groups

10 A group of users have inadvertently deleted the group to which they belong, and they can no longer access the resources of a folder. You create a new group with the same name as the group that was deleted. However the group users are still unable to access the folder. What might be the cause of this problem?

When you create a group, the system assigns a new unique identifier to this group, even if the name of the group is identical to that of a former group. Consequently, you must add the members again to this new group.

11 Can you create a global group on a workstation?

No. You can define global groups only on domain controllers.

12 Which two types of group are available in native mode? Which two types of group are available in mixed mode?

Security groups and distribution groups exist in both native mode and in mixed mode.

13 Which group scopes are available in native mode? Which group scopes are available in mixed mode?

In mixed mode, you can create domain local groups and global groups. In native mode, you can create local groups, global groups and univeral groups.

14 What can a domain local group contain in mixed mode?

In mixed mode, a domain local group can contain users and global groups that come from any domain in the forest.

15 What can a domain local group contain in native mode?

In native mode, a domain local group can contain global groups and universal groups from any domain in the forest. It can also contain other local groups that come from from its own domain.

16 What can a global group contain in mixed mode?

In mixed mode, a global group can contain users that come from its own domain.

17 What can a global group contain in native mode?

In native mode, a global group can contain users and global groups that come from its own domain.

18 What can a universal group contain in mixed mode?

There are no universal groups in mixed mode.

19 What can a universal group contain in native mode?

In native mode, a universal group can contain user accounts and global group accounts. It can also contain other universal groups that come from any other domain in the forest.

20 Can you change the scope of a group in mixed mode?

No.

21 Can you change the scope of a group in native mode?

Yes. You can transform a domain local group into a universal group, provided that the group does not already contain any other domain local groups. A global group can become a universal group provided that it does not belong to any other global groups.

22 You are the administrator of a company that has several thousand objects in the Active Directory account database. You want to make some modifications to a group that is called RAS. You cannot remember in which OU you created this group. How can you quickly find this group?

*You can go into the use the **Active Directory Users and Computers** console, open the **Action** menu and then select **Find**.*

23 What is the role of the predefined group that is called Account Operators?

Members of this group allows you to grant its members the permission to manage user accounts.

24 Which group scope allows you to organize users in a domain?

Global groups.

25 Which computers store local and global groups?

Global groups are available on domain controllers. Local groups are available on domain controllers, on workstations, and on member/stand-alone servers.

Profiles

26 Where are local profiles stored on a Windows 2000 machine?

In the directory <disc_letter>:\documents and settings\.

27 A user regularly changes workstations within a domain. What will happen if you do not configure a roaming profile for this user? How can you ensure that the user will be able to work in his/her environment on each computer without implementing a roaming profile?

If you have not configured any roaming profile, that the user will not be able to work in his/her environment. In this case, the user must log on to each machine, in order to set up his/her profile.

28 How do you create a mandatory roaming profile?

You can create a mandatory roaming profile by renaming the ntuser.dat profile file as ntuser.man.

29 Is it possible to create a local roaming profile?

Yes. You can create a local roaming profile by changing the name of the local profile file to ntuser.man.

30 Can you create a non-mandatory roaming profile for a group? What will be the consequences of such an action?

Although this action is not recommended, there is nothing to stop you doing it. In this case, any modifications that are made by any of the group members will apply to the other group members.

31 You have configured mandatory roaming profiles in a domain. However, the server that stores these profiles is unavailable. Will the users concerned be able to log on to the domain? If so, in which case?

Users will be able to log on, only if they are logging on from a machine for the first time, as no local profile will exist in this case. On the other hand, if the profile is already in the cache, the ntuser.man file will be present and the logon will be refused on the domain.

32 How can you quickly create home directories for around a hundred accounts?

You can do this by creating a template account by using the %username% variable. You can then copy this account in order to create new accounts. The system will transform the variable into the user name automatically, and it will create the home directory with Full Control permission for the user, provided that the disc is in NTFS.

Prerequisites for this chapter

☒ Knowledge of the Windows 2000 environment.

☒ Working knowledge of the use of browsers in the Internet or on an intranet.

☒ Basic networking knowledge.

Objectives

At the end of this chapter, you will be able to:

☒ Understand the difference between a printer, a print device and a print server.

☒ Install a printer either locally, or via the network.

☒ Connect a printer to different types of port (such as local, TCP/IP, and LPR ports).

☒ Install print services for UNIX and for Macintosh.

☒ Connect to a printer from different platforms.

☒ Add other drivers.

☒ Connect to a printer via the Internet, or via an intranet.

☒ Publish a printer in the Active Directory database.

☒ Redirect print jobs to another printer.

☒ Set the availability and the priorities that apply to a printer.

☒ Set up the print spool.

☒ Apply permissions to printers.

☒ Implement a printer pool.

☒ Locate printers using Active Directory.

☒ Administer a printer via the WEB.

☒ Troubleshoot print problems.

Printer management

Contents

A. Terminology

First, this chapter will define a few terms that are used in the Windows 2000 environment:

Print server
> This is the Windows 2000 computer that receives the documents that must be printed.

Printer
> The printer is defined on the print server. It is the software interface between the application the print device.

Print device
> This is the physical peripheral that produces the final document. It can be either a **local device** or a device that is equipped with a network interface card: a **network-interface print device**.

A print device can have two types of connection:

Local connection
> With this type of connection, your device is physically connected to the parallel port, or to the serial port of your computer.

Remote, network connection
> With this type of connection, the device is connected either to another network computer, or to a Windows 2000 server, or to a print server. Several users can use such a connection to send their documents for printing.

B. Installing a printer

With Windows 2000, all the operations that can be carried out on the printers that are located in the **Printers** folder or in the **My Computer** console of your computer can also be carried out remotely, via the network, from other Windows NT or Windows 2000 machines (provided that you have sufficient permissions). Thus, an administrator can remotely install or configure printers from his/her machine, as if the administrator had logged on to each of the machines concerned.

In order to do this you must open My Network Places and access the **Printers** icon of the remote computer.

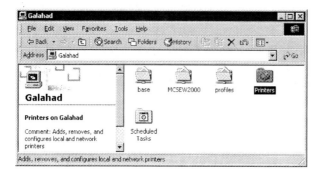

1. Local printer

> Open the Control Panel, and double-click the **Printers** icon. Alternatively, you can click the **Printers** folder that is situated in the **Start - Settings** menu.

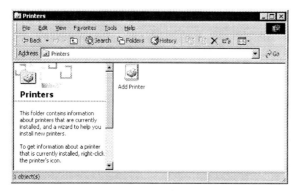

> Double-click the **Add Printer** icon in order to start up the Add Printer Wizard.

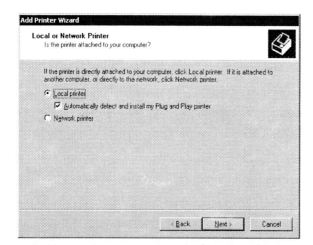

➢ In order to install a printer that is connected to this computer, select **Local printer**, and then click **Next**.

☞ *Note that the Add Printer Wizard can automatically detect your Plug and Play printers.*

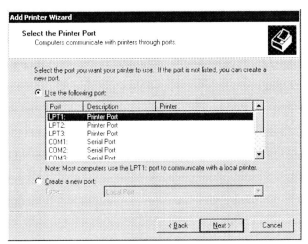

The dialog box shown above, allows you to specify the port on which your print device is connected. You can choose one of the different parallel ports (LPT1, LPT2, LPT3), or one of the different serial ports (COM1, COM2, COM3). Alternatively, you can choose to print to a file, or to the Microsoft FAX port in order to send faxes.

You can also add other ports. If you have a network-interface print device, then you should add the port that corresponds to this peripheral. Such print devices are more convenient to use, because they do not require your server to act as a print server, and the information transfer is quicker on the network cable than on a parallel cable.

Windows 2000 supports the following ports:

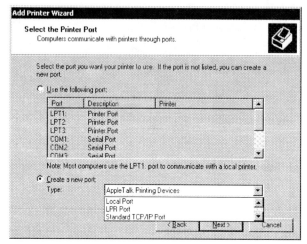

Apple Talk Printing Devices

As the title indicates, this option allows you to use Apple Talk print devices.

Local Port

This option allows you to connect a print device to a parallel port, to a serial port or to specify a file. This port also allows you to redirect print jobs, either to a UNC path (***remote_computer\device_share_name***), or to the NULL port.

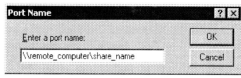

LPR Port

This option allows you to connect print devices that are attached to UNIX servers. It also allows your server to act as an LPD server.

Other Network File and Print Services

To add or remove a component, click the check box. A shaded box means that only part of the component will be installed. To see what's included in a component, click Details.

Subcomponents of Other Network File and Print Services:

- ☑ File Services for Macintosh   0.0 MB
- ☑ Print Services for Macintosh   0.0 MB
- ☑ **Print Services for Unix**   0.0 MB

Description: Enables UNIX clients to print to any printer available to this computer.

Total disk space required: 1.8 MB   [Details]
Space available on disk: 2037.9 MB

[OK] [Cancel]

Standard TCP/IP Port

This option allows you to connect print devices that are directly attached to the network.

Add Standard TCP/IP Printer Port Wizard

Add Port
For which device do you want to add a port?

Enter the Printer Name or IP address, and a port name for the desired device.

Printer Name or IP Address: 10.10.2.15

Port Name: IP_10.10.2.15

[< Back] [Next >] [Cancel]

Port for Netware

This option allows you to use Netware print devices. It becomes available after you have installed the NWLink protocol and the client service for Netware.

Hewlett-Packard Network Port

This option allows you to use print devices using old HP Jetdirect adapters. This option is available only after you have installed DLC protocol.

By default, only the **Local Port** and the **Standard TCP/IP Port** are available. If you want to use the **LPR** or the **Apple Talk** port, you must install the corresponding services. Here are the steps that you must follow in order to do this:

➢ Open the Control Panel and double-click the **Add/Remove Programs** icon.

➢ Select the **Add/Remove Windows Components** icon. Then click the **Components** button, and select **Other Network File and Print Services**.

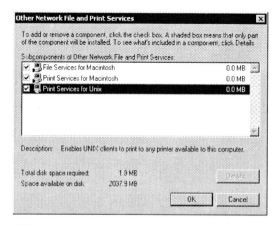

☞ *In the UNIX world, LPR is used to send print requests to a remote spooler. These print requests are received by the remote LPD service. When you have installed print services for UNIX, Windows 2000 is equipped with the following two services: **LPDSVC.DLL** which receives the requests that come from UNIX hosts, and **LPRMON.DLL** which allows you to send print jobs to the LPD service of a UNI host.*

➢ When you have chosen the port that you wish to use, click **Next**.

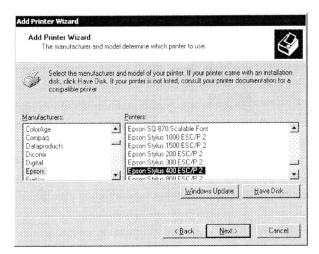

➤ In the left hand pane, select the manufacturer of your print device. Then, in the right-hand pane, select its model reference. Click the **Next** button.

➤ Enter a name for your printer (by default, the model reference will be used). Click **Next**.

➤ For the operation that is shown here, on the next screen select the **Do not share this printer** option (printer sharing will be discussed later on in this chapter). Then click the **Next** button.

Windows 2000 then offers to print a test page. This test page comprises a graphic illustration together with the list of drivers that are used. This option allows you to check that the drivers are suitable for your printer.

➤ Click the **Next** button, followed by the **Finish** button.

If you decide to use your computer as a print server, then it is strongly recommended that your machine play only this role, if it will be required to handle large volumes of print jobs. You can use Windows 2000 Professional as a print server, provided that you will not have more than 10 simultaneous connections, including any that are set up by UNIX clients. If you will have a large number of connections, including Macintosh, UNIX and Netware connections, you must use Windows 2000 Server, Windows 2000 Advanced Server or Windows 2000 Datacenter Server.

2. Network printer

Once a printer is shared, network clients can use it.

a. Connecting from a Windows 2000, 95/ 98 or NT machine

In order to install a network printer on a Windows 2000 machine, you must first locate the printer using My Network Places, or using Active Directory. When you have located the printer, right-click its icon and then select **Connect**.

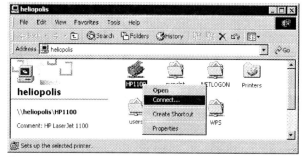

The driver is then automatically downloaded and the printer is installed. When this has been done, the printer appears in the **Printers** folder where it is represented with a network printer icon.

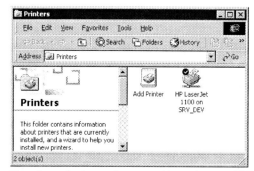

For other clients, such as machines that run Windows 95/98, Windows NT 4.0 or Windows NT 3.5x, you must install the drivers that correspond to the system on the print server. Thereby, clients can download the driver automatically.

In order to add other drivers, go into the properties of the printer, and select the **Sharing** tab. Click the **Additional Drivers** button so as to display the following dialog box:

The drivers for Windows 2000 versions that run on Intel platforms are installed. In order to add additional drivers, activate the check boxes that correspond to the drivers you wish to add.

b. Connecting from other clients

In order to allow other clients (such as those that run Windows 3.x or MSDOS, for example) to use a shared printer, then you must manually install the appropriate driver on the machines concerned.

For non-Microsoft clients, you must install the appropriate services on the print server.

c. Connecting via the Web

If the print server to which you want to connect runs Microsoft Internet Information Server 5, then you can install a printer via your company's intranet, or via the Internet.

In order to do this, open your browser, and go to the address http://*IIS_server_name/printers*.

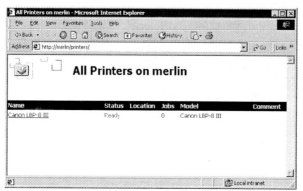

The browser displays all the printers that are installed on the target machine destination. Click the printer that you wish to install.

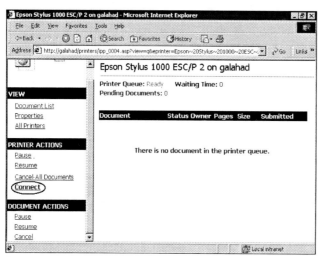

Then click the **Connect** link, in the left-hand pane of the browser window.

C. Configuring a printer

You can configure a printer by adjusting its properties:

➤ Right-click the icon of the printer that you want to configure, and then select the **Properties** option.

1. General tab

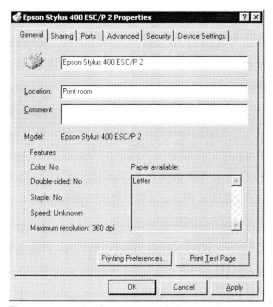

The **General** tab allows you to define the following items:
– Name of the printer: by default the printer name is that which was suggested when you installed the printer. However, you can specify any name that you like. Your choice of name is important as it may be used in order to search for this printer via Active Directory.
– Location: this information can help in an Active Directory search.
– Comment: this field allows you to indicate other information concerning the printer. This information can also help in an Active Directory search.

The **Printing Preferences** button allows you to specify the **Orientation** of your documents (Portrait or Landscape), the **Page Order** for printing and the number of **Pages per Sheet**. In addition, you can indicate **Advanced** options concerning a certain number of settings that are specific to the printer concerned.

As the name suggests, the **Print Test Page** allows you to print a test page at any time in order to check that your printer is working properly. Following your print attempt, you can start up the Print Troubleshooter, in order to solve any problems.

2. Sharing tab

The **Sharing** tab allows you to make the printer available for clients who want to print via the network (by connecting to the printer).

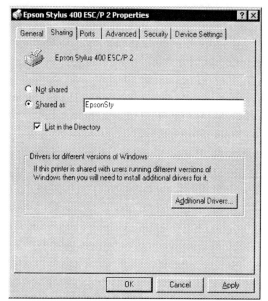

The name that you enter in the **Shared as** text box is the name that the clients will see via the network.

As mentioned above, the **Additional Drivers** button allows you to add other drivers so as to allow other machines that do not run Windows 2000, automatically to download the drivers that they will need in order to connect to this printer. The clients will automatically download the appropriate driver from the shared directory on the print server (the **print$** directory, under **%systemroot%\system32\spool\drivers**).

The **List in the Directory** check box, allows you to include the printer in the Active Directory database. This check box is enabled by default. This approach allows you easily to find a printer without needing to know the name of the print server on which it is connected.

3. Ports tab

This tab allows you to configure the printer ports (cf. B. Installing a printer).

This tab allows you to redirect print jobs to another printer, in order to disconnect your printer so that you can carry out maintenance work on it.

➢ Select the port that you wish to redirect, and then click the **Add Port** button.

➢ Select **Local Port**, and then click **New Port**.

➢ Enter the UNC path that leads to the new printer.

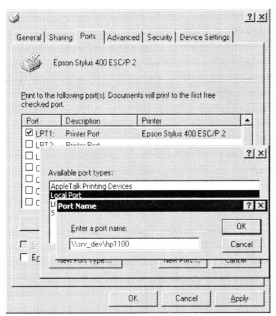

All the print jobs that are sent to the former printer will be redirected to the new share, without the users noticing any difference.

4. Advanced tab

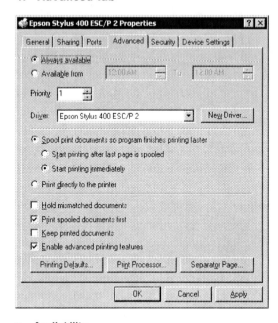

a. Availability

You can restrict the time periods during which print jobs can be sent to the printer. This is particularly useful if some of your users print large documents that can prevent other users from printing. In this case, you can install on the same print server, two identical printers that point to the same print device. Connect the users who have high volume print jobs onto one of the printers, and connect the other users onto the other printer. Then, leave the default option, **Always available** for the printer that will be used by the other users, and, for the printer that will be used by the high volume print users, apply a time period restriction so that their documents will be printed only during the night time. With this approach, these large documents will be placed in the print queue, and they will be printed only during the time period that you specify.

b. Priority

You can assign a priority level for the documents that are sent to the printer. Windows 2000 will compare this priority level with that of an alternative printer (such as that which was implemented in the example above). The lowest priority level is priority 1, and the highest priority level is priority 99.

c. Changing the driver

You can change the driver that is associated with your print device. You can also add a new driver, by clicking the **New Driver** button.

d. Spool

A spool is also known as a **queue**. When you start printing a large document, the computer processes your document first, in order to convert it into the language format of the printer concerned. Then, your document is processed again so that it can be sent page by page in the printing rhythm of the print device. By putting your document into a queue, the system can allow the application to resume processing quicker. Windows 2000 puts the document into the background, so as to allow current processes to continue working normally.

On the other hand, the **Print directly to the printer** option makes you wait until the printing has finished, before you can carry on working with your application. In addition, this option is possible only if your printer is not shared, as only in this case is the spool bypassed.

The **Spool print documents so program finishes printing faster** option allows two sub-options:

Start printing after last page is spooled
   Allows you to specify that the printing can be started, only after the entire document has been put into the spool.

Start printing immediately

☞ *The first of these sub-options is very useful when documents require the user to enter information before they can be printed. If you do not choose this option, then such documents can stay blocked in the spool, awaiting input/output, and thereby stop everyone from printing.*

Clients of Windows 2000, Windows NT and Windows 95 can use a second local spooler. Unlike the drivers of other clients, which process documents completely into a format that the print device can understand, the drivers of Windows 2000, Windows NT and Windows 95 clients process the document only partially before forwarding it to the remote spooler. As soon as the spooler of the remote server is able to accommodate it, the document is transmitted to the remote spooler, where it is processed completely. Then, the document is placed in the print queue, before being sent to the print device.

☞ *When a document is blocked in the spool, as you can no longer delete the document, you often have to stop, and then restart the **Print Spooler** service using the **Services** console in the Administrative Tools menu.*

e. Options

There are four options that help you to manage your documents:

Hold mismatched documents
   This option is useful with Postscript documents, for which different language versions can provoke minor errors.

Print spooled documents first

This option allows you to optimize print processing. With this option, the priority of a document is based not only on the priority level that you specified further up in this dialog box. In addition, a document that has already been placed in the spool will have priority over documents that have yet to be placed in the spool (even if the new document has a higher priority level).

Keep printed documents

This option allows you to specify that all documents that have already been printed will be kept in the print manager (in the spool). If this option is disabled then when the document has been printed, it will be deleted from the print queue, and its equivalent in printer language will be deleted from the hard disk.

Enable advanced printing features

This option allows you to use advanced features such as **Page Order** and the number of **Pages per Sheet**. You must disable this option if you have any compatibility problems.

The **Printing Defaults** button allows you to view the advanced features. It allows you to view and to modify the properties that are available by clicking the **Printing Preferences** button under the **General** tab.

The **Print Processor** button allows you to select the data type of the print processor. The role of the print processor is to send the spooled document from the hard disk to the print device, with the help of the driver. For PCL printers the print processor data type by default is EMF (*Enhanced MetaFile*). Postscript printers use the RAW (ready to print) data type. Windows 2000 supports 5 different print processor data types.

The **Separator Page** button allows you to add separator pages between documents. This technique helps you to find your document amongst all the other documents that have been printed by the device. Separator pages also allow you to modify the printing mode.

Four separator pages are available. They are located in **%systemroot%\system32**:

- **sysprint.sep**: adds a separator page before each document. This separator page is compatible with Postscript printers.
- **pcl.sep**: allows HP printers to go into PCL mode, and adds a separator page before each document.
- **pscript.sep**: allows HP printers to go into Postscript mode, but does not add separator pages.
- **sysprtj.sep**: is similar to sysprint.sep, except that it uses Japanese characters.

You can modify the code of each page in order to customize the separator page.

5. Security tab

The **Security** tab allows you to specify the actions that users, and user groups, can carry out on the printer.

By default, the **Everyone** group has **Print** permission.

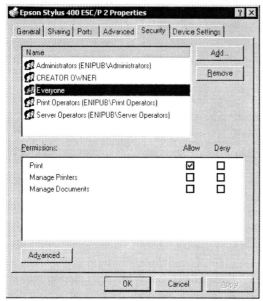

Printers that run on Windows 2000 offer three standard permissions:

Print

This permission allows users to connect to the printer and to manage their own print jobs (for example, they can remove their documents from the spool).

Manage Documents

This permission does not allow users to print, but it does allow users to manage all the documents.

Manage Printers

This permission provides full control on all documents that are submitted to the printer. It also provides full control on the printer itself. Users that have this permission can share the printer, change its permissions, delete the printer change its properties, pause the printer, and manage all the documents that are submitted to it (including deleting the documents, and modifying their properties).

As with permissions on shared, or NTFS, folders, you can choose from two options for each permission: **Allow** and **Deny**.

If a user belongs to a group with permissions that are different from the user's own permissions, then the user will have the combination of all these permissions, with the exception of any permissions that have been denied, as the Deny option takes priority.

The **Advanced** button allows you to view access control settings including the attributes of the permission entries. It also allows you to create your own permissions by combining attributes together.

The **Owner** tab of these access control settings allows you to designate a user with **Manage Printers** permission, as the new owner of the resource.

The **Auditing** tab of the access control settings allows you to monitor the use of the printer (the implementation of audits will be covered in Chapter 12 of this book, which deals with security).

6. Device settings tab

The **Device Settings** tab allows you to adjust the settings that are specific to the printer. These settings vary according to the printer model concerned.

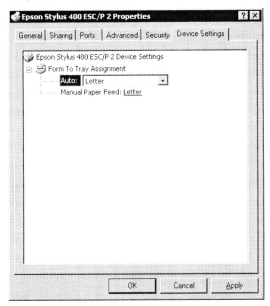

D. Implementing a printer pool

1. Introduction

A printer pool allows you to have a logical printer that points to several print devices that work with the same driver.

This technique provides printing power that is suitable for large networks. It allows you to manage several print devices (with identical properties) using a single print queue (or a single printer).

With this approach, it is the printer that decides which of the available ports to use, according to their order of creation.

For example, if you have a fast print device, then you should associate it with the first printer port so that it will be favored.

☞ *It is often more convenient for the users if you place all the print devices in the same geographical location. It is also useful to define print banners in order to ease the identification of the different printed documents.*

2. Configuring the pool

➢ Open the **Start** menu, then select **Settings** followed by **Printers**.

➢ Right-click the icon that represents the printer for which you want to create a print pool.

➢ Select **Properties**, and then select the **Ports** tab.

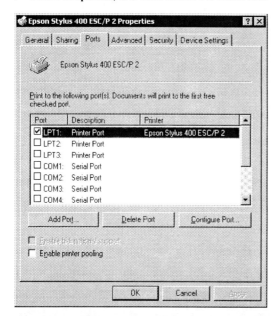

➤ Activate the **Enable printer pooling** check box. Activating this check box allows you to select several ports.

➤ Select all the ports that must be used in the pool, and click the **OK** button.

E. Managing priorities

1. Introduction

On the same print server, you can create several printers that will access the same print device.

This technique allows you to specify different accesses to the same device, in order to accommodate a certain number of constraints:

– Print during specific time periods.
– Define printing priorities (by granting permissions for specific groups on each of the printers).
– Change the print processing mode for the document (for example, you can choose to **Start printing immediately** for one printer, and to **Start printing after last page is spooled** for another printer).
– Define specific print formats (for instance, for photocopy printers that are equipped with different paper trays, and that use different paper formats).

For example, if you want to assign different priorities to two different user groups, for the same print device, you must create two printers that point to the same physical device. Then, assign different priorities on the printers, and apply specific permissions to the user groups.

☞ It must be noted that these printers must be created on the same print server. However, you can locate the devices in different places (you can even place these devices on different shared local ports).

2. Configuring the priorities of two printers

Whether you have one printer, or whether you have several printers, the operating principle stays the same. You can even work with several printers that access several print devices. This approach combines the technique of priority management, with that of the printer pool.

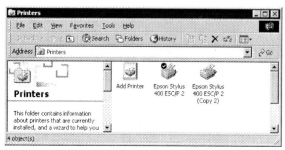

For each printer, associate a specific priority (using the **Advanced** tab), and apply specific permissions.

Example: The **Accountants** group must use the Epson Stylus 400 ESC/P2 with Priority level 12.

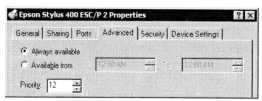

On the Epson Stylus 400 ESC/P2 (Copy 2) you must set the Priority to level 99 for the Managers group.

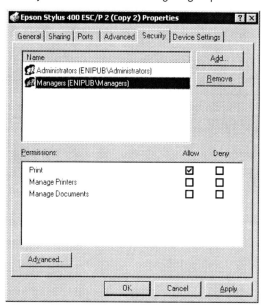

Then, you must connect the members of the Managers group onto the Epson Stylus 400 ESC/P2 (Copy 2) printer, and the members of the Accountants group onto the Epson Stylus 400 ESC/P2 printer.

F. Print management

When you print a document, it is first placed in the print queue. Each printer is associated with a print queue, which itself is managed by the print manager.

When the document is placed in the print queue, it is in fact, stored on the hard disk of the computer on which the logical printer is situated. The spool folder that is on the disk grows larger, and the extent to which it is accessed will vary according to the sizes of the documents that are placed in the queue. In order to reduce any disc access delays due to printing operations, it may be useful to move the spool directory from the system disk onto another volume. This will help to spread the disk access workload.

There are two ways of changing the path of the spool folder:

➢ Open the registry.
   HKEY_LOCAL_MACHINE\SYSTEM\CurrentControlSet\
   Control\Print\Printers.
   Modify the DefaultSpoolDirectory value.

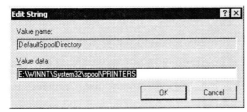

Alternatively:

➢ Open the **Printers** folder, then open the **File** menu, and
   select **Server Properties**.

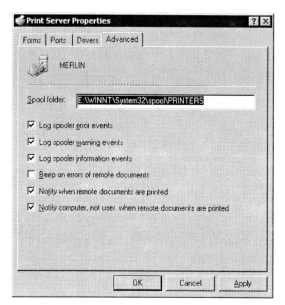

> Click the **Advanced** tab. Note the different options that you may choose. For example, these options allow you to receive the following type of message when a document has been printed:

In order to access the print manager, double-click the icon that represents the printer concerned.

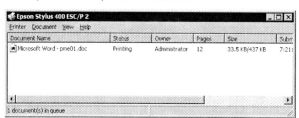

The print manager provides a menu bar and a display pane that provides details concerning the documents that have been placed in the print queue.

Each entry in the print queue is made up of the name of the document, the status of the document (for example **Printing, Paused printing, Spooled, Printer offline**), the owner of the document, the number of pages, the size of the document, the date and time at which the document was submitted, and the physical port.

The **Document** menu allows you to:
- Pause a print job (so that you can insert the correct envelope, or change the ink cartridge, for example).
- Resume a print job.
- Restart the printing of documents, provided they are not deleted from the print queue after they have been printed.
- Cancel the printing of a document.
- Display the properties of a document.

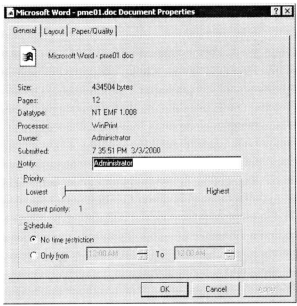

The properties of a document cover all the settings that are used for the document. These settings concern not only the processing of the print job. They also concern the physical configuration of the printer.

You can specify that a user must be notified when the document has been printed, you can alter the priority of the document, and you can even define a printing schedule.

Amongst other options, the **Printer** menu allows you to:
- Pause the printing for all the documents (**Pause Printing**). This option stops the physical printing, but it still allows new print jobs to be submitted to the printer, and placed in the print queue. This option is useful when you must carry out maintenance work on the print device.
- **Cancel All Documents**: this option removes all the documents from the print queue.

☞ *In order to suspend printing rapidly, you can put the printer offline.*

G. Publishing and searching for printers in Active Directory

One of the roles of the Windows 2000 directory database is to allow you easily to find network objects. You can locate print devices very easily and very quickly, without needing to know the name of the server onto which the device is connected.

By default, when you share a printer, it is automatically published in Active Directory (the **List in the Directory** check box is enabled).

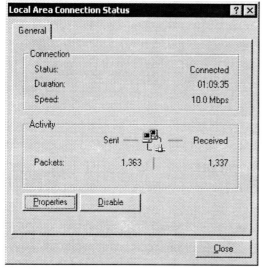

You can search for a printer as follows:

➢ Open the **Start** menu, and select **Search**.

➢ Then select **For Printers**.

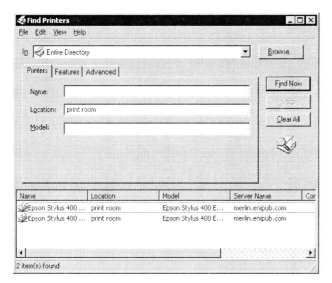

> ➤ You can search according to one or another of the fields that you entered when you configured the printer (for example, **Name**, **Location**, or **Model**). You can also search according to such items as the server name, or the owner name.

> ➤ Click the **Advanced** tab in order to search according to other fields:

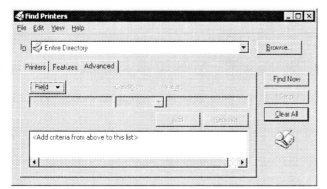

Click the **Field** button, in order to select the fields that you wish to use as criteria in order to carry out your search.

When you have located the printer, provided that you have the necessary permissions, you can connect to it, and you can view its properties, and possibly modify them (for example, its ports, or its permissions).

H. Administering a printer via the Web

One of the new features that Windows 2000 offers, is to allow you to print via the Internet or via your company's intranet. Windows 2000 supports the IPP (*Internet Printing Protocol*) protocol that allows you to print to a URL address. This protocol is encapsulated in the http protocol.
In order to use this feature, IIS version 5 (*Internet Information Server*) must be installed on the server on which the shared printers reside. On small networks (with up to 10 connections) you can also use Peer Web Services (PWS) on a Windows 2000 Professional machine.
Here are the steps that you must follow in order to connect to a printer via the Internet or via intranet :

➢ Open the **Printers** folder and double-click the **Add Printer** icon.

➢ Select **Network printer**, followed by **Next**.

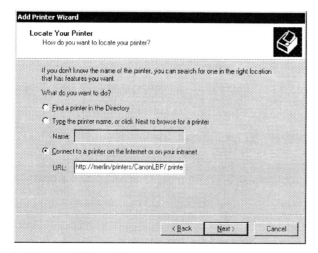

➢ Enter a URL address in the format: http://*servername/printers/printer_sharename*/.printer, then click **Next**.

➢ Select whether or not this printer must be your default printer.

➢ Click **Next**, followed by **Finish**.

➢ The printer appears in the Printers window in the following

format: .

When you access a printer via the Web, you use the authentication that is supplied by the IIS server.

Provided that you have the necessary permissions, you can manage your documents and your printers using your web browser. When you install IIS 5, you create a virtual directory that points to **%systemroot%\web\printers**. You can access this directory by entering the URL address: http://*web_ server_name*/Printers.

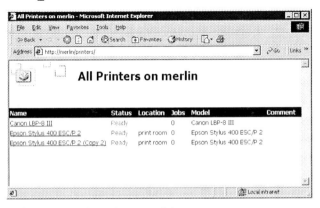

➢ Select the printer that you wish to manage.

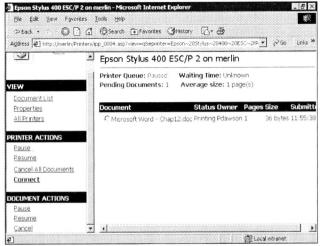

You can then manage documents that are on the spooler, and on the printer itself.

If you attempt to carry out an action for which you do not
have the necessary permissions, you will be asked to
provide authentication:

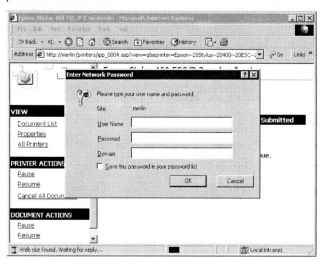

➤ If you no not have an account and password with the
necessary rights, then the following message will appear:

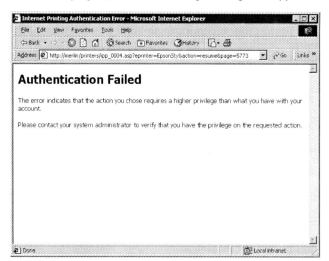

I. Troubleshooting print problems

You are unable to print a document. Here is a list of possible causes:

⇨ *The port is incorrect.*

⇨ *The device is disconnected.*

⇨ *The driver that is being used is unsuitable.*

⇨ *The device has no more paper, or no more ink, or the paper is jammed.*

⇨ *The format that you have selected is incorrect for the paper tray.*

⇨ *The printer is paused.*

⇨ *The spooler that is on the servers does not work or has not been declared.*

⇨ *The printing period is badly configured.*

⇨ *The user does not have the required permissions, or the printer is not shared (or is no longer shared).*

A document that you send from an MS DOS application does not print:

⇨ *Check that the local driver is installed.*

⇨ *Some DOS applications will not print until the application is closed.*

You have problems with 16-bit Windows applications:

⇨ *There is a "memory error" upon startup.*

⇨ *You cannot select a font.*

⇨ *No default printer is selected.*

Your document does not print completely or the print is deteriorated:

⇨ *Check that you are using the appropriate driver.*

⇨ *The print processor does not support the data type concerned, or the data type has been changed.*

The hard disk starts racing and your document never reaches the server:

⇨ *There is not enough disk space on the print server. Move the spool directory, or free up some space on the partition concerned.*

You are unable to print on the server. The print jobs do not execute and you cannot delete them:

⇨ *Stop and restart the Spooler Service.*

PostScript text appears on the printer:

⇨ *Check that your print device is able to manage PostScript.*

⇨ *Check that your print device is correctly configured in order to manage Postscript (you could possibly use PostScript.SEP in order to switch to PostScript mode).*

Labs

To be absolutely sure that you have assimilated this chapter, work through the corresponding labs. These are set out from page 654 to page 656.

☒ Printers.

Assessing your skills

Try the following questions if you think you know this chapter well enough.

Printing

1 The documents that are located in the spooler of the print server are blocked. You would like to cancel the document printing in order to empty the spooler, but you are unable to do this. How will you solve this problem?

....

....

2 What is the difference between a printer and a print device?

....

....

3 Which port would you use in order to print to an LPD server?

....

....

4 What is the default location for a print spooler?

....

5 How do you redirect print jobs from one printer to another?

....

....

....

....

6 You want to connect several print devices on your print server, using the same printer. When you try to select several ports, you are able to activate only one. What must you do in order to create a printer pool?

....

....

7 You are unable to print a document because there is not enough disk space. What must you do on the print server?

....

....

....

....

8 You want to use a print device that has an old HP Jetdirect adapter. What must you do so that you will be able to use this print device?

....

9 You want to use a Netware print device. When you install your printer, the port for Netware is not available. What might be the cause of this problem?

....

....

....

....

10 You want your Windows 95 clients to be able to connect to your shared printer on your Windows 2000 server. What must you do so that the clients will be able to download the driver automatically?

....

....

....

....

....

....

11 What condition must be applied to a print server in order to enable your to connect to a printer via the Web?

....

....

12 Which protocol allows you to print via the Internet?

....

Printer management

13 Some of your users must print large documents, but you do not want them to block the printer for long periods. In addition, these users do not need their printed documents urgently. What must you do in order to achieve your objective?

....
....
....
....
....

14 You do not want your printer to be listed in Active Directory. What must you do in order to ensure this?

....
....

15 What is the lowest priority value? What is the highest priority value?

....

Results

Check your answers on pages 324 to 326. Count one point for each correct answer.

Number of points   /15

For this chapter you need to have scored at least 11 out of 15.

Look at the list of key points that follows. Pick out the ones with which you have had difficulty and work through them again in this chapter before moving on to the next.

Solutions

Printing

1 The documents that are located in the spooler of the print server are blocked. You would like to cancel the document printing in order to empty the spooler, but you are unable to do this. How will you solve this problem?

*You must use the **Services** console so as to restart the Print Spooler service.*

2 What is the difference between a printer and a print device?

A printer is a software interface between the application and the print device, which is a piece of hardware.

3 Which port would you use in order to print to an LPD server?

You must use the standard TCP/IP port.

4   What is the default location for a print spooler?

%systemroot%\system32\spool\printers.

5   How do you redirect print jobs from one printer to another?

*You can replace a port that is configured locally on the printer, with a **local port**, and you can specify, as a UNC name, the share name of the second printer.*

6   You want to connect several print devices on your print server, using the same printer. When you try to select several ports, you are able to activate only one. What must you do in order to create a printer pool?

*You must go into the properties of the printer concerned, activate the **Ports** tab, and then activate the **Enable printer pooling** check box.*

7   You are unable to print a document because there is not enough disk space. What must you do on the print server?

*You must free disc space on the partition that contains the spool directory. Alternatively, you can change the location of the spool directory by going into the **Printers** console, opening the **File** menu, selecting **Server Properties**, and activating the **Advanced** tab.*

8   You want to use a print device that has an old HP Jetdirect adapter. What must you do so that you will be able to use this print device?

You must install the DLC protocol.

9   You want to use a Netware print device. When you install your printer, the port for Netware is not available. What might be the cause of this problem?

In order to use the port for Netware, you must install the NWLink protocol, and the Client Services for Netware.

10   You want your Windows 95 clients to be able to connect to your shared printer on your Windows 2000 server. What must you do so that the clients will be able to download the driver automatically?

*You must go into the **Properties** of your printer, select the **Sharing** tab, and click the **Additional Drivers** button. In the list of drivers, enable the check box that corresponds to Windows 95/98 for an Intel environment, and then click **OK**. You must then supply the Windows 2000 Advanced Server installation files.*

11   What condition must be applied to a print server in order to enable your to connect to a printer via the Web?

You must have installed Internet IIS 5 on the print server.

12   Which protocol allows you to print via the Internet?

IPP (Internet Printing Protocol).

Printer management

13 Some of your users must print large documents, but you do not want them to block the printer for long periods. In addition, these users do not need their printed documents urgently. What must you do in order to achieve your objective?

You must install two identical printers on the print server. For one of these printers, you must define its activity schedule so that it will print the documents during the night. For the other printer you must not specify any such scheduling restrictions. Then, you must connect the users who print large documents to the printer on which there are time restrictions, and you must connect the other users onto the other printer.

14 You do not want your printer to be listed in Active Directory. What must you do in order to ensure this?

Go into the properties of your printer and activate the Sharing tab, and disable the List in the Directory check box.

15 What is the lowest priority value? What is the highest priority value?

The lowest priority value is 1 and the highest priority value is 99.

Prerequisites for this chapter

☒ Knowledge of the Windows 2000 environment.

☒ Basic knowledge of file systems.

☒ Essential networking knowledge.

Objectives

At the end of this chapter, you will be able to:

☒ Compare FAT16, FAT32 and NTFS file systems.

☒ Choose the most suitable file system in a given situation.

☒ Share folders and apply permissions.

☒ Connect to shared folders.

☒ Describe administrative shares.

☒ Create shares remotely.

☒ Stop sharing a folder.

☒ Check shares.

☒ Send administrative messages.

☒ Define NTFS permissions.

☒ Apply NTFS permissions to files and to folders.

☒ Manage multiple permissions.

☒ Manage NTFS permission inheritance.

☒ Take ownership of data.

☒ Determine the effective permissions when you access a shared folder via the network.

☒ Organize the availability of data using DFS topologies.

☒ Manage stand-alone DFS topologies and fault tolerance.

☒ Access DFS topologies from 2000, Windows NT, Windows 95 and Windows 98 platforms.

☒ Implemente and managing disk quotas.

☒ Manage disk compression.

Managing disk resources

Contents

A. File systems

1. FAT16

This file system is present on a large number of operating systems:
- OS /2
- MS-DOS
- Windows 3.x
- Windows 95/98
- Windows NT
- Windows 2000

The FAT system was designed for low-volume partitions (nowadays, for partitions of up to 500 MB). For partitions of this size, FAT uses only a very small amount of disk space for its internal management.

The FAT structure is very simple. One reason for this simplicity is that the FAT does not manage an Access Control List (ACL) for each file and folder.

2. FAT32

Fat32 is a development of FAT16 file systems. Whereas FAT16 does not support partitions of over 2 GB, FAT32 allows you to go beyond this limit. This file system is used with OSR2 versions of Windows 95, and also with the Windows 98 operating system. Windows NT 4.0 does not recognize FAT32. However, Windows 2000 does support this file system.

3. NTFS 5.0

NTFS *(NT File System)* allows you to manage security locally using ACLs. NTFS also supports, individual compression, disk quota management, and file encryption by public key/private key.

NTFS offers a transactional mode at file system level. This mode allows NTFS to ensure that the internal structures will be coherent, in most cases. This is possible because all actions that are carried out on the file system are logged. In addition, NTFS supports 64-bit addressing. This feature allows NTFS to divide its partitions into elementary allocation units, which are known as clusters. Not only does this technique allow NTFS to manage larger partitions, but it also allows this file system to waste less disk space when it manages small files.

Managing disk resources

With NTFS, search operations are much quicker thanks to the use of a B-tree structure. This structure, which is complicated to set up, allows you to write algorithms that have Log N complexity, whereas classical algorithms offer a complexity that is a function of N/2.

In other words, if you want to look for an item amongst N items (for example, N=100), then with classical algorithms you will need to search for a length of time that is proportional to N/2 (for example 100/2 = 50). On the other hand, with B-tree structures you will need to search for a length of time that is proportional to Log N (for example Log 100, which equals 2). Suppose that your reference time is one second. Then, with classical N/2 algorithms your search will take 50 seconds, whereas with B-trees your search will take only 2 seconds.

☞ *The higher the value of N, the greater this difference will be.*

When a file is fragmented, then fewer disk accesses that will be necessary in order to re-assemble it with NTFS, than would be necessary with FAT.

NTFS uses a particular table called the *Master File Table*. This table allows you to accommodate small files, and to access them very quickly.

You can extend an NTFS volume, or an NTFS disk stripe. This technique allows you to increase the size of a data volume, without losing information.

Finally, with NTFS, there is no specific limitation on the number of directories that you can create.

4. Choosing the most suitable file system (FAT or NTFS)

For partitions that are smaller than 500 MB, the FAT file system is the most suitable.

NTFS is particularly suitable for high-volume disks. You must use NTFS when you want to:
– implement data security (for files or for folders),
– compress individual items,
– have a stable file system,
– manage data encryption,
– apply disk quotas,
– make your server a domain controller (in order to store Active Directory).

B. Sharing folders

The main purpose of a network is to allow you to access files that are situated on another computer, a workstation or a server. By default, operating systems such as Windows for Workgroups, and the different versions of Windows 95, do not share directories (folders) or files that are on the hard disk, for security reasons. The administrator must set up the sharing of the resource in order to allow users to access it via the network. According to the users who must access it, this resource is shared with different rights (for example, write, read, or delete).

Resource level security

On Windows for Workgroups operating systems, access security is ensured by a password. A password is allocated per resource and per type of access, independently of the users. For example, no password is necessary for read-only access, whereas a password is necessary in order to allow full access (read and write).

User level security

With Windows 98, you can operate with user level security, or with resource level security.

With Windows NT and Windows 2000, only user level security can be used. In this mode, initial authentication is compulsory. Thereby, a user is designated as being authorized to access a resource, according to a particular type of access. For any given resource, you can designate several users, and/or groups of users, and you can define a specific type of access for each of them.

It must be noted that, with Windows for Workgroups and Windows 98, you can share resources only if you have explicitly enabled this feature by activating the options **I want to be able to give others access to my files** and **I want to be able to allow others to print to my printers**.

When you have activated these options, and after you have restarted your machine, the server service that allows you to share these resources is loaded into memory.

☞ *With FAT, sharing folders is the only means of ensuring the security of network access to resources.*

1. Sharing a folder

On Windows 2000, the files are not shared. Only the folder that contains the files can be shared.

By default, certain resources are shared on Windows 2000. These are administrative shares that are reserved for the configuration management of remote workstations. These files are hidden, and only the administrator can access them.

Shared Folder	Shared Path	Type
ADMIN$	E:\WINNT	Windows
C$	C:\	Windows
D$	D:\	Windows
E$	E:\	Windows
IPC$		Windows
print$	E:\WINNT\System32\spool\drivers	Windows

C$, D$, E$, device_letter$	This share provides the administrator with full access to drives. The administrator can connect to a remote machine by entering \\computer_name\c$.
Admin$	This share is used in order to manage a workstation via the network. This refers to the %systemroot% directory.
IPC$	This share allows processes to communicate with each other. It is used in order to administer a workstation remotely, or in order to consult a shared directory.
Print$	This share is used in order to administer printers remotely.

It must be noted that the names of administrative shares finish with a **$** sign, which causes them to be hidden. You can add this symbol at the end of a share name so as to hide the share concerned.

In order to share a folder, right-click the folder that you want to share, and then select the **Sharing** option.

Enable the **Share this folder** option. You can then change the name of your share, if you wish. This is the name that will be seen via the network. By default, the share name is the same as that of the folder, but this is obligatory. You can also add a comment that is useful in order to describe the folder's contents.

On Windows 2000, a shared folder is reserved for certain users. In order to access a shared folder on a domain controller, you must be either a member of the administrators group, or a member of the server operators group. On a Windows 2000 member server, or an a Windows 2000 Professional workstation, you must be either a member of the administrators group, or of the power users group.

You can choose to restrict the number of simultaneous connections on this share.

If you have MS DOS or Windows for Workgroups clients, then you must use short names (in the 8.3 character format).

In order to modify network access permissions, click the **Permissions** button.

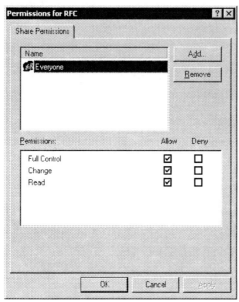

This dialog box displays the share permissions that are currently applied to the folder. Note that the system grants **Full Control** permission to the **Everyone** group, by default.

Under **Permissions**, the list of permissions that apply to the shared folder is displayed. These permissions are as follows:

- **Read**: The user that has this permission is allowed to read the files, to run the programs, and to browse the subfolders.
- **Change**: The user that has this permission, has the **Read** permission, plus the right to modify, and to delete, folder and files.
- **Full Control**: The user that has this permission, has the **Change** permission, plus the right to change share permissions.

In order to apply these permissions to the users, you can use two columns of check boxes:

In order to grant a permission, click the corresponding check box in the **Allow** column. In order to deny a permission, click the corresponding check box in the **Deny** column.

If a user is a member of several groups to which different permissions have been granted, then the users permissions will be the combination of the permissions that have been granted to the different groups. However, this rule does not apply in the case of a permission for which the **Deny** check box has been enabled. The **Deny** check box always takes priority over the **Allow** check box (you must be careful of this consequence of using the **Deny** check box).

In order to add a group or a user, click the **Add** button. In order to delete a user or a group, select the account concerned and then click the **Remove** button.

You can create several share names for the same folder. In order to do this, you can click the **New Share** button (in order to make this button appear, you may need to click **OK** in order to close this dialog box, and then re-open it and reselect the **Sharing** tab).

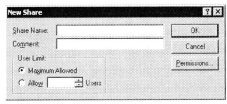

Alternatively, you can use the **Computer Management console** in order to share a folder.

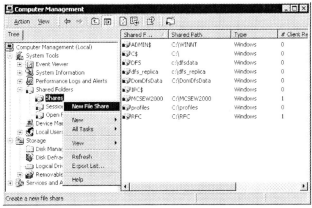

Right-click the **Shares** folder and then select **New File Share**.

Fill in the different fields and then click **Next**.

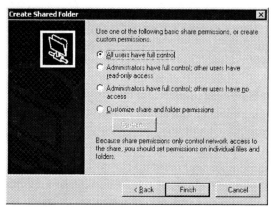

You can then specify the share permissions that must be applied to this folder.

2. Ceasing to share a folder

When you cease the sharing of a folder, you stop the access to this folder via the network, and you withdraw all its share permissions.

➤ Right-click the name of the shared folder concerned, and select the **Sharing** option.

➤ If there are several shares, then select the share that you wish to remove.

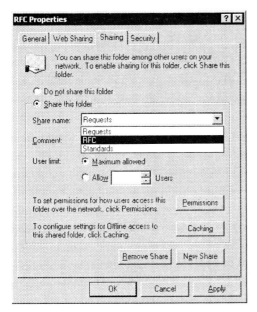

> Click the **Remove Share** button, then click **OK**.

> If you have only one share name for the folder, or if you want to stop sharing the folder, whatever the share name, then click the **Do not share this folder** option.

Alternatively, you can cease a share using the **Computer Management** console:

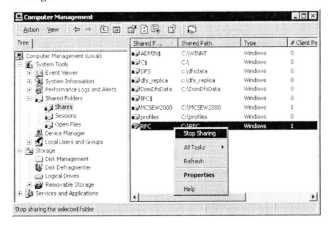

3. Connecting to a shared resource

Once a folder is shared, it is accessible via the network.

➢ Double-click the **My Network Places** icon, followed by the **Entire Network** icon. Then select the machine on which the shared resource is located (select the domain or the workgroup, followed by the machine concerned).

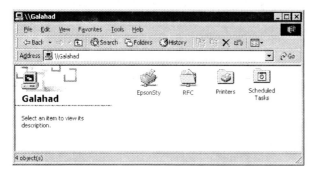

➢ Double-click the icon that represents the computer concerned. You will be able to access a shared resource if you have the necessary permissions.

In order to connect a drive letter to a shared resource, right-click the **My Network Places** icon, or, go into Windows Explorer and open the **Tools** menu, then select the **Map Network Drive** option.

The following dialog box appears:

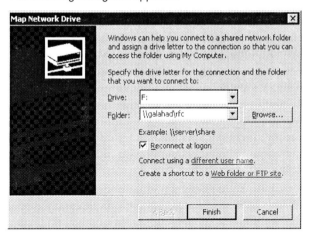

> ➤ Choose the drive letter that you want to use as a reference to the shared resource on the target computer.

> ➤ Enter the path that leads to the resource concerned. This must be a UNC path (\\server\share).

> ➤ Enable the **Reconnect at logon** check box if you want to continue using this drive letter the next time that you logon.

> ➤ You can connect to the resource using the permissions of another user account. In order to do this, click **different user name**, and then, in the dialog box that appears, enter the user name and the password for the account that you want to use for this connection.

> ➤ The **Web folder or FTP site** option allows you to add the connection to this shared folder, into My Network Places.

You can now access the shared directory by double-clicking the **My Network Places** icon. You can also add network places using the **Add Network Place** icon. In addition to paths that lead to shared directories, you can also add as network places, URLs that point to Web sites or to FTP sites.

4. Checking shares

Checking shares allows a user or the administrator to display the list of network users who are accessing the shared resources, and to control the access to these resources.

➢ Open the **Computer Management** console.

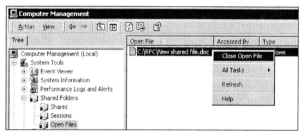

- The **Open Files** folder allows you to view the list of all the files from shared folders that are open on the server. It also allows you to close these shared resources. If you close a file that was open in read/write mode, then any modifications that had been made will be lost. The user still has the right to access the resource. The disconnection is temporary however, as the user can re-access the resource immediately.

☞ *This passive disconnection technique allows the system to ensure fault tolerance even when the network temporarily fails.*

- The **Sessions** folder allows you to view all the sessions that are open on the computer. This folder then, lists all the people who have logged on to the computer via the network. All the connections that a user has made are represented by a single session, no matter how many times the has logged on to the machine. This feature is particularly useful when you want to shutdown a computer, as it allows you to warn all the users who are currently logged on to it.
- The **Shares** folder allows you to share, or to cease sharing a resource (as discussed earlier in this chapter).

☞ *This console allows you to connect to remote computers in order to administer them. For example, you can create new shares remotely, or cease sharing remote resources.*

Sending administrative messages

If you want to stop a service in order to carry out maintenance work, then you must warn the users who are connected so that they will be able to save their data.

You can send a message to all the users who are connected
to your server.

➢ Open the **Computer Management** console, and right-click
Shared Folders.

➢ Select **All Tasks**, followed by **Send Console Message**.

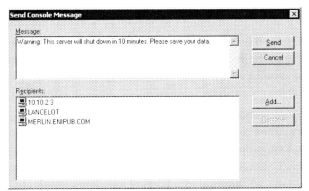

Your message will be sent to all the machines that are listed
under **Recipients**.

5. Advice for sharing folders

In order to ease the access to resources via the network, you
must take into account the following points:
- Choose share names carefully and provide comments on
   the shares. On the client machines, specify explorer
   viewing in **Detail** mode so as to display the associated
   comments.
- Remember that if the share name exceeds 8.3 characters,
   then the users of machines that run MSDOS, Windows 3.x
   or Windows for Workgroups will not see the shares and
   will not be able to access them.

6. Implementing the different types of shares

a. Sharing folders for network applications

According to the size of the company network, one or more
servers will be needed in order to store the applications that
are used.

➢ Wherever possible, create a shared folder (called APPS,
for example) that contains one subdirectory per
application.

➢ For each application, create a group with a name that
represents the application in question (for example,
WORD or EXCEL). These groups will simplify the
management of the users who have access to the specific
applications concerned.

> Attribute the following permissions:

Read   for the users group that must use the
                     application,

Change   for the users group that must update
                     and troubleshoot the application,

Full Control   For the administrators.

b. Sharing data folders

Data folders allow users to exchange information via a
centralized folder that is reserved for this purpose.
Data folders can be divided into two categories:

Public data

These folders allow users that come from different groups to
exchange information.

> You could apply **Change** permission to the **Domain Users**,
  for example,

> Create a tree structure so that you can backup the data
  very easily.

Working data

These folders allow specific user groups to share a private
data space.

> Create a basic directory, which you can call DATA, for
  example.

> You could apply **Change** permission to specific groups on
  specific DATA subfolders. For example, the
  ACCOUNTANTS subfolder could be created for the
  Accountants group.

c. Sharing home directories

The home directories of all the users can be grouped
together into one folder.

> Create a folder that is called USERS and share this folder
  using the same share name.

> Create a subfolder for each user and give it the name of
  the user in question.

> If you are working in NTFS, create a **USER** share with
  Full Control permission for **Everyone**. On each of the
  user's subfolders, grant **Full Control** permission for the
  user alone.

☞ *When you create the user, if you specify %USERNAME% in order to create the user's home directory on an NTFS volume (for example, specifying the path \\Servername\USERS\%USERNAME%), then the appropriate permissions will be applied automatically.*

➢ If you are working in FAT, then you must share each user's home directory with **Full Control** permissions for the user alone.

C. Access security

The permissions that have been described so far in this chapter are applied to enable users to access resources via the computing network. They do no provide protection when users access a computer locally.

This chapter will now cover the security features that allow users to protect their own data from unauthorized access, both locally and via the network. These security features also allow you to protect the operating system from accidental deletion by uninformed users, or by users who are insensitive to system warnings when the system is about to delete files. In order to use these Windows 2000 features, you must be using the NTFS file system. Only NTFS allows you to implement security and to audit attributes on folders and files.

NTFS allows you to keep each file and folder up to date with an Access Control List, or ACL. This ACL maintains at file system level, the user numbers (SID) and the user permissions on the resource.

1. NTFS Permissions

NTFS distinguishes between folder permissions and file permissions.

a. Conditions for attributing NTFS permissions

In order to apply NTFS permissions for a file or for a folder, you must either be the owner of the item concerned, or you must be the administrator, or you must have the necessary permissions. The permissions that are required are **Full Control**, **Change Permissions** or **Take Ownership** (which allows you to become the owner of the object).

b. Permissions for a folder

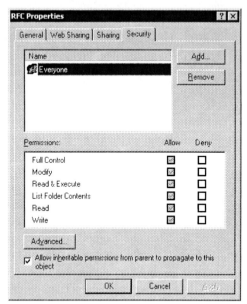

In order to apply NTFS permissions for a folder, right-click the folder concerned, select **Properties,** and then select the **Security** tab.

The following permissions appear:

– **Write**: users who have this permission can create files and folders, and they can also modify the attributes of these items (for example: **Read-only,** and **Hidden**).

☞ *A user who has this permission must also have read permission so as to be able to access the folder.*

– **Read**: users who have this permission can read the contents of the folder and also the contents of the files that are in the folder. This permission also allows users to read the attributes.

– **List Folder Contents**: this permission covers **Read** permission, plus the right to browse the folder's contents

– **Read & Execute**: this permission covers **Read** permission, plus **List Folder Contents** permission, plus the right to navigate across folders so as to reach other folders and files.

– **Modify**: this permission covers **Read & Execute** permission, and it also allows you to delete the folder.

– **Full Control**: this permission allows you to change permissions for the folder, to take ownership of the folder, to delete the folder, and it covers all the other NTFS permissions as well.

☞ *If permissions are not applied explicitly to a user's account, or to one of the groups to which the user belongs, then the user will not be able to access the resource.*

In reality, each of these permissions is an association of NTFS attributes. In order to find out the list of attributes, apply a permission to a user, click the **Advanced** button. Then, select the **Permission Entry** for the user that has this permission and click the **View/Edit** button.

c. Permissions for a file

– **Write**: allows you to write in the file, to change its attributes, and to display the permissions and the owner of the file.
– **Read**: allows you to read the file contents, its attributes, the permissions that are associated with the file, and the name of its owner.
– **Read & Execute**: This permission provides **Read** permission, and it also allows you to run programs.

- **Modify**: This permission provides **Read & Execute** permission, and it also allows you to delete the files.
- **Full Control**: This permission covers **Modify** permission, and it also allows you to take ownership of the file and to change its permissions.

d. Advanced permissions

If the standard permissions do not fully meet your needs, then you can create your own permissions by combining NTFS attributes. However, you must ensure that your new permission is coherent.

You can customize your permissions as follows:

➢ Display the properties of the resource for which you want to apply NTFS permissions.

➢ Under the **Security** tab, add the user, or the user group, to which the permission must apply.

➢ Select this user, or this group, and then click the **Advanced** button.

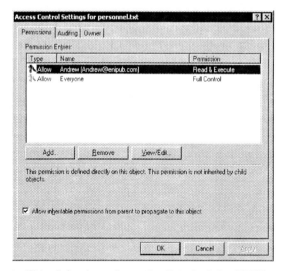

➢ This dialog box shows the list of all the NTFS attributes that have been granted to each user.

➢ Click the **View/Edit** button.

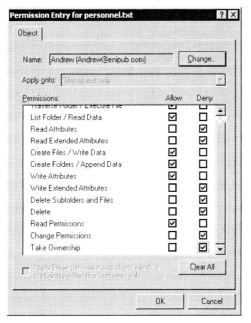

➢ Choose the NTFS attributes that you require.

➢ You can also specify the scope of your permissions.

e. Applying NTFS permissions

Multiple application

You can apply NTFS permissions for a file or for a folder, to users or to groups of users.

When a user is a member of several groups to which different permissions have been attributed, then the user's permissions that will be effectively applied to the user will be the combination of all the permissions that are applied to the user's groups.

An exception to this rule occurs when a permission has been denied to the user or to one of the user's groups. In this case, the deny always takes priority.

For example: suppose you want all domain users to have **Full Control** permission for a file. You apply this permission:

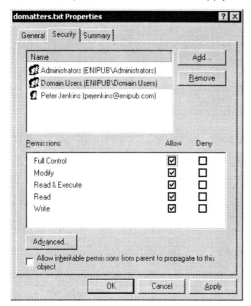

However, you do not want the user Peter Jenkins to be able
to access this file. You deny **Full Control** permission for this
user:

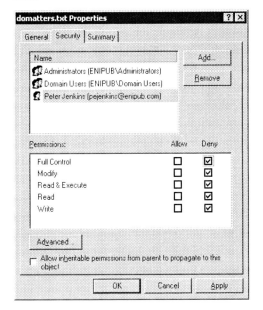

Inheriting permissions

When you create a file or a folder, then the file or the folder
inherits the permissions of the parent container. This
inheritance is represented by a series of check boxes that
are grayed-out.

In order to cancel this inheritance, disable the following
check box:

☑ Allow inheritable permissions from parent to propagate to this
object

The following message then appears:

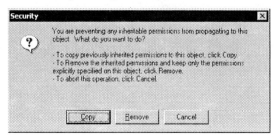

In response to this dialog box, you can choose one of several options:

- You can choose to keep the inherited permissions, and to make their check boxes appear with a white background so that you will be able to change them. In this case click **Copy**.

- Alternatively, you can choose to remove the inheritance, and to keep only those permissions that you have attributed for the file or the folder. In this case click **Remove**.

☞ *If you remove an inheritance, you can recover it again by re-enabling the **Allow inheritable permissions from parent to propagate to this object** check box.*

☞ *By default, the permissions for folders and for files are inherited from the parent container.*

2. Taking ownership of files and folders

Each file or folder that is located on an NTFS volume has an owner. By default, the owner of a resource is the user that created the resource, who is automatically a member of the **CREATOR OWNER** group. When a user is the owner of a resource, he/she can always modify the permissions, such as those that allow users to read or to write.

A user cannot become the owner of a resource, unless he/she has the special **Take Ownership** permission. Although a user that has this permission can become the owner of a resource, he/she cannot make another user the owner of the resource.

Here are the steps that you must follow in order to take ownership of a resource:

➢ Right-click the name of the file, or of the folder, of which you want to take ownership, and select the **Properties** option.

➢ Select the **Security** tab and then click the **Advanced** button.

➢ Select the **Owner** tab.

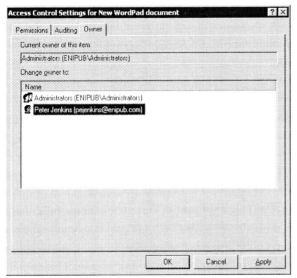

If the user has **Take Ownership** permission, then the user's account will appear in the list under **Change owner to**. The user must select his/her account and then click the **Apply** button.

Unlike with Windows NT 4.0, when a user who belongs to the administrators group takes ownership of a resource, then it is the user's account that becomes the owner.

3. Copying and moving files and folders

In order to copy or move an item to an NTFS partition, a user must have the necessary permissions.

For example, a user can move a file between NTFS partitions only if the user has **Write** permission for the destination folder, and **Modify** permission for the source folder.

If you copy a file or a folder to a different NTFS partition, or to the same NTFS partition, then the file or the folder will inherit the permissions of the destination container folder.

If you <u>move</u> a file or a folder to a different NTFS partition, then the file or the folder will also inherit the permissions of the destination container folder. However, if you move a file or a folder to the same NTFS partition, then the file or the folder will keep the same permissions.

If you copy or move files or folders from an NTFS partition to a non-NTFS partition, then the file or the folder will lose its permissions, as these permissions are supported only on NTFS partitions.

When you copy a file or a folder, then you become the owner of the copy that you have made.

When you move a file or a folder from one partition to another, then you copy the item first, and then you delete the source item.

D. DFS

DFS (*Distributed File System*) allows you to group together into one tree structure, several directories that are physically situated at different places in the network. This technique allows you to group together all the information that a set of users require into one structure, without the users having to worry about where their data is physically located.

You can configure two types of DFS systems:
- Stand-alone DFS, with which the DFS topology resides on a single server.
- Fault-tolerant DFS (or domain DFS), with which the DFS topology is recorded in the Active Directory database.

a. Terminology

A DFS topology comprises at least two items:
- A root node, which provides the entry point.
- Child nodes that point to different shared folders.

When you create a DFS topology, the first thing that you must do is to create a root node under which all the child nodes will be created. You can create a DFS topology an NTFS file system, or on a FAT file system. However, you must remember that if you use an NTFS system, then you will enhance the security of your data.

b. Stand-alone DFS

You can create a stand-alone DFS structure as follows:

➤ Open the **Distributed File System (DFS)** console, open the **Action** menu, and select **New Dfs Root**.

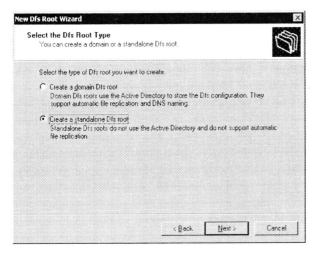

➤ Select **Create a standalone Dfs root**, and click **Next**.

➤ Then enter the name of the server that must accommodate the DFS topology.

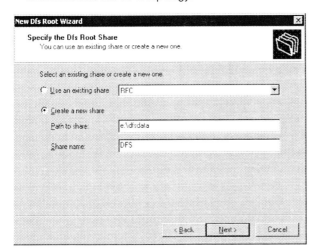

➤ In order to specify your DFS root share, you can either select an existing share, or you can choose to create a new share.

When the operation is finished your root will be created. All that you need do now is to create the child nodes.

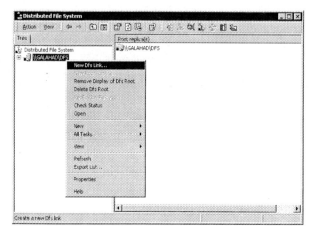

> Right-click the DFS root and then select **New Dfs Link**.

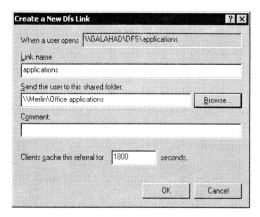

> Give a name to the child node. This name will be that which the users will view when they browse the DFS topology. Then, indicate a UNC path for the shared folder to which you want to point. You can add a comment, and you can change the length of time that the child node reference will be kept in the cache of the client computers.

> Use the same procedure in order to add your other child nodes.

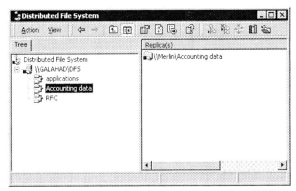

When users access the share that is called DFS on the Galahad server, via the network, they will see the following window:

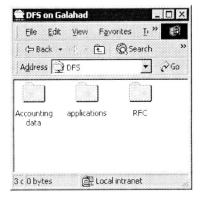

☞ *Clients that run Windows NT 4.0, Windows 98 and Windows 2000 can access DFS topologies. Clients that run Windows 95 must install the DFS client software. In order to do this you must install the Active Directory client for Windows 95 that is located on the 2000 Advanced Server CD-ROM Windows. This client allows you to use DFS, and it also allows you to carry out searches in Active Directory. However, the Windows 95 workstation must be equipped with IE4.01 (or later version) and the Active desktop snap-in must be enabled.*

c. Fault-tolerant DFS

The fault tolerance is obtained because the DFS structure is recorded in Active Directory. As the directory database is replicated on all the domain controllers, then if the topology host server fails then Active Directory allows you to recover the DFS topology. All the changes that are made to the topology are recorded in the directory database.

Managing disk resources

You can create a fault-tolerant DFS structure as follows:

➢ Open the **Distributed File System (DFS)** console, open the **Action** menu, and select **New Dfs Root**.

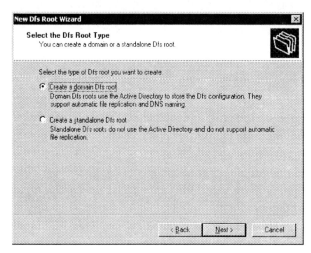

➢ Select **Create a domain Dfs root**.

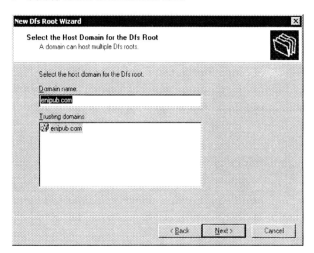

➢ Select the domain that must accommodate the DFS topology.

> Then, indicate the domain server that must accommodate your DFS topology.

> As with the creation of a stand-alone DFS structure, you must now specify the path of the DFS root share, along with its share name.

> Then, create the child nodes in the same way as you created them for the stand-alone DFS topology.

After you have installed a DFS topology, you can create replicas of your root. The purpose of a replica is to provide fault tolerance in case a client is unable to connect to a DFS root. When this happens, the system will automatically connect the user to the DFS root replica.

In order to create a replica you must carry out the following steps:

> Right-click the domain DFS structure.

> Select **New Root Replica**.

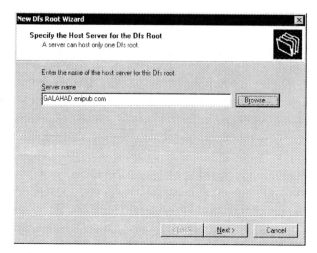

> Enter the name of the host server for the replica.

> Finally, you must indicate the shared folder on the server that you indicated above that must host the DFS root replica.

☞ *When you configure Active Directory, you define the sites that group together the computers in your network that communicate over fast links. The purpose of these sites is to regulate the traffic that runs over slow links. As the DFS system recognizes these sites, then it will always try first to connect the user to a replica that is located on the users site.*

This section has just described how you can introduce fault tolerance using a DFS root. If a user connection to a DFS root fails, then the connection will be set up with a replica of this root. However, what will happen if a user is able to connect to a DFS root, only to find that the servers that host the child nodes are unavailable? In this case, the user will be unable to access the required resources. In order to safeguard against this situation, you must create replicas of the child nodes. This technique will then provide you with fault tolerance that is reasonably complete.

You can create a replica of a child node as follows:

➢ Right-click the child not for which you want to create a replica, and select **New Replica**.

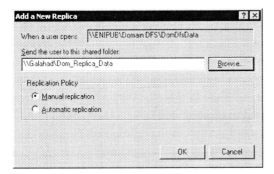

➢ Enter the path for the folder to which the users must be redirected, when necessary.

➢ When you have finished configuring your replicas, all that you need do is to replicate the contents of the child nodes to all the replicas (you can do this either manually, or automatically).

In order to ensure that you have identical data in each replica, you must configure the replication. To do this, right-click the child node, and select **Replication Policy**. Then, select the share that must be the master replica, and click the **Set Master** button. When you have done this, select the other replicas that must participate in the replication and click the **Enable** button. If you do not want to replicate with one of the replica members, then select it and click the **Disable** button. You can replicate only with members that are situated on NTFS partitions, and on machines that run the replication service.

☞ *In addition to providing fault tolerance, creating replicas of child nodes allows you to spread the workload. This is because the DFS topology server will forward the client queries to all the servers that act as child node replicas.*

Each child node can have up to 32 replicas.

Managing disk resources

E. Managing disk quotas

With a network environment in which the users save their data on the servers, it is useful to be able to control the amount of disk space that is used by each user.

Thanks to its NTFS file system, Windows 2000 allows you to manage disk quotas on each partition. Not only can you limit the amount of data that the users can store, but you can also set alerts, and monitor for each user, the amount of disk space that has been used, and the amount of disk space that remains available.

Windows 2000 uses file and folder ownership in order to calculate its quotas. Thereby, when a user takes ownership of a file or a folder, then the space that is required by the file or the folder is added to the amount of space that is already occupied by this user.

In its quota calculations, Windows 2000 does not take into account any compression that you may have carried out. Also, although you can apply disk quotas to compressed partitions, the space that is calculated by Windows 2000 will not take account of this compression.

a. Enabling disk quotas

Disk quotas are not enabled by default. In order to enable them, you must carry out the following steps:

➢ Right-click the drive letter that corresponds to the partition to which you want to apply the disk quotas. Select **Properties** and then select the **Quota** tab.

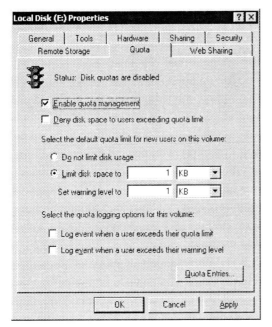

➤ As the quotas are not enabled by default, activate the **Enable quota management** check box.

The 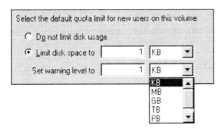 icon is at red whilst the quotas have not been enabled. When you have activated the **Enable quota management** check box, click **Apply** and watch what happens to this icon. It shows amber to indicate the initialization of the quotas, and finally it turns to, and stays on, green when the quotas are enabled.

Activate the **Deny disk space to users exceeding quota limit** check box in order to to implement this option.

When the disk quota system is active, you can define the amount of disk space that must be allocated to each user. For any users that have no quota entries, you can choose not to limit the amount of disk space that they use. Alternatively, you can set a limit that must be applied to all of these users.

The warning level defines the amount of information that can be stored before Windows 2000 writes an error message in the quota entries.

If you wish to log any occurrences either of users who exceed their quota limits, or of users who exceed their warning levels, then activate the corresponding check boxes:

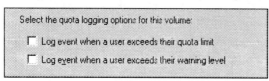

Here is an example of such a message:

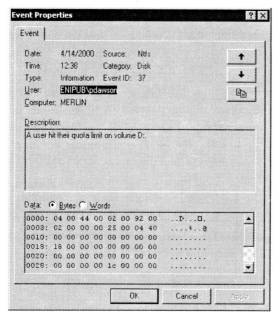

b. Creating a new entry

Creating an entry allows the administrator to define the amount of disk space that a user is allowed to occupy on a partition.

➢ In order to create a new entry, click the **Quota Entries** button.

➢ Open the **Quota** menu, and select **New Quota Entry**. Then select the user(s) to whom you wish to apply the entry.

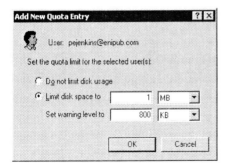

> Select the disk space limit, and the warning level, and then click **OK**.

The use then appears in the quota entries list.

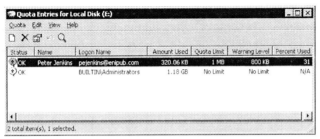

This list tells you for each user, how must disk space is currently occupied, the limit that is set by the quota, the warning level, and the percentage used.

In the **Status** column, an icon indicates that the user is under his/her warning level, an icon indicates that the user has exceeded his/her warning level, and an icon indicates that the user has exceeded his/her quota limit.

The **Quota Entries** window allows you to delete documents so as to free up disk space.

In order to do this, right-click the user for whom you wish to free the disk space, and click **Delete**.

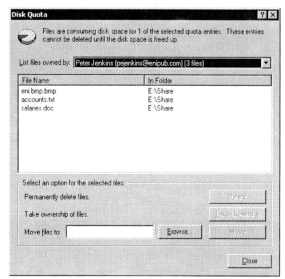

Select the files, either that you want to delete, or for which you want to take ownership, or that you want to move.

☞ *You cannot delete the administrator's documents in this way.*

F. Compressing

The NTFS file system supports the compression of files and of folders. The purpose of this compression is to optimize disk space. A file that is compressed takes up less space than the same file when it is not compressed.

You can compress a whole partition as well as a file or a folder.

In order to compress a file or a folder that is situated in an NTFS partition, right-click the file or the folder and select the **Properties** option.

Then, click the **Advanced** button so as to display the following dialog box:

Activate the **Compress contents to save disk space** check box, and click **OK**.

☞ *You can choose either to compress a file or a folder, or you can choose to encrypt the file or the folder. You cannot choose both at once!*

When you have compressed a file, the users can continue to use the file, just as they did before. You can access these files from any type of client, whether it is a Windows client or an MSDOS client.

In order more easily to recognize a file or folder that has been compressed, without having to look at its attributes, you can make your compressed file or folder appear in your Windows Explorer, in a different color than non-compressed items.

➤ Open the **Tools** menu of your Windows Explorer, select **Folder Options**, and then select the **View** tab.

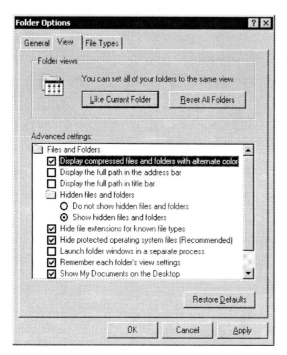

> Activate the **Display compressed files and folders with alternate color** option.

The names of compressed files and folders now appear in blue.

If you choose to compress a folder, you must indicate whether you want to compress only this folder, or whether you want to compress any files and subdirectories that are contained in the folder, as well.

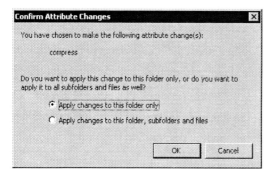

Copying and moving compressed files

Here are some rules concerning the compression attribute when you copy or move a file or a folder:

	Onto the same NTFS volume	Between different NTFS volumes
Copy	Inherits the compression attribute of the destination	Inherits the compression attribute of the destination
Move	Retains its compression attribute	Inherits the compression attribute of the destination

For example, if you move a compressed file that is located on the path c:\data\file.txt, to the path d:\applications\file.txt, and the destination folder, "applications", is not compressed, then the file "file.txt" will lose its compression attribute.

On the other hand, if you move the same file, c:\data\file.txt, to c:\backup\file.txt and the destination folder, "backup" is not compressed, then the file "file.txt" will keep its compression attribute.

☞ The **compact.exe utility** allows you to manage your compression operations from the command prompt.

☞ When you copy a non-compressed file into a compressed folder, then the file will be compressed after it has been copied. Consequently, the partition that contains the destination folder must have enough available disk space in order to be able to receive the initial non-compressed file.

Labs

To be absolutely sure that you have assimilated this chapter, work through the corresponding labs. These are set out from page 657 to page 667.

☒ Shared resources.

☒ NTFS Permissions.

☒ Combining shared folder permissions and NTFS permissions.

☒ Distributed file system (Dfs).

☒ Managing individual compression.

☒ Managing disk quotas.

Assessing your skills

Try the following questions if you think you know this chapter well enough.

File systems

1   On a FAT file system with Windows 2000, can you create files with names that contain spaces?   ☐

....

....

2   Which file systems does Windows 2000 manage?   ☐

....

3   For a disk of 200 MB, is the performance better with FAT or with NTFS?   ☐

....

Sharing

4   You want to make files available for a certain number of users via the network. The users must be able to consult these files, but they must not be allowed to modify them. How will you achieve this, given that the FAT 32 file system is used on the partition on which the data is stored?   ☐

....

....

....

....

5 You wish to share a folder for which you are the only user who has access. You do not want the folder to be visible in My Network Places. How can you achieve this?
....

6 Is it possible to share the same folder using several different names?
....
....
....

7 What are the three shared folder permissions?
....

8 The Managers group has the **Read** shared folder permission for the information directory. You do not want one of the members of this group to be able to access this folder at all. How can you achieve this, given that the managers group has several permissions for other resources in the network?
....
....
....
....

9 Is it possible to create shares on a remote computer, even when the folder that you want to share has not yet been created?
....
....
....
....
....

10 You want to stop a server in order to carry out maintenance operations. You wish to warn users who may have files that are open on this server. How will you achieve this?
....
....
....

NTFS

11 What do you need in order to be able to assign NTFS permissions to a file or to a folder?
....
....
....
....

Managing disk resources

12 Can you prevent a folder from inheriting permissions from a parent folder?

....
....
....
....
....

13 A user that he/she cannot access a shared folder. The user received an Access is denied message. When you check the permissions for the shared folder, you notice that the user's account has **Read** permission on the folder, and that the user is a member of a group that has **Full Control** permission. What is causing this problem?

....
....

14 You have taken ownership of a file. However, you want the users to think that one of your colleagues is the owner of this document. How can you achieve this?

....
....
....
....

Distributed file systems

15 What is the role of Dfs?

....
....

16 Give two examples of Dfs types.

....

17 What must you do in order to enable a Windows 95 client to access a Dfs topology?

....
....

18 How can you ensure that the resources of a DFS topology will always be accessible even if the server that is storing the Dfs topology breaks down, or if the servers that are storing the resources of the child nodes break down?

....
....

Optimizing disk storage

19 You want to limit the amount of disk space that is available for each user on the D: drive. How will you achieve this objective?

....

....

....

20 Is it possible individually to compress files on a FAT partition?

....

21 What will happen if you move a compressed file that is on an NTFS partition, to another directory on the same NTFS partition?

....

Results

Check your answers on pages 372 to 374. Count one point for each correct answer.

Number of points | /21 |

For this chapter you need to have scored at least 16 out of 21.

Look at the list of key points that follows. Pick out the ones with which you have had difficulty and work through them again in this chapter before moving on to the next.

Key points of the chapter

☐ File systems.

☐ Sharing.

☐ NTFS.

☐ Distributed file systems.

☐ Optimizing disk storage.

Solutions

File systems

1 On a FAT file system with Windows 2000, can you create files with names that contain spaces?

Yes. You can do this even on FAT, thanks to the management of long file names.

2 Which file systems does Windows 2000 manage?

FAT 16, FAT 32 and NTFS.

3 For a disk of 200 MB, is the performance better with FAT or with NTFS?

A disk that has this small capacity will perform better in FAT.

Sharing

4 You want to make files available for a certain number of users via the network. The users must be able to consult these files, but they must not be allowed to modify them. How will you achieve this, given that the FAT 32 file system is used on the partition on which the data is stored?

*In order to do this you must share the folder that contains these files. As the partition that stores the information is not in NTFS, you cannot apply security measures at file level. Consequently, you must attribute only **Read** share permission on the folder for the users that will have access to these documents via the network.*

5 You wish to share a folder for which you are the only user who has access. You do not want the folder to be visible in My Network Places. How can you achieve this?

You must add the $ sign at the end of the folder's share name.

6 Is it possible to share the same folder using several different names?

*Yes. In order to do this, go into the **Properties** of the folder, activate the **Sharing** tab, activate the **Share this folder** option (if necessary), and click the **New Share** button.*

7 What are the three shared folder permissions?

***Full Control, Change** and **Read**.*

8 The Managers group has the **Read** shared folder permission for the information directory. You do not want one of the members of this group to be able to access this folder at all. How can you achieve this, given that the managers group has several permissions for other resources in the network?

*Go into the properties of this folder, activate the Security tab, and, in addition to the Managers group, add the user account in question. Then activate the **Read** check box that is in the **Deny** column.*

9 Is it possible to create shares on a remote computer, even when the folder that you want to share has not yet been created?

*Yes. In order to do this, go into the **Computer Management** console, connect to the remote computer concerned, right-click the **Shares** folder, and select **New File Share**. If the file that you want to share does not exist, then the system will create it.*

10 You want to stop a server in order to carry out maintenance operations. You wish to warn users who may have files that are open on this server. How will you achieve this?

*Go into the **Computer Management** console, right-click **Shared Folders**, and then select **All Tasks – Send Console Message**.*

NTFS

11 What do you need in order to be able to assign NTFS permissions to a file or to a folder?

*You must either be the owner of the file or the folder, or you must be the administrator, or you must have **Full Control**, or **Change Permissions** or **Take Ownership** permissions for the file or the folder.*

12 Can you prevent a folder from inheriting permissions from a parent folder?

*Yes. You can do this by going into the properties of the resource, activating the **Security** tab, disabling the **Allow inheritable permissions from parent to propagate to this object** check box, and then clicking the **OK** button.*

13 A user that he/she cannot access a shared folder. The user received an Access is denied message. When you check the permissions for the shared folder, you notice that the user's account has **Read** permission on the folder, and that the user is a member of a group that has **Full Control** permission. What is causing this problem?

This user probably does not have the NTFS permission that is necessary in order to access this folder.

Managing disk resources

14 You have taken ownership of a file. However, you want the users to think that one of your colleagues is the owner of this document. How can you achieve this?

This is not possible. You can take ownership of a resource, provided that you have the permission that is necessary in order to do this. However, you cannot designate another user as the owner of a resource.

Distributed file systems

15 What is the role of Dfs?

The role of Dfs is to present in a single tree, a set of resources that are dispersed in the network.

16 Give two examples of Dfs types.

Stand-alone Dfs and Fault-tolerant Dfs.

17 What must you do in order to enable a Windows 95 client to access a DFS topology?

You must install the Active Directory client, which is located on the Windows 2000 Advanced Server CD-ROM.

18 How can you ensure that the resources of a Dfs topology will always be accessible even if the server that is storing the Dfs topology breaks down, or if the servers that are storing the resources of the child nodes break down?

You can ensure this by creating new replicas of the root and of the child nodes.

Optimizing disk storage

19 You want to limit the amount of disk space that is available for each user on the D: drive. How will you achieve this objective?

In order to do this, you must enable the disk quotas on the D: drive, and then you must create a quota entry for each of the users.

20 Is it possible individually to compress files on a FAT partition?

No. Only NTFS partitions support individual compression.

21 What will happen if you move a compressed file that is on an NTFS partition, to another directory on the same NTFS partition?

The file will keeps its compression attribute.

Prerequisites for this chapter

☒ Familiarity with the terms, disk and partition.

☒ Ability to handle consoles.

Objectives

At the end of this chapter, you will be able to:

☒ Distinguish between a basic disk and a dynamic disk.

☒ Manage basic disks.

☒ Transform your basic disks into dynamic disks.

☒ Manage dynamic disks.

☒ Create mount points.

☒ Implement software fault tolerance.

☒ Defragment and clean your disks.

Configuring disks, partitions and volumes

Contents

The disk management of Windows 2000 has evolved with respect to earlier Windows versions. Although there is nothing new about the contents of primary partitions, extended partitions and other logical drives, you can now optimize your disks by creating volumes.

A. Basic disks

With Windows 2000, a basic disk is a disk structure on which you can create primary partitions and extended partitions.
There is a limit to the number of partitions that a basic disk can support. On a basic disk, you cannot have more than:
– 4 primary partitions,
– or, 3 primary partitions and 1 extended partition. In this extended partition you can create one or more logical drives.
On Windows 2000, you can manage your disks using the **Disk Management** snap-in that is situated under the **Storage** node of the **Computer Management** console tree.
Alternatively, you can create your own console and add the **Disk Management** snap-in into it.
You can manage the disks of any computer by selecting the **Connect to another computer** option, or by creating a console that points to the computers that you want to manage, provided that you are a member of the administrators group, or of the server operators group.
In order to do this, open an MMC and add the **Disk Management** snap-in.

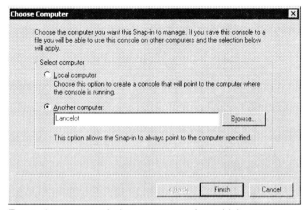

Enter the name of the computer for which you want to manage the disks, and then repeat the operation for any other machines for which you want to manage the disks.

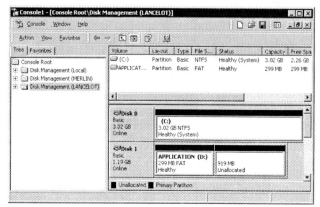

You can now use this console in order to carry out operations on your physical disks such as creating and deleting partitions.

1. Creating a primary partition

In order to create a primary partition, right-click an unallocated disk space:

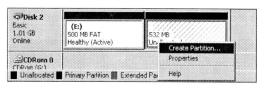

Then, select **Create Partition** so as to start up the **Create Partition** Wizard.

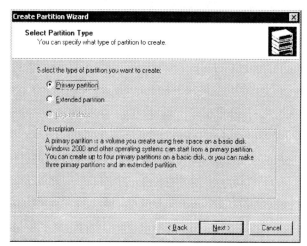

Select **Primary partition**. Note that the **Logical drive** option is grayed out. This is because you can create a logical drive only within an extended partition.

Create Partition Wizard

Specify Partition Size
How big do you want the partition to be?

Choose a partition size that is smaller than the maximum disk space.

Maximum disk space: 919 MB

Minimum disk space: 1 MB

Amount of disk space to use: 500   MB

< Back   Next >   Cancel

Enter the size that you want for the principal partition. If you decide to create a partition that will occupy all the available disk space, then you should leave at least 1 MB of free space, as you will need this is you want to convert your basic disk into a dynamic disk. This is because the conversion processes will need this space in order to store their working information.

Create Partition Wizard

Assign Drive Letter or Path
You can assign a drive letter or drive path to a partition.

• Assign a drive letter: E

○ Mount this volume at an empty folder that supports drive paths:

○ Do not assign a drive letter or drive path

< Back   Next >   Cancel

By default, Windows 2000 suggests a drive letter for this partition. If you wish, you can choose another letter that is not being used by the other drives. You can change this drive letter after the partition has been created.

You can choose to mount your partition in an empty folder in an NTFS partition. Alternatively, you can choose not to assign either a drive letter or a drive path. In this case Windows Explorer will not be able to access this partition (you can always assign a drive letter later).

The next step consists of formatting the partition.

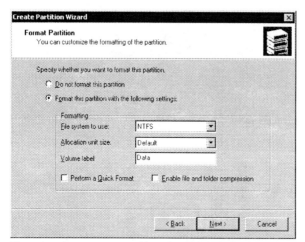

You can choose to use either the FAT, FAT32 or NTFS file systems. In addition, you can customize the size of the allocation unit. If you choose to format your partition in FAT with a cluster size of over 32 KB, then your partition will not be compatible with previous operating system versions. Be careful of this point then, if you have a multiple boot facility. However, pre-Windows 2000 operating systems would still be able to access the resources that are located on this partition via a network share.

Note that you can choose to enable file and folder compression if you format your partition in NTFS.

When you have finished indicating your settings, the system will format your partition. When your partition is ready to be used it will be marked as being **Healthy**.

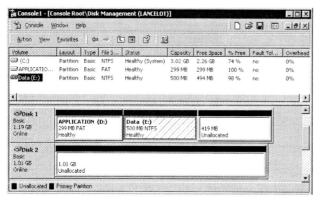

In addition to allowing you to carry out such operations as creating and deleting partitions, this **Disk Management** program provides information concerning disk type (basic or dynamic), file systems, capacities, free space, percentage of free space, and whether or not your partitions belong to a fault-tolerance set.

2. Creating an extended partition

If you have already three primary partitions on your disk, then your extended partition must occupy the rest of the available space (leaving 1 or 2 MB in order to allow for possible conversion to a dynamic disk). Otherwise, you will lose any remaining space because you cannot create more than four partitions on your disk.

In order to create an extended partition you must carry out the following steps:

➢ Right-click an unallocated space and then select **Create Partition**.

➢ Select **Extended partition** and then click **Next**.

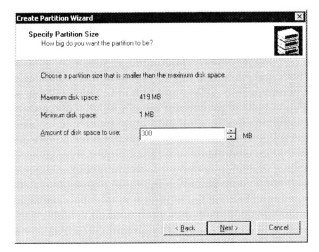

➢ Enter the size that you require for your extended partition and click **Next**.

The extended partition is then created and appears in the Disk Management console in green (when standard colors are used).

This extended partition is no longer considered as being **Unallocated**, but it is considered as **Free Space** (free for the creation of a logical drive).

3. Creating logical drives

After you have created an extended partition, you must create one or more logical drives. You can create as many logical drives as you have drive letters that are available.

In order to create a logical drive, right-click the extended partition and then select **Create Logical Drive** so as to start the Create Partition Wizard.

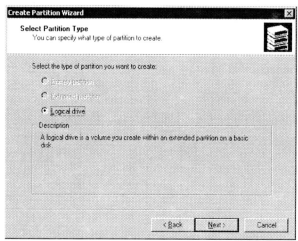

The **Logical drive** option is then selected automatically.

➢ Choose the size that must be allocated to this logical drive. If you wish to create several logical drives within this extended partition, then do not take up all the available space in order to create the first one!

➢ The following step involves either choosing the letter that you want to assign to this drive, or deciding not to assign a letter, or mounting the drive at an empty folder in an NTFS partition.

➢ Then, define the type of formatting (FAT, FAT32, NTFS, and the cluster size) and click **Finish**.

The system then formats the logical drive. If you have not used all the free space for the creation of this logical drive, then you can use the rest of the free space in order to create other logical drives. Once the drive has been formatted it is marked as **Healthy**.

☞ *You can change the letters that are attributed to your partitions or to your logical drives at any time. In order to do this, right-click the partition or the drive for which you want to change the drive letter and select* **Change Drive Letter and Path**.

Removable storage devices contain only primary partitions. You can create neither extended partitions nor volumes on this type of storage device. In addition, you cannot mark as active, a partition that is on a removable storage device.

You can alter the colors and the schemes that are used to represent the different partitions using the **View – Settings** menu.

B. Dynamic disks

A dynamic disk does not have partitions, it has volumes. A volume is a part of a disk that runs like a separate physical disk. The information concerning the disk is not written in the registry, but on the disk itself.

Here are the advantages of dynamic disks:
- You can use fault tolerance (without having to restart the computer),
- You can create as many volumes as you like,
- You can extend NTFS volumes.

You can still use the partitions on basic disks, which ensures compatibility with existing configurations. However, volumes cannot be read by pre-Windows 2000 systems.

1. Upgrading to a dynamic disk

You can upgrade from a basic disk to a dynamic disk without losing data. However, once you have upgraded to dynamic disks, if you wish to return to basic disks, then you will have to delete all the disk volumes (therefore, you must remember to back up your data first).

On a dynamic disk, you can have the following volume types:
- Simple volumes
- Striped volumes
- Spanned volumes
- Mirrored volumes
- RAID 5 volumes

If there are partitions on your basic disks when you upgrade them to dynamic disks, then they will become volumes as follows:

- A primary partition will become a simple volume.
- Each logical drive of an extended partition will become a simple volume.
- The free space of an extended partition will become unallocated space (you can then create volumes using this space).
- A partition mirror will become a mirrored volume.
- Stripe sets with parity will become RAID 5 volumes.
- Stripe sets will become striped volumes.
- Partition stripes will become spanned volumes.

In order to upgrade from a basic disk to a dynamic disk, go into the **Disk Management** program and right-click the disk that you want to upgrade:

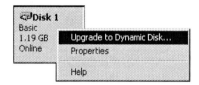

➢ Then, select **Upgrade to Dynamic Disk**.

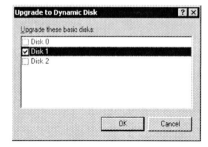

➢ Select the disk(s) that you wish to upgrade, and then click **OK**.

➢ In the dialog box that appears, If you click the **Details** button, a further dialog box appears that indicates all the partitions of the disk that must be upgraded.

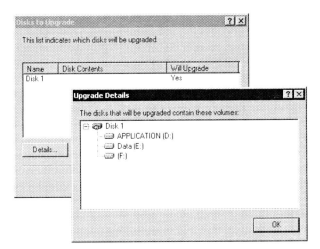

> Click **OK** so as to return to the previous dialog box, and then click the **Upgrade** button in order to start the upgrade process.

When the upgrade operation has finished, the modifications are updated in the **Disk Management** console.

2. Simple volume

A simple volume corresponds to the space of a single disk. Unlike partitions, volumes are limited neither to a maximum size neither to a maximum number.

On a dynamic disk, simple volumes can be formatted in NTFS, FAT 16 or FAT 32.

A simple volume that is formatted in NTFS can be extended in order to create a volume that will cover the initial space of the volume, plus one or more unallocated disk spaces that can either be contiguous or not.

In order to create a simple volume, right-click part of a dynamic disk that is not allocated.

> Select **Create Volume** so as to start up the Create Volume Wizard.

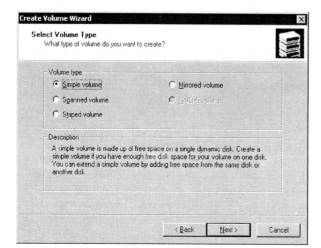

> Select **Simple volume** then click **Next**.

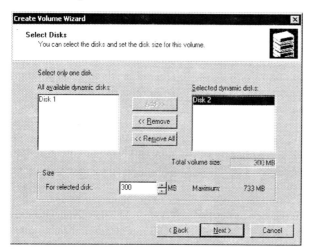

In order to create a simple volume, you must select only one disk and set the size for this volume.

> The next step consists of assigning a drive letter (or not assigning a drive letter), or mounting the volume at a folder.

> Then, select the file system that must be used for this volume.

3. Extending a simple volume

If your volume is formatted in NTFS, you can extend it by combining the disk space that is occupied by the volume with one or more unallocated spaces.

The new size of the volume will then be the initial size of the volume, plus the sum of all the spaces that have been added.

In order to extend your volume, right-click it and then select **Extend Volume**.

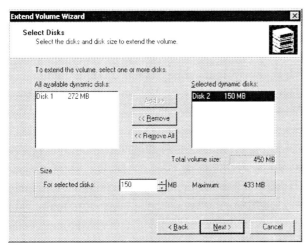

As you can extend your volume over unallocated portions of dynamic disks, you must select the disk(s) on which you want to extend your volume. When you have selected a disk, click the **Add** button so as to add the disk concerned under **Selected dynamic disks**. Then, set the extra size that you want to add to your initial volume. If you are extending your volume using unallocated spaces from several disks, you can define a different size that must be added from each space.

If you extend your volume over unallocated spaces on another disk, then your volume will become a spanned volume.

You cannot extend a volume that is the result of an upgrade from a partition. The volume must have been created on a dynamic disk. This means that you cannot extend system volumes or boot volumes.

4. Spanned volume

A spanned volume is a composed of unallocated spaces that have been grouped together from a minimum of 2 disks, and a maximum of 32 disks. Data is written first to free space on one disk and, when this disk is full, data is written to free space on the next disk.

In order to create a spanned volume, right-click an unallocated space and then select **Create Volume**.

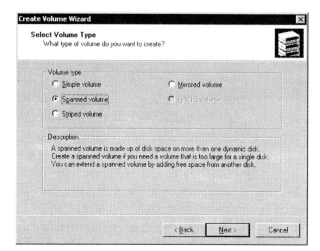

> Select **Spanned volume** and then click **Next**.

You must select at least two dynamic disks so as to create a spanned volume. Indicate the size that you want to use for each disk, and then click **Next**.

Assign a drive letter or a mount point. Finally, you must specify the file system that must be used for this spanned volume so as to finish the operation.

As with simple volumes, you can extend a spanned volume.

You cannot re-use a space that is situated on a disk that is included in a spanned volume, without deleting all the volume. Before you carry out this operation then, you must back up the volume, as all the data will be lost.

5. Striped volumes

A striped volume groups together into one logical volume, unallocated space from at least 2 disks and at most 32 disks. The data is written to stripes of 64 KB. This means that 64 KB will be written to the first disk, the next 64 KB will be written to the second disk, and so forth. This type of volume optimizes read and write access.

However, it must be noted that this type of volume does not provide fault tolerance. If a disk fails, then all the data that is written to all the member disks of the striped volume will be lost.

As all the data is written in striped sets, each of the stripe members must have the same amount of disk space. For example, if you want to create a striped volume on three disks, for which the first disk has 300 MB of free space, the second disk has 350 MB of free space, and the third disk has 280 MB of free space, then your striped volume will be created according to the smallest amount of disk space. In this example, the size of the striped volume will be 840 MB (3 x 280 MB).

In order to create a striped volume, right-click an unallocated space and then select **Create Volume**:

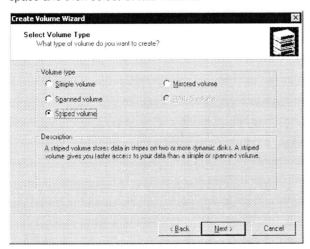

➢ Select **Striped volume**, and then click **Next**. If this option is grayed out, then you do not have unallocated spaces on at least two different dynamic disks.

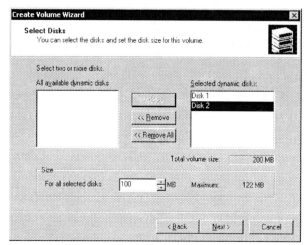

Add the disks on which you want to create the striped volume.

Then select either a drive letter for your striped volume, or a mount point.

Finally, choose the format for your volume (FAT16, FAT32 or NTFS).

You can neither extend nor mirror a striped volume.

C. Fault tolerance

With Windows 2000 fault tolerance can be implemented only on dynamic disks. Windows 2000 supports software fault tolerance.

1. Overview of RAID technology

RAID (*Redundant Array of Inexpensive Disks*) was devised when people realized that it is less costly to have several disks that are reasonably priced and that contribute to system security, than it is to use a single disk that is built to a high specification.

There are 6 RAID levels that vary according to the management method that is used. Some of these levels are variations, or intermediate phases, of the primary levels. Amongst the RAID levels 0 to 5, the two levels that are used most are RAID 1 and RAID 5.

☞ *It must be noted that RAID 0 corresponds to the implementation of a striped volume and it does not implement fault tolerance!*

2. RAID 1: disk mirroring

This solution is expensive in terms of storage space with respect to cost. On the other hand, it is easy to implement and to manage.

The data is written identically to two disks, in a way that is transparent to the user.

If an incident occurs, the mirror is broken, the defective disk is replaced, and the mirror is re-implemented. Consequently, no information is lost.

Two mirroring strategies can be used:

Mirroring

This solution involves one disk controller and two disks. Consequently, it has a vulnerable link!

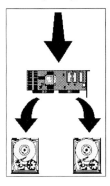

Duplexing

This solution involves two disk controllers and two disks. As a separate controller handles each disk, this method offers improved reliability and performance. This strategy is used with SCSI controllers.

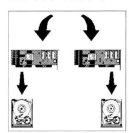

Windows 2000 manages both of these methods in such a way that their operation is transparent to the user.

☞ *A further advantage of RAID 1 is that it can cover the system partition.*

3. Implementing mirrorsh

➢ Right-click the volume that you want to mirror.

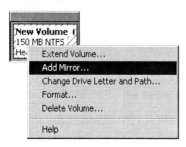

➢ Select **Add Mirror**. If this option is unavailable then you do not have a dynamic disk that has enough free space in order to create a mirror.

➢ Select the disk on which you want to set up your mirror, and the click the **Add Mirror** button.

The system then regenerates the data that is situated on the initial disk, onto the mirror disk.

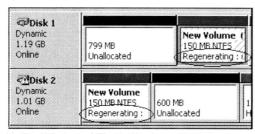

Unlike Windows NT4.0, Windows 2000 does not require you to restart your computer after you have created a mirror.
You can check that the mirroring was implemented:

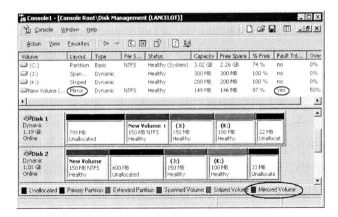

a. Breaking and removing a mirror

You can break or remove a mirror at any time. When you break a mirror, you keep the data intact on both members of the mirror. The mirror then, is separated into two volumes that contain identical information. However, this configuration no longer provides fault tolerance.

In order to break a mirror, you must right-click the mirrored volume that you wish to break and then select **Break Mirror**.

A new drive letter is then assigned to the volume on which you carried out this operation.

When you remove a mirror, you delete the data from one of the mirrored volumes. This volume then becomes unallocated space.

In order to remove a mirror, right-click the mirrored volume that you wish to remove, and then click **Remove Mirror**.

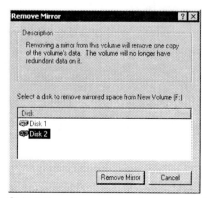

Select the mirror volume that you want to remove, and then click the **Remove Mirror** button.

4. Booting on a secondary mirror disk

As you can mirror the system partition, you must be able to boot on the secondary mirror disk if the primary mirror disk fails.

In order to do this you must create a bootable diskette. This diskette must be formatted using a Windows 2000 or a Windows NT 4.0 operating system. For an INTEL type machine, this diskette must contain the following files:

– NTLDR
– NTDETECT.COM
– NTBOOTDD.SYS (in the case where the BIOS of the SCSI controller is disabled)
– BOOT.INI

ARC names

ARC names have the following structure:

```
SCSI(x)disk(y)rdisk(0)partition(n)
```
or,
```
MULTI(x)disk(0)rdisk(z)partition(n)
```

SCSI(x) or MULTI(x)	x is the SCSI controller number, in initialization order. Some SCSI disks are called MULTI, according to the BIOS management mode.
DISK(y)	With multi-bus SCSI adapters this corresponds to bus number. It is always zero for MULTI controllers.
RDISK(z)	z indicates the logical disk number on the adapter for MULTI controllers. It is always zero for MULTI disks.

PARTITION(n) n indicates the partition number on the disk, from 1 to n.

Here is an extract from the boot.ini file on the C disk:

```
[boot loader]
timeout=1
default=multi(0)disk(0)rdisk(0)partition(1)\
WINNT
[operating systems]
multi(0)disk(0)rdisk(0)partition(1)\WINNT=
"Microsoft
Windows 2000 Advanced Server" /fastdetect
```

Here is an extract from the boot.ini file that must be contained by the bootable diskette:

```
[boot loader]
timeout=1
default=multi(0)disk(0)rdisk(0)
partition(1)\WINNT
[operating systems]
multi(0)disk(0)rdisk(0)partition(1)\
WINNT="Microsoft Windows 2000 Advanced
Server" /fastdetect
multi(0)disk(0)rdisk(1)partition(1)\
WINNT="Microsoft Windows 2000 Advanced
Server" /fastdetect
```

5. Repairing an original system disk

When mirrored volume fails, the other mirrored volume will continue to run, but it will no longer provide fault tolerance. Consequently, you must repair the mirror. When a disk fails, it is marked in the **Disk Management** console as **Missing**, **Offline**, or **Online (Errors)**.

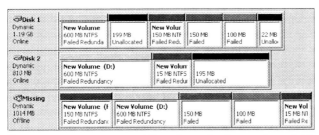

If an error occurs on one of the mirrored volumes, then right-click the volume concerned, and select the **Reactivate Volume** option.

If this technique is ineffective, then you must remove the mirror and then re-create it.

This is a delicate operation. It is described here for information purposes only, and if you decide to carry it out, then you must do so at your own risk! You must use this solution then, only as a last resort when all else fails, and you must try it out first on a test machine before you use it on an operational machine.

➢ Boot the machine using a bootable diskette, and select the partition on the disk that is still intact.

➢ Start up the **Disk Management** program.

➢ Select the mirrored volume that is missing or defective, and then select **Remove Mirror**.

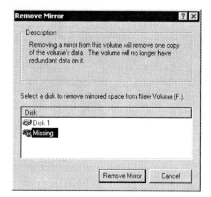

➢ Check that you have selected the disk that has the problem, and the click the **Remove Mirror** button.

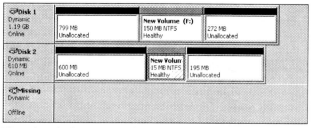

The mirror is then removed.

➢ Modify the boot.ini file as necessary, then replace the defective disk so that you can recreate the mirror.

6. Mirroring a basic disk

When you upgrade from Windows NT 4.0 to Windows 2000 then any disk mirroring that was implemented on the machine will be conserved. This is the only case in which you can have RAID 1 fault tolerance on basic disks with Windows 2000. Your mirror will continue to operate as it did before you upgraded your system.

You can carry out the following actions on a basic disk:

- Repairing: if you wish to repair your mirror, then you will need another basic disk for your new mirrored-member. You cannot use a dynamic disk in order to repair a mirror that is situated on a basic disk.
- Resynchronizing a mirror: When you have repaired a mirrored disk, if the disk does not return to **Healthy** status, then you must resynchronize the mirror in order to update the information on mirrored members.
- Breaking a mirror: If you no longer want to implement fault tolerance for the information that is concerned on your disks, then you can break your mirror at any time. In order to do this, right-click the mirror and then select **Break Mirror**. The two halves of the mirror then become two independent partitions that contain the same data.
- Removing a mirror: in order to be able to re-use both partitions independently of each other, right-click the mirror and then select **Remove Mirror**. The mirrored information is then deleted.

7. RAID 5: stripe set with parity

This solution is less expensive than mirroring, in terms of the disk space that is occupied by the security information. However, it requires at least three disks, as the parity information must be stored for each stripe. This solution allows you to record extra parity information that is calculated using saved data. This technique enhances read/write performance.

The disadvantage of a software solution such as that offered by Windows 2000, is that it is unable to cover the system partition. However, a number of vendors do offer hardware solutions that cover the system partition, and that cover it in a fully transparent manner.

Nevertheless, the software solution is much more affordable, from a financial point of view.

a. Creating stripe sets with parity

Right-click an unallocated space, and select **Create Volume**.

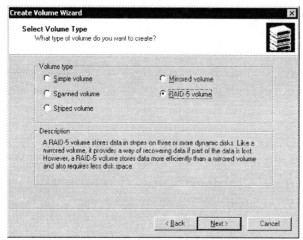

Then, select **RAID-5 volume**, and click **Next**.

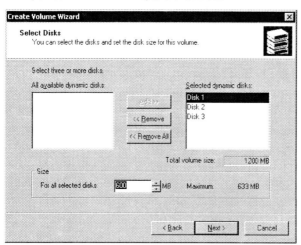

In order to create a RAID 5 volume you must, have at least three disks. As with stripe sets, the volumes that must be used for RAID 5 must all be the same size. If you have unallocated spaces of 800 MB on the first disk, 750 MB on the second disk and 600 MB on the third disk, then the stripe set with parity will have a size of 3 x 600 which equals 1800 MB (this calculation is based on the smallest space that is available on any of the disks that will be used for RAID 5).

As with the creation of other types of volume, you must then choose a drive letter and a file system format.

b. Repairing a defective RAID 5 volume

If you have a problem with one of the stripe set members, then you will still be able to access the data. However, the fault tolerance driver, **ftdisk.sys**, must regenerate the missing parts (using the parity information), which will result in a slight deterioration in system performance.

In order to solve the problem, you must repair the defective stripe set member. If the volume concerned has either an **Offline** or a **Missing** status, right-click it and select the **Reactivate Volume** option.

If the volume status is **Online (Errors)**, then try following the same procedure as for the other defective statuses. However, if the operation is ineffective, then you must replace the defective disk. In order to do this, right-click the RAID 5 volume that is on the faulty disk, then select **Repair RAID-5 volume**. A dialog box then asks you to select the disk that must replace the defective disk.

c. RAID 5 on basic disks

As with RAID 1, you will conserve your stripe sets with parity when you upgrade from Windows NT 4 to Windows 2000. Your stripe sets with parity will be implemented on basic disks, and this is the only way in which you can obtain RAID 5 level fault tolerance with this type of disk on Windows 2000.

You can carry out the following actions:

- Removing: when you remove a stripe set with parity on a basic disk then the data is deleted along with the partitions that make up the stripe set with parity.
- Repairing: in the case of **Failed Redundancy**, you must repair the stripe set with parity. In order to do this you must have another basic disk. You cannot use a dynamic disk in order to repair a stripe set with parity that is implemented on basic disks. In order to repair your stripe set with parity, right-click it and then select **Repair Volume**. If the status of the stripe set with parity does not return to **Healthy** when this regeneration is finished, then right-click the stripe set with parity and select **Regenerate Parity**.

8. Choosing the best fault tolerance solution

a. RAID 1 versus RAID 5

Both of these solutions support FAT and NTFS.

Mirroring :

- can be used with system volumes and boot volumes,
- requires two hard disks,
- offers good read/write performance.

Stripe set with parity :
- can be used only with data volumes,
- requires at least 3 hard disks and at most 32 hard disks,
- offers excellent read performance.

b. Data backup strategies

Data must still be backed up with either of these fault tolerance solutions.

With either of these solutions, and notably with a RAID 5 solution, if more than one of the disks fails then you can repair the problem only by restoring the data that you must have backed-up previously.

c. Cost of RAID 1 and RAID 5 solutions

For both of these solutions, it is useful to measure the cost in terms of the percentage of the disk that is used. For the mirror solution, disk consumption is important, as the data is written twice, which means that only 50% of the available space is *useful* disk space

With a RAID 5 solution, the more disks that you have, the more the cost decreases. If you have n disks, then this 'useful' disk space ratio is $(n-1)/n$.

For example, with a RAID 5 solution that uses 5 disks each which has a size of 1 GB, the disk space that is effectively available is 4 GB (the 'cost' ratio is 4/5).

d. Choosing the best fault tolerance method

You can implement both RAID 1 and RAID 5 solutions on the same server.

It is common practice to use a mirror solution for the boot volume (the volume that contains the system files), and to use a stripe set with parity solution in order to protect the data volumes.

D. Mounting volumes

In order to go beyond the limit that is imposed by drive letters (due to there being only 26 alphabetical letters), you can mount volumes in empty directories that are in local NTFS partitions or volumes. Although these volumes are mounted in NTFS partitions or volumes, they can themselves be formatted in NTFS, in FAT or in FAT32.

You can mount your partitions or your volumes when you create them. Alternatively, you can mount them at any time after you have created them.

➢ Right-click the volume or the partition that you want to mount.

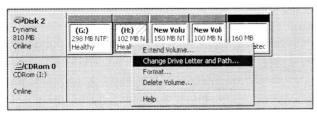

➤ Click **Change Drive Letter and Path.**

➤ Click the **Add** button so as to display the dialog box that will allow you to select the directory in which you want to mount this volume.

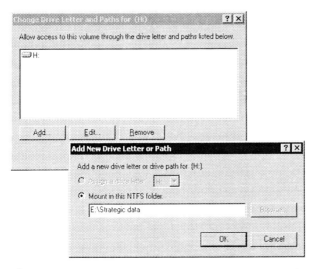

☞ *Remember to delete the drive letter that you associated with the volume or the partition when you created it.*

E. Adding disks

If the computer on which you want to add a disk does not support hot plugging (the feature that allows you to add and remove disks without stopping the machine), then you must stop your computer, add your disk(s), and then restart your computer. Windows 2000 then recognizes the new disk(s) and adds them to the **Disk Management** console.

On the other hand, if your hardware supports hot plugging, just add or remove your disk(s), then select **Action – Rescan Disks**:

The new disk(s) then appear in the console without you having to restart your computer.

☞ *If however, your disks do not appear, then restart your computer!*

If you add a disk that comes from another computer, it should be recognized automatically. If it is not recognized for any reason, then it will be marked as **Foreign**. In this case, you must right-click this disk and then select **Import Foreign Disks**.

If you import a disk from another computer and the Disk Management displays a **Failed: incomplete volume** message, then the disk was taken from a spanned volume, or from a stripe set.

On the other hand, if a **Failed Redundancy** message appears, then your disk was taken from a RAID 1 or a RAID 5 configuration. You will still be able to access the data on the disk. However, you will not have the fault tolerance, unless you add, either the other mirrored member in the case of RAID 1, or the other stripe set members in the case of RAID 5.

F. Monitoring and optimizing disks

1. Disk Defragmenter

When you use a disk heavily, it can become fragmented (this occur when files and folders are saved on non-contiguous disk spaces). This does not prevent you from accessing these files and folders, but your server will perform better if your files and folders are stored in contiguous disk spaces.

Windows 2000 provides a utility that allows you to defragment volumes, whether they are formatted in FAT, FAT32 or NTFS.

In order to start up this utility, go into Windows Explorer, activate the properties of the volume that you want to fragment, and select the **Tools** tab.

Then click the **Defragment Now** button.

Alternatively, you can use the **Computer Management** console:

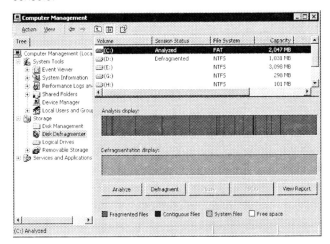

➢ Click the **Analyze** button in order to find out whether or not you need to defragment your disk. In addition, this option tells you which of your files are fragmented.

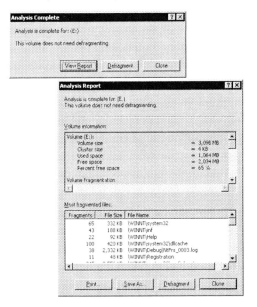

> Click the **Defragment** button in order to start defragmenting.

2. Checking a disk

Under the **Tools** tab of the volume properties dialog box, you can error-check your volume by clicking the **Check Now** button.

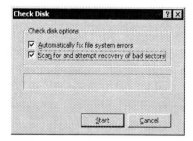

3. Cleaning up a disk

The volume properties dialog box also allows you to clean up your volume, by clicking the **Disk Cleanup** tab.
The Disk Cleanup program examines the volume in order to determine how much space it will be able to free up:

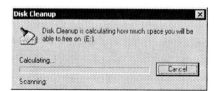

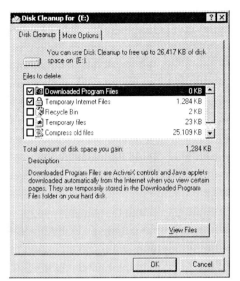

Select actions that you want to carry out, and then click OK.

Labs

To be absolutely sure that you have assimilated this chapter, work through the corresponding labs. These are set out from page 668 to page 670.

☒ Updating basic disks to dynamic disks.

☒ Implementing fault tolerance.

Assessing your skills

Try the following questions if you think you know this chapter well enough.

Managing disks

1   Which two types of disk does Windows 2000 support?   ☐
....

2   How many partitions can you create on a basic disk?   ☐
....
....

3   Which types of partition can you create on a basic disk?   ☐
....
....
....
....

4 Can you remotely manage the disks on a machine? ☐
....
....
....
....

5 What conditions do you need in order to be able to mount ☐
a volume?
....
....
....

6 What type(s) of file system(s) can you use as a mount ☐
point on an NTFS partition?
....

7 After you have added a CD-ROM drive, you notice that ☐
the system has attributed the letter F to your drive. Can you
change this letter so that users will be able to access the
drive using the letter D, even though the system has already
attributed this letter to another partition that contains only
data?
....
....
....
....

8 Can you transform a basic disk into a dynamic disk ☐
without losing data? If so, how can you do this?
....
....
....

9 Can you transform a dynamic disk into a basic disk? ☐
....
....
....
....

10 What are the peculiarities of a dynamic disk? ☐
....
....
....

11 You want to extend a primary partition. However, you are ☐
unable to do this, even though your partition is formatted in
NTFS. What might be the reason for this?
....
....

12 Can you install new disks on a server without switching it ☐
off?
....
....
....

Fault tolerance

13 On which type of disk can you implement fault tolerance on Windows 2000? ❑

....

....

14 Can you implement RAID 1 on basic disks with Windows 2000? ❑

....

....

....

15 What is the difference between mirroring and duplexing? ❑

....

....

....

....

16 What is the minimum number of disks that you require in order to implement RAID 5? ❑

....

17 You have four disks, each of which has 200 MB of free space. You want to implement RAID 5 in order to protect your data. What disk space will effectively be available for your data? ❑

....

....

18 Which solution allows you to ensure fault tolerance on your disk system? ❑

....

....

19 What is the difference between a striped volume and a RAID 5 volume? ❑

....

....

....

....

20 One of your mirrored disks has failed. This disk contained the system partition, and you can no longer start your server. How will you solve this problem? ❑

....

....

....

....

....

....

....

Configuring disks, partitions and volumes

Results

Check your answers on pages 408 to 410. Count one point for each correct answer.

Number of points | /20 |

For this chapter you need to have scored at least 15 out of 20.

Look at the list of key points that follows. Pick out the ones with which you have had difficulty and work through them again in this chapter before moving on to the next.

Key points of the chapter

☐ Managing disks.

☐ Fault tolerance.

Solutions

Managing disks

1 Which two types of disk does Windows 2000 support?

Windows 2000 supports basic disks and dynamic disks.

2 How many partitions can you create on a basic disk?

On a basic disk you are limited to 4 partitions. You cannot create partitions on a dynamic disk. You can create only volumes.

3 Which types of partition can you create on a basic disk?

You can create primary partitions and extended partitions. On a basic disk, you can create up to 4 primary partitions, or you can create 3 primary partitions and one extended partition. This extended partition can by divided into logical drives.

4 Can you remotely manage the disks on a machine?

Yes. In order remotely to manage a Windows 2000 machine, go into the Computer Management console, right-click the Computer Management icon in the Tree pane, and then select Connect to another computer.

5 What conditions do you need in order to be able to mount a volume?

The destination partition or volume must be formatted in NTFS, and the destination directory that must accommodate the mount point must be empty.

6   What type(s) of file system(s) can you use as a mount point on an NTFS partition?

FAT16, FAT32 or NTFS.

7   After you have added a CD-ROM drive, you notice that the system has attributed the letter F to your drive. Can you change this letter so that users will be able to access the drive using the letter D, even though the system has already attributed this letter to another partition that contains only data?

*Yes. In order to do this you must right-click the partition that has the letter D, and then you must select **Change Drive Letter and Path**. Then you must assign another letter to this partition in order to free the letter D for your CD-ROM. Carry out the same operation on your CD-ROM drive.*

8   Can you transform a basic disk into a dynamic disk without losing data? If so, how can you do this?

*Yes. In order to do this, go into the **Disk Management** console, right-click the disk that you want to transform, and select **Upgrade to Dynamic Disk**.*

9   Can you transform a dynamic disk into a basic disk?

This can be done, but all the data that is contained on your disk will be destroyed. Consequently, you must backup your data before you carry out this operation, or else all your data will be lost.

10   What are the peculiarities of a dynamic disk?

A dynamic disk does not contain partitions. It contains volumes. It allows you to overcome the limits that basic disks impose. In addition, the system considers each volume as a part of the disk that functions as a separate physical disk.

11   You want to extend a primary partition. However, you are unable to do this, even though your partition is formatted in NTFS. What might be the reason for this?

You can extend NTFS volumes only on dynamic disks.

12   Can you install new disks on a server without switching it off?

*Yes. You can do this provided that your hardware supports this operation. This technique is called hot plugging. In order to do this, add your disks, and then go into the **Disk Management** console. Open the **Action** menu and then select **Rescan Disks** in order to make your disks appear in the console.*

Fault tolerance

13   On which type of disk can you implement fault tolerance on Windows 2000?

On dynamic disks.

14 Can you implement RAID 1 on basic disks with Windows 2000?

Yes. When you upgrade a machine that implements RAID 1 to Windows 2000, the system will preserve the RAID 1 solution on the basic disks.

15 What is the difference between mirroring and duplexing?

With mirroring, two disks are arranged into a mirror configuration, which will have only one disk controller. On the other hand, duplexing allows you to put your disks into a mirror configuration with each disk having a separate controller.

16 What is the minimum number of disks that you require in order to implement RAID 5?

In order to implement RAID 5, you need at least three disks.

17 You have four disks, each of which has 200 MB of free space. You want to implement RAID 5 in order to protect your data. What disk space will effectively be available for your data?

Only 600 MB will be effectively available, as the system will use the equivalent of one of these disks in order to store the parity information.

18 Which solution allows you to ensure fault tolerance on your disk system?

Only RAID 1 allows fault tolerance. RAID 5 volumes do not allow you to cover the system partition.

19 What is the difference between a striped volume and a RAID 5 volume?

Although both of these volume types allow you to write data in striped sets, a striped volume does not provide fault tolerance. RAID 5 offers fault tolerance by writing parity information on the disks.

20 One of your mirrored disks has failed. This disk contained the system partition, and you can no longer start your server. How will you solve this problem?

In this case you must create a boot diskette that contains the files: NTLDR, NTDETECT.COM, BOOT.INI. It must also contain NTBOOTDD.SYS if you have a SCSI with BIOS deactivated. This diskette must have been formatted on a Windows 2000 system. You must modify the ARC names of the boot.ini so that you will be able to boot on the second mirror member. When you have started your machine, you must regenerate the mirror.

Prerequisites for this chapter

- ☒ Knowledge of the Windows 2000 operating system.
- ☒ Knowledge of the NTFS 5 file system.
- ☒ Knowledge of TCP/IP.
- ☒ Knowledge of group policies.

Objectives

At the end of this chapter, you will be able to:
- ☒ Encrypt your data.
- ☒ Make IP traffic secure.
- ☒ Recognize secure IP frames.
- ☒ Create security templates.
- ☒ Apply security templates.
- ☒ Implement a security policy for accounts and passwords.
- ☒ Implement an audit strategy.
- ☒ Analyze the security.

Security

Contents

A. Encrypting documents

1. Introduction

In order to enhance resource security, Windows 2000 allows you to encrypt your data in the context of NTFS file systems. This technique ensures that the contents of your documents will be accessible only by users who have the key that allows them to decrypt them.

Once you have encrypted a document, users who are authorized to decrypt it will have transparent access to it. Although this encryption is applied using NTFS permissions, it is independent of the NTFS permissions that are applied to the same document.

The encryption that is used on Windows 2000 is called EFS (*Encrypting File System*). In response to an increasing need for security, EFS allows you better to protect sensitive data. Even though it is difficult to by-pass NTFS permissions, an element of risk is always involved. For example, on the Internet you can obtain utilities that allow you to access NTFS partitions by booting your computer on a simple MSDOS diskette. In this case, NTFS permissions no longer apply.

EFS uses symmetric encryption (this means that the same keys are used for encryption and for decryption). The list of these keys itself is encrypted with a public key from the user's X.509 v3 certificate. This list is integrated into the document. In order to decrypt the document, you must use the user's private key that was used to encrypt the document so that you can extract the list of keys that are used. Only the user knows this private key. This technique is known as asymmetric encryption (the public key that is used in order to encrypt the document is different from the private key that is used in order to decrypt the document).

☞ *Files are encrypted block by block, and each block is encrypted using a different encryption key.*

☞ *EFS allows you to encrypt files or folders that are on a computer. It does not allow you to encrypt data that is transferred on the network. For this purpose, Windows 2000 offers solutions such as IPSec and SSL (Secure Sockets Layer). IPSec will be covered later on in this chapter.*

2. Implementation

a. Encrypting

➢ Open Windows Explorer and then right-click the file or the folder that you want to encrypt on an NTFS partition or volume. Then select **Properties**.

➢ Click the **Advanced** button.

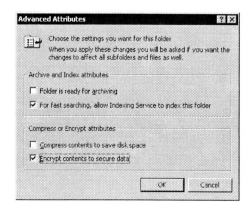

➢ Activate the **Encrypt contents to secure data** option, and then click **OK**.

If you encrypt a folder that contains files or subfolders, then you must choose whether you want to encrypt only the folder, or whether you want to encrypt the folder and its contents.

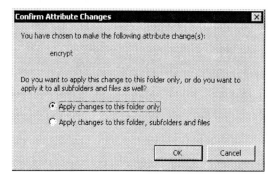

☞ *You cannot encrypt a file or a folder, and compress it. If you encrypt a file that is compressed, then the file will lose its compression attribute.*

You can also use a command prompt utility in order to encrypt or decrypt files or folders. This utility is called **cipher.exe**.

Using cipher.exe

/e   Encrypts the folders that are specified, and encrypts also any files or folders that will be added later to the specified folders.

/d   Decrypts the specified folders. Any folders or files that are added later to the specified folders will not be encrypted.

/s:dir   When combined with /E or /D, this switch encrypts or decrypts the folders and subfolders that are specified in the command line.

/i   By default cipher stops when an error occurs. This switch forces cipher to continue its operations.

/q   Reports only important information.

/k   Generates a new encryption key for the user that is running cipher.

If you run the cipher utility without specifying any switch, then cipher will return the status of the current encryption.

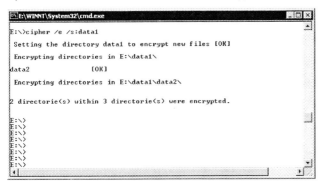

If you decide to encrypt a file that is located in a directory that is not encrypted, then you can choose either to encrypt only the file, or to encrypt the file and its parent folder.

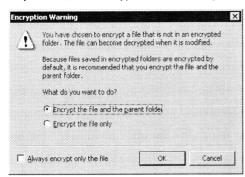

b. Stop encrypting

If you want to stop encrypting (decrypt) a file or a folder, go into Windows Explorer, right-click the folder or the file that you want to decrypt, select **Properties** then click the **Advanced** button. Then, deactivate the **Encrypt contents to secure data** option.

If you decrypt a folder that contains files or subfolders, then you must choose whether or not you want to decrypt the contents of the folder.

You can also use the **cipher.exe** utility for this purpose, specifying the switch /**d**.

c. Copying and moving

When you copy or move an encrypted document, then the document will stay encrypted, whether the destination folder is encrypted or not.

Similarly, if you backed up encrypted documents using the Windows 2000 backup utility, then these documents will remain encrypted after you have restored them.

If you copy, or move, an unencrypted file to a folder that is encrypted, then the file will also be encrypted. You can apply a policy that will prevent the encryption of files that are moved to an encrypted folder that is situated on the same volume.

In order to do this, you must use the policy:

Do not automatically encrypt files moved to encrypted folders

that is situated in the **Group Policy** snap-in, in the folder **Computer Configuration - Administrative Templates - System**.

It must be noted that if you copy or move an encrypted file to a file system other than NTFS, then the file will not be encrypted at the destination. You may find this technique useful so as to issue a document that you have encrypted.

☞ *When a document has been encrypted by another user, you can copy or move only to an NTFS file system.*

☞ *A user who has the right to delete a file will be able to delete an encrypted file.*

3. Recovery agents

Only the user who has encrypted a document can read it. But, what happens if the user account of the person who encrypted the document is deleted? It would appear that the data would be permanently lost!

In order to deal with such situations, **recovery agents** allow you to decrypt documents. Each encrypted document contains the list of the keys that were used in order to encrypt the document. This list is itself encrypted with the user's public key, and normally, it can be decrypted only with the private key of the user who encrypted the document. However, this list is also encrypted with the recovery agent's public key. Consequently, it can be decrypted by the recovery agent's private key. Thereby, when a user's private key fails, you can use the recovery agent in order to recover the documents concerned.

a. Who are they?

The first administrator who logs on to a domain after the domain has been created becomes the recovery agent for that domain.
The first administrator that logs on to a workstation, or to a stand-alone server, becomes the recovery agent for the workstation or the server.

b. Recovering a document

A recovery agent decrypts a document using his/her private key:
- Either, you must copy the recovery agent's private key onto the computer on which you want to recover the encrypted document (you are strongly advised not to use this method for security reasons),
- Or, you must send the document that must be decrypted to the recovery agent, so that the recovery agent can use his/her private key that is located on its own machine.

If you decide to send the document to the recovery agent, then back up the document using the Windows 2000 backup utility, and then send the backup to the recovery agent, who can restore it on his/her own machine. Then, the recovery agent will be able to open the document transparently.

B. Security of IP network traffic

With Windows 2000, Microsoft allows you to encrypt the IP traffic that circulates on your LAN, or even across extended networks. The main objective of this feature is to provide security for data that circulates on a network that is not itself secure, like Internet for example.

Windows 2000 uses **IPSec** (*IP Security*) for this purpose. This is an open standard, and not a proprietary invention. Because of this, a Windows 2000 machine is able securely to communicate with any type of computer (client, server, or router) that runs IPSec.

☞ *IPSec is described in RFC 1825.*

1. Implementing IPSec

It is very simple to implement IPSec. You can implement IPSec, either machine-by-machine, or using group policies.

➢ Right-click **My Network Places** and then select **Properties**.

➢ Right-click the **Local Area Connection** for the network interface card on which you want to enable IP security.

➢ Select **Properties**, then select **Internet Protocol (TCP/IP)**, and click the **Properties** button.

➢ Then, click the **Advanced** button.

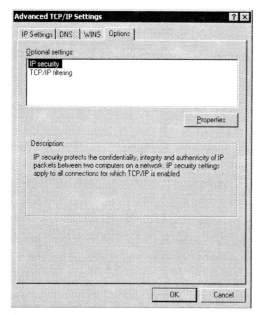

➢ Click the **Options** tab, then select **IP security** and click **Properties**.

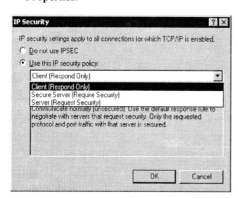

By default, IP security is not enabled. You can choose from three security levels:

Client (Respond Only)
This option allows IP traffic to circulate normally. Encrypted response is provided to clients that request it.

Secure Server (Require Security)
This option does not allow unsecured communication.

Server (Request Security)
This option implements encrypted messages, but accepts unencrypted client requests.

☞ *You can implement IPSec with the Group Policy snap-in. For this purpose use* **IP Security Policies on Active Directory** *that is located in* **Computer Configuration - Windows Settings - Security Settings**.

2. Example

The **Network Monitor** allows you to capture frames. This tool can be used to show how IPSec works. You can install Network Monitor as follows:

➢ Open the Control Panel, double-click the **Add/Remove Programs** icon, and then click the **Add/Remove Windows Components**, followed by the **Components** button.

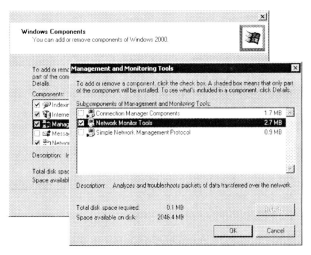

➢ Activate **Management and Monitoring Tools**, and then click the **Details** button.

➢ Then, activate the **Network Monitor Tools** check box, click **OK** and then **Next**.

When the installation has finished the **Network Monitor** program will be available in the **Administrative Tools** menu.

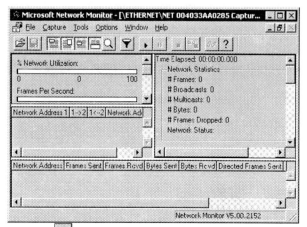

Click the ▶ button so as to start the capture. From now on, all the frames that your machine sends or receives will be captured.

☞ *The Network Monitor version that is supplied with Windows NT 4.0 or with Windows 2000 is restrained so that it will capture only the frames that are input or output by your computer. A complete version is available with SMS.*

The next step is to provoke IP traffic without having implemented IP security. You can do this by sending a message using the **net send** command (you can use NetBIOS on TCP for this purpose).

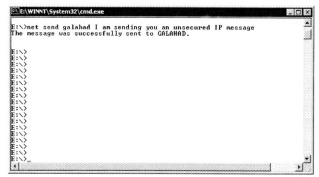

Galahad, the destination machine, then receives the following message:

> In the Network Monitor, click the button in order to stop the capture and view it.

> Look in the list of captured frames, and locate the frame that contains your message. This list entry should include the following four field:

```
LOCAL      SMB      C send message, from MERLIN to GALAHAD      MERLIN
```

> Double-click this frame so as to display its contents.

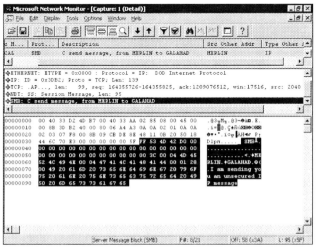

Note that the data was transferred in a clear format!

Your next step is to carry out the same operation, but this time encrypting the IP packets. In order to do this activate IP security, on both source and destination machines, such that only secured communication is accepted.

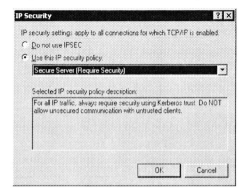

When you have repeated the previous capture and send operation, your network monitor should display a frame list similar to the following:

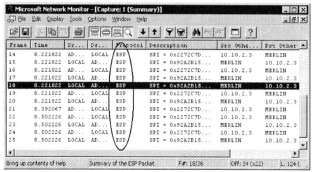

Note the name of the protocol: *ESP (Encapsulated Security Payload)*. This is the IPSec encapsulation protocol.

If you double-click one of these frames then the contents will appear as follows:

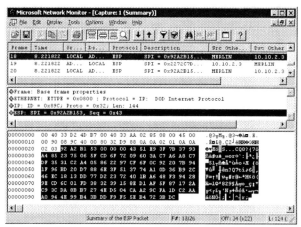

The IP traffic is secured.

C. Accounts and password security

You can define accounts and password security using group policies. Several templates are provided that offer different levels of security. You can modify existing templates, or you can create new ones, in order to meet your own specific security needs.

Once you have configured a template it is imported into the group policy so that it can be applied to users or to computers.

You can access security templates by creating an MMC and adding into it, the **Security Templates** snap-in.

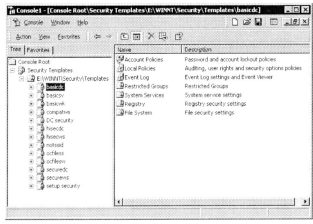

The security templates are text files that have **.inf** name extensions. They are located in the directory %systemroot%\security\templates.

☞ *You can display a description of the contents of a template by right-clicking the template concerned and selecting the Set Description option.*

In order to create a new template, right-click %systemroot%/security/template, and then select **New Template**.

Give a significant name to your new template, along with a description that will help you quickly to remember its purpose.

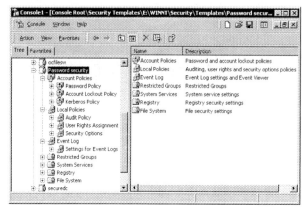

Finally, you must set up the security actions that your template must implement.

In order to apply a security model to a group policy, you must use either the **Active Directory Sites and Services** console, or the **Active Directory Users and Computers** console.

➢ Right-click the container for which you want to apply the policy.

➢ Select **Properties** then select the **Group Policy** tab.

➢ Select, or create a policy, then click the **Edit** button.

➢ Right-click **Security Settings** (under **Computer Configuration - Windows Settings**), then select **Import Policy**.

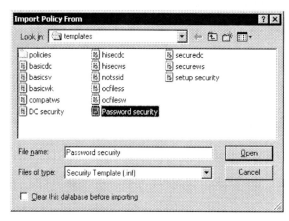

➢ Select the security template that you wish to import and then click the **Open** button.

1. Account lockout policy

Now that this chapter has described how to apply a security template to a group strategy, it will cover more closely the settings that must be applied to an account policy.

Account policies allows you to define the conditions in which user accounts will be locked out. When an account has been locked, no one can use it until it has been unlocked.

Account lockout duration

Activate the **Define this policy setting in the template** check box so that you will be able to define the length of time for which the account will be locked out.

If you want to retain full control over account lockouts, then do not activate this check box.

Reset account lockout counter after

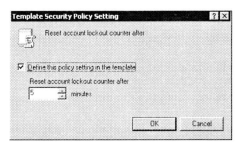

A counter and a duration are associated with the account lockout. The counter allows you to count the number of unsuccessful logon attempts. The duration, which is associated with the account lockout counter, allows you to define the time that must elapse before this counter is reset.

Suppose you define a policy that stipulates that an account must be locked out after 3 unsuccessful logon attempts, along with a reset of the account lockout counter after 5 minutes. In this case, if a user unsuccessfully tried to log on twice, then the user would have to wait for 5 minutes before the account lockout counter was reset. After this period has elapsed, the user will be able twice to try to logon again before being locked out once more. However, when the account is locked out, this value does not apply.

Account lockout threshold

In this dialog box, indicate the number of unsuccessful logon attempts before the account is locked out.

If a user reaches this number of consecutive unsuccessful logon attempts, then the user will receive a message saying that his/her account has been disabled and that the user must contact the administrator. In the properties of this account, the **Account is locked out** check box will no longer be grayed out, and will be activated.

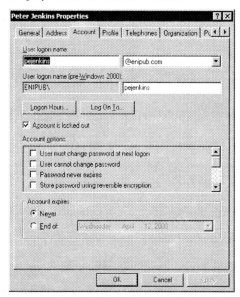

Before you unlock the account, check the user's identity along with the reasons for which the account was locked out. In order to unlock the account, deactivate the **Account is locked out** check box.

2. Password policy

Enforce password history
Maximum password age
Minimum password age
Minimum password length
Passwords must meet complexity requirements
Store password using reversible encryption for all users in the domain

Maximum password age

This setting allows you to indicate the time period for which a user's password will remain valid. When this period has elapsed, the user must change password.

Enforce password history

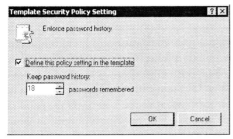

The purpose of stipulating that passwords must expire is to ensure that users change their passwords regularly, so that should a pirate discover a password, he/she will be unable to continue infiltrating the network with this user account. It is useful then, to ensure that when a user has to change password, the user cannot choose the same password again. For this purpose, you can keep a password history. In the example above, a user will not be able to re-use any of the user's last 18 passwords.

Minimum password age

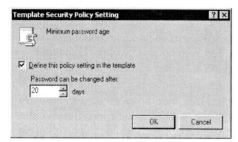

This setting indicates the period of time during which the users do not have to change their passwords. If you defined a policy that remembers former passwords, then, when the user changes password, he/she will not be able to use a password that is stored in the password history. However, there is nothing to stop the user from changing his/her password immediately afterwards and in this case, there is nothing to stop the user from re-using a former password. In order to prevent this, you can forbid users from modifying their passwords for x days. The value of x should be as close as possible to the number of days that must elapse before the password expires.

Minimum password length

Longer passwords are more difficult to guess. Remember that passwords are case sensitive.

Passwords must meet complexity requirements

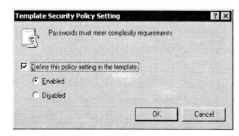

If you enable this setting then passwords must contain lower case and upper case characters, along with numbers or punctuation marks. A password cannot be the user's account name nor can it be the user's full name.

Store passwords using reversible encryption for all users in the domain

You must use this parameter if you have Macintosh clients who do not use the Microsoft client software. Macintosh clients cannot encrypt passwords by using the same method as that used by Windows 2000. Consequently, the password is stored in Active Directory, and the server can decrypt it so that it can compare it with the password that the client sends.

D. Audit

The audit is a system tool that allows you to log the events and the activities that are carried out by the system or the users that you want to monitor. Events can be audited when they are successful, and/or when they are unsuccessful.

The results of these audits are stored in the **Security** log of the **Event Viewer**. They provide information on the action that was carried out, they tell you by whom it was carried out, and they tell you whether the action was successful, or whether it was unsuccessful.

You can define an audit policy by defining a security template and then importing it into a group policy. Alternatively, you can define your audit policy directly in the group policy, using the **Active Directory Users and Computers** console. As audit policies must be applied computer by computer, then it is better to define a group policy for an organizational unit that contains the computers that must be audited (these are generally the servers).

➢ Open the console **Active Directory Users and Computers** console, and right-click the container to which you want to apply the audit policy.

➢ Select **Properties** and activate the **Group Policy** tab.

➢ Create a new policy, or select and existing one and then click the **Edit** button.

➢ Expand **Computer Configuration, Windows Settings, Security Settings, Local Policies,** and **Audit Policy.**

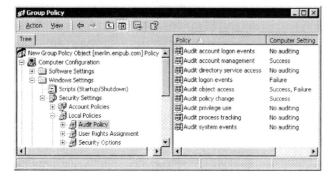

➢ Double-click the event that you want to audit.

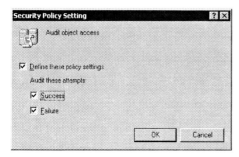

➢ Activate the **Success** check box, and/or the **Failure** check box.

☞ *Do not choose to audit all the types of event on success and on failure, as this will make it more difficult to extract relevant information from the Event Viewer.*

If you want to audit the actions that are carried out on your resources (such as files, folders, printers and drives), then you must activate the **Audit object access** policy, and set up the audit on the resource concerned. You can do this as follows:

➢ Edit the properties of the resource.

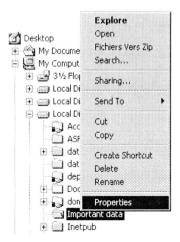

☞ *You can audit only files and folders that are located on NTFS partitions or volumes.*

➢ Select the **Security** tab, and click the **Advanced** button.

➢ Select the **Auditing** tab, and click the **Add** button.

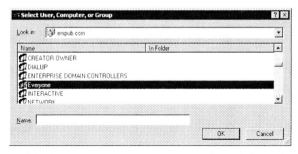

➢ Add the users that you want to audit and then click the **OK** button.

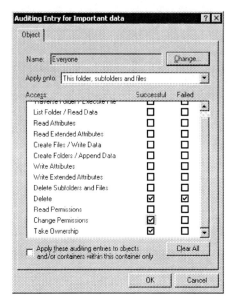

> Enable the actions that must be audited when they are successful, and/or when they fail, and then click **OK**.

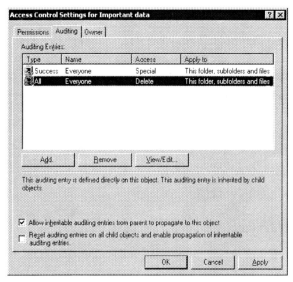

> Click **OK** in order to finish the operation.

 Important note: If you select only **Failure** for the **Audit object access** policy, then you will not be able to audit the events that are successful, even if you define them as such at resource level.

☞ *You can audit a printer for invoicing purposes, for example. You can audit the following actions for a printer: Print, Manage Printers, Manage Documents, Read Permissions, Change Permissions and Take Ownership.*

Auditing Active Directory

Audit policies allow you to audit actions that are carried out on the Active Directory database. In order to do this, set up the **Audit directory service access** event in the Audit Policy. Similarly to Audit object access, you must go into the directory database in order to specify the items that you want to audit.

➢ Open the **Active Directory Users and Computers** console.

➢ Right-click the object that you want to audit, and select **Properties**.

➢ Select the **Security** tab, and click the **Advanced** button.

➢ Select the **Auditing** tab, and click the **Add** button.

➢ Add the users that you want to audit (you are advised to add the **Everyone** group), and then click the **OK** button.

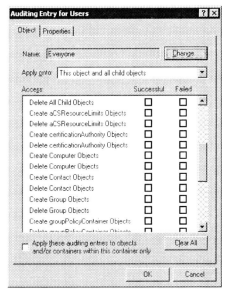

➢ Enable the check boxes that correspond to the events that you want to audit, and the click **OK** twice so as to confirm you choice.

Viewing the audited events

You can consult the audited events using the **Security** log of
the **Event Viewer**.

The 🔒 icon represents failure, and the 🔑 icon represents
success.

➢ Open the **Event Viewer** console that is situated in the
Administrative Tools menu.

➢ Click the **Security Log**. The list appears of all the actions
that have been audited.

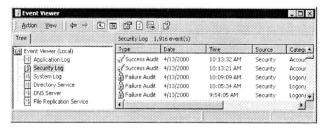

➢ Double-click the event for which you want to view the
details.

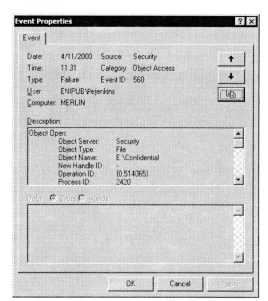

This dialog box shows information on the action concerned,
and provides the name of the user that carried it out. If you
click the ⬛ button, then you will take a copy of the
description that you can then insert into a text file.

```
Event Type:      Failure Audit
Event Source:    Security
Event Category:  Object Access
Event ID:        560
Date:            4/11/2000
Time:            11:31:16 AM
User:            ENIPUB\Pejenkins
Computer:        MERLIN
Description:
Object Open:
        Object Server:    Security
        Object Type:      File
        Object Name:      E:\Confidential
        New Handle ID:    -
        Operation ID:     {0,641816}
        Process ID:       1124
        Primary User Name:       Pejenkins
        Primary Domain: ENIPUB
        Primary Logon ID:        (0x0,0x108BF)
        Client User Name:        -
        Client Domain:  -
        Client Logon ID:         -
        Accesses        DELETE
                        READ_CONTROL
                        SYNCHRONIZE
                        ReadAttributes
```

In this description, note that the user Pejenkins of the ENIPUB domain, tried unsuccessfully to delete the folder e:\Confidential on 04/11/2000 at 11:31 on the computer that is called Merlin.

You define audit policies in order to monitor your network so as to counter any intrusions or incorrect usage. Consequently, it is important that you cover all the relevant events. Group policies allow you to set up the Event Viewer in order to:

- Stop the computer when the security log is full. This technique allows you to ensure that you will not miss any event audit.
- Set a maximum size for the security log, the system log and the application log.
- Set a time period, during which log data will be stored in the different logs.
- Define how you want to store the different logs (by overwriting events that are older than a certain number of days, by overwriting events when necessary, or by not overwriting events at all).

You can define these settings in the group policies in the **Event Log**, of the security settings.

E. User rights

You can use group policies, in order to modify certain rights on the operating system. These user rights include the rights to log on locally, change the system time, shut down the system, add workstations to domain and manage auditing and security log.

In order to modify these rights, select the container concerned, and then go into the group policies.

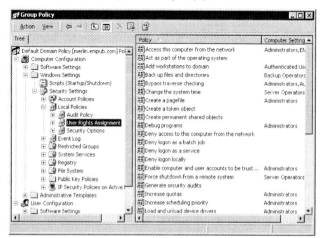

For example, suppose you want to grant the right to log on locally onto a domain controller to a specific user (by default, only the administrators and the operators have this right on domain controllers). In order to do this, select the organizational unit that represents the domain controllers, then modify this group policy in order to add the user concerned for the **Log on locally** right, in the **User Rights Assignment** that is situated under **Local Policies**.

F. Security options

In addition to account, password and auditing options, group policies allow you to add an extra security level using the **Security Options**, which are situated under the **Local Policies**. These security options allow you:
- not to display the log on name of the user who last logged on. This policy allows you to prevent users from guessing the name of the administrator, in the case where you renamed this account,
- to display a logon message title,
- not to allow unsigned drivers to be installed,
- automatically to log off users when their logon time expires,

- to prevent users from installing printers,
- to warn users that they must change their passwords, before their passwords expire,
- to rename the administrator account and the guest account,

and they also allow you to carry out many other actions.

G. Analyzing the security

When you have set up and applied your security templates, you cannot be completely sure that the actions that will be applied are really the ones that you wanted.

In order to check the security that is applied against the security that you planned, a snap-in is provided that allows you to carry out this diagnosis.

➤ Open an MMC. Then, add the **Security Configuration and analysis** snap-in.

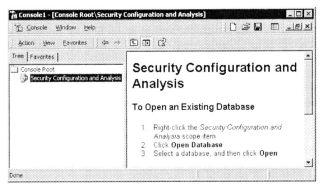

➤ Right-click **Security Configuration and Analysis** and select **Open Database**.

➤ Enter a name for your database. Then click **Open** and select the template that you want to analyze.

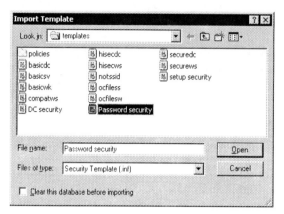

> Click the **Open** button.

> Right-click **Security Configuration and Analysis** and select **Analyze Computer Now**.

> Enter a name for your log file, into which the analysis results will be stored, and then click **OK**. The security analysis can then begin:

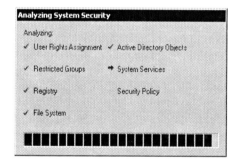

> ➤ The result appears in your console:

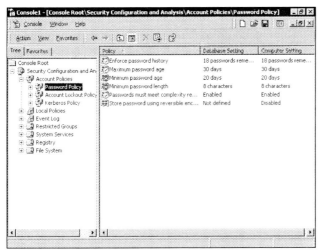

The difference between the status of your computer and the settings that are required by your template, is shown for each of the elementary policies. A ▓ symbol indicates that your computer setting is different from that of the template, and a ▓ symbol indicates that your computer setting is the same as that of the template.

If the security that is applied to your computer is not the one that you wanted, then right-click **Security Configuration and Analysis** and select **Configure Computer Now**. The system will then apply your security template as you intended.

Labs

To be absolutely sure that you have assimilated this chapter, work through the corresponding labs. These are set out from page 671 to page 677.

☒ EFS encryption.

☒ IPSec.

☒ Account policies.

☒ Analysing security.

☒ Audit policy.

Assessing your skills

Try the following questions if you think you know this chapter well enough.

EFS encryption

1 Which method can you use on an NTFS partition or volume in order to enhance the security of files or folders that are located on a computer that runs Windows 2000?   ❏
....

2 What does EFS mean?   ❏
....

3 What is the difference between symmetric encryption and asymmetric encryption?   ❏
....
....
....
....

4 Is it possible to encrypt a document that is compressed?   ❏
....
....
....

5 Which command prompt utility allows you to encrypt and to decrypt a set of files or folders?   ❏
....

6 After having encrypted a document, a user can no longer open it. How can the user recover the information in this document?   ❏
....
....
....
....
....
....

Traffic security

7 You want to use the Internet over long distances in such a way that your company's roaming users will be able securely to connect to your company's network. Which method will you use so as to secure the traffic, given that the remote access server is a Windows 2000 Advanced Server, and that all the remote users work with Windows 2000 Professional?   ❏
....

Security using group policies

8   You wish to configure the security on all the domain
controllers in your domain identically. Which method will you
use for this purpose?

....
....
....
....
....
....
....

9   You wish to monitor the actions that are carried out on
objects in the Active Directory database. How will you do
this?

....
....
....
....
....
....
....
....
....

10   Which tool allows you to monitor audited events?

....
....

Results

Check your answers on pages 442 to 443. Count one point
for each correct answer.

Number of points | /10 |

For this chapter you need to have scored at least 8 out of 10.
Look at the list of key points that follows. Pick out the ones
with which you have had difficulty and work through them
again in this chapter before moving on to the next.

Key points of the chapter

☐   EFS encryption.

☐   Traffic security.

☐   Security using group policies.

Solutions

EFS encryption

1   Which method can you use on an NTFS partition or volume in order to enhance the security of files or folders that are located on a computer that runs Windows 2000?

Document encryption using EFS.

2   What does EFS mean?

Encrypting File System.

3   What is the difference between symmetric encryption and asymmetric encryption?

With symmetric encryption, the same key is used in order to encrypt a document and to decrypt it. With asymmetric encryption, different keys are used in order to encrypt a document and to decrypt it.

4   Is it possible to encrypt a document that is compressed?

If you specify that a compressed document must be encrypted, then it will be automatically decompressed before it is encrypted.

5   Which command prompt utility allows you to encrypt and to decrypt a set of files or folders?

*The **cipher.exe** command.*

6   After having encrypted a document, a user can no longer open it. How can the user recover the information in this document?

Apparently, the user is unable to open this encrypted document, because the user's private key is damaged. In order to solve this problem, the user must send the document to a recovery agent (this is the first administrator who logged on to the domain). The recovery agent can decrypt the document using his/her own key.

Traffic security

7   You want to use the Internet over long distances in such a way that your company's roaming users will be able securely to connect to your company's network. Which method will you use so as to secure the traffic, given that the remote access server is a Windows 2000 Advanced Server, and that all the remote users work with Windows 2000 Professional?

IPSec allows you to secure all your IP traffic.

Security using group policies

8   You wish to configure the security on all the domain controllers in your domain identically. Which method will you use for this purpose?

The most effective method is to create a security template for your specific needs. Then, you must associate this template with the group policy that is applied to the OU that contains all the domain controllers. In order to check that this template meets your needs you must use the Security configuration and analysis snap-in.

9   You wish to monitor the actions that are carried out on objects in the Active Directory database. How will you do this?

Select the OU that contains your domain controllers, and use group policies in order to configure the Audit directory service access setting for success and failure. Then go into the Active Directory Users and Computers console, right-click the objects that you want to audit, select Properties, activate the Security tab, click the Advanced button, activate the Auditing tab, and indicate the users that you want to monitor. In order to ensure that you do not miss any actions, you must add the Everyone group.

10   Which tool allows you to monitor audited events?

The Security log in the Event Viewer.

Prerequisites for this chapter

☒ General networking knowledge.

Objectives

At the end of this chapter, you will be able to:

☒ Install and configure a server and DHCP clients.

☒ Define the new features that are offered by the Windows 2000 DHCP service.

☒ Install and configure a WINS server and WINS clients.

☒ Install and configure an Internet/intranet server.

☒ Configure a Windows 2000 server as a remote access server in a VPN.

☒ Configure incoming and outgoing calls.

☒ Describe ths interconnection solutions that you can use with Windows 2000.

☒ Describe and implement remote access security.

☒ Implement a RADIUS authentication server.

☒ Start up the Windows 2000 Telnet service.

Contents

Network services

A. Dynamic Host Configuration Protocol

In the preceding chapters, you will have noticed the main difficulty that you meet when you implement TCP/IP on a network of any reasonable size. Each machine must be perfectly configured, and the risk of conflicting addresses will always be present. Another point that is even more important is that you must change the addresses of portable machines each time that you move them to another network.

The DHCP protocol, which is defined in the RFC 1533, 1533, 1534, 1541 and 1542, allows you centrally to configure the machines in a network. It does this by providing the local network with a server that is able to supply the client machines with their TCP/IP settings. These settings include:
- IP address,
- Subnet mask,
- Default gateway,
- Addresses of name servers (NetBIOS/WINS or Internet/DNS),
- NetBIOS node type (the way in which a network interface card resolves a NetBIOS name into an IP address),
- Internet domain name.

This technique reduces the risk of conflicting addresses. In addition, when you use DHCP you no longer have to reconfigure your portable computers each time they are used in another network.

In addition, when you configure an IP workstation you need activate only one check box, as the server provides all the IP settings.

The administrator can easily find out the addresses that have been allocated to DHCP clients. The addresses are allocated according to a **lease** that can run either for a limited time period, or for an unlimited time period. Each machine keeps the same address until the end of the lease, and will renew the lease with the same address if this address is available.

The following machines can be DHCP clients:
- Windows 2000 Professional, and Server versions,
- Windows NT, Server and Workstation,
- Windows 95,
- MS-DOS 3.0 Client,
- Windows for Workgroups 3.11.

Network services

Implementation issues

You can search for a DHCP server using a broadcast. You must have one DHCP server per segment, unless you use a DHCP relay agent. It is advisable that you have two DHCP servers available, for fault tolerance reasons.

☞ *Some routers can let through DHCP broadcasts that are based on BOOTP (RFC n°1542). In this case, a DHCP server can provide addresses to machines throughout the whole network.*

Address query mechanism

The client must request the lease, which it will obtain in a number of phases. But, how can the client communicate with a DHCP server in order to obtain its IP settings, when you need IP so as to be able to do this?

This problem is solved in a very simple way. In the first phase, the user initializes a restricted version of TCP/IP that allows the user simply to send a **broadcast** (255.255.255.255) to all the DHCP servers that are present on the local network. This broadcast contains a lease query for the different IP settings.

In the second phase, the DHCP servers that are present receive the query and send offers to the client, if the DHCP clients have address scopes that are suitable for the client. The client will then select the first offer that it receives, and broadcast a message that selects the offer concerned. All the DHCP servers will receive this message. Those DHCP having made offers that were not selected will then withdraw their offers so that they will be able to propose these settings to another machine. The DHCP server that made the offer that was accepted will send to the client by broadcast, the configuration settings, along with a confirmation of the lease. The client will then be able to complete its IP configuration and use all the network features just like any ordinary machine.

The client will try to renew its lease when half of the lease period has elapsed. Then, if necessary, it will try again after 87,5% of the lease period has elapsed.

If the DHCP server is able to renew the client settings, then it will send a new confirmation to the client.

Whilst the lease has not expired, the machine can continue to use its IP settings. If the lease does expire, then the client must make a new lease query. If this new lease query is refused, then the machine can no longer use TCP/IP.

It must be noted that this approach is very convenient for portable machine, as it allows them to change networks, and hence to change DHCP servers, and to have their IP configuration automatically modified upon expiry of the preceding lease.

Lease period
Why is it useful to provide leases with limited durations? These types of leases are useful for machines that frequently move from one network to another, as this makes available addresses that can be used by other machines. In this case, these freed addresses will be available to be offered to other machines upon expiry of the lease.

However, the IPCONFIG or the WINIPCFG utility allows you to force the freeing of the lease, or to force a renewal query for the lease.

1. Installing DHCP server

➢ On the Windows 2000 server, go into the Control Panel and double-click the **Add/Remove Programs** icon.

➢ Click the **Add/Remove Windows Components** icon, click the **Components** button, select **Networking Services**, and then click the **Details** button.

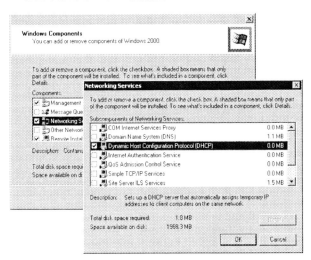

➢ Enable **Dynamic Host Configuration Protocol (DHCP)** check box, and click the **OK** button.

➢ Click the **Next** button in order to launch the installation.

When you have installed the DHCP server service, you can start creating address scopes that will be attributed to clients who ask for them. However, before clients will be able to obtain IP configurations from a DHCP server, the DHCP server must first be authorized in the Active Directory to attribute IP leases.

2. Authorizing a DHCP server

It is important to control the machines that are able to act as DHCP servers, and consequently to control the machines that are able to attribute IP leases that could conflict with the IP addresses of the other DHCP servers. For this purpose, a member of the **Enterprise Admins** group (in the root domain of the forest) must authorize DHCP servers to attribute IP configuration to clients. In addition, this approach allows the administrator to control the IP addresses that will be distributed to clients.

The following steps allow you to authorize a DHCP server in Active Directory:

➢ Log on as a member of the Enterprise Admins group, open the Administrative tools menu and launch the DHCP console. Alternatively, you can right-click the **DHCP** icon, select the **Run as** option, and then enter the account name and password of one of the members of the Enterprise Admins group.

➢ If your server does not appear in the **Tree** pane, right-click **DHCP**, and then select the **Add Server** option. Enter the name of your server and then click the **OK** button.

➢ Select your server under **Tree**. An 🗔 icon (which shows a red arrow pointing downwards) indicates that your server is not authorized to attribute IP leases.

➢ Right-click **DHCP** and select **Manage Authorized Servers.**

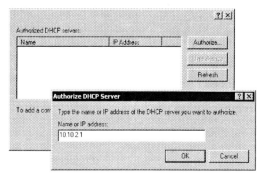

➢ Click the **Authorize** button and enter either the name of the DHCP server that you want to authorize, or its IP address. Then click the **OK** button.

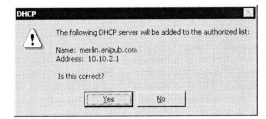

➢ If the information is correct, then click the **Yes** button.

➢ The icon that appears before the name of the DHCP server then appears as follows  (a green arrow pointing upwards).

☞ *A DHCP server sends broadcasts regularly so as to check that the authorization status has not changed*

Your next step is to configure the IP settings that must be attributed to the DHCP clients.

3. Creating address scopes

An address scope contains the IP addresses that must be allocated to the client, the subnet mask, the lease period of this scope, along with any addresses that must be excluded, if any machines already use addresses that are contained in this scope.
If there are several DHCP servers in the network, then they must not have scopes that overlap each other or else the dynamic address allocation could offer conflicting addresses.
You can create an address scope as follows:

➢ Go into the **DHCP** console, right-click the name of the DHCP server, and select **New Scope**.

➢ Click the **Next** button, and give a name and a description that corresponds to your scope.

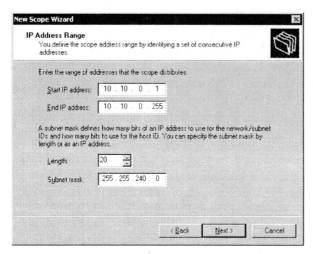

> ➢ Enter the start address and the end address of your scope. By default, a mask is assigned that corresponds to the class of your addresses. However, you can change this mask so that you will be able to create subnets. In this case, indicate the number of bits that you want to use for your mask. Alternatively, you can enter the value of the mask directly in decimal.

> ➢ Click the **Next** button.

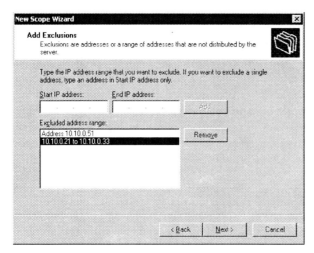

> ➢ Enter any addresses or address ranges that you want to exclude from your scope, and then click the **Next** button.

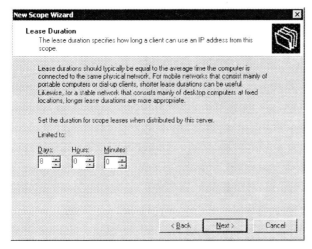

➢ Indicate the duration of your scope, and then click the **Next** button.

☞ *Remember that a DHCP client will try to renew its IP lease half way through its lease period, and again when 87,5% of the lease period has elapsed, if it was unable to release its lease half way through the lease period. Consequently, the longer the lease, the less traffic that will be generated by these lease renewal queries. On the other hand, you must be careful net to set the lease period too long if you have a lot of mobile clients. In any case, lease renewal queries do not generate a very high volume of network traffic!*

The next screen asks you whether you want to continue your configuration by specifying further scope options now, or whether you prefer to configure these options later.

➢ Enable **No, I will configure these options later**, and then click the **Next** button, followed by the **Finish** button.

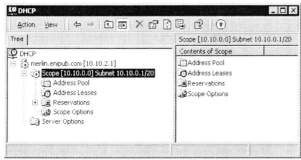

By default, when you create a scope, your scope is not activated. In order to make your scope operational, you must activate it by right-clicking it and then selecting **Activate**. Until you carry out this operation, the DHCP clients will not be able to obtain an IP lease. When you activate the scope, its icon changes from 🖳 to 🖳.

☞ *When you install the DHCP service, two new groups are created. The **DHCP Users** group allows its members to access the information in the DHCP console in read-only mode. The **DHCP Administrators** group allows its members to administer the DHCP server.*

a. Adding options to a scope

This chapter has described how you can attribute a standard IP configuration to DHCP clients. However, it is also useful to provide DHCP clients with other settings, such as their default gateway address, and the addresses of their DNS and WINS servers.

You can do this in two ways:
- Either, you can configure identical settings for all the scopes.
- Or, you can configure different settings for each scope.

b. Creating specific options for each scope

One of the scope options is the IP address of the gateway.

➤ Right-click the **Scope Options** folder that is situated under the scope folder concerned, and select **Configure Options**.

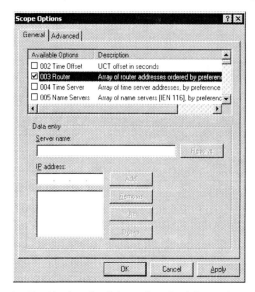

➤ Enable the check box of each of the options that you wish to add, and then indicate its value.

c. Creating global options for all the scopes

Unlike the scope options, the global options, or **Server Options** apply to all the scopes that are created on the server.

➢ Right-click the **Server Options** folder and select **Configure Options**.

➢ Enable the check box of each of the options that you wish to add, and then indicate its value.

d. Principal DHCP options

Option	Role
003 Router	Default gateway address.
006 DNS Servers	Addresses of name servers.
015 DNS Domain Name	Name of Internet domain.
028 Broadcast Address	Allows you to specify a broadcast address.
033 Static Route Option	Allows you to distribute static routes to clients. For this option, you must specify pairs of addresses. The first address of the pair indicates the network that must be reached, and the second address of the pair the interface address of the router by which you must pass.
035 ARP Cache Timeout	Lifetime of ARP mappings.
044 WINS/NBNS Servers	Address of WINS server(s).
046 WINS/NBT Node Type	NetBIOS node type.

Some options of these options have been introduced by the DHCP RFC n°2132 implementation. These new options include the means of indicating one or more default Web servers to clients, and of listing the addresses of SMTP, POP3, or NNTP servers that are available for DHCP clients.

e. Reserving a specific address for a client

If you want a client to obtain a specific IP address, you can reserve an address for the client using the clients MAC (physical) address. You can do this as follows:

➢ Right-click the **Reservations** folder that is situated under the scope from which you want to reserve an address, and then select **New Reservation**.

➤ You must enter the following items: the IP address that you want to reserve, the MAC address that is defined on 48 bits with Ethernet, a reservation name and a description. Note that you can specify whether this reservation will be used for a DHCP and/or for a BOOTP client.

➤ By right-clicking this reservation, you can configure options that are specific to this address.

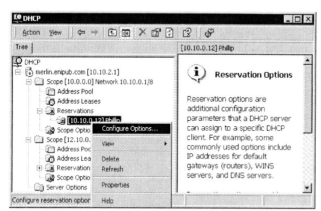

☞ You can find out the MAC address of a machine by entering **ipconfig /all** in the command prompt.

f.   Lease renewal or freeing by the user

You can force your computer to free its lease. In order to do this on a Windows 2000 or Windows NT machine, you can use the **Ipconfig/Release** command. In order to do this on a Windows 98, you can run the WINIPCFG.EXE program and click the **Release All** button, which is provided for this purpose.

You can use the **Ipconfig/Renew** command in order to obtain a new IP lease.

4. Configuring a client machine to use DHCP

a.   Windows 2000 machines

➢ Edit the TCP/IP properties of the machine.

➢ Enable the **Obtain an IP address automatically** option. Note also that you can manually enter the IP address of a DNS server, even if you obtain your IP configuration via a DHCP server. In order to obtain the IP address of the DNS server using the scope options of the DHCP server, select **Obtain DNS server address automatically**.

☞ *The TCP/IP properties that are manually defined on the client machines take priority over the DHCP options.*

b. Windows NT machines

➢ Go into **Network Neighborhood** and select the **Protocols** tab.

➢ Select **TCP/IP Protocol** and click the **Properties** button.

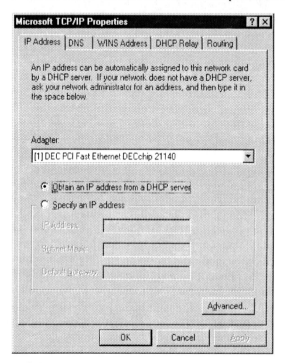

➢ Select **Obtain an IP address from a DHCP server**.

c. Windows 98 machines

➢ Go into the **Properties** of **Network Neighborhood**.

➢ Double-click the TCP/IP protocol that corresponds to the local network interface card, or select TCP/IP protocol and click the **Properties** button.

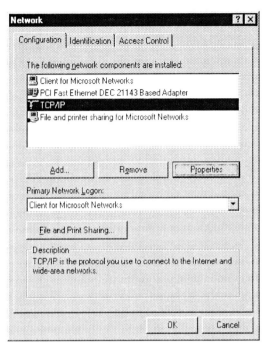

➢ In the dialog box that appears, select **Obtain an IP address automatically**, and click **OK**.

Network Services

> Then, restart the machine as the system requests you to. The machine will request its first lease upon initialization of TCP/IP.

d. MSDOS machines or network client 3.0 on MSDOS

You can also configure network client 3.0 on MSDOS as a DHCP client.

Before you can do this, you must first install TCP/IP protocol. In order to install TCP/IP protocol, you must first rename the **oemtcpip.inf** file as **oemsetup.inf**.

> Launch the network client installation program from a floppy disk that contains a copy of the \Clients\Msclient\Disks\Disk1 directory from the CD-ROM: Windows NT Server 4.

> Specify the default directory for the installation (for example **C:\NET**) and then select your network interface card. You can then install TCP/IP.

> The list of available protocols includes **NWLink IPX**, **Microsoft NetBEUI** and **Microsoft TCP/IP**. Select **Microsoft TCP/IP**.

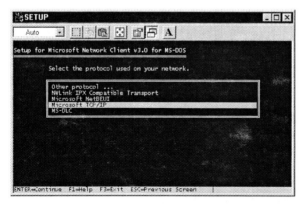

> Then, you must specify the location of the **oemsetup.inf** file that contains information on the protocol that must be installed. Choose the directory that is proposed by the diskette.

➢ You can then set up the TCP/IP protocol:

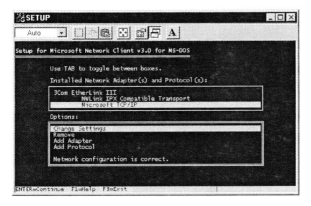

Finally, the following screen appears:

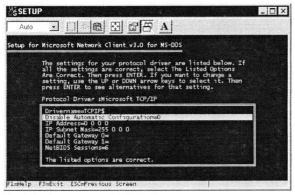

By default, you are a DHCP client.

➢ Validate the configuration in order to complete the installation.

5. Processing DHCP queries

a. Queries

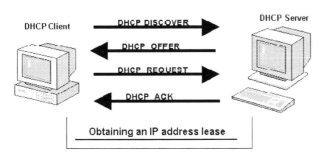

Obtaining an IP address lease

DHCP Discover

Strange as it may seem, even when a client has no TCP/IP settings, it will still execute a limited version of these protocols in order to obtain these configuration setting.

The DHCP client broadcasts a first frame so as to look for the DHCP server. This frame is called **DHCP DISCOVER**.

The client sends a broadcast to look for the DHCP Server because it does not know which machine it is: physically, this broadcast frame is sent to the MAC address FF.FF.FF.FF.FF.FF, and logically it is sent to the address 255.255.255.255.

As a sender, the client identifies itself with its own physical MAC address, and with a logical IP address of 0.0.0.0, whilst the client does not have its IP address.

☞ *When a DHCP client renews its lease before it expires, it can work with all its settings and it does not need to send a broadcast.*

☞ *The client uses the UDP protocol in order to send the broadcast. This protocol allows you to connect to UDP port 67 (BOOTP server), as a BOOTP client (UDP port 68).*

This process is carried out each time that it is needed. Notably, it is used in the following circumstances:

– When TCP/IP is initialized for the first time on a DHCP client,
– When the DHCP client requests a specific IP address, and this address is refused. In this case the DHCP client must send a new Discover in order to find another server,
– When the client's lease expires and the client must request a new one.

DHCP Offer

All the DHCP servers in the network must make an offer to the client, provided that it has IP addresses that are available for the IP network number that is requested.

☞ *The scope is chosen according to the origin of the IP packet. For example, for a server that has several IP addresses, then the scope is chosen according to the IP network number that is associated with the network interface card that received the broadcast. In the case of a DHCP Relay Agent, the scope will be chosen according to the agent's IP address.*

This is the **DHCP OFFER** step. In principle, the client can choose to take up the offer of any of the servers. However, the client will finally proceed with the first offer that it receives.

The DHCP servers transmit the following information in this frame:
- The client's MAC address,
- The IP address that is offered,
- The associated mask,
- A lease duration,
- The DHCP Server's own IP address.

☞ *It must be noted that this frame is also broadcast on the network and that the client's MAC address is not used directly.*

If none of these attempts are successful, then it tries again every 5 minutes.

DHCP Request

The client responds to one of the offers from one of the servers. It does this by sending a broadcast in which it indicates that it accepts the offer. This is called a **DHCP REQUEST**. The client sends this broadcast so as to inform all the DHCP servers of the choice that it has made. In fact, the client chooses the first offer that it receives.

Following this broadcast, each of the DHCP servers whose offer has not been chosen by the client withdraws its offer.

DHCP Acknowledgement

Finally, when the DHCP Server receives the DHCP request from the client accepting the offer that was made by the Server, it confirms the lease by sending a **DHCP ACK** (or **DHCP Acknowledgement**). The DHCP Acknowledgement stipulates the lease duration, and it includes the DHCP options if these are necessary.

☞ *DHCP ACK must not be confused with DHCP NACK. A DHCP NACK is sent by a DHCP Server in order to withdraw TCP/IP settings that have been leased. For example, the DHCP Server will do this when the lease expires, or if the client has moved to a different physical network. Thereby, the server no longer acknowledges the lease that it allocated previously. Then, the client must restart the lease query process, as the client no longer has an IP address.*

The client can now set up its TCP/IP using all the information that it has received.

This information is stored in HKEY_LOCAL_MACHINE\ System\CurrentControlSet\Services*Network_Interface_card _name*\Parameters\Tcpip.

On Windows NT, you can view these settings using the **ipconfig /all** *command.*

b. Renewing a lease

At the beginning

At the beginning of the lease, a DHCP client will try to renew its lease with the same server, using the same settings that it obtained previously, making a **DHCP REQUEST**.

If the request is unsuccessful, then the client will continue to use these settings until the lease expires.

Half way through the duration

When half of the lease duration has elapsed, the DHCP client will try to renew its lease, before it is no longer able to use its IP settings. In this way, the client can exchange frames directly, without having to make costly broadcasts on the network.

This approach greatly simplifies the DHCP query procedure, as the client can make its renewal query by sending a **DHCP REQUEST** directly to the server with which it set up its current lease.

If the server is available, it responds by returning a **DHCP ACK** acknowledgement, along with any settings that may have changed.

If the server is not available, then the client will not be able to renew its lease. However, the client will be able to continue to work with its IP settings until its lease expires.

7/8ths of the way through the duration

If the client was unable to renew its lease half way through its duration, then it will make a final attempt to renew its lease when 87.5% of the duration has elapsed. In this case, the client will send its DHCP query to all the DHCP servers. The client no longer sends its request specifically to its previous DHCP server, as this server did not renew its lease upon the previous request.

Thus, a **DHCP REQUEST** message is broadcast in order to contact any server that is available.

If the DHCP lease is not renewed before the end of the lease, then the client will lose its IP settings and it will no longer be able to use IP communication.

You can monitor the IP leasing mechanism by running the **Network Monitor** so as to capture the frames that are exchanged between the DHCP client and the DHCP server.

6. New features offered by the Windows 2000 DHCP service

a. Dynamic update of DNS servers

When a DHCP server allocates an IP address to a machine, then, provided that the DNS server supports the dynamic update protocol, it will inform the DNS server so that this server can update the DNS Server database.

By default, the client updates the host name "A" resource record, and the DHCP server updates the "PTR" resource record.

When the lease expires, the DHCP server deletes both of these records in the DNS database.

➢ Go into the DHCP console, right-click the DHCP server name and select **Properties**. Then activate the **DNS** tab.

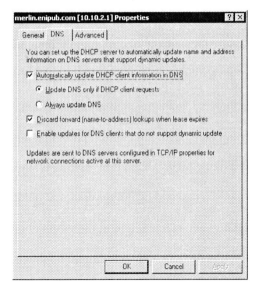

➢ Enable the **Automatically update DHCP client information in DNS** check box (this check box is enabled by default).

– The **Update DNS only if DHCP client requests** option means that the DHCP server will update the PTR record, and the DHCP client will update the "A" record.

– The **Always update DNS** option indicates that the DHCP server will update both records (A and PTR).

☞ *If you disable this dynamic update feature, then the DHCP clients will try to update both A and PTR records. However, if the DHCP client computer updates the PTR record, then the DHCP server will not be able to delete it. This can result in a build-up of old, out-of-date records in the DNS database.*

☞ *The clients that are allowed to update their DNS records are those for which the extension 81 appears in the DHCP query frame. Windows 2000 DHCP clients have frames with this extension.*

b. Superscopes

Superscopes, or global scopes, allow you to attribute IP addresses from several logical subnets, to DHCP clients that are situated on the same physical segment. Thereby, you can administer all the scopes that belong to the global scope, in the same way as you would administer a single scope. Superscopes are useful when you do not have enough addresses for a subnet.

You can configure a superscope as follows:

➤ In the **DHCP** console, right-click the server name, and select **New Superscope**.

➤ Enter a name for your superscope, and then click the **Next** button.

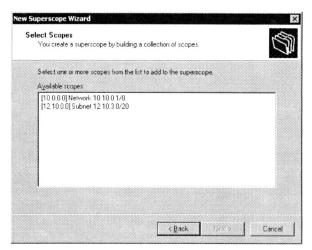

➤ Select the scopes that must be included in the superscope. You can use the Ctrl key in order to help you select to select several scopes.

➤ Click the **Next** button followed by **Finish**.

Once your superscope has been created, you can add new scopes to it at any time by simply right-clicking it and selecting **New Scope**.

When you delete a superscope you do not delete the scopes that it contains.

c.   Multicast scopes

The Windows 2000 DHCP service allows you to use class D multicast addresses (from 224.0.0.0 to 239.255.255.255). This type of address is used by videoconference type applications. The objective is to broadcast information to different clients by sending a single message. This approach also allows you to avoid using broadcasts that needlessly use the resources of all the machines.
You can create a multicast scope as follows:

➢ Go into the **DHCP** console, and right-click the DHCP server name.

➢ Select **New Multicast Scope**.

➢ Click the **Next** button and enter a name and a description for your multicast scope. Then click the **Next** button.

➢ Enter the start IP address and the end IP address, and then click the **Next** button.

➢ Indicate any addresses that you wish to exclude from this scope, and then click the **Next** button.

➢ Specify the duration of your multicast scope lease, and click **Next**. Then select the **Yes** option in order to activate your multicast scope.

➢ Click the **Next** button, followed by the **Finish** button.

☞ *In its properties, you can indicate a time to live for your multicast scope.*

☞ *Multicast runs on IGMP (Internet Group Management Protocol) protocol.*

d.   Option classes

Option classes allow you to customize the attribution of IP settings. They allow you to group together clients according to their computers, or simply according to common needs. There are two types of option class:
- Classes that are defined by the vendor. These classes manage the DHCP options that are attributed to clients with a common vendor type.
- Classes that are define by the user. These classes manage DHCP options that are attributed to clients with a common configuration. You must manually configure this type of class on the client machine.
Classes are defined using an identifier.
You can find out all the DHCP Class IDs that are authorized for an adapter by entering the command **ipconfig /showclassid**.

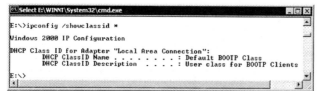

You can apply specific options for a class as follows:

➢ Right-click the **scope option** folder for the scope to which you want to apply a specific class, and then select **Configure Options**.

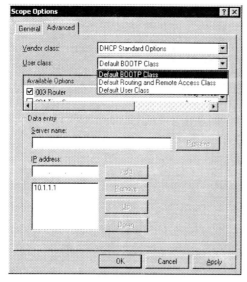

➢ Activate the **Advanced** tab and then select the vendor class for which you want to apply the option. Indicate the option.

➢ Indicate the user class for which you set up the options on the client machines. In order to help you with this choice, you can use the following command:
ipconfig / setclassid *connection_name class_name*.

e. Automatic private IP addressing

As with Windows 98, Windows 2000 allows you to allocate an IP address to a workstation without having to manually configure the workstation, and without even having a DHCP server. In order to do this, you must configure the client as a DHCP client in the TCP/IP properties. If no DHCP server responds then Windows 2000 will automatically apply an IP address from the range 169.254.0.1 – 169.254.255.254. With such an address, a machine can communicate with all the other machines to which IP addresses have been allocated using the same method. In order to prevent the same address being allocated to several machines, when a machine generates an address in this way it broadcasts it. Then, if no computer responds then the machine will apply the address. The DHCP client will continue to use this address for as long as it does not detect a DHCP server on the network.

☞ *Automatic private addressing provides only an IP address and its mask. It does not provide any other information. Because of this, clients that have obtained such an address are able to communicate only with machines that have received an address by the same mechanism, and that are on the same network segment.*

☞ *You can use the registry in order to deactivate the allocation of an automatic private address. In order to do this you must reset the **IPAutoconfigurationEnable** value of the **REG_DWORD** type, to zero. This value is located under **KKLM\SYSTEM\CurrentControlSet\Services\Tcpip\Parameters\Interfaces\Network_Interface_Card_GUID**.*

Network services

7. DHCP relay agent

DHCP clients obtain a lease by broadcasting for a DHCP
server. If you have several network segments that are
separated by routers, then you must normally have one
DHCP server per segment. However, you can overcome this
constraint by having a server that acts as a DHCP relay
agent.

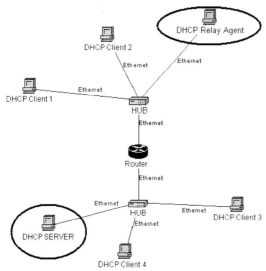

A DHCP relay agent must be configured with a static IP
address, and it must know the IP address of the DHCP
server. It interprets the DHCP broadcasts that are sent by
the clients, in order to route then to the DHCP server. The
DHCP server knows from which scope it must select an
address to be returned to the DHCP relay agent, as the
server knows the agent's IP address. When the DHCP relay
agent receives this address it broadcasts it on its segment.
In this way, the DHCP relay agent is able to attribute an IP
address that corresponds to its own IP address scope.

You can implement a DHCP relay agent as follows:

➢ Open the **Routing and Remote Access** console.

➢ If the routing is not active on your server, then right-click
the name of your server and select **Configure and Enable
Routing and Remote Access**.

➢ Select **Manually configured server** and then click the **Next**
button.

➢ Click the **Finish** button in order to start the service.

➢ Expand the icon that represents your server, followed by the **IP Routing** folder.

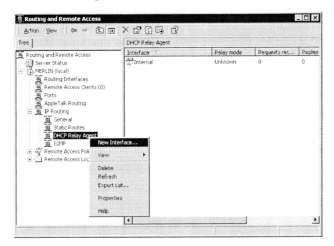

➢ Right-click **DHCP Relay Agent**, and select **New Interface**.

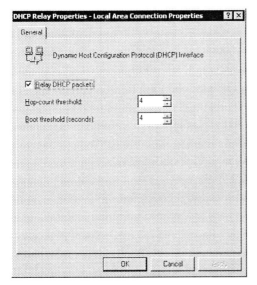

➢ Enable the **Relay DHCP packets** check box.

☞ *If the **DHCP Relay Agent** does not appear under IP Routing, then right-click the **General** folder and select New Routing Protocol. Select DHCP Relay Agent and click the OK button.*

Now, you must indicate the DHCP server to which the agent must relay the packets.

➢ Right-click the **DHCP Relay Agent** icon, and then select **Properties**.

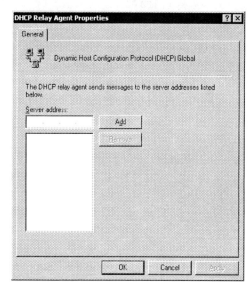

➢ Enter the address of the DHCP Server(s).

B. Windows Internet Name Service

The WINS service (NetBIOS name server, or NBNS), resolves NetBIOS names into IP addresses. This service is an Internet standard, and it has been part of the Microsoft implementation of TCP/IP for a long time. Each Windows machine has a NetBIOS name and a host name. Therefore, you must not confuse the WINS service with the DNS service. By default, the host names correspond to the NetBIOS names of the machines. However, this is not compulsory, and these two services are complementary.

When a Windows machine starts up, it registers its name with its WINS server. Then, each WINS client can call the server so as to resolve a NetBIOS name into an IP address. For example, this happens when you start Network Neighborhood on Windows NT, or My Network Places on Windows 2000. The WINS service allows you to install DNS very easily. If DNS is unable to resolve a name, it queries the WINS server so as to resolve it. As all clients automatically register with WINS, then DNS is able to resolve all names, and you do not need manually to provide this information to the DNS server. However, it must be noted that this feature is valid only in an environment in which the machines run with NetBIOS (these are essentially Microsoft machines, and Unix machines that use SAMBA).

When a machine registers its name with its WINS server, then the WINS server consults its database so as to check that another machine has not already registered with this name. The WINS server returns to the client, a message confirming the registration. This confirmation message contains a value called TTL (*Time To Live)* that indicates for how long the registration will be valid. If the client does not renew its registration before the TTL elapses, then it will be deleted from the WINS server database. Similarly, when a WINS client shuts down, it informs the WINS server so that the Wins server can delete the registration. By default, the client renews its name when half of the TTL has elapsed. Also by default, the TTL is set at six days, and the client renews its name after three days. When the client renews its name, it receives from the server a new confirmation message with a TTL of six days.

When a client needs to resolve a NetBIOS name into an IP address (after entering a **net view**, or a **net use** command) it must first consult its local NetBIOS cache. If the name does not appear in its cache (because the name has not previously been resolved), then it must interrogate its WINS server. If the WINS server cannot answer the query, then the client will send a broadcast so as to resolve the name.

Although the Windows 2000 WINS service is an improved version, it is compatible with pre-Windows 2000 versions. In fact, in an environment that is entirely composed of Windows 2000 components, the main name resolution method is DNS, which runs dynamically. In addition, this book indicated at the beginning, NetBIOS is no longer compulsory with Windows 2000, and it is quite possible to deactivate it.

1. Installing the WINS service

Before you install the WINS server, check that the WINS server has a static IP configuration.

➢ Go into the control panel, and double-click the **Add/Remove Programs** icon.

➢ Click the **Add/Remove Windows Components** icon, and then click the **Components** button.

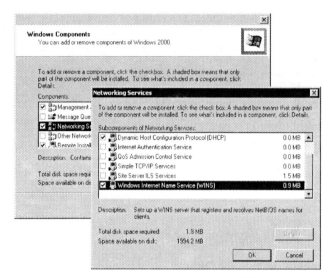

> Select **Networking Services** and then click the **Details** button.

> Enable the **Windows Internet Name Service (WINS)** check box, and then click the **OK** button, followed by the **Next** button.

2. Static configuration of WINS clients

When a machine does not use DHCP in order to obtain its IP configuration, you must manually configure the address of its WINS server(s).

a. On Windows NT

> Display the properties of **Network Neighborhood**, and then click the **Protocols** tab.

> Select **TCP/IP Protocol** and click the **Properties** button.

> ➤ Activate the **WINS Address** tab, enter the IP address of the **Primary WINS Server**, and the IP address of any **Secondary WINS Server**.

When you enter the **IPCONFIG /ALL** command, the NetBIOS node type is automatically changed to "Hybrid":

b. On Windows 2000

➢ Display the TCP/IP **Properties**.

➢ Click the **Advanced** button.

➢ Click the **WINS** tab, and then click the **Add** button.

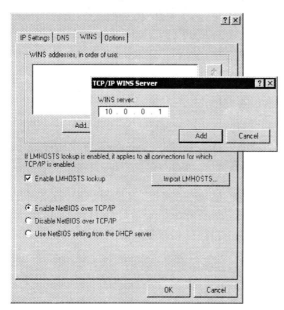

➢ Enter the address of the primary WINS server, and repeat the operation if you want to add other WINS servers (for fault tolerance reasons). You can add up to 12 WINS servers.

☞ *Unlike Windows NT, on Windows 2000 you do not need to restart your machine after you have configured your WINS.*

c. On Windows 95/98

As with Windows NT and Windows 2000, on Windows 98/98 you can configure your WINS server using the TCP/IP properties.

3. Dynamic configuration of WINS clients

You can attribute one or more WINS servers with the DHCP console, either using scope options or using server options.
In this case you must add the 044 option and the 046 option:

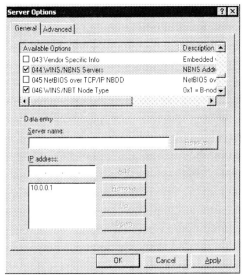

> ➢ Enable the **044 WINS/NBNS Servers** check box, and indicate the IP address(es) of the WINS server(s).

➢ Enable the **046 WINS/NBT Node Type** check box and indicate the value that corresponds to the node type that you want to assign to the client for name resolution:

- **0x1: B-node**. Clients will use broadcasts in order to resolve NetBIOS names into IP addresses.
- **0x2: P-node**. Clients will use a name server so as to register, and so as to resolve NetBIOS names into IP addresses.
- **0x4**: **M-node**. With mixed mode, clients will first try broadcasting. Then, if this is not enough, they will use a name server.
- **0x8**: **H-node**. With hybrid mode, clients will use a name server, followed by a broadcast, if necessary.

☞ *The node type corresponds to an entry in the registry database in* **HKLM\System\CurrentControlSet\Services \Netbt\ Parameters**. *This is the* **NodeType** *value, which has a REG_DWORD type.*

4. Configuring static entries

If you have any non-WINS clients in your network, then you can register them manually in the WINS database so that their names can be resolved.

➢ Open the **Administrative Tools** menu and then activate the **WINS** console.

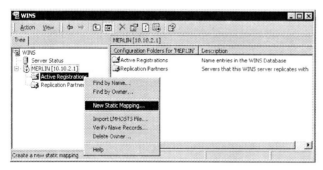

➢ Right-click the **Active Registrations** folder and select **New Static Mapping**.

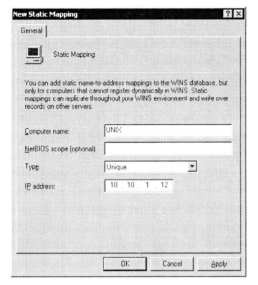

> Enter the name of the machine along with its IP address, and then click the **OK** button.

☞ *As the name implies, it must be noted that static mappings are not dynamic! Consequently, they must be updated as soon as any change occurs.*

5. Displaying the WINS Server database

As the network administrator, you can consult the WINS names database at any time. In order to do this, you can use the **WINS** console.

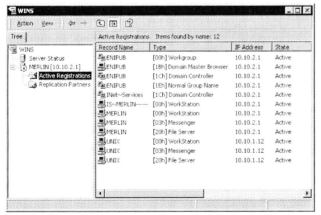

You can make searches by right-clicking the **Active Registrations** folder.

This console allows you to find out which network resources the machines are using. For example, when a workstation registers with its WINS server, in addition to NetBIOS name and its IP address, it registers a NetBIOS name that corresponds to the server service and to the workstation service of the machine. This service is identified by the 16th byte of the NetBIOS name. Here is the list of the main NetBIOS names:

– **computer_name [00h]**: the name that is registered for the workstation service of the WINS client.
– **computer_name [03h]**: the name that is registered for the Messenger Service on the WINS client.
– **computer_name [20h]**: the name that is registered for the Server Service on the WINS client.
– **user_name [03h]**: the name of the user who logged on to the computer. The 16th byte of this record has the value of 03h. The **net send** command uses this record in order to send a message to a user.
– **domain_name [1Bh]**: the name of the domain that is registered by the domain controller that is acting as Domain Master Browser.

6. Using a WINS proxy agent

The WINS relay agent, or WINS proxy agent, is used when NetBIOS clients are not WINS clients, but send broadcasts in order to resolve IP addresses into names. This server receives queries to resolve names into IP addresses and redirects them to a specific WINS server. Thereby, the WINS relay agent finds out the IP address of the WINS that must be used.

The machine that plays the role of the WINS proxy agent is a client of a WINS server. You need only use the registry editor in order to create a value with the **REG_DWORD** type, rename it as **EnableProxy**, and then allocate the value of **1**. This value must be situated in **HKLM\System\Current ControlSet\Services\NetBT\ Parameters**.

7. Replication partners

You can add a replication as follows:

➢ Open the **WINS** console. Right-click **Replication Partners** and then select **New Replication Partner**.

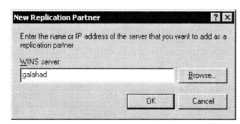

> Enter the name or the IP address of the server that you wish to add as a replication partner (a name can be used only if the LMHOSTS file contains the necessary information, or if the WINS server is in the same network).

> When you click **OK**, the replication partner server appears in the list in the right-hand pane of the **WINS** console.

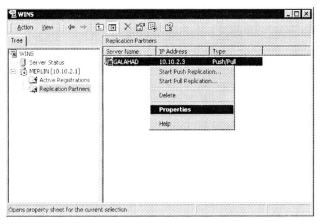

> Right-click this list entry, and select **Properties** so as to set up the role that the server must play in the replication (by default it is a **Push/Pull** server).

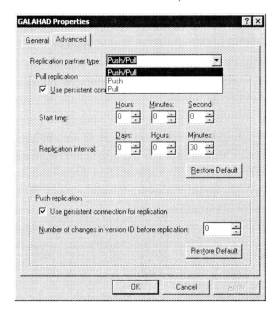

> Activate the **Advanced** tab, and select **Push/Pull** so that this server will send notifications to the other WINS server, and so that it will also obtain information when its replication partner sends it a query in order to notify it that a modification has been made.

> Carry out the same operation on the other replication partner.

> Indicate the replication start time and the replication interval.

> For replication partners that are mutually configured as **Push/Pull**, indicate the number of changes that must be made before the replication is started.

> In order to force a replication, right-click the server name in the **WINS** console, and then select **Start Push Replication** or **Start Pull Replication**.

8. Setting up the WINS server

You can configure a set of intervals for a WINS server:
- **Renew interval**: This is the **Time To Live** value (the frequency with which a WINS client must renew its name).
- **Extinction interval**: This is the duration that must elapse after an entry is marked as released, until it is marked as extinct.
- **Extinction timeout**: This is the duration that must elapse before an entry that is marked as extinct is finally deleted from the database.
- **Verification interval**: Upon expiry of this interval, a WINS server will check that the names of its partners are still active.

In order to configure these settings, right-click the server name in the **WINS** console, select **Properties** and activate the **Intervals** tab.

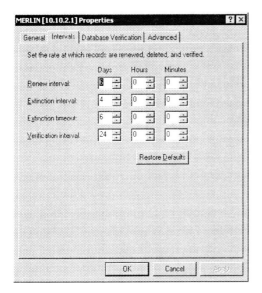

☞ *You can stop and restart the WINS service by right-clicking the server name in the WINS console.*

C. Internet Information Services (IIS 5.0)

1. Introduction

With its server versions, Windows 2000 provides as a core product, a service that allows you to use Web features, either within your company, or on the Internet. When you install Internet Information Services on a Windows 2000 server, you transform it into a Web and FTP server.

A Web server is a computer that runs the TCP/IP protocol and that sends Web pages to clients that ask for them. The HTTP (*HyperText Transfer Protocol*) protocol is used, for this purpose. HTTP is encapsulated within TCP/IP. Thereby, your Windows 2000 server can accommodate Web sites so that they can be consulted all over the world via the Internet network. However, providing information via a Web server does not necessarily imply that that the information will be available on the Internet. Thus IIS 5.0 (*Internet Information Services 5.0*) allows you to provide information within a company, in the same way as the information that is provided on the Internet. Such a configuration is called an intranet.

When you implement an intranet, you use the same techniques as those that are used on the world network, except that they are limited to a network (which is generally that of the company) and there is no entry point via the Internet. Users consult the information using a browser. A browser is an application that you can use in order to consult Web pages. Some browsers, such as Internet Explorer, also allow you to view graphics, to listen to sounds, to read video and to run programs such as Java applets or ActiveX controls.

When you consult a Web site using your browser, you can enter the name of the Web server that you want to consult, such as www.editions-eni.com. Such addresses are used because they are easier to remember than addresses such as 132.145.0.1. However, when you run a query on a full name such as www.editions-eni.com, then a DNS server transforms this name into an IP address.

The Windows 2000 Internet Information Services are a great improvement over previous versions. This chapter will provide you with some key points concerning IIS administration, but it is by no means an in-depth study of this service. A complete book is necessary in order to allow you to master this service.

2. Installing

For the Web server, you must use the TCP/IP protocol with a static IP configuration. It is preferable to use a DNS server so that you will be able to use Internet names, and an NTFS partition in order to secure the data that your server will accommodate.

When you install Windows 2000 Server, or Windows 2000 Advanced Server, then the Internet Information Services (IIS 5.0) will be installed by default. However, if you chose not to install these services at this time, then you can always install them later, at any time.

➢ Go into the Control Panel, double-click the **Add/Remove Program** icon, click the **Add/Remove Windows Components** button, and then click the **Components** button.

➢ Enable the **Internet Information Services (IIS)** check box, and then click the **Details** button in order to select the IIS options that you wish to install.

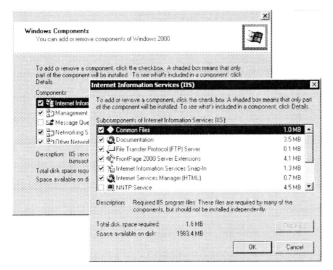

> Click the **OK** button, followed by the **Next** button.

> When the installation is finished, you will be able to use a new console that allows you to manage **Internet Information Services**:  Internet Services Manager

☞ *When you install **Internet Information Services**, you create a tree in which the parent directory is **Inetpub**.*

3. Accommodating Web sites

You can create a Web site using the **Internet Services Manager** console. This is the first step that must be taken in order to allow users to access your server via the Internet or via the intranet.

By default, an example site is created in the **Inetpub\wwwroot** directory when you install IIS. This site allows you to test your installation of Internet Information Services on your server by using a browser in order to connect to the address: http://*ip address of your server*.

You can create a new site as follows:

> Go into the **Internet Services Manager** console.

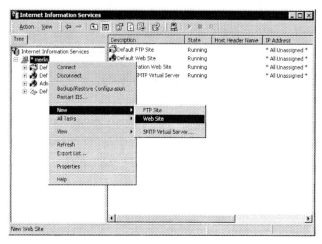

> Right-click the name of your Web server, select **New**, and then **Web Site**.

> Enter a meaningful description of your Web site and then click the **Next** button.

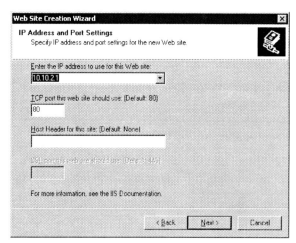

> Indicate the IP address of the server, and the TCP port. The Web service listens to the TCP 80 port. If you change this port, then the users must indicate this new port number in the http address. For example, if you specify a Web port number of 1200, then the users must connect as follows:

Address 🛂 http://www.10.10.2.1:1200/

> Click the **Next** button.

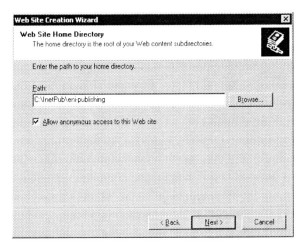

> ➢ Enter the path in which you want to store the files that will make up your site. It is advisable to store sites on NTFS partitions for security reasons.

> ➢ Click the **Next** button.

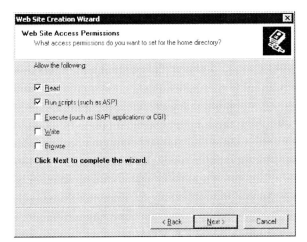

> ➢ Indicate the permissions that users must have on your site's home directory. Be careful here, as these permissions are independent from those of NTFS.

> ➢ Click the **Next** button, followed by the **Finish** button.

You can now access your site, either by entering the IP address of the server http://10.10.2.1, or by entering the host name, provided that you use a name resolution method.
In addition, you can modify the properties of a site. In order to do this, right-click the site concerned, and then select **Properties**.

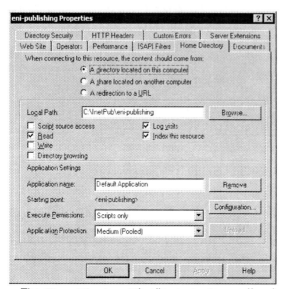

- The **Home Directory** tab allows you to specify where the site information must be stored. If the folder that contains this site is not located on the Web server, then you must indicate **A share located on another computer**.
- The **Performance** tab allows you to limit the bandwidth that will be used for this Web site. This feature is especially useful if your Web server accommodates several sites. In addition, you can limit the percentage of the CPU that this site will use. When you activate the **Enable process throttling** check box, then the system will add an event into the Event Viewer, as soon as the site uses more CPU than it is allowed to use. You can force the site to keep within its CPU limit by enabling the **Enforce limits** check box.
- The **Documents** tab indicates the page that must be loaded when users connect to the site.
- The **Custom Errors** tab allows you to modify error messages in order to make them more understandable by the users who receive them.

4. Authenticating access

When you install Internet Information Services, you create an account called **IUSR_your-computer-name**. This account allows users to consult information without having to enter a name and a password. This account uses anonymous authentication. This means that anonymous users can access documents for which permissions have been granted to the **IUSR** account. Consequently you must be careful not to grant too much permission to this account.

If you do not want to allow anonymous access to your site, you can choose other authentication methods.

a. Basic authentication

When you define basic authentication, you force users to enter a user account and a password before they can access the information. You can apply such "filtering" at site level or at folder or file level. This authentication method is based on Windows 2000 accounts. The user can access the resource only if the user supplies the name of a user account and the corresponding password.

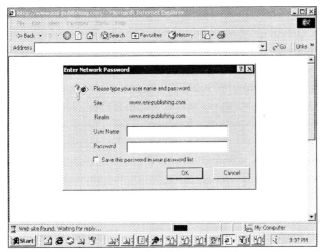

It must be noted however, that this method does not encrypt the account information when it transmits it from the client to the server.

You can configure this authentication method as follows:

➢ Go into the **Internet Services Manager** console, right-click the Web site that you want to secure, and then select **Properties**.

➢ Select the **Directory Security** tab, and then click the **Edit** button that is under **Anonymous access and authentication control**.

➤ Deactivate the **Anonymous access** check box and the **Integrated Windows authentication** check box, and enable the **Basic authentication** check box. Click **Yes** in response to the warning message that appears and then click **OK** twice in order to complete the operation.

b. Integrated Windows authentication

As with the previous method, this integrated Windows authentication forces users to enter the name of a user account and the password that is associated with it, in order to access the database concerned. In this case, passwords are not transmitted on the network and authentication information is encrypted.

☞ *In order to use this method, you need a browser that will support it. At the time of publication, Internet Explorer (version 2.0 or later) is the only browser that supports this authentication method.*

c. Digest authentication for Windows domain servers

This method runs only with accounts that are in Windows 2000 domains, and it requires that passwords are stored in clear text. The password is not transmitted on the network and only a hashed value is sent to the server. At the time of publication, only Internet Explorer 5 is able to use this method.

5. Setting up an FTP (File Transfer Protocol) site

FTP is a file transfer protocol. You can create an FTP site using IIS 5. Thereby, you can provide users with access to documents, and you can even allow them to download applications.

By default, you create an FTP site when you install IIS. This site is empty when it is created and you can add documents that you wish to publish by copying them into the directory **inetpub\ftproot**. You can also create a new FTP site by right-clicking the name of your server, and then selecting **New** followed by **FTP site**. A wizard then helps you to create your site.

You can modify the configuration of the FTP site that is created by default by right-clicking **Default FTP Site** in the **Internet Services Manager** console, and then selecting **Properties**.

– The **FTP Site** tab allows you to configure the port that is used by FTP (port 21 by default), and the maximum number of simultaneous connections that can be made to the FTP site.

– The **Security Accounts** tab allows you to set up the access to the FTP site (by default, anonymous connections are allowed).

– The **Messages** tab allows you to indicate a message that must be displayed when a user connects to, or disconnects from, the FTP site.

– The **Home Directory** tab allows you to specify the path to which users are directed when they connect to the FTP site. This tab also allows you to display the results of FTP queries in either an MSDOS or a UNIX listing style.

Here is an example of the Unix listing style:

```
E:\WINNT\System32\cmd.exe                                        _ | □ | X |

E:\>ftp merlin
Connected to merlin.enipub.com.
220 merlin Microsoft FTP Service (Version 5.0).
User (merlin.enipub.com:<none>): administrator
331 Password required for administrator.
Password:
230-Welcome to my FTP site
230 User administrator logged in.
ftp> dir
200 PORT command successful.
150 Opening ASCII mode data connection for /bin/ls.
-r-xr-xr-x   1 owner      group          4 Mar 21 11:30 RFC1812.txt
-r-xr-xr-x   1 owner      group          4 Mar 21 11:31 RFC2131.txt
-r-xr-xr-x   1 owner      group          4 Mar 21 11:31 RFC2136.txt
226 Transfer complete.
ftp: 216 bytes received in 0.01Seconds 21.60Kbytes/sec.
ftp> quit
221  See you later
```

- The **Directory Security** tab allows you to specify IP addresses that will be granted or denied access to the FTP site.

☞ *Make sure that you apply suitable NTFS permissions to documents that can be accessed via FTP.*

You do not have to copy or move the documents that you want to appear on your FTP site. You can create virtual directories that point elsewhere in the network. Users who connect will not notice any difference. In order to create a virtual directory, right-click your FTP site, then select **New** followed by **Virtual Directory**. Enter an alias (this is the name that the users will see) and enter the path where the data is located. Finally, you must grant suitable permissions. In order to make this virtual directory operational, you must create a directory with the alias name in the directory that accommodates the FTP site (on the IIS server).

D. Remote access

Windows 2000 allows users to access a company's network remotely (from a hotel, or from home, for example). You can configure a Windows 2000 server so that it will act as a remote access server and a VPN server. On the client side, the user will connect to the server using the remote access client. The two sides must be linked using a communications medium that is suitable for remote communication. Therefore, a WAN link must be used. This can be a Switched Telephone Network (STN), an Integrated Services Digital Network (ISDN), an X25 medium (packet switching), a frame relay (frame switching) or an Asynchronous Transfer Mode (ATM) connection. You can even use a serial cable in order to link together the two computers. A WAN link communication protocol must be used on this physical medium. With Windows 2000, you can use PPP, Microsoft RAS, ARAP and SLIP protocols.

1. Transport methods

In order to send data between the remote client and the server, you must encapsulate it in a suitable protocol.

a. WAN link protocol

You need a specific protocol in order to transmit information across remote links. Microsoft allows you to use several protocols:

- **SLIP** (*Serial Line Internet Protocol*): You must use this protocol in order to connect to a SLIP server via a modem. This is an old communication standard that is used in UNIX environments. It was originally written in order to support low throughput networks. It does not support automatic negotiation of the network configuration and can encapsulate only the IP. It does not support encrypted authentication either.

☞ *Windows 2000 includes a SLIP client but it does not support the role of SLIP server as this lacks the security and the efficiency of PPP.*

- **PPP** *(Point to Point Protocol)*: This is an improvement on SLIP. Unlike SLIP, which supports only IP, PPP allows you to encapsulate other protocols such as IPX/SPX, and NetBEUI, in addition to TCP/IP. The great advantage of PPP is that it is not a proprietary protocol. Because of this, any client that supports PPP can connect to a Windows 2000 remote access server.
- **Microsoft RAS**: This proprietary protocol allows Windows for Workgroups clients, Windows NT 3.1 clients, MSDOS clients and Lan Manager clients that use NetBEUI protocol to access a Windows 2000 remote access server. The Windows 2000 remote access server acts as a gateway for these clients in order to allow them to access the server, even if the server uses another protocol.
- **ARAP**: Windows 2000 can act as a remote access server for Macintosh clients. Macintosh clients use the ARAP protocol to connect to Windows 2000 servers.

☞ *Windows 2000 clients cannot connect to an ARAP remote access server.*

b. LAN protocol

The section above describes the different protocols that allow you to set up a connection with the remote access server. Once the connection has been set up, the client uses resources as if it is located on the local network. In order to allow this, the data is encapsulated in a local network protocol. Windows 2000 allows you to use TCP/IP, Nwlink IPX/SPX, NetBEUI and AppleTalk protocols. In turn, these LAN protocols are encapsulated into a WAN link protocol such as PPP so that they can be transmitted on the remote links.

Thereby, you can use Windows 2000 remote network access services in order to allow a client that runs the NetBEUI protocol for example, to communicate with a UNIX server that is located on the company's local network. In this way, the remote access server acts as a NetBEUI / TCP-IP gateway. However, both of these protocols must be installed on the remote access server.

c. Virtual Private Networks (VPN)

The main advantage of virtual private networks is that you can use them in order to connect together two computers irrespective of the physical level (LAN or WAN connection). Thereby, you can create a VPN between two machines using either the Internet, or simply the local network, as the communication medium. VPNs use tunneling protocols. Windows 2000 allows you to use VPNs with PPTP or with L2TP. The purpose of these two protocols is to provide an encrypted tunnel in an insecure network (such as the Internet).

- **PPTP (Point to Point Tunneling Protocol)**: This protocol allows you to interconnect networks using an IP network.
- **L2TP (Layer Two Tunneling Protocol)**: This protocol allows PPTP to interconnect networks when the tunnel offers a packet oriented point-to-point connection. They allow you to operate on an IP network using Frame Relay, X25, ATM, and IP Permanent Virtual Circuits (PVC).

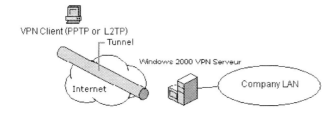

VPN Client (PPTP or L2TP)

Both PPTP and L2TP use PPP protocol in order to transfer data (IP, IPX/SPX...). They provide an extra envelope for data transport via VPNs. This envelope adds headings that allow you to transport the information.

L2TP offers the following advantages:
- They allow you to compress headers (4 bytes, instead of 6 bytes with PPTP)
- They allow authentication to take place in the tunnel.

These two protocols offer different levels of security. PPTP uses the encryption that is offered by PPP. L2TP uses IPSec in order to encrypt data. However, IPSec and L2TP are totally independent from each other. You can use L2TP without IPSec.

If you use IPSec in a PPTP tunnel then the PPTP will provide authentication in the tunnel, in the same way as L2TP does.

2. Configuring a remote access server

Windows 2000 provides two utilities that allow you to configure remote network access:
- **Network and Dial-up Connections**

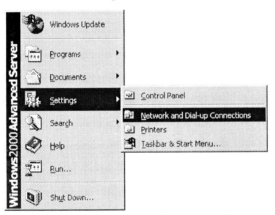

- and the **Routing and Remote Access** console.

You can use this console in order to configure incoming connections when you server is a domain controller or a domain member.

If this is not the case, then you can configure both incoming and outgoing connections using the **Network Connection Wizard**. You can access the **Network Connection Wizard** by opening the **Start - Settings** menu and then selecting **Network and Dial-up Connections**.

a. Incoming connections

Network and dial-up connections

When you authorize incoming calls, you configure your server as a remote access server. On a server that is not a domain controller and that does not belong to a domain, you can authorize incoming calls as follows:

➢ Open the **Start - Settings** menu and then select **Network and Dial-up Connections**.

➢ Double-click the **Make New Connection** icon.

➢ The welcome screen of the **Network Connection Wizard** appears. Click the **Next** button.

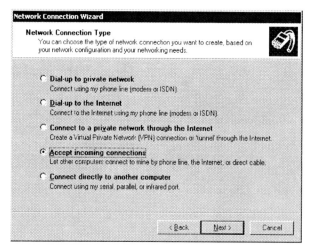

➢ Select **Accept incoming connection**, and then click the **Next** button.

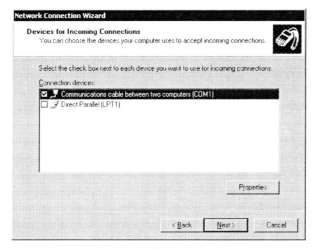

> Select from the list, the devices that you want to use for your incoming connections. If your modem does not appear in the list, then you can install it using the **Phone and Modem Options** program that is located in the Control Panel. Click **Next**.

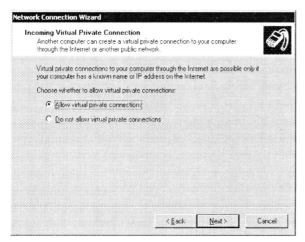

> Indicate whether or not you want to allow VPN connections, and then click the **Next** button.

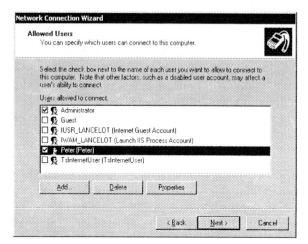

> Select the users that will be allowed to use the remote
  access. You can grant permission to other users at any
  time by displaying the properties of the accounts
  concerned, and selecting the **Dial-in** tab.

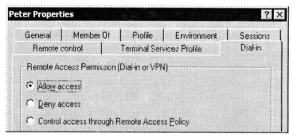

Users who dial in to a server that is not a domain controller
must have an account in the SAM database of this server.

> The next step allows you to modify the dial-in properties,
  such as the LAN protocol that must be used.

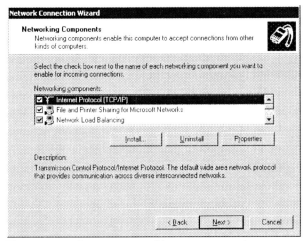

This screen allows you to add a new protocol, or to set up the addresses that must be used by remote access clients. In order to do this, select the TCP/IP protocol and then click the **Properties** button.

You can use DHCP in order automatically to attribute IP addresses to remote clients or to specify a range of addresses for these clients. In this case, the first address in the range will be assigned to the remote access server. This technique allows you to use a different network address in order to communicate with remote clients.

➢ Click the **Next** button, and then click the **Finish** button so as to complete the operation.

Network services

Routing and Remote Access

In order to accept incoming connections on a domain controller or on a member server, you must use the **Routing and Remote Access** console.

When you use this console for the first time, you must enable the Routing and Remote Access service.

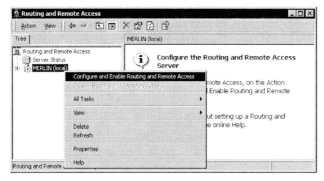

> Right-click the name of your server, and select **Configure and Enable Routing and Remote Access**.

> Click the **Next** button in the welcome window that appears.

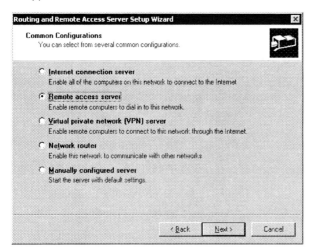

> Select **Remote access server**, and click the **Next** button.

> Then, check the list that appears in order to make sure that it contains all the protocols that you require, and click the **Next** button.

➢ Indicate whether you use a DHCP server so as to assign IP addresses to your remote clients, or whether you prefer to specify a range of addresses. If you prefer the latter option, then enable **From a specified range of addresses**, and click the **Next** button.

➢ Click the **New** button, and then enter a start address and end address for your address range.

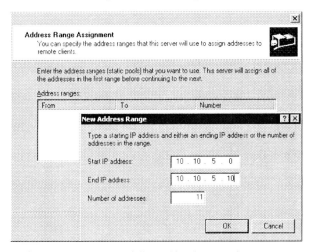

➢ Click the **OK** button, followed by the **Next** button.

➢ For the last step, you are asked if you want to install the RADIUS server. Select **No, I don't want to set up this server to use RADIUS now**, and click the **Next** button followed by the **Finish** button.

☞ *This chapter will cover the use of a radius server in the section that is entitled RADIUS authentication server.*

If you have used this console already for a reason other than for the remote access service (for example in order to configure a DHCP relay agent, or to configure a router), then you can configure your remote access server by right-clicking it's icon in this console and selecting **Properties**.

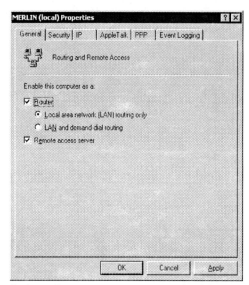

Activate the **Remote access server** check box.

☞ *When the remote access service is started for the first time, it automatically creates 5 PPTP ports and L2TP ports. The number of these ports is not limited and you can configure them using the **Ports** icon in the **Routing and Remote Access** console.*

b. Outgoing connections

In order to access a remote access server, you must configure an outgoing connection. You must use the **Network Connection Wizard** for this purpose. In order to access this wizard, you must open the **Start – Settings** menu, select **Network and Dial-up Connections** and double-click the **Make New Connection** icon.

You can configure three types of outgoing connections:

– Remote access connection (which covers the options, **Dial-up to private network** and **Dial-up to the Internet**).

– Connection to a virtual private network.

– Direct connection using a cable.

Remote access connection

The **Dial-up to private network** option allows remote clients to connect directly to the remote access server using a modem.

In this case you must know the telephone number of the server to which you want to connect.

Network Connection Wizard

Phone Number to Dial
You must specify the phone number of the computer or network you want to connect to.

Type the phone number of the computer or network you are connecting to. If you want your computer to determine automatically how to dial from different locations, check Use dialing rules.

Area code: Phone number:
                  0208 956 2321

Country/region code:

☐ Use dialing rules

‹ Back   Next ›   Cancel

The **Dial-up to the Internet** option allows you to connect to an Internet Service Provider (ISP). The **Internet Connection Wizard** will help you to set up this connection. You can connect via your LAN, in which case you must indicate the address of your proxy server. Alternatively, you can use your modem in order to connect to your ISP.

Connecting to a Virtual Private Network (VPN)

In order to create a virtual private network you need to know only the IP address of the destination machine. Select the **Connect to a private network through the Internet** option, and then click **Next**.

Network Connection Wizard

Destination Address
What is the name or address of the destination?

Type the host name or IP address of the computer or network to which you are connecting.

Host name or IP address (such as microsoft.com or 123.45.6.78):
10.10.2.1

‹ Back   Next ›   Cancel

Network services

➢ Indicate the host name or the host IP address, and click the **Next** button. Then, indicate whether only you must be able to access the connection that you are creating, or whether you want to share it with other users, who will then be able to log on to your machine.

➢ The next step allows you to share this connection with other users of your LAN. Click **Next**, enter a name for this connection, and then click the **Finish** button.

The wizard creates a new icon in the **Start** menu:

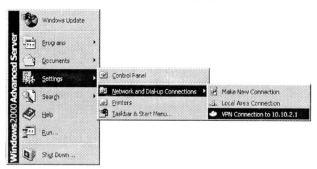

In order to connect, click the icon that represents the connection.

Enter a user name and a password for an account that has dial-in permission, and then click the **Connect** button.

When the connection has been set up you will receive the
following message:

Connecting directly using a cable

You can link two computers together by connecting a cable
to the serial ports, to the parallel ports or to the infrared
ports. In this case, select **Connect directly to another
computer**, and then click the **Next** button.

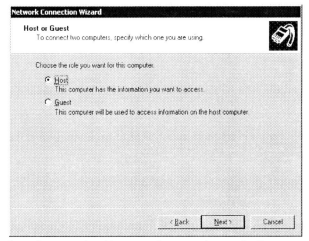

In order to make this type of connection work, then one of
the computers must be configured as a **Host**, and the other
computer must be configured as a **Guest**. The host computer
will act as a sort of access server, and the guest computer
will act as the client. With both of these configurations, you
must specify the device that will be used for the connection
(and also the port that will be used for the connection). In
addition, for the host you must indicate the users that will be
allowed to connect.

3. Authentication

When you allow remote network access connections, you must implement an authentication mechanism that will run during the logon process, so as to prevent any unauthorized people from getting into your company's network.

Logging on via a WAN can be divided into three parts:

- Setting up a physical link. This first phase allows the two parties to negotiate the connection by sending LCP (*Link Control Protocol*) packets. These packets contain the connection's negotiation settings on the physical level, such as the compression, the type of authentication that is used, and whether links are shared or not.
- The second phase covers the authentication. It runs after the line has been set up, and before the network level set up.
- When the authentication has been completed, then the network level-3 protocol that must be used (IP for example) is negotiated. NCP (*Network Control Protocol*) packets are sent for this purpose.

Here are layers of the PPP architecture:

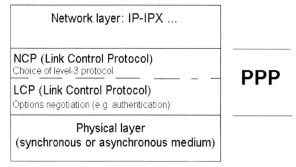

Windows 2000 supports several authentication methods that offer differing security levels. You can configure these authentication methods using the **Routing and Remote Access** console.

➢ Right-click the name of your remote access server and then select **Properties**.

➢ Select the **Security** button and then click the **Authentication Methods** button.

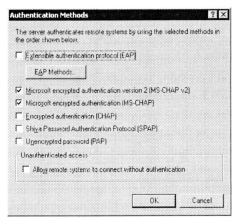

Several authentication protocols are o ffered:

- **PAP (*Password Authentication Protocol*)**: This method is relatively simple, and not very secure. The remote client sends the password as clear text. The client sends the user name and password to the remote access server. The remote access server then checks this information against its own information.
- **SPAP (*Shiva Password Authentication Protocol*)**: This is a proprietary protocol that is supplied by the vendor Shiva. It allows a Shiva client to connect to a Windows 2000 remote access server, or a Windows 2000 client to connect to a Shiva server. The passwords are encrypted.
- **CHAP (*Challenge Handshake Authentication Protocol*)**: This is a sophisticated authentication protocol. The remote access server sends a "challenge" to the client after the first phase of the logon has completed. This is an identifier that is sent to the client after being randomly generated by the server. Only the remote access server knows this identifier. The client sends its password in a hashed format, together with the "challenge" that was sent by the server. This method is called hashing (it is used by MD5: *Message Digest*). The server restores the message and checks that the password corresponds to the user name.
- **MS-CHAP (*Microsoft Challenge Handshake Authentication Protocol*)**: This protocol uses the same principle as CHAP. In addition, MS-CHAP allows you to use MPPE (*Microsoft Point-to-point Protocol*) encrypting in order to secure data on PPP or PPTP links.
- **MS-CHAP version 2**: This is a development of MS-CHAP. It is more secure than MS-CHAP v1. It is the most secure authentication protocol that Windows 2000 offers. You can use this protocol only if you have Windows 2000, NT 4.0 or Windows 95/98 clients.

– **EAP** *(Extensible Authentication Protocol)*: This is not a single protocol. It is a set of protocols that provide other methods in order to authenticate PPP protocol. Notably, this method is used for smart-card authentication by TLS (*Transport Layer Security*) protocol, by MD5-CHAP protocol, and by other authentication methods that have not yet been developed such as biometric recognition.

☞ *As with the MS-CHAP protocol, you can use MPPE encryption with the TLS protocol.*

4. RADIUS authentication server

RADIUS (*Remote Authentication Dial-in User Service*) is a protocol that allows you to centralize the authentication, and the authorization, of remote users. It is a standardized service and is therefore completely independent of remote access clients and servers.

In addition to controlling access, a RADIUS server records events, and sends alerts in order to find out if non-authorized users are trying to connect to the network.

In order to use RADIUS authentication, you need a RADIUS client and a RADIUS server. The RNA Server *(Remote Network Access Server)* acts as the client, and the Windows 2000 server acts as the server, and accommodates the IAS *(Internet Authentication Service)*.

Installing a RADIUS server

A Windows 2000 server can act as a RADIUS server. For this purpose, the IIS service must be installed.

➤ Open the Control Panel, double-click the **Add/Remove Programs** icon, click the **Add/Remove Windows Components** button, and then the **Components** button.

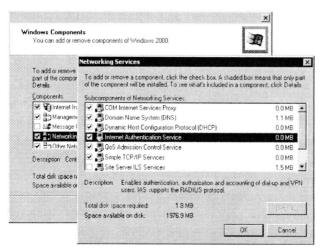

> Select **Networking Services**, and then click the **Details** button. Activate the **Internet Authentication Service** then click **OK** followed by **Next**.

You now have a new console in the **Administrative Tools** menu that allows you to manage the RADIUS server:

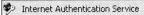 Internet Authentication Service

Configuring the RADIUS server

You can configure the RADIUS server as follows:

> Go into the **Internet Authentication Service** console, right-click the **Clients** folder, and then select **New Client**.

> Enter a name for the client, and click the **Next** button.

> Enter the IP address of the RADIUS client (you can enter its DNS name and then resolve it by clicking the **Verify** button). In the **Client-Vendor** list, select **Microsoft**. Enter a password in the **Shared secret** textbox, and then repeat it in the **Confirm shared secret** textbox. This password allows the system to check RADIUS clients for this server. Clients need to know this secret in order to send their authentication requests.

> Click the **Finish** button.

Configuring the RADIUS client

You must carry out the following configuration on the remote access server:

> Open the **Routing and Remote Access** console, right-click the name of your remote access server, and select **Properties**. Activate the **Security** tab.

> Under **Authentication provider**, select **RADIUS Authentication**, and then click the **Configure** button.

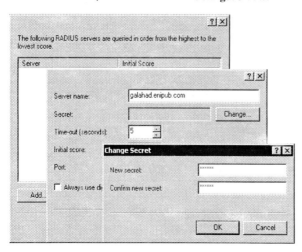

> Click the **Add** button in order to identify the RADIUS server. Enter the name of the IAS server, and then click the **Change** button so as to enter the password that will be used between the RADIUS client and the RADIUS server.

This is the secret that was indicated when you configured the RADIUS server.

➤ When you have finished, you must restart the Routing and Remote Access server.

5. Remote access policy

The remote access server and the IAS sever use remote access policies in order to control how users log on. Unlike group policies, remote access policies are not stored in Active Directory. This means that you can apply different remote access policies on different remote access servers.

These policies are combinations of **conditions**, of **authorizations** and of a **profile**.

a. Conditions

The conditions of a policy are a set of attributes that allow you to decide whether or not the connection must be accepted.

You can set up conditions as follows:

➤ Open the **Routing and Remote Access** console. Right-click **Remote Access Policies**, and then select **New Remote Access Policy**.

➤ Enter a name that represents your policy, and then click the **Next** button.

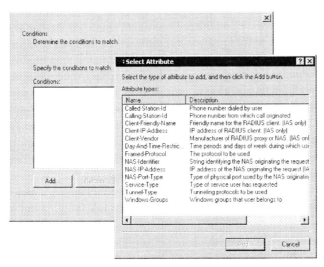

➤ Click the **Add** button, then add the attributes that you want include in your policy. For example, you can specify the type of the connection. In order to do this select **Tunnel-Type** and then click the **Add** button.

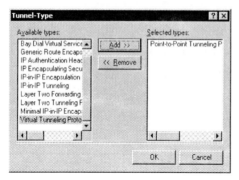

> Select the protocol(s) that will be used as conditions from the list in the left-hand pane, then click the **Add** button.

> Repeat the operation with all the conditions that you want to add to your policy. All the conditions that you specify will appear in the following window:

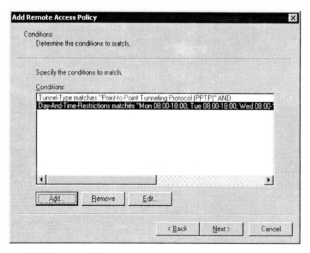

> Click the **Next** button.

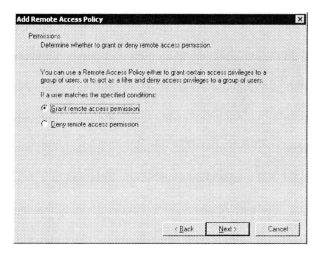

> Indicate whether you want to grant, or to deny, the connections that correspond to your conditions, and then click the **Next** button.

> Then, you can choose to edit your profile, or to click the **Finish** button. You can always modify your profile later.

Here is a list of some of the attributes that are offered:

- Attributes that you can apply only for the IAS server: **Client-IP-Address** allows you to specify the IP address of the RADIUS client, **Client-Friendly-Name** allows you to specify the name of the RADIUS client, and. **Client-Vendor** allows you the make of the RADIUS client (for example Microsoft, Cisco, or 3COM).

- Attributes that you can apply only for the RNA server: **Calling-Station-ID** that specifies the telephone number that must be dialed by the remote client, **Caller-Station-ID** that corresponds to the caller's telephone number, **Day-And-Time-Restrictions** that allow you to specify a connection schedule, **Windows groups** that allow you to apply restrictions or authorizations to the users that belong to a group.

b. Authorizing

On Windows 2000 you can define remote access permissions in the properties of user accounts, and you can also define them in remote access policies.

In order to change the connection permissions for a user, display the **Properties** dialog box for the user account and select the **Dial-in** tab.

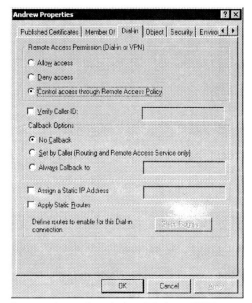

Remote Access Permission (Dia-in or VPN)

You can allow, or deny, access to a user explicitly. However, as user access permissions are defined both in the user account properties and in the remote access policies, if you explicitly allow access to a user, then the user may still not be able to connect, as this will also depend on the conditions and on the profile of the policy. Notably, this approach allows you to allow access to a group of users, but to deny access to one specific user who is a member of this group. In order to do this, you must specify the **Windows Groups** attribute as a condition of the remote access policy, and then explicitly **Deny access** to the user in the properties dialog box for the user account. For the other members in the group, you can explicitly **Allow access** in their user account properties, or you can simply allow them access using the remote access policy.

The **Control access through Remote Access Policy** is available only for user accounts in a domain that is in **native mode**. It allows you to allow or to deny access according to the permissions that are defined in the remote access policy.

☞ *The permissions that are defined at remote access policy level correspond to the options* **Grant remote access permission** *or* **Deny remote access permission** *according to whether or not the users fulfill the conditions of the policy.*

Verifying Caller-ID

If you activate the **Verify Caller-ID** check box, then you can specify the caller's telephone number. Then, the user will not be able to connect from another telephone number.

☞ *Use this option only if you are sure that all the elements of in your connection will accept the caller ID. If this is not the case then the connection will fail.*

Callback Options

Callback options allow you to call back a user when the user tries to connect. This option allows a user, who is working at home, to connect to the company network without having to meet the communication expenses.

In addition, you can force the callback to a predetermined number. This provides an additional level of security, as you will be sure that user who is connecting is situated at the specified number. If this is not the case, then the connection will fail.

IP routing

You can assign an IP address to a user that connects to the remote access server by activating the **Assign a Static IP Address** check box.

You can also update the routing table of the remote client by adding static routes that the client may need. In order to do this, you must activate the **Apply Static Routes** check box.

☞ *When you are in mixed mode you cannot check the caller's ID, as the options that allow you to assign IP addresses and static routes are not available. Neither can you control access via the remote access policy.*

c. Profile

You can set up profiles using the **Routing and Remote Access** console. A profile allows you to specify the connection settings that must be applied to the client, once the conditions have been validated.

➤ Go into the **Routing and Remote Access** console and select **Remote Access Policies**.

➤ In the right-hand pane, right-click the policy for which you want to modify the profile.

➤ Select **Properties** and then click the **Edit Profile** button.

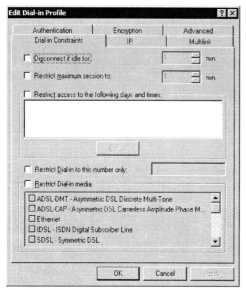

Dial-in Constraints

Using this tab you can specify how long users can stay connected, and you can indicate the idle time that must elapse before a session is disconnected. You can also restrict access to certain time periods, to a certain telephone number, and to a certain types of de medium (such as X25, Ethernet, VPN, or ISDN).

IP (Filtering IP traffic)

Using the **IP** tab, you can filter packets that come from clients, or that go to clients. You can apply these filters according to the type of protocol (for example, ICMP, UDP, or TCP). You can apply these filters either according to the port number of the source, or according to the port number of the destination. This tab also allows you to configure the way in which IP addresses must be assigned to clients.

Authentication

You can use the **Authentication** tab in order to specify the protocol that must be used for connections that use this policy. The protocol that you select must be configured in the properties of the server.

Encryption

The **Encryption** tab allows you to specify the type of encryption that must be used for connections that use this policy. You can apply two different types of encryption:

– MPPE (*Microsoft Point-to-Point Encryption*), which is used by PPP and PPTP connections.
– IPSec (*IP Security*), which is used by VPN L2TP connections.

Enable the **Basic** check box in order to activate 56-bit DES encryption for IPSec and 40-bit encryption for MPPE.

Enable the **Strong** check box in order to activate 56-bit DES encryption for IPSec and 56-bit encryption for MPPE.

Multilink

Windows 2000 allows you to use several physical links in order to create a single logical link, so that you can increase the bandwidth. You can use this feature only if PPP Multilink Protocol has been installed on both the server, and on the clients.

In order to allow multilinks, go into the **Routing and Remote Access** console, display the **Properties** of the server, activate the **PPP** tab, and enable the **Multilink connections** check box.

Windows 2000 has improved the basic principles of multilinks by adding the BAP (*Bandwidth Allocation Protocol*). This protocol allows you dynamically to allocate bandwidth according to needs. This protocol then, allocates bandwidth on demand. BAP runs in combination with PPP.

Consequently, the **Multilink** tab allows you to set up the BAP protocol.

d. Application order of conditions, permissions and profile

When you try to connect, the system consults policy conditions first, followed by the permissions, and finishes with the profile. The following diagram illustrates the different phases of setting up a connection.

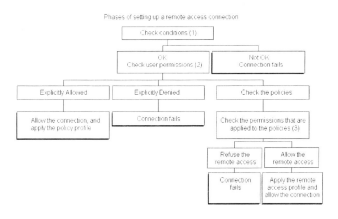

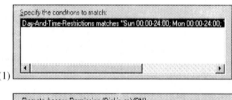

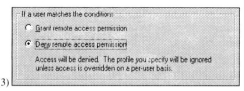

When you install the **Routing and Remote Access** service, then you create a policy by default. This policy refuses access for all uses that have **Control access through Remote Access Policy** permission. In fact, the default policy stipulates that connections will be refused 24 hours a day. In order that users will be allowed to connect then, either you must grant explicit permission in the **Dial-in** tab of their account **Properties** dialog box, or you must change the policy. This rule applies only if your domain is in native mode. It does not apply in mixed mode because users cannot have **Control access through Remote Access Policy** permission in mixed mode. However, remote access policies will still be applied in a mixed mode domain, as even if you explicitly allow users to connect, then they will still have to fulfill the policy conditions in order to be able to connect.

☞ *When you change from mixed mode to native mode, then the explicit Deny access permissions become **Control access through Remote Access Policy** permissions, and the explicit Allow access permissions stay the same.*

You can create several remote access policies. However, if you do this you must ensure that all the users who must have remote access are in accordance with at least one of the policies.

E. Telnet

Telnet is a TCP/IP service that allows you to emulate terminals. The Telnet client program has always been supplied with the different versions of Windows. The Telnet client program allows you to connect to a remote host in order to emulate a terminal. It has often been used to connect to such machines as UNIX servers, and routers.

With Windows 2000, the Telnet server service is also provided. This service allows a remote host to run a Telnet session on a Windows 2000 server. It is not started by default. You can activate this service as follows:

➢ Go into the **Administrative Tools** menu, and open the **Services** console.

➢ Double-click the **Telnet** service.

> Click the **Start** button (note the **Manual** startup type). If you want the service always to be activated when you start up your server, then replace the **Manual** startup type by **Automatic**.

You can now connect to a Windows 2000 server using a command prompt:

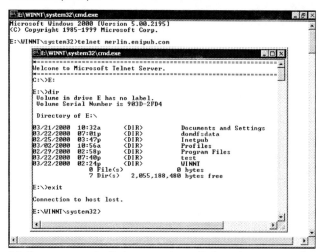

All the commands that you enter will then be run on the **Telnet** server.

Labs

To be absolutely sure that you have assimilated this chapter, work through the corresponding labs. These are set out from page 678 to page 687.

☒ DHCP.

☒ WINS.

☒ IIS 5.

☒ Remote access.

☒ Virtual private network.

Assessing your skills

Try the following questions if you think you know this chapter well enough.

DHCP

1   What is the purpose of DHCP?   ☐
....
....
....

2   What information must you supply so that a client can   ☐
become a DHCP client?
....
....
....

3   A DHCP client obtains an IP configuration from the only   ☐
DHCP server that is on the network. Normally, the client
should receive an address from a DNS name server in its
configuration, as the 006 DNS Servers option was
configured for the scope. However, the client does not
receive the correct address. What might be causing of this
problem?
....
....
....
....
....

4   What are the minimum items of information that are   ☐
obtained by a DHCP client?
....

5   Can a DHCP server be its own client?   ☐
....

6   Can you have several DHCP servers on the same   ☐
network?
....
....

7   A DHCP server has an IP address of 132.147.0.1/16.   ☐
Can you define a 132.148.0.0 scope (with a mask of
255.255.0.0) on the same server? If so, how are these
addresses attributed?
....
....

8 A DHCP client obtains an IP configuration with a 3-day lease. One hour later, the DHCP server breaks down. The client then restarts. What will happen to the client? How will the client be affected?

....
....
....
....

9 How would you configure the duration of the DHCP lease, if only a limited number of IP addresses are available? Would you set a very short lease duration, or a very long lease duration?

....
....
....

10 You have just installed a DHCP server. You configured your clients as DHCP clients. However, none of them receives an IP configuration from your DHCP server, even though you checked that the scope was activated. What might be causing this problem?

....
....
....
....
....
....

11 Can a Windows 2000 DHCP service update A and PTR records of clients in the DNS database of the names server?

....
....
....

12 What is the purpose of a superscope?

....
....
....

13 What is the purpose of option classes?

....
....
....

14 Which types of option class can you create?

....
....
....

15 A DHCP client user, who has a Windows 2000 Professional machine, complains that he/she cannot access a resource that is situated on a server, which has an IP address of 192.168.1.1. The scope that is configured on the DHCP server covers the range 192.168.1.10 -192.168.1.200. When you run the **ipconfig** command on the client machine, you notice that the machine has an IP address of 169.254.0.23. What might be causing this problem, and from where did this address come?

....
....
....
....
....
....
....

16 What is the role of the DHCP Relay Agent?

....
....
....
....
....

WINS

17 What is the role of the WINS Server?

....

18 When you run the **ipconfig /all** command on the client machine, you notice that the machine is configured as a hybrid node. What does this signify?

....
....
....
....

19 Why are static entries added into a WINS database?

....
....
....
....

20 Which two actions must a WINS client carry out with its server?

....
....
....
....

Network services

21 How must you configure a computer so that it will become a WINS client? ☐

....

....

....

22 Can a WINS server be a DHCP client? ☐

....

....

Internet and intranet

23 What is the difference between Internet and intranet? ☐

....

....

....

24 You have just installed IIS on your server, which is called Merlin. Which new user have you created on your server? ☐

....

25 You want to share within your company, general information on the company's users. You have a heterogeneous network that includes Windows, UNIX and Macintosh clients. How can you make these documents available in a simple way? ☐

....

....

....

....

26 You are in charge of the intranet Web site of your company. You want to allow all the users to access the public information on this site, but you want to restrict access to confidential information on the same site. How will you achieve these objectives? ☐

....

....

....

....

....

....

....

....

Remote network access

27 Which two tunneling protocols does Windows 2000 support? ☐

....

28 What is the use of a VPN? ☐

....

....

....

....

29 Which type of encryption can you use with the L2TP ☐
protocol in order to secure the tunnel?

....

30 Which console would you use on a Windows 2000 server ☐
in order to configure a RNA Server or a VPN?

....

....

31 What information do you need in order to set up a VPN ☐
connection?

....

....

....

....

32 Which types of outgoing connections can you configure ☐
on a Windows 2000 machine?

....

....

....

33 Which types of authentication methods are offered by the ☐
Windows 2000 remote access service?

....

34 Which is the most secure authentication protocol? ☐

....

35 What is the role of a RADIUS server? ☐

....

....

....

36 How do you implement remote access security? ☐

....

37 Why are remote access policies stored on the remote ☐
access server and not in Active Directory?

....

....

Network services

38 You have installed a RNA Server in your domain in native mode. You accept all the default values of the remote access policy options. However, you notice that the user account with which you are going to test the connection has the **Control access through Remote Access Policy** permission. After several attempts to connect to the server from a client, you receive a message that tells you that you do not have connection rights. What might be causing this problem?

....
....
....
....
....
....
....

39 In a mixed mode domain, you cannot use a remote access policy in order to control access. However, can you still use remote access conditions and profile?

....
....
....
....

Results

Check your answers on pages 527 to 531. Count one point for each correct answer.

Number of points | /39 |

For this chapter you need to have scored at least 29 out of 39.

Look at the list of key points that follows. Pick out the ones with which you have had difficulty and work through them again in this chapter before moving on to the next.

Key points of the chapter

☐ DHCP.

☐ WINS.

☐ Internet and intranet.

☐ Remote network access.

Solutions

DHCP

1   What is the purpose of DHCP?

The DHCP service allows you dynamically to attribute complete IP configurations to clients who request them.

2   What information must you supply so that a client can become a DHCP client?

You need only specify on the client machine that the client must obtain an IP configuration from a DHCP server.

3   A DHCP client obtains an IP configuration from the only DHCP server that is on the network. Normally, the client should receive an address from a DNS name server in its configuration, as the 006 DNS Servers option was configured for the scope. However, the client does not receive the correct address. What might be causing of this problem?

A DNS server address was probably assigned manually. TCP/IP property options that are chosen manually on the client machine have priority over the DHCP options.

4   What are the minimum items of information that are obtained by a DHCP client?

An IP address, and a subnet mask.

5   Can a DHCP server be its own client?

No.

6   Can you have several DHCP servers on the same network?

Yes. However, their IP address scopes must not overlap.

7   A DHCP server has an IP address of 132.147.0.1/16. Can you define a 132.148.0.0 scope (with a mask of 255.255.0.0) on the same server? If so, how are these addresses attributed?

Yes. In this case a DHCP Relay Agent that is situated on another IP network will reference the server.

8   A DHCP client obtains an IP configuration with a 3-day lease. One hour later, the DHCP server breaks down. The client then restarts. What will happen to the client? How will the client be affected?

When the client restarts it will try, unsuccessfully, to renew its lease. The client will be unaffected until the lease expires.

9 How would you configure the duration of the DHCP lease, if only a limited number of IP addresses are available? Would you set a very short lease duration, or a very long lease duration?

The lease must be short, in order that the IP addresses can be freed quickly after they have been used so that they will be available for other clients.

10 You have just installed a DHCP server. You configured your clients as DHCP clients. However, none of them receives an IP configuration from your DHCP server, even though you checked that the scope was activated. What might be causing this problem?

*Before a DHCP server can attribute IP leases, it must be authorized to do so. As a member of the administrators group you can use the DHCP console so as to authorize the server. In order to do this, you must right-click **DHCP**, and then select **Manage authorized servers** so as to add the server to the list of those servers that are authorized to attribute IP leases.*

11 Can a Windows 2000 DHCP service update A and PTR records of clients in the DNS database of the names server?

*Yes. In order to do this you must go into the **DHCP** console, display the properties of the DHCP server concerned, select the **DNS** tab, enable the **Automatically update DHCP client information in DNS** check box, and select the **Always update DNS** option.*

12 What is the purpose of a superscope?

A superscope allows you to attribute IP addresses from several logical subnets to DHCP clients that are located on the same physical segment. This approach allows you to administer the superscope as if it was a normal single scope.

13 What is the purpose of option classes?

You can use DHCP option classes in order to manage configuration details of DHCP clients within a scope.

14 Which types of option class can you create?

You can create option classes that are defined by the vendor, and option classes that are defined by the user.

15 A DHCP client user, who has a Windows 2000 Professional machine, complains that he/she cannot access a resource that is situated on a server, which has an IP address of 192.168.1.1. The scope that is configured on the DHCP server covers the range 192.168.1.10 -192.168.1.200. When you run the **ipconfig** command on the client machine, you notice that the machine has an IP address of 169.254.0.23. What might be causing this problem, and from where did this address come?

When the machine restarts it will probably not be able to contact a DHCP server. It will therefore be assigned an automatic private IP address from the address range 169.254.0.1 - 169.254.255.254. However, as the server has an IP address of 192.168.1.1, then the workstation will not be able to communicate with the server.

16   What is the role of the DHCP Relay Agent?

It allows clients to obtain an IP configuration from a DHCP server that is located on a different network segment. The DHCP Relay Agent intercepts all the DHCP broadcasts and forwards them explicitly to the DHCP server, of which it knows the IP address.

WINS

17   What is the role of the WINS Server?

To resolve NetBIOS names into IP addresses.

18   When you run the ipconfig /all command on the client machine, you notice that the machine is configured as a hybrid node. What does this signify?

The node type corresponds to the resolution method that is used for NetBIOS names. Hybrid, or H-node, indicates that the clients will first try to use a names server in order to resolve names, and will then use broadcasts, if necessary.

19   Why are static entries added into a WINS database?

They allow you to resolve the names of non-WINS clients, such as UNIX hosts, for example.

20   Which two actions must a WINS client carry out with its server?

First, the client will ask to register its name on the server. Then, it will ask the server to resolve names into IP addresses.

21   How can you configure a computer so that it will become a WINS client?

You must specify the address of one or more WINS servers, either manually using the TCP/IP properties, or using a DHCP server.

22   Can a WINS server be a DHCP client?

No. A WINS server must have a fixed IP address so that its clients can communicate with it.

Internet and intranet

23   What is the difference between Internet and intranet?

The Internet is a public network, whereas an Intranet is a private network. In order to communicate, both of these networks use TCP/IP and its associated tools.

24   You have just installed IIS on your server, which is called Merlin. Which new user have you created on your server?

IUSR_MERLIN.

Network services

25 You want to share within your company, general information on the company's users. You have a heterogeneous network that includes Windows, UNIX and Macintosh clients. How can you make these documents available in a simple way?

You must install IIS on a Windows 2000 server in order to publish your documents that have been converted to HTML format. Thereby, users can access these documents using a browser.

26 You are in charge of the intranet Web site of your company. You want to allow all the users to access the public information on this site, but you want to restrict access to confidential information on the same site. How will you achieve these objectives?

Configure your Web site so that it will use the basic authentication method. Grant Read and Execute permissions to the IUSR account, for public information. Grant access permissions for the confidential information, to specific users or to groups of users. In this way, when users connect to the confidential information, the site will authenticate them.

Remote network access

27 Which two tunneling protocols does Windows 2000 support?
PPTP and L2TP.

28 What is the use of a VPN?

You can use a VPN to connect together two computers, without taking into account the physical medium. This technique allows you securely to transmit data across an insecure network.

29 Which type of encryption can you use with the L2TP protocol in order to secure the tunnel?
IPSec.

30 Which console would you use on a Windows 2000 server in order to configure a RNA Server or a VPN?

*For this purpose, you can use the **Routing and Remote Access** console that is situated in the Administrative Tools menu.*

31 What information do you need in order to set up a VPN connection?

When you create a VPN connection, you need know only the IP address of the VPN server. Then, when you connect, you will be required to authenticate (with a user name and a password).

32 Which types of outgoing connections can you configure on a Windows 2000 machine?

You can configure remote access connections, VPN connections, direct cable connections, and Internet connections.

33 Which types of authentication methods are offered by the Windows 2000 remote access service?

EAP, MS-CHAP (v1 and v2), CHAP, SPAP and PAP.

34 Which is the most secure authentication protocol?

MS-CHAP version 2.

35 What is the role of a RADIUS server?

A RADIUS server allows you to centralize the authentication, and the permissions, of remote users.

36 How do you implement remote access security?

Using remote access policies.

37 Why are remote access policies stored on the remote access server and not in Active Directory?

This technique allows you to have several remote access servers that have different policies.

38 You have installed a RNA Server in your domain in native mode. You accept all the default values of the remote access policy options. However, you notice that the user account with which you are going to test the connection has the **Control access through Remote Access Policy** permission. After several attempts to connect to the server from a client, you receive a message that tells you that you do not have connection rights. What might be causing this problem?

*The cause of the problem is that the default policy does not allow clients to connect, when the **Control access through Remote Access Policy** permission is activated in the **Dial-in** tab of the **Properties** dialog box for the user accounts concerned. In order to allow these users to connect, you must either modify the policy, or specifically allow distant access to the users concerned.*

39 In a mixed mode domain, you cannot use a remote access policy in order to control access. However, can you still use remote access conditions and profile?

*Yes. Even though the **Control access through Remote Access Policy** permission is not available in mixed mode, the system will still take into account the remote access conditions and the profile in order to decide the permissions that must be applied.*

Network services

Prerequisites for this chapter

☒ Understanding of the network services concept.

☒ Knowledge of the Windows 2000 operating system.

Objectives

At the end of this chapter, you will be able to:

☒ Install Windows 2000 terminal services.

☒ Configure client machines so that they can connect to the terminal server.

☒ Create and manage a multiple user environment.

☒ Set up RDP connections.

☒ Administer user sessions.

☒ Configure user accounts in a terminal server environment.

Contents

Terminal services

A. Introduction

The server versions of Windows 2000 offer a new feature: several user sessions are supported on the same server. Windows Terminal Server Edition (TSE) provides terminal emulation for the Windows NT 4.0 environment. Windows 2000 terminal services provide the Windows 2000 multi-session feature. In addition, Windows 2000 terminal services offer new features that are not provided by Terminal Server Edition. These new features include the following:
– the administrator can take charge of a user session,
– the clipboard is shared between the local session and the remote session,
– Windows for Workgroups 3.11 clients are supported,
– you can spread the workload,
– you can print locally.
A user with Terminal Services client can log on to the Windows 2000 server. A user session is created on the Windows 2000 server. Everything runs on the server, and only the result of the execution is returned to the client. The client sends only mouse movements and keyboard entries. The actions that the client undertakes are executed on the server. The server then returns to the client the results of the client's actions in graphic form. RDP (*Remote Desktop Protocol*), which runs on TCP/IP, handles this communication. You can also use the Terminal Services in order to run sessions on a remote network. As RDP returns only the results of the queries that are run on the server, this technique is very suitable for slow links. This mechanism must not be confused with a client-server application. With client-server applications, part of the processing is run on the client and the rest of the processing is run on the server. With Terminal Services all the processing is carried out on the server.
Several modifications have been made to the Windows 2000 kernel in order to allow it to manage this service. Previously, servers accepted only one session, that of the user who was physically connected to the computer. The Win32 subsystem now allows you to manage several user sessions on the same machine. In fact, what happens is that a Win32 subsystem is run for each session. This approach ensures that different sessions will not share the same information, and avoids any sharing violation problems.

Terminal Services offer a number of advantages:
- users can run 32-bit applications when they have neither a 32-bit system, nor enough power to support them.
- Obsolete computers can use the Windows 2000 environment. For example, you can use the Terminal Server client on an old 386 machine and thereby take advantage of the Windows 2000 environment, and of all the applications that run in it.
- System administration is simplified because all the user applications are centralized on the same server, and only one installation is required for all the users.

The only constraint that is set by these services is that your server machine must have a relatively high-grade hardware configuration. However, the cost of such a server is quickly recovered thanks to the savings that can be made at the client level, and thanks to the reduced system administration costs.

☞ *The Citrix Metaframe layer that you can install on the Terminal Server allows you to extend certain features. These features include automatic read mapping in client sessions, and the transport of sound between the server and the client.*

B. Installing

In order to use Terminal Services, on the server side you need the **Terminal Services**, and on the client side you need client software that can set up a connection to the server.

So as to optimize the use of the Terminal Server, you must take into account the following recommendations:
- Install the Terminal Services on a member server. Although you can install the Terminal Services on a domain controller, this approach may affect system performance as the domain controller may play one or more roles that consume resources. For similar reasons, you should not install the Terminal Services on a server that plays such roles as DHCP, WINS, and DNS.
- Use the NTFS file system so as to ensure enhanced system security. If you use the FAT system, all the users who log on to the server will be able to access the local resources.
- If possible, you must use fast hard disks (such as SCSI, FAST SCSI or SCSI-2 disks).
- You should use one or more powerful network interface cards.

1. Terminal Services

The configuration that you will need in order to install Terminal Services will depend on the number of users that log on to the server. You must allow at least 4 to 8 MB of extra RAM per user (the addition of 16 MBs of RAM per user is recommended). The more RAM that you add, the better performance that you will obtain.

For example, a Pentium Pro running at 200 MHz can support approximately 20 simultaneous sessions.

You can install this service as follows:

➢ Go into the Control Panel, double-click the **Add/Remove Programs** icon and click the **Add/Remove Windows Components** button, followed by the **Components** button.

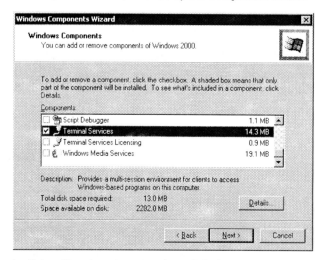

➢ Select **Terminal Services**, then click the **Details** button in order to add or remove any subcomponents as required.

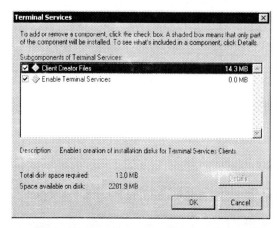

➤ The **Client Creator Files** option provides a diskette creation wizard in order to install the client software. Click **OK** followed by **Next**.

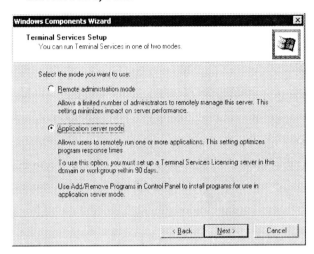

➤ Select **Application server mode**, if you want to use the server as a terminal server. Alternatively, select **Remote administration mode**, if you want to run remote sessions simply in order to administer your servers.

➤ Click **Next**.

If any applications are already installed, Windows 2000 warns you that you will need to re-install these applications so that they will run properly in a multi-user environment. The list of these applications is provided.

➤ When you have noted this list, click **Next** in order to continue with the installation.

➤ When the installation is finished you must restart the computer.

You will now have three new programs in order to administer the Terminal Services:

Terminal Services Configuration	This program allows you to set up the connections, and to define the server settings.
Terminal Services Manager	This program allows you to manage user sessions.

Terminal Services Client Creator	This program allows you to create TS client installation disks according to the client platform concerned.

2. Terminal Services clients

In order to logon to a server that runs Terminal Services, users need a client program. The client program that is required will depend on the client operating system: this can be Windows CE, Windows 2000, Windows NT 4.0, Windows 95/98 or Windows for Workgroups 3.11.

☞ *In addition, the Citrix Metaframe layer allows you to use MSDOS clients or UNIX hosts in order to log on to Terminal Server.*

You can install the client part in several ways:
– You can create installation disks using the **Terminal Services Client Creator** program.

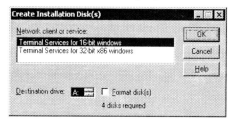

➢ Select the type of platform (16-bit Intel, or 32-bit Intel). The number of disks that you require in order to install the client is indicated (4 disks for 16-bit Intel clients, or 2 disks for 32-bit Intel clients).

➢ Specify whether or not the disks must be formatted before the installation program is copied to them, by activating or deactivating the **Format disk(s)** check box.

– During the installation of Terminal Services, Windows 2000 creates a folder called **Clients** under the *%systemroot%\system32* tree. This folder contains the client installation files. If you share this directory you will be able to access it directly from the client machine via the network.

Under the **Clients** folder, the **Tsclient** subfolder is located, which in turn contains three further subfolders:

Net

> This folder must be used for installation via the network. It contains two subfolders that correspond to the different types of platform (Win16 for 16-bit Windows clients, and Win32 for 32-bit Windows clients).

Win16

This subfolder holds the installation disk contents for 16-bit Windows clients.

Win32

This subfolder holds the installation disk contents for 32-bit Windows clients.

When you have chosen your installation method, run the **setup.exe** installation program and then carry out the following steps:

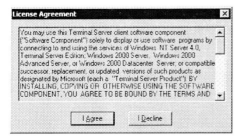

➢ Agree to the terms of the License Agreement.

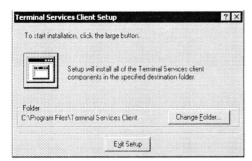

➢ Either accept the proposed location for the installation of the client program, or modify it.

So as to continue, click the [ ] button.

➢ Click **Yes** if you want all users of this machine to have access to the Terminal Services client. In this case, the installation program will copy all the necessary files and the installation will be complete.

Alternatively, if you click the **No** button, then the installation program will ask you where you want to place the client program in the **Start** menu.

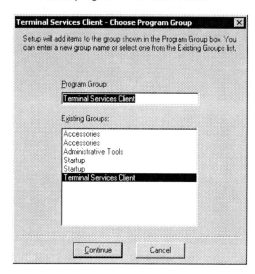

> ➤ Click **Continue** in order to copy the files and to complete the installation.

In your **Start - Programs** menu, you will now have a folder named **Terminal Services Client** that contains the client program, along with an uninstall program and a program that allows you to create client connections.

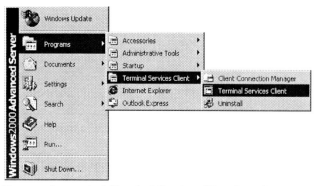

You can then select **Terminal Services Client** in order to set up a connection to the server.

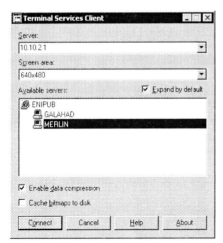

Select the server to which you want to log on. If your network does not have named servers and the Terminal Server is not on your LAN (and therefore not accessible by broadcast), then you can input the IP address of the remote server.

➤ Click the **Connect** button.

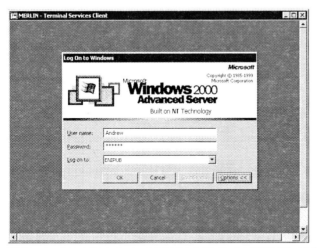

Then you can enter your user name and your password, and you can work as if you were connected locally.

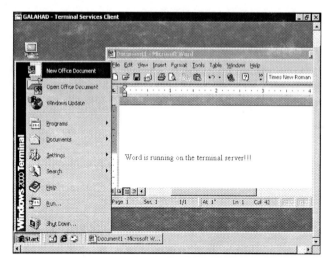

Some Windows 2000 shortcut keys have equivalent sequences in a Terminal Services session. This is the case for the shortcut combination, Ctrl Alt Del, which displays the **Windows Security** dialog box in a Windows 2000 session:

- Ctrl Alt Del is replaced by Ctrl Alt End in a Terminal Services session.
- Alt ⇄ is replaced by Alt Pg Up.
- Alt Esc is replaced by Alt Ins.

You can close your Terminal Services session in several ways:

- You can click the close button of your session window.

In this case, you will log off, but the applications and processes of your session will continue to run on the server. When you log on again, you will be able to continue your session, starting from the state in which you left it.

- Alternatively, you can open the **Start** menu and select **Shut Down**.

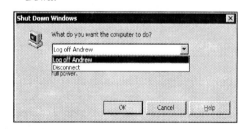

If you select **Log off** *user_name*, then you will close your session along with all its applications.

If you select **Disconnect**, then you will log off without stopping the processes that are currently running. These processes will continue to run on the server.

C. Installing applications

If you install Windows 2000 server with a view to using it as a terminal server, then you should install **Terminal Services** when you install Windows 2000. In this way you can avoid re-installing any applications that you would have installed before you installed these services.

In fact, the applications must be installed in a specific mode so that they can be used in multi-session mode.

In order to install the applications correctly, you must double-click the **Control Panel - Add/Remove Programs** icon, and then you must click the ![button] button.

Alternatively, you can use the **Change user** /**install** command from a command prompt, in order to go into install mode. When you have completed your installation you can return to execute mode by running the **Change user** /**execute** command.

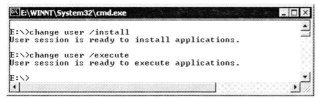

When you add applications using the **Add/Remove Programs** utility, Windows 2000 automatically goes into install mode, and then automatically returns to execute mode when the installation is complete.

☞ *Before you install any application, make sure that no user is currently logged on.*

Some applications that were not initially designed so as to run in a multi-user environment need scripts that allow them to run correctly in this type of environment.

When you install **Terminal Services**, you create a folder that contains several application scripts in **%systemroot%\\ Application Compatibility Scripts\\Install**. These scripts must be applied after you have installed the applications.

All applications do not need scripts in order to run with Terminal Services. However, if you do need scripts in order to allow an application to run correctly in a multi-user environment, then the vendor of the application must supply them. Microsoft offers a certain number of scripts for applications such as Office 95, Office 97, Outlook 97, Outlook 98, Netscape Navigator, Netscape Communicator, MS Project 95 and MS Project 98, Lotus SmartSuite, and many others.

You can edit these scripts in order to know which changes they implement. For example, here is an extract from the script for Outlook 98:

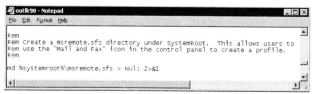

In order to run these compatibility scripts, you must carry out the following steps:

➢ Find the script that is associated with the application concerned in the folder %systemroot%\Application Compatibility Scripts\Install.

➢ Make a copy of the script so that you will be able to modify it, and still keep the original version.

➢ Edit the script and check that the paths are coherent with those that you used when you installed the application. Modify them, if necessary.

➢ Open a command prompt and run the script.

➢ If there is a logon script for the application, modify the paths, if necessary.

➢ Edit the **User.cmd** file, and call each logon script in the same way as the examples of such calls that are already included in the User.cmd file. Delete the remarks concerning the applications that you want to install.

➢ Copy the **User.cmd** file into the directory %systemroot%\ system32.

➢ Open a command prompt and run the **User.cmd** script. You need run this script only once. You do not need to repeat this operation when you add a new application.

D. Configuring

When you install the Terminal Services, users can log on by themselves without any action being required on your part. However, there are several consoles that allow you to set up the connections, and the users' actions.

1. Connection settings

You can use the **Terminal Services Configuration** console in order to set up the connections.

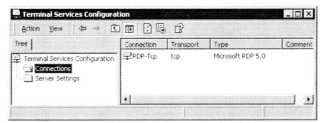

You can use the **Server Settings** folder for the following purposes:

– You can find out in which mode the Terminal Services server is running. In order to do this, double-click the ⊞Terminal server mode icon.

– You can specify that temporary folders must not be deleted when users log off. When users log on, the system creates a different temporary folder for each session. By default, the system deletes these temporary folders when the user logs off. However you can set up the system so that it will not delete these folders. In order to do this, double-click the ⊞Delete temporary folders on exit icon.

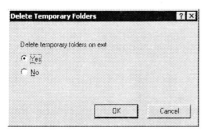

– By default, the system creates a different temporary folder for each session. You can disable this setting by double-clicking the ⊞Use temporary folders per session icon.

– You can disable Active Desktop for client sessions in order to improve the performance of the system. In order to do this, double-click the ⊞Active Desktop icon, and activate the **Disable Active Desktop** check box.

- You can use Internet Connector Licensing for all Terminal Services clients. For this purpose, double-click 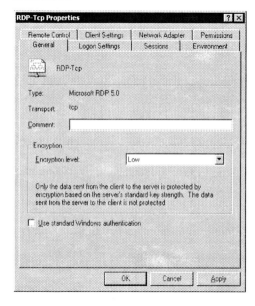Internet Connector licensing , and then select **Enable**. Internet Connector Licensing provides anonymous access to your server so that you can demonstrate your programs to your clients via the Internet, without you having to rewrite your programs to allow access via the Web.

The **Connections** folder allows you to set up your connections. For this purpose, double-click the connection that you want to modify. All the modifications that you make here will be applied to all the users that use the connection concerned.

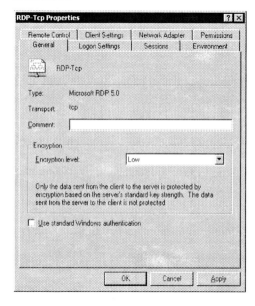

Encryption level

The **General** tab allows you to define the encryption level.

Logon Settings

The **Logon Settings** tab allows you to provide logon information, such as the user name, the user password and the domain. If you enter information into all of these fields then the user will no longer need to authenticate with the server. This approach is useful if you want to use the Terminal Server solely in order to allow users to access a single application that will be made available as soon as the users log on. However, you must be careful with this technique, as all the users will log on with the same user account. Consequently, you must choose an account that has limited permissions.

Sessions

The **Sessions** tab allows you to control the duration of user sessions. If you activate the **Override user settings** check box for an option, then the setting that you indicate for the connection will have priority over that which is set up for the users.

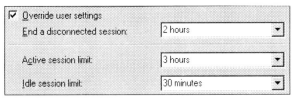

Active session limit

> This value indicates the maximum time that a user can stay logged on. When this time expires, the user is warned that he/she has 2 minutes in order to save his/her files before he/she is logged off by the system.

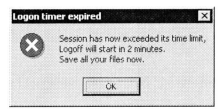

Idle session limit

> This value indicates the maximum time that the user can remain idle before being logged off by the system. Before the user is logged off he/she is sent a message warning that if the user has still made no action after 2 minutes then he/she will be logged off.

End a disconnected session

> By default, when a user is logged off after expiry of a time limit, or even when the user logs off by opening the **Start − Shut Down** and choosing the **Disconnect** option, communication between the client and the server is stopped, but the session stays active on the server. When the user logs on again, the user will go back into his/her environment and all the processes that the user left will still be running. The value that you specify for the **End a disconnected session** option indicates the time that the session will stay active on the server, before the session is re-initialized (or in other words, before the session's processes are stopped).

☑ O̲verride user settings

When session limit is reached or connection is broken:

   ⊙ D̲isconnect from session

   ○ En̲d session

When a connection is broken, or when the user session limit is reached, you can specify that the session will be definitively stopped along with all the session's processes. In order to do this, activate the **End session** option. On the other hand, if you want the users to recover their applications as they left them, when they log on again, then you must activate the **Disconnect from session** option. The **Disconnect from session** option is useful when you use slow or costly links. Thereby, users can remotely start a job, they can then logoff, and logon later in order to analyze the results. However, you must be careful with this approach, as a disconnected session will still use resources on the server.

Executing programs upon logon

You can use Terminal Services in order to provide users with a Windows 2000 Desktop. Alternatively, you can use Terminal Services so as to run a single application when a user logs on. In order to do this, select the **Environment** tab, activate the **Override settings from user profile and Client Connection Manager wizard**, and enter the path that leads to the application that must be started when the user logs on.

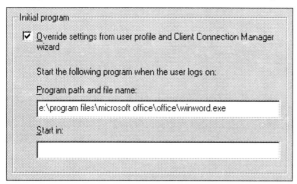

☞ *You can also use the Client Connection Manager that is located in the Start – Programs - Terminal Services Client menu on the client machine, in order to create a new connection that will automatically run a program. In addition, you can include a shortcut that points to the application on the user's desktop.*

Remote control

When users are logged on to the Terminal Server, you can monitor what they are doing. In addition, you can take control of their sessions, in order remotely to solve a problem, or even to demonstrate an operation to the users.

For this purpose, you must use the **Remote Control** tab.

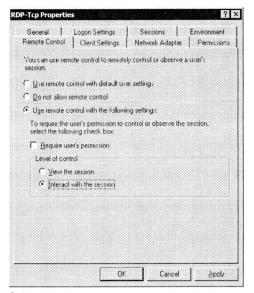

Select the **Use remote control with default user settings** option
in order to assign different control settings for each user. The
setup will then be carried out in the user accounts properties.
In order to assign the same options for all the users, select
Use remote control with the following settings, and then
indicate what you want to do:

Require user's permission

> If you activate this check box, then, when you attempt
> remotely to control a user session, the user will receive a
> message that asks him/her whether or not he/she
> accepts this remote control.

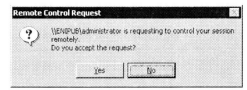

Level of control

> You can select **View the session**, in which case you will be
> able to monitor the session, but you will not be able to
> intervene in the session. Alternatively, you can select
> **Interact with the session**. This will allow you to monitor the
> session and it will also allow you to interact with the
> session.

In order to take remote control, go into the **Administrative
Tools** menu and open the **Terminal Services Manager**
console. Then, right-click the session that you want to
control.

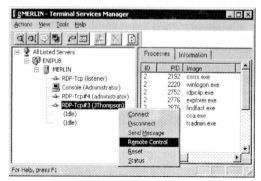

Select **Remote Control**.

☞ *You cannot take control directly from the Terminal Server. If you are on the Terminal Server and you want remotely to control a session, then you must use the client program so as to open a session on your own machine, and then go into the Terminal Services Manager console from this session.*

Client ports and printers

By default, when a user logs on to the Terminal Server, the user can use his/her local printers in his/her session. In addition, the user can use a clipboard that is common to the user's Desktop and to the user's Terminal Server session. These two options, along with the remote control feature, were not available with the Terminal Services RDP4 protocol. They have become available with the RDP5 protocol of Windows 2000.

You can disable printer mapping, port mapping and clipboard mapping using the **Client Settings** tab.

Choosing a network adapter for the connections

If you have several network cards on the terminal server, then by default, the same connection properties will be used for all the network adapters. The **Network Adapter** tab allows you to specify different settings for the clients of different subnets.

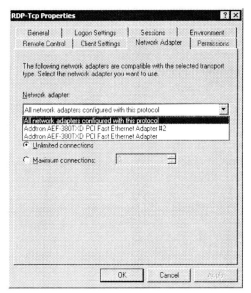

In addition, you can limit the number of connections for each interface.

In order to specify different settings for each subnet, you must create a new connection for each network adapter. In order to do this, go into the **Terminal Services Configuration** console, right-click the **Connections** folder, and then select **Create New Connection**. A wizard will then help you to create a new connation.

2. Setting up user actions

In order to be able to log on to a Terminal Server, users must have the necessary permission. By default, all users have this permission. You can withdraw this permission for a user, by going into the user's properties, activating the **Terminal Services Profile** tab, and deactivating the **Allow logon to terminal server** check box.

Whereas the **Terminal Services Configuration** console allows you to configure connections for all the users who log on, the **Properties** dialog box for a user account allows you to assign different settings for different users. You can specify the following settings:

- Starting a program when a user logs on. For this purpose you must use the **Environment** tab of the user account properties dialog box.
- Disconnecting client printers upon logon.
- Specifying, or not specifying an active session limit, an idle session limit, and the end of a disconnected session.
- Remote control.
- Assigning a profile for a Terminal Services session. When a user logs on to Terminal Services, the user will use his/her user profile, unless a specific profile has been

defined for the Terminal Services session. You can create such a profile in the same way as you would create a profile for a standard Windows 2000 connection. You can use the **Terminal Services Profile** tab in order to declare your profile. You can also use this tab in order to specify a user's home directory.

E. Managing sessions

You can manage sessions from any machine, by using the **Terminal Services Manager** console. You can install this console on your machine using the administrative tools installation program **Adminpack.msi**. Alternatively, you can log on to Terminal Services as the administrator.

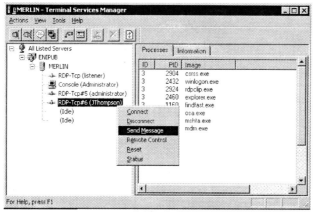

This console shows the status of all Terminal Services connections. When you select a connection, the processes that are used by this connection appear in the right-hand pane of the window. You can close an application remotely by right-clicking a process ID. You can obtain information such as the workstation from which a user logged on, the user's display resolution, and the user's IP address, by selecting the user connection, and then clicking the **Information** tab in the right-hand pane.

1. Sending messages

In order to carry out administrative tasks (such as installing new programs on the Terminal Server, or shutting down the Terminal Server) you will need to warn the users that you are about to disconnect, or to re-initialize their sessions. You can do this by right-clicking the connections and selecting **Send Message**.

2. Disconnecting a user

You may wish to disconnect a user for maintenance reasons, or when a breakdown occurs. In order to do this, right-click the connection that you want to disconnect, and then select **Disconnect**. You must remember that, when you disconnect a user you do not close the applications on which the user was working. When the user logs on again, then the user will recover his/her desktop in the state that it was in before being disconnected. When the session has been disconnected, it appears in the **Terminal Services Manager** console under the name of *disconnected (username)*. For example: Disconnected (JThompson) .

The user's session window closes and the following message appears:

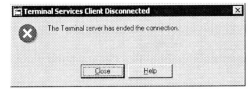

3. Resetting a connection

When you reset a session, you close all the applications that are running in the session. However, you must be careful when you do this because the user will lose all the information that has not been saved! When you reset a session, it no longer appears in the **Terminal Services Manager** console. You can re-initialize a session that is in a disconnected state by right-clicking it and then selecting **Reset**.

F. Remote administration

You can use **Terminal Services** solely in order remotely to administer your servers. If you want to do this, then you must select the **Remote administration mode** during the installation process of Terminal Services. This option requires fewer server resources than the **Application server mode** option.

With **Remote administration mode**, only administrators can log on to the Terminal Server. However, you can authorize other users to log on by permissions in the user connection properties.

When you install Terminal Services, then a certain amount of memory is reserved for each user session. However, if you use Terminal Services with the sole objective of remotely administering, then you can free much of this reserved space, as you will certainly have few administrators who will wish to log on to the same server at the same time so as to administer it. In order to limit the amount of memory that is used by Terminal Services, you must set to 0, the value of the **IdleWinStationPoolCount** registry that is located in **HKLM\System\CurrentControlSet\Control\TerminalServer** if you install Terminal Services in remote administration mode, then this value is set to 0 automatically).

The following measures will help to optimize the performance of your Terminal Server in remote administration mode:

- Disable Active Desktop in the **Server Settings** folder of the **Terminal Services Configuration** console.
- Disable the wallpaper for Terminal Server sessions using the **Environment** tab in the connection properties.
- Adjust the **Idle session limit** and **End of a disconnected session** values, just in case the administrators forget to log off.

☞ *Make sure that you specify a high encryption level in remote administration mode, in order to ensure that transmitted data will be thoroughly encrypted.*

Labs

To be absolutely sure that you have assimilated this chapter, work through the corresponding labs. These are set out from page 688 to page 691.

☒ Installing Terminal Services.

☒ Installing Office 97.

☒ Configuring connections.

☒ Installing Terminal Services Client.

☒ Switching from application server mode to remote administration mode.

Assessing your skills

Try the following questions if you think you know this chapter
well enough.

Terminal Services

1 Which protocol does the system use in order to transport ☐
information such as mouse movements and keystrokes,
between the terminal client and the terminal server?
....

2 Is the Terminal Services application, a client-server ☐
application?
....
....
....
....

3 How can you transform your server into a terminal ☐
server?
....
....
....
....

4 What are the different installation modes that you can ☐
use for Terminal Services?
....

5 What does a client need so that it can log on to a ☐
terminal server?
....

6 How can you install Terminal Services Client on a ☐
machine that runs Windows 98?
....
....
....
....

7 Can you use Terminal Services Client on non-Intel ☐
platforms?
....

8 What is the difference between disconnecting a session ☐
and resetting a session?
....
....
....
....

9 How must you install an application so that it will run on a terminal server? ❑

....
....
....
....
....
....
....

10 What is the role of an application script? ❑

....
....
....

11 Where are the application scripts situated? ❑

....
....
....
....
....
....
....

12 You want to ensure that all users that are logged on to Terminal Services will be disconnected if they are idle for 30 minutes. How can you do this? ❑

....
....
....
....

13 Can you monitor a session without the session user knowing about it? ❑

....
....
....
....
....
....

14 You have two subnets, and you want to apply different logon settings to users, according to the subnet via which the users log on. How can you achieve this? ❑

....
....
....
....
....

Results

Check your answers on pages 557 to 559. Count one point for each correct answer.

Number of points   /14

For this chapter you need to have scored at least 11 out of 14.

Look at the list of key points that follows. Pick out the ones with which you have had difficulty and work through them again in this chapter before moving on to the next.

Key points of the chapter

☐ Terminal Services.

Solutions

Terminal Services

1 Which protocol does the system use in order to transport information such as mouse movements and keystrokes, between the terminal client and the terminal server?

RDP (Remote Desktop Protocol) version 5.

2 Is the Terminal Services application, a client-server application?

No. With client-server applications, part of the application is run on the client, and the rest of the application is run on the server. However, with Terminal Services, the client part consists solely of logging on to the server, and all the processes run entirely on the server. The client sends only the graphical inputs.

3 How can you transform your server into a terminal server?

*You can specify that Terminal Services must be installed when you install Windows 2000. Alternatively, after you have installed your system you can go into the **Control Panel** and then open **Add/Remove Programs** - **Add/Remove Windows Components**, and click the **Components** button, and then select the **Terminal Services** component.*

4 What are the different installation modes that you can use for Terminal Services?

Remote administration mode and Application server mode.

5   What does a client need so that it can log on to a terminal server?

TCP/IP protocol, and Terminal Services Client.

6   How can you install Terminal Services Client on a machine that runs Windows 98?

*You can create installation diskettes using the **Terminal Services Client Creator** program that is located on the server. Alternatively, you can install Terminal Services Client directly from the Windows 98 client by connecting to the **clients** directory on the terminal server, which must previously have been share, and then running **setup.exe** that is located in **clients – tsclient – net - win32.***

7   Can you use Terminal Services Client on non-Intel platforms?

No, not at the present time.

8   What is the difference between disconnecting a session and resetting a session?

When you disconnect a session, you close the network connection between the client and the server. However, all the applications of the session will continue to run, and will continue to consume server resources. When you reset a session, not only do you stop the communication between the client and the server, but you also free all the resources on the server that were being used by the session.

9   How must you install an application so that it will run on a terminal server?

*You must place the server in install mode. You can do this in two ways: You can use the **Add/Remove Programs** icon in the **Control Panel**. Alternatively, you can enter the **change user /install** command into a command prompt. If you use this latter method, you must remember to return to execute mode by entering the **change user /execute** command.*

10   What is the role of an application script?

Application scripts allow applications that were not designed for a multi-session environment, to modify a certain number of their settings so that they will be able to run in this type of environment.

11   Where are the application scripts situated?

When you install Terminal Services, Windows 2000 creates a directory that contains these scripts. This directory is situated in the tree %systemroot%\Application Compatibility Scripts\Install. If the application that you want to install in multi-session mode does not have a script in this directory, then you must ask the vendor of your application to supply you with this script.

12 You want to ensure that all users that are logged on to Terminal Services will be disconnected if they are idle for 30 minutes. How can you do this?

*Go into the **Terminal Services Configuration** console and set the **Idle session limit** to 30 minutes. This option is located in the connection properties, under the **Sessions** tab. You must activate the corresponding **Override user settings** check box so as to apply this option to all the users.*

13 Can you monitor a session without the session user knowing about it?

*Yes. You can do this by deactivating the **Require user's permission** check box. If you want to monitor access to Terminal Services of all the users, then you must use this check box that is situated under the **Remote Control** tab of the connections properties. Alternatively, if you want to monitor access to Terminal Services by specific users, then you must use this check box that is situated under the **Remote Control** tab of the user account properties for each of the users concerned.*

14 You have two subnets, and you want to apply different logon settings to users, according to the subnet via which the users log on. How can you achieve this?

*The Terminal Server must have two network interfaces, one for each of the subnets. You must use the **Terminal Services Configuration** console in order to create a new connection. Then, you must apply the different settings to the different connections.*

Prerequisites for this chapter

☒ Knowledge of PC hardware components.

☒ Knowledge of network software and hardware components.

☒ Knowledge of Active Directory objects.

Objectives

At the end of this chapter, you will be able to:

☒ Backup your data and that of the system.

☒ Restore Active Directory objects.

☒ Use different startup modes in order to troubleshoot your
system.

☒ Use the Event Viewer and the Performance Monitor in
order to monitor your system.

☒ End a process that has failed.

**Backing up, restoring, trouble-
shooting and analysing**

Contents

A. Backing up

Windows 2000 provides a tool that allows you to backup and to restore system data (such as the Active Directory, and the registry). This utility is called **Backup** and is located in the **Start - Programs - Accessories - System Tools** menu. The Backup utility is very easy to use and provides a graphic interface that is very user friendly and intuitive. Not only does it allow you to backup and to restore, but also it allows you to schedule these activities. This tool has been greatly improved since the Ntbackup tool of Windows NT 4.0.

You can backup to tape devices, to logical drives, to removable disks or to CD-ROM writer drives. You can backup from volumes that are formatted either in FAT or in NTFS.

You can backup and restore manually. Alternatively, you can use a wizard that will guide you step by step through the procedure of creating the necessary jobs. This wizard also allows you to create an emergency repair disk.

It is, of course, extremely important that you back up regularly, system data, and other essential information. In addition, it is just as important that you test your backups. You must regularly carry out restore tests, so as to be sure that your storage devices will operate correctly on the day when you need to restore.

1. Backing up data

Every file and every folder has an archive attribute. When this attribute is set, it indicates that the file or the folder has not been modified since the last backup. When you modify a file, the system sets this attribute, and will backup this file when it runs the next backup procedure.

You can access this attribute by opening the properties of the file, or of the folder, and then clicking the **Advanced** button.

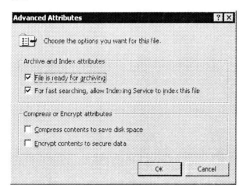

If the **File is ready for archiving** check box is enabled, then the archive attribute is set. If this attribute is disabled for a file or a folder then the system will automatically enable it when you modifiy the file or the folder.

You can make five types of backup:

Normal

Backs up all the files that you have selected and sets their archive attribute.

Copy

Backs up all the files that you have selected and does not set their archive attribute.

Incremental

Backs up all the files that you have selected that have been modified since the last backup. This type of backup sets the archive attribute.

Differential

Backs up all the files that you have selected that have been modified since the last backup. This type of backup does not set the archive attribute.

Daily

Backs up all the files that have been modified during the day that the backup is made. This type of backup does not set the archive attribute.

☞ *A differential backup takes longer than an incremental backup. However, a differential backup takes less time to restore than an incremental backup.*

In order to back up data you must carry out the following steps:

➤ Go into the **Start - Programs - Accessories - System Tools** menu, and then select **Backup**.

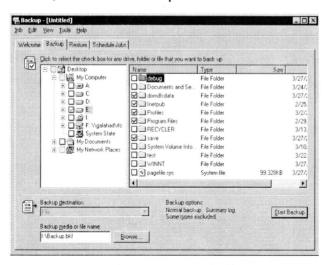

➢ Activate the **Backup** tab, and then select the folders and the files that you want to back up.

➢ Open the **Tools** menu and select **Options**.

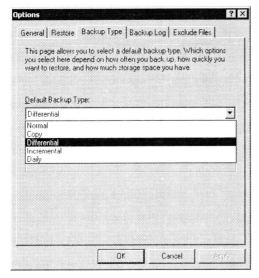

➢ Activate the **Backup Type** tab and select the backup type that you want to implement.

➢ The **Backup Log** tab allows you to specify the level of detail that you want to log during the backup process.

➢ Click the **OK** button.

➢ Enter the name of the backup file, along with the identification of the drive onto which you want to back up.

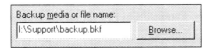

➢ Click the **Start** button in order to start the backup.

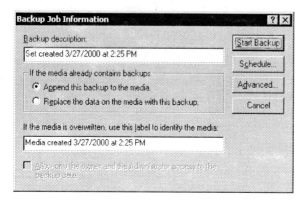

> ➤ Enter a description for your backup (the description by
>   default includes the creation date and time). The **Ad-
>   vanced** button allows you to select the backup type. This
>   button is useful if you have not already selected the
>   backup type using the **Tools** menu.

> ➤ Click the **Start Backup** button. When you backup has
>
>   finished it is represented by an ⬛ icon.

☞ *If you back up NTFS files, the NTFS permissions that
  are associated with the files and the folders will be
  maintained when these files and folders are restored
  onto an NTFS partition. Similarly, files that have been
  encrypted will remain encrypted after you have restored
  them.*

☞ *Before you carry out your backup, make sure that no-
  body is using the files that you have selected. The
  backup process will ignore any files that are being used.
  These files will be indicated in the backup log. Nevertheless, Windows 2000 can backup files that are being
  used by the system when it backs up the System State.*

2. Backing up the system state

The Windows 2000 Backup utility allows you to backup the
data that concerns the state of your system. This comprises
the registry database, the system startup files, the Active Directory, the sysvol files, the certificates service database and
the COM+ Class Registration database.
You cannot back up these components individually.
In order to back up these components, go into the **Backup**
utility, and activate the **System State** check box.

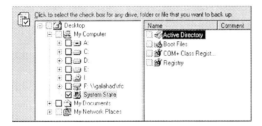

3. Scheduling

One of the improvements that the Windows 2000 Backup utility offers, with respect to the Windows NT version, is that Windows 2000 Backup allows you to schedule your backup jobs, using a graphic interface.

➤ Click **Schedule Jobs**, in the **Backup** utility.

➤ Click **Add Job** button in order to start the Backup Wizard.

➤ Follow the steps of the Backup Wizard.

In this schedule, the system will carry out a normal backup every Monday, and an incremental backup every other day in the week.

B. Restoring

1. Restoring data

In order to restore data, you can use the Restore Wizard, or you can restore manually. For this purpose, activate the **Restore** tab in the **Backup** utility. Then, select the backup that you want to restore. If no backup media appear in the list, then this is probably because you have deleted the catalog that corresponds to the media catalog by selecting **Delete Catalog** from the **Tools - MediaTools** menu. In this case you must import the catalog that corresponds to the backup. You can do this by opening the **Tools** menu and then selecting **Catalog a backup file**.

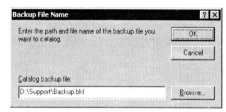

➢ Enter the name of the path that leads to your backup files and then click **OK**.

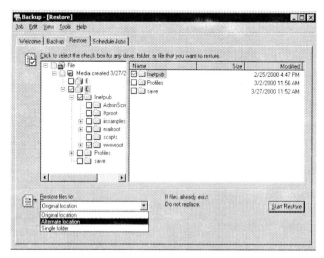

➢ Open the media and select the files that you want to restore from the backup set, then indicate whether you want to restore your backup to the original location, or whether you want to restore your backup to an alternate location.

➢ Click the **Start** button.

> Click the **Advanced** button if you want to specify advanced settings, and click **OK** in order to start restoring.

2. Restoring the system state

When you restore the system state, Windows 2000 deletes the current system state and replaces it with the system state from the backup. Consequently, you must backup the system state regularly in order to avoid losing data.

So as to restore the state of your system on a domain controller, you must restart your server in **Directory Services Restore** mode. In order to do this you must press the F8 key when the system prompts you to do so and then select the **Directory Services Restore Mode (Windows 2000 domain controllers only)** menu. Log on using the local administrator account that you created when you installed Active Directory. This startup mode allows you to start Windows 2000 without loading Active Directory. In fact, if you want to restore it, then the Active Directory database must not be loaded. Then, you can use the **Backup** utility so as to restore Active Directory (System State). Restart the server so that Windows 2000 will re-index and update the Active Directory database.

a. Restoring Active Directory objects

If you want to restore Active Directory objects that you have inadvertently deleted, then you must follow another procedure.

Windows 2000 marks all deleted objects and stores them in the directory database for 60 days. Each object has a serial number that is called the USN (*Update Sequence Number*). This USN is used for replication. If you restore an object in Active Directory, then you will restore it with a USN that is less than that of the object that you deleted. Therefore, during the replication process, the object will be marked as deleted.

The mechanism that allows you to restore objects into Active Directory is called forced restore. When you force a restore, the objects have the largest USN numbers. This allows you to restore them and to replicate them without any problems.

In order to restore individual objects, you must carry out the following steps:

> Restart your domain controller in **Directory Services Restore Mode (Windows 2000 domain controllers only)**.

> Restore the latest backup that concerns the system state using the **Backup** utility.

> When the restore has finished, close the **Backup** utility, and open a command prompt.

> In the command prompt, enter **ntdsutil**.

> In the command prompt, enter **authoritative restore**.

> Then type:
> **restore subtree** *full_object_name*.

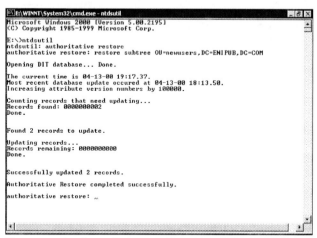

The example above illustrates the restore of the GROUPS organizational unit, in the ENIPUB.COM domain.

> Quit the ntdsutil program by entering the **Quit** command twice, and then restart the server.

b. Restoring the system on a new server

If your server breaks down completely, and you must re-install it, then you can restore the system state of the old server, onto the new server so that it will have exactly the same characteristics (for example, it will have the same name, the same registry database and the same directory database).

In order to do this, re-install the Windows 2000 system. You must accept the default install options, as you will set up your system again later. Make your server a stand-alone server and re-install all the applications that were present on the server previously. Then, go into the **Backup** utility and re-store the system state from the latest backup.

C. Troubleshooting

1. Startup steps

After your computer has tested its hardware components (using the POST, or Power On Self Test, sequence on Intel platforms), the first action that it will carry out is to read the MBR: Master Boot Record. Then, this MBR will examine the partitions table in order to find the active partition in this table that contains four entries. The boot sector in the active partition is run: this is the operating system preloader. The preloader then loads the operating system loader, which will then load the operating system.

Here are the steps of a Windows 2000 boot:

- **Step 1**

  Reading NTLDR (for MSDOS, IO.SYS is the first file that is read). **Ntldr** switches the processor from real mode to 32-bit linear memory mode. Then it starts up the FAT and NTFS system drivers, which allow it to access the file systems in order to start up Windows 2000 fully. **Ntldr** then reads **BOOT.INI** so as to build the boot loader menu.

- **Step 2** - BOOT.INI: This a text file that allows Windows 2000 to boot, or to start up on another operating system.

Here is an example of the boot.ini file. You can use this file in order to boot Windows 2000:

```
[boot loader]
timeout=30
default=multi(0)disk(0)rdisk(0)partition(1)\WINNT
[operating systems]
multi(0)disk(0)rdisk(0)partition(1)\WINNT="Microsoft Windows 2000
Advanced Server" /fastdetect
```

ARC Names

ARC names have the following structure:

```
SCSI(x)disk(y)rdisk(0)partition(n) or
MULTI(x)disk(0)rdisk(z)partition(n)
```

```
SCSI(x) or MULTI(x)
```

The value x denotes the SCSI hardware controller number in their initialization order. It must be noted that some SCSI discs appear with the name MULTI (those for which the SCSI controller BIOS has not been disabled), according to the BIOS management mode.

DISK(y)   For Multibus SCSI adapters, this corresponds to the bus number. It is always equal to zero for MULTI controllers.

RDISK(z)   For MULTI components, z indicates the disk number on the adapter. For SCSI disks it is always equal to zero.

PARTITION(n)   n indicates the partition number on the disk, from 1 to n.

Thereby, on a disk that is handled by an IDE controller, or by a SCSI (BIOS activated) controller, the second partition that is on the second physical disk of the first controller will be referenced by: multi (0) disk (0) rdisk (1) partition (2). In this case disk (0) is a constant.

☞ *Important note: an incorrect ARC name will generate the following message,*
"Windows 2000 could not start because the following file is missing or corrupt:
%Systemroot%\System32\ntoskrnl.exe
Please re-install a copy of the above file"
In most cases, you can solve this problem simply by editing the boot.ini file.
An incorrect ARC name can occur after you have created a new main partition, when the Windows 2000 boot partition is in a logical drive of an extended partition.

– Step 3
NTDETECT.COM: hardware detection program.

☞ *NTDETECT.COM allows you to generate the HARDWARE volatile key.*

☞ *If you select an operating system other than Windows 2000, then the BOOTSECT.DOS allows you to run the preloader of this other system (BOOTSECT.DOS is a copy of the former boot sector before Windows NT was installed).*

– Step 4
The **Hardware Profile/Configuration Recovery** startup menu, followed by loading of the Windows 2000 system.

2. Contents of the BOOT.INI sections

This file is hidden, and is in read-only mode (S, H, R attributes). With Intel platforms, it is created automatically on the system partition when Windows 2000 is installed.

a. [boot loader] Section

`timeout` Defines the number of seconds that must elapse before Windows 2000 loads the default operating system.
A value of 0 causes the system to start immediately.

☞ *You can modify boot.ini directly, and set a value of –1. In this case the system will wait indefinitely for you to select an option.*

☞ *In most cases, you should use the **Control Panel – System** icon, activate the **Advanced** tab, and then click the **Startup and Recovery** button, in order to modify this value.*

☞ *If you want to modify this file after you have started MS DOS, then you must simultaneously disable the three attributes S,H, and R using the following command:*
attrib -S -H -R BOOT.INI, *before you modify the file. After you have modified the file, you must reset these attributes using the following command:*
attrib +S +H +R BOOT.INI

> `default` This parameter corresponds to the path of the default operating system. This path must be present in the [operating systems] section.

b. [operating systems] section

This section allows you to define the paths to the boot sectors of the different operating systems that are available, such as: Windows 2000, Windows NT, Windows 95/98, MSDOS and OS/2.

3. Last known good configuration

Internally, Windows 2000 manages several sets of system configurations (it manages three in general).
In most cases, Windows 2000 starts up with the default configuration, or CurrentControlSet (see HKEY_LOCAL_MACHINE\System).

☞ *In fact, Windows 2000 records a configuration as the last known good configuration as soon as a user is able to log on with it (even if it generates many errors!)*

When a problem occurs following a new installation, then the message **At least one driver or service failed during system startup** will warn you of the problem, before you log on. In this case, you must stop and restart the machine, without logging on, so as to restart using the **Last known good configuration** option.
You can access this option as follows:
– When you start up Windows 2000, press the `F8` key when you are prompted to do so. Then, use the arrow keys in order to select the **Last known good configuration** option.
When you apply the last known good configuration, you lose all the configurations from the previous session.

4. Starting from a floppy disk

You can start up Windows 2000, whether Windows 2000 uses FAT or whether it uses NTFS!
For this purpose, you must use a diskette that you have formatted on a Windows NT 4.00 system, or on a Windows 2000 system (this is necessary so that the NT preloader will be installed on the diskette, and ready to load NTLDR). You must then copy the files NTLDR, BOOT.INI, NTBOOTDD.SYS (if the BIOS of the SCSI controller is deactivated) and

NTDETECT.COM, which are situated in the root of the Windows 2000 system partition. Startup steps 1 to 3 are carried out on the diskette instead of the hard disk.

5. Using an emergency repair disk

As the administrator, you can repair the system by starting up on the Windows 2000 installation startup diskettes. You can create these 4 diskettes by selecting the bootdisk directory on the Windows 2000 CD-ROM, and entering the command **makeboot a** in a command prompt:

After you have inserted the fourth diskette, you can carry out an emergency repair by pressing the **R** key. However, in order to do this you need previously to have created an emergency repair diskette on the system that you want to repair. You can create this diskette using the **Welcome** tab of the **Backup** utility. You can also repair the installation using the recovery console (by pressing the **C** key).

After you have pressed the **R** key, you can repair manually, in order to choose the options that you want to repair. Alternatively, you can choose to carry out a fast repair. In this case the following options will be chosen for you:

Inspect startup environment

This option checks the presence of the files that are needed in order to start up Windows 2000 (such as boot.ini, and ntldr).

Verify Windows 2000 system files

This option is needed if any Windows 2000 files have been deleted, or if the disk has been altered. The SETUP.LOG file that is contained on the emergency repair disk allows the program to copy the files from the CD-ROM onto the hard disk.

Inspect boot sector

This option recreates the boot sector (so that it will point to the first NTLDR file).

☞ *You can also run an emergency repair by booting on the Windows 2000 CD-ROM, without using the startup diskettes.*

6. Other startup options

Windows 2000 can run in different modes. This feature allows you to troubleshoot any operational problems that the system may have. You can access the menu that allows you to choose these modes by pressing the ⌈F8⌋ key when you are prompted to do so during the startup process of your system.

Safe Mode
> This option allows you to start up your system by loading the essential drivers that you need for this purpose. A file called **Ntbtlog.txt** is created in the %systemroot% directory. This file allows the system to detect the drivers that have been loaded, and the drivers that have not been loaded.

Safe Mode with Networking
> This is the same as Safe Mode, except that the drivers that the system needs for networking are loaded as well.

Safe Mode with Command Prompt
> When you choose this option, Windows 2000 runs in Safe Mode without loading the graphic interface.

Enable VGA Mode
> With this option, Windows 2000 runs with the standard VGA graphic drivers. You must choose this option when you have a problem with you graphic card driver.

Enable Boot Logging
> When you choose this option Windows 2000 starts up normally, and produces a report on all drivers and services that have been loaded during the start up. This report is written to the **Ntbtlog.txt** file that is located in the %systemroot% directory.

Directory Services Restore Mode (Windows 2000 domain controllers only)
> As we saw previously, this mode allows you to start up Windows 2000 without loading Active Directory, so that you will be able to restore it.

Debugging Mode
> When you choose this option, the system sends debugging information to another computer via a serial cable.

7. Recovery console

The recovery console is a text mode interface that allows you to repair your system when you can no longer boot Windows 2000. You can use this console, in order to stop or to start services that could prevent the system from starting up, in order to format hard disks and in order to read data that is situated on FAT or NTFS disks. So that you can go into this console, you must indicate the installation you wish to repair, along with the password of the local administrator of the server (if your machine is a domain controller, this is the local administrator that you indicated when you installed Active Directory).

You can run the recovery console in two ways:
- You can start up the system, either using the 4 startup diskettes, or using the Windows 2000 CD-ROM. Then, when you are prompted to do so, you must press the **C** key so as to start up the recovery console.

– Alternatively, you can access the recovery console using the Windows 2000 startup menu. However, before you can do this, you must first install this console.

a. Installing the recovery console

➢ Start up a command prompt.

➢ Access the **I386** directory of the Windows 2000 CD-ROM.

➢ Input the command **winnt32 /cmdcons**.

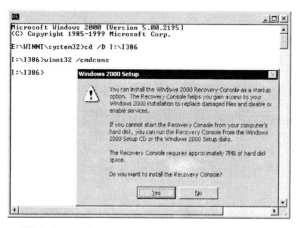

➢ Click the **Yes** button.

➢ Restart your computer. You will notice that the **Microsoft Windows 2000 Recovery Console** option now appears in the startup menu along with other options such as **Microsoft Windows 2000 Advanced Server**, for example.

☞ *The boot.ini file has been modified and will now look like the following example:*

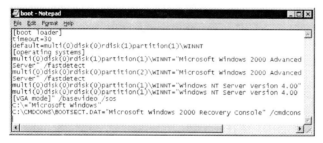

☞ *When you have entered the recovery console, enter the **Help** command in order to display the list of available commands.*

Here are some of the commands that you can use in the recovery console:

listsvc: lists all the services and drivers, and indicates
whether they are started or not.

Disable: allows you to stop a service.

Enable: allows you to start a service

Systemroot: sets systemroot as the current directory.

Fixboot: writes a new boot sector onto the system partition.

Fixmbr: repairs the master boot record of the main boot
sector of the partition.

8. Processes

Loss of control on your system is rarely caused by failure of
the system itself. It is generally caused by the failure of an
application. This does not prevent the other applications from
running, but it can affect system performance. So as to
remedy this situation, you must stop the process that is
causing the problem. In order to do this, run the **Task
Manager**, using the shortcut key sequence: Ctrl Alt Del.
Then click the **Task Manager** button in the **Windows Security**
dialog box that appears. You can also access the Task
Manager by right-clicking the task bar.

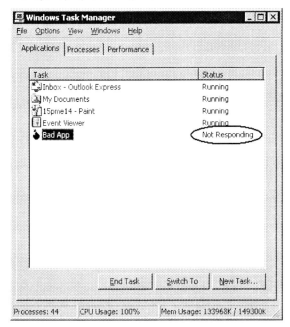

➢ Click the **Processes** tab, or right-click the name of the application that has failed, and then select **Go To Process**.

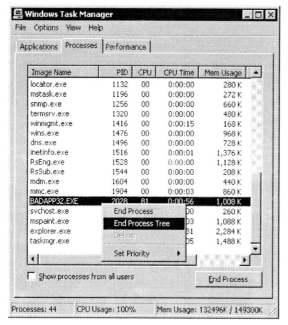

➢ Right-click the process that corresponds to the application that has failed and then select **End Process**. Note that you can also select **End Process Tree**, which allows you to delete all the processes that are associated with the process that you have selected.

Each process has a run priority level. There are 6 different priority levels:
- Realtime
- High
- AboveNormal
- Normal
- BelowNormal
- Low

By default, every application that you start has a **normal** priority level. You can set different priority levels so that one application will run faster than another. In order to do this, right-click the process for which you want to change the priority level and select **Set Priority**.

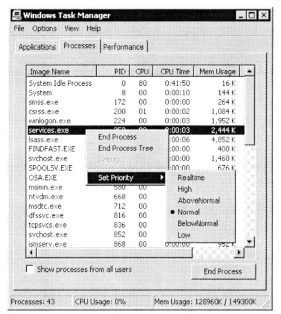

Then, select the priority to which you want to set the process.

☞ *Be careful not to set a process priority level to **Realtime**, as, if this process fails, the system would not be able to regain control.*

9. Event Viewer

Windows 2000 traces many actions and events in the operating system. The Event Viewer console can be started from the **Administrative Tools** menu.

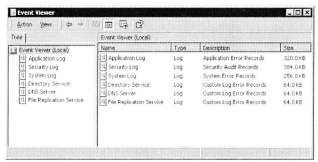

Several logs are available that allow you to record the events:

– **Application Log**: application developers use this log in order to write the information that is returned by their applications.

- **System Log**: This log contains information that is returned by the system, such as a notification that the system is unable to find a domain controller. Both of these logs generally contain error records, which are represented by the icon : 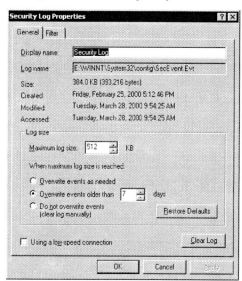Error , and information records, which are represented by the icon : ⓘInformation and warning records, which are represented by the icon: ⚠Warning .
- **Security Log**: This log contains the return messages from your audits (🗝Success Audit and 🔒Failure Audit).

The **Action - Properties** menu allows you to set up the recording of events in the log that you have selected.

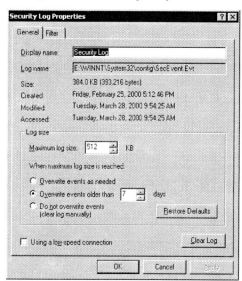

By default, the maximum size of the log is 512 KB. You can change this maximum size, and you can define the actions that must be taken when the log is full. These actions are as follows:
- Overwrite events.
- Overwrite events that are older than a specific number of days. However, you must note that if the log is full and no event that is recorded in it is older than this number of days then new events will not be written to the log.
- Do not overwrite events. This option implies that you must clear the log manually.

☞ *You can define a group policy that will stop the machine as the log becomes full. The objective of this technique is to ensure that no audit records will be lost.*

☞ *Your event viewer will contain other logs according to the roles that your server plays (for example, Active Directory, or DNS).*

If you have many records, then you can apply filters in order to help you to find items for which you are looking. For this purpose, you must go into the **Properties** of the log concerned and select the **Filter** tab.

In order to find out the cause of an error, you can double-click the event concerned.

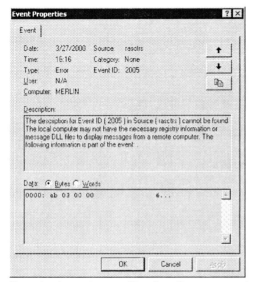

If you implement an audit policy, then you must remember to consult the security log regularly. You can save the security log so as to monitor the security. In order to save a log, right-click the log concerned, and then select **Save Log File As**. The file will be saved in .evt format (you can also save it in text format if you prefer). This allows you to read it later using the event viewer. You can also save your logs in .csv format, which allows you to use these files with applications that handle delimiters.

D. Performance utility

The performance utility allows you to monitor the activities of one or more computers, in a detailed way. The monitored information is stored in text files. You can view it in graphic form, and you can associate it with minimum and maximum alert thresholds. The **Performance** console can be started from the **Administrative Tools** menu.

1. Counters

Windows 2000 considers as **objects**, such items as devices, files, disks, processors and virtual memory.

You can monitor each object in a number of different ways. For example, for the *Processor* object, the **Performance** console offers different **counters** such as the number of **Interrupts/sec**, the percentage of processor use in **User** mode and in **Privileged** mode.

Four objects are especially important: the processor, the physical disk, the memory, and the network interface.

An object can be present several times with the Windows 2000 system. In this case it is said to have multiple instances: a dual processor computer will have two **instances** of the **Processor** object. If the **NetBEUI** protocol is linked to two network cards, then it will also have two instances. The purpose of detailed system analysis is to find bottlenecks. In other words, so as to find devices that slow down the whole system because they do not have enough performance in order to deal with the workload that the system is asking of them.

☞ *One bottleneck can hide another bottleneck. For example, heavy disk activity will slow down the running of Windows 2000. This slowing down may be connected with the hard disk (due to disk fragmentation, or poor access time and data transfer time, for example). However, it might also be masking a lack of RAM, for which the system must compensate with excessive paging between the swap file and volatile memory.*

2. Graphs

Graphs are useful for short term monitoring.

☞ *The Performance utility provides many counters by default. You can add other counters by installing a program or by installing extra features.*

The first counter that you must monitor for a given object is the counter that is most general for the object. This is also the most meaningful counter for the object. For example, for the Processor object, you must choose the %Processor Time; for NetBEUI, you must choose Bytes Total/sec.

In order to monitor a counter, click the 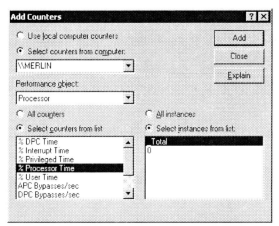 button:

This dialog box allows you to choose the network computer that you want to monitor, and the counter of the object instance. For each new counter, the **Performance** console displays a different description entry.

When you want to measure network performance on a computer, it is often useful to configure the **Performance** utility on the remote machine.

☞ *It is advisable to start the Performance utility with a Realtime priority level in order to ensure that you do not distort the measurements.*

☞ *In order to view the TCP/IP protocol family, you must first install the **SNMP** (Simple Network Management Protocol) **Agent** on the computer that you want to study with the Performance utility.*

You can delete a counter from the graph by selecting it and then clicking the ☒ button.

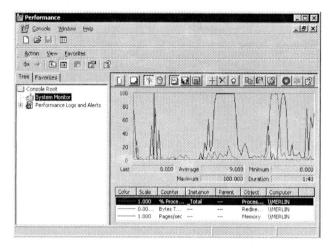

In order to highlight a counter, you can select it in the counter list and then press the shortcut key [Ctrl] **H**.

Finally, you can access the properties of the graph using the 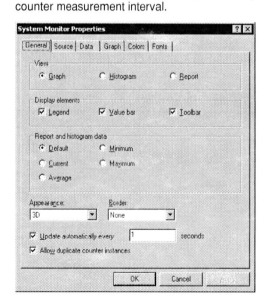 button. This button allows you to configure such settings as the type of view (**Graph, Histogram** or **Report**) and the counter measurement interval.

3. Alerts

You can apply alerts to the measurements that are made on Windows 2000 objects. Thereby, each measurement can trigger an alert according to maximum and minimum thresholds that you define as the administrator. An interesting feature of these alerts is that you can associate them with an action: for example, you can send a warning message across the network, or you can stop a process.

In order to use alerts, go into the Performance console, and carry out the following steps:

➤ Right-click the **Alerts** folder.

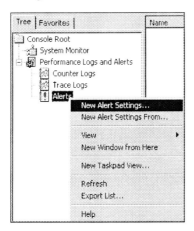

➤ Select **New Alert Settings** and enter a meaningful name for your alert.

➤ Click the **Add** button so as to add a counter onto which you want to apply your alert.

For example, the **Processor** object and the **%Processor Time** counter characterize processor workload. When the system carries out some operations, this counter can reach 100%. However, if the processor returns to an activity level of between 0% and 80%, with a few occasional peaks, then the processor is certainly not a bottleneck for the system.

On the other hand, if the **Processor Queue Length** counter (the number of threads that are waiting to run) of the **System** object is permanently greater than 2, then the processor may be a bottleneck.

Each of the counters that you add, allows you to monitor with respect to a maximum and a minimum threshold. For each alert, you can run a program, either upon the first alert that is associated with the counter, or upon each alert that is associated with the counter.

➢ Specify the action that the system must carry out if the threshold is reached by selecting the **Action** tab. You can specify actions such as: sending a message to a user or to a computer, adding an entry in the event viewer, and running a program.

➢ Indicate when the scanning must start and when it must stop, using the **Schedule** tab. You can choose to start and to stop scanning manually, at any time. In this case, right-click the alert that you want to start or to stop, and select **Start Stop**.

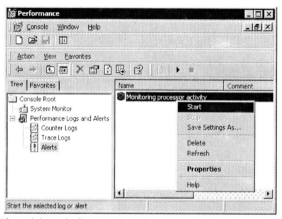

A red icon indicates that the scanning is stopped, and a green icon indicates that the scanning is running.

4. Reports

You can also view counter activity in text format. In this view mode, you configure and use the Performance utility in the same way as in Graph view mode.
In order to switch to Report mode:

➢ Click the 🗐 button.

➢ The ➕ and ✖ buttons allow you respectively to add and to delete the counter that you have selected.

5. Exporting data

Exporting data allows you to work with your measures using another application, such as a spreadsheet or a word-processor.

➢ Right-click the graph, the histogram or the report and select **Save As**.

> You can save your data in .tsv format (in this format the fields will be delimited using tabs). Alternatively, you can save your data in .htm format. In this case you can re- motely run your graph using your browser.

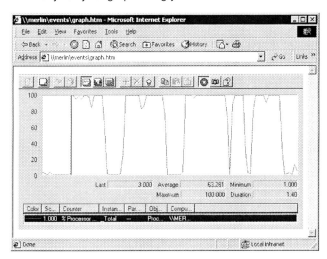

E. Identifying bottlenecks

1. Memory

With Windows 2000, the component that is the most likely to cause bottlenecks is the RAM.

a. Paged and non-paged memory

Windows 2000 memory is divided into two categories: **paged** and **non-paged**.
Paged memory is virtual memory.
Unlike with paged memory, data that is stored in non-paged memory stays in RAM and is never written to disk. Examples of such data are the internal structures that are used by the operating system.

b. Principle of virtual memory

On Windows 2000, virtual memory covers the RAM, the file-system cache and the disk, as a single means of storing information.
The code and the data that is not used are transferred to disk when the RAM space is needed. The more the system lacks RAM, the more the system uses the disk, and the more the system slows down. In this case, the memory is a bottle-neck for the system.

c. Hardware page faults

A high rate of **Page Faults** is a sign that the memory is a bottleneck. A page fault occurs when a program needs data that is not in the physical memory and that must be read from the disk (from the swap file).

If you obtain a report with:

Memory   **Page Faults/sec >>5**

then you have a clear indication that the memory is a bottleneck for the system.

You can use other counters in order to identify a bottleneck:

Memory   **Pages/sec >>5**

This counter indicates the number of requests for pages that are not immediately available in RAM, and that must be read from disk, or that must be written to disk in order to free the RAM so that it can be used by other pages. If this value stays over 5, then the memory is certainly a bottleneck for the system.

2. Processor

Most of what happens on a server involves the processor. The CPU on an applications server is generally more heavily used than on a file server, or on a print server. Thus, whether processor activity is *normal* or not on a server, will depend on the role that the server plays.

The two most common causes of processor bottlenecks are calls that are made by applications and by device drivers, and excessive interrupts that are generated by unsuitable disks, or by unsuitable network subsystem components.

The counters that are associated with the **Processor** object will help you to find out whether or not the processor is a bottleneck:

Processor   **% Processor Time**   **>>80**

This counter measures the time that the processor is occupied. A value of this counter that is constantly over 80%, indicates that the processor is a bottleneck.

You can then fine-tune your measures in order to identify the process that is using the processor. In order to do this, you must monitor each process individually.

If the system has several processors, then you must use the counter:

System   **% Total Processor Time**   **>>80**

The following counter:

Processor   **Interrupts/sec**

Indicates the number of interrupts coming from applications or from hardware devices that the processor handles per second.

System   Processor Queue Length   >>2
This counter indicates the number of requests that are waiting to be handled by the processor. In other words, it shows the number of threads that are ready to run and that are awaiting the processor. In general, a value of this counter that is greater than 2 indicates a bottleneck. In this case, you will then need to look for the component that is overloading the processor.

3. Disk

Disks store the programs and the data that the applications use. A disk can often become a bottleneck when it is waiting for a response from the computer.

a. Activating disk counters

By default, the disk counters are activated (with disk management set up for automatic startup). If this is not the case then you must activate the counters or else they will stay empty. In order to do this you must enter the following command in the command prompt:
diskperf –y [\\computer_name]
Note that the **-n** switch allows you to deactivate the counters.

☞ *You must restart your computer for any changes to take effect.*

When you study the disk subsystem, you must use the following counters:

%Disk Time

This counter indicates the activity level of the disk : it shows the time that is spent reading and writing information.
A %Disk Time that approaches **100%**, indicates that your disk is very heavily used. In this case you must identify the process that is responsible for the disk activity.

Current Disk Queue Length

This counter indicates the number of input/output requests that are waiting. A **Current Disk Queue Length** that is constantly over 2, indicates that the disk is a bottleneck.

b. Solutions when the disk is a bottleneck

If you find that your disk subsystem is a bottleneck, you can take a number of actions:
– You can add a quicker controller, such as a FAST SCSI-2, or a controller that has an integrated cache.
– You can add extra disks, if you are working in a RAID environment. This approach allows you to distribute the data workload over several physical disks. It also allows you to enhance performance, especially read performance.

－ You can offload your system by distributing certain users, certain applications and even certain services onto other computers in the network.

4. Network

A Network bottleneck is one of the most difficult bottlenecks to analyze. Several elements can disrupt the smooth running of a network.

You can use a certain number of objects in order to monitor the network: **Server**, **Redirector**, and **Network Interface** along with the protocols. The object that you must analyze depends essentially on the environment.

Here are the counters that are most commonly used:

Server Bytes Total/sec

> This counter indicates the number of bytes that are sent and received by the server via the network. It shows the activity level of the server concerning reception and transmission of data.

Server Logon/sec

> The Logon/sec counter shows the number of instantaneous logon attempts. This counter is useful in order to find out the number of validations that a domain controller is carrying out.

Network segment　　%Network Usage

> This counter indicates the percentage of the network bandwidth that the local network uses. It is useful in order to add a service onto a server.

☞ *This counter is added at the same time as the network monitor agent. It allows you to put the network interface card into promiscuous mode. This mode allows your network interface card to accept all the packets that circulate on the network, including those that are not being sent to your machine. This approach allows you to analyze these packets.*

Labs

To be absolutely sure that you have assimilated this chapter, work through the corresponding labs. These are set out from page 692 to page 697.

☒ Backing up data.

☒ Restoring data.

☒ Backing up the system state.

☒ Restoring an object to the Active Directory.

☒ Installing the recovery console.

☒ Using the Performance utility.

Assessing your skills

Try the following questions if you think you know this chapter well enough.

Troubleshooting

1 After having modified the registry database on your server, you are no longer able to start it. How can you solve this problem?

....
....
....

2 After you have started a Windows 2000 domain controller, you receive a message telling you that Active Directory is malfunctioning. How will you solve this problem?

....
....
....
....
....

3 You start your computer using an MSDOS diskette, and then you run the SYS C: command. However, following this operation, the Windows 2000 startup menu no longer appears. What must you do in order to regenerate the boot sector that has been damaged?

....
....
....
....

4 A user has installed a new driver. Then, when the user logs on, he/she goes into the event viewer and notices that there are a large number of messages concerning this new driver. The user tries applying the last known good configuration, but this does not change anything. What might be causing this problem?

....
....
....
....
....

5 You want to install the recovery console so that it will appear in your startup menu, as you want to use it in the event of a problem occurring on your server. How will you do this?

....
....

Backing up, restoring, trouble-shooting and analysing

6 An application has failed, and you want to stop the process that is associated with this application so as to free CPU time in order to make it available for other applications. How will you do this?

....
....
....
....
....

7 What are the different levels of process run priority? What is the default run priority for applications? ☐

....
....
....

Backing up

8 You want to backup files that have NTFS permissions. Will permissions be maintained when you restore these files? ☐

....

9 You want to backup a file that has been encrypted using EFS. Will the file still be encrypted after you have restored it onto an NTFS partition? ☐

....

10 What are the five types of backup that you can carry out with Windows 2000? ☐

....
....

11 You want to back up the Registry and the Directory database on your domain controller. How will you do this? ☐

....
....
....
....
....
....

12 After having inadvertently deleted an organizational unit, you want to restore it from a recent backup. Which utility must you use for this purpose? ☐

....
....
....

Monitoring the system

13 Which tool allows you to monitor the results of an audit? ☐

....

14 Which tool allows you to identify possible causes of ☐
bottlenecks?

....

15 You have configured your Performance utility in order to ☐
monitor the Processor object. You suspect that the
processor may be a bottleneck and, if you need to act, you
want to act as quickly as possible. What is the best way to
make sure that the system will notify you in the event of a
problem occurring?

....

....

Results

Check your answers on pages 593 to 596. Count one point
for each correct answer.

Number of points | /15 |

For this chapter you need to have scored at least 11 out
of 15.

Look at the list of key points that follows. Pick out the ones
with which you have had difficulty and work through them
again in this chapter before moving on to the next.

Key points of the chapter

☐ Troubleshooting.

☐ Backing up.

☐ Monitoring the system.

Solutions

Troubleshooting

1 After having modified the registry database on your server, you
are no longer able to start it. How can you solve this problem?

During the startup process, press the ⌗F8⌗ *key when you are
prompted to do so, and then select* **Last Known Good Configuration** *from the menu that appears.*

2 After you have started a Windows 2000 domain controller, you receive a message telling you that Active Directory is malfunctioning. How will you solve this problem?

During the startup process, press the F8 *key when you are prompted to do so, and then select **Directory Services Restore Mode** from the menu that appears. You will then restart the domain controller without loading Active Directory. This technique will allow you to restore your active directory from a recent backup.*

3 You start your computer using an MSDOS diskette, and then you run the SYS C: command. However, following this operation, the Windows 2000 startup menu no longer appears. What must you do in order to regenerate the boot sector that has been damaged?

You can repair this sector, either using the Windows 2000 CD-ROM, or using the 4 startup diskettes.

4 A user has installed a new driver. Then, when the user logs on, he/she goes into the event viewer and notices that there are a large number of messages concerning this new driver. The user tries applying the last known good configuration, but this does not change anything. What might be causing this problem?

When you log on, you validate your configuration as the last known good configuration. The user should have stopped the system, before logging on, as soon as the message appeared advising the user to consult the Event Viewer, as a driver is causing this problem.

5 You want to install the recovery console so that it will appear in your startup menu, as you want to use it in the event of a problem occurring on your server. How will you do this?

*You must run the command **winnt32 /cmdcons** from the I386 directory of the Windows 2000 CD-ROM.*

6 An application has failed, and you want to stop the process that is associated with this application so as to free CPU time in order to make it available for other applications. How will you do this?

*In order to stop a process, you must go into the **Task Manager**, right-click the application that you wish to stop, and select **Go To Process**. Then, you must right-click the process concerned and select **End Process**.*

7 What are the different levels of process run priority? What is the default run priority for applications?

Realtime, high, above normal, normal, below normal, and low

Backing up

8   You want to backup files that have NTFS permissions. Will permissions be maintained when you restore these files?

Yes. These permissions will be maintained, provided that you restore these files to an NTFS partition.

9   You want to backup a file that has been encrypted using EFS. Will the file still be encrypted after you have restored it onto an NTFS partition?

Yes.

10   What are the five types of backup that you can carry out with Windows 2000?

Normal, copy, differential, incremental and daily.

11   You want to back up the Registry and the Directory database on your domain controller. How will you do this?

*You must go into the Windows 2000 Backup utility, and backup the **System State**. Not only will this action back up, your Registry and Active Directory, but it will also back up the shared system volume, the startup files and the COM+ Class Registration database.*

12   After having inadvertently deleted an organizational unit, you want to restore it from a recent backup. Which utility must you use for this purpose?

*You must go into **Directory Services Restore Mode**. Then, you must restore your organizational unit using the Backup utility, and then run the command **ntdsutil.exe**.*

Monitoring the system

13   Which tool allows you to monitor the results of an audit?

The security log of the Event Viewer.

14   Which tool allows you to identify possible causes of bottlenecks?

The Performance utility.

15   You have configured your Performance utility in order to monitor the Processor object. You suspect that the processor may be a bottleneck and, if you need to act, you want to act as quickly as possible. What is the best way to make sure that the system will notify you in the event of a problem occurring?

You must use the alert mode of the Performance utility so that the system will notify you when a problem occurs.

Prerequisites for this chapter

☒ Knowledge of Windows NT 4.

☒ Knowledge of Windows 2000.

☒ To have read Chapter 5, concerning DNS.

☒ To have read Chapter 6, concerning Active Directory.

Objectives

At the end of this chapter, you will be able to:

☒ Upgrade Windows 95/98 workstations to Windows 2000 Professional workstations.

☒ Upgrade Windows NT 3.51 and Windows NT 4.0 servers to Windows 2000 servers.

☒ Design the logical and physical structure of your Windows 2000 domain(s).

☒ Define the different Windows 2000 domains starting from your Windows NT domains.

☒ Upgrade your primary domain controller.

☒ Upgrade your backup domain controllers.

☒ Change your Windows 2000 domains from mixed mode to native mode.

Upgrading a network to Windows 2000

Contents

Upgrading a network to Windows 2000 requires particular care and attention. Although with Windows NT 4.0 it was simple to create a domain, in-depth planning is required in order to upgrade your domain to Windows 2000. This chapter will provide you with the elements that you will need in order to start your planning.

A. Upgrading member servers and client computers

You can upgrade member servers and client computers at any time (you can do this either before or after you upgrade your domain controllers). In fact, you can benefit from the many advantages that are offered by Windows 2000 versions (Professional and Server), without running your machine in a Windows 2000 domain environment. Windows 2000 Professional clients and Windows 2000 member servers can run without Active Directory.

1. Windows 95 and Windows 98

When you upgrade your Windows 95/98 workstations, you will make them more flexible and more reliable, in addition to enhancing their security.

In order to upgrade your clients, you must execute the Windows 2000 Professional installation program. Unlike Windows 95/98 clients, Windows 2000 Professional workstations that are members of a domain must have a computer accounts in this domain. Consequently, you must create a computer domain account for all the workstations that you upgrade to Windows 2000.

In addition, if you transform your FAT partitions to NTFS, then you will provide a higher level of security.

☞ *However, if you are unable to upgrade to Windows 2000 for hardware reasons, you can still install Active Directory client for Windows 95 and 98. This approach will allow you to use the DFS system, and to search information in Active Directory, when you have upgraded your Windows NT domain controllers to Windows 2000 domain controllers.*

2. Windows NT 3.51 and Windows 4.0

You can upgrade Windows NT 3.51 and Windows NT 4.0 clients in the same way as you upgrade Windows 95/98 clients. These Windows NT clients already have computer domain accounts, and therefore you do not need to recreate them.

It is not advisable to continue to use machines that run Windows NT 3.51 in a Windows 2000 domain, as Windows 2000 domains cannot authenticate groups and users in domains that are different from the logon domain using transitive trust relationships.

☞ *Before you upgrade your machines, you must check that the hardware that is contained in the client computers is referenced in the hardware compatibility list. If your upgrade does not run correctly, then you must check the **Winnt32.log** file that is situated in **%systemroot%**. This file is created during the upgrade procedure and provides information on the cause of any problem that occurred during this procedure.*

☞ *Go into a command prompt on the client machine, select the Windows 2000 CD-ROM, and run the command **winnt32 /checkupgradeonly**. This command will generate a report that allows you to identify and hardware and software items that are not compatible with Windows 2000.*

3. Windows 3.1 or Windows 3.5

If you want to upgrade a Windows 3.1 machine or a Windows 3.5 machine, to Windows 2000, then you must first upgrade your machine to Windows NT Workstation 3.51 or Windows NT Workstation 4.0. Alternatively, you can re-install your machine as a Windows 2000 Professional directly (however, in this case you will lose all your data because you must re-format your disk).

B. Planning the logical structure of a network

Before you upgrade your domain controllers, you must plan the structure of the Windows 2000 forest that you will create. In most cases, a single Windows 2000 domain will be sufficient to meet your needs. However, you may prefer to maintain a correspondence between your existing Windows NT domains and your future Windows 2000 domains.

This chapter will study the different types of Windows NT domain, and it will discuss how they must be transformed into Windows 2000 domains.

a. Single NT domain model

With this type of Windows NT model, you use a single domain in order manage the accounts and the resources. This is the simplest architecture. One domain controller replicates its SAM database on to its backup controllers.

You must migrate this type of model into a single Windows 2000 domain.

b. Single NT account domain model

This type of model has an account domain that contains all the user and group accounts. The other domains are called resource domains. These domains trust the account domain by a non-transitive, one-way trust relationship.

In this case, the account domain can become the root domain of the forest, and the resource domains can become child domains of the root domain. In this case, the trust relationships will be two-way and transitive.

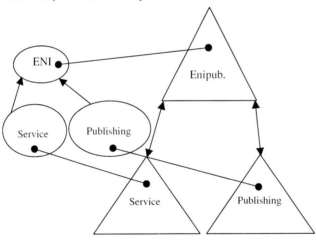

Windows NT Domains / Windows 2000 Forests

c. Multiple NT account domain model

This type of Windows NT model contains several account domains and one or more resource domains. The resource domain(s) trust each account domain using a non-transitive, one-way trust relationship. Each account domain trusts the other account domain(s) using the same type of trust relationship.

You can upgrade this structure to a structure that has a new root domain that has all the account domains as child domains. The resource domains become child domains of the former account domains. As the trust relationships are two-way and transitive, a child domain of an account domain will automatically trust another child domain of another account domain.

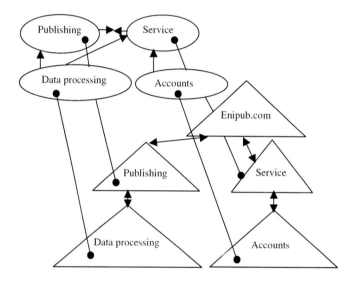

Windows NT Domains / Windows 2000 Forest

However, this model can very well become as follows:

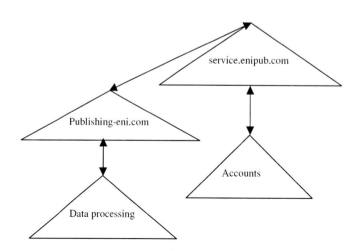

d. Total trust, domain-to-domain model

With this type of **NT** domain model, all the domains are account domains and trust each other using non-transitive, one-way trust relationships.

All these domains can become child domains of a new root domain.

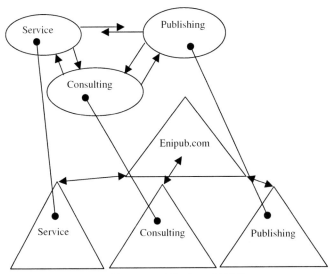

Windows NT Domains / Windows 2000 Forest

C. Planning the physical structure of a network

When you have planned the logical structure of your network, you must plan its physical structure. All the machines that are connected together with fast links are grouped together on the same site. This approach allows you to control the traffic that is caused by replicating Active Directory via the slow links.

Next, you must plan the inter-site replication.

Replicating the directory database does not cause most of the traffic that circulates on the network. You must also consider the transmission of logon information, and the transmission of Active Directory queries. For this reason, you may find it useful to have one domain controller per site. In addition, if you have several domains, then you may also find it useful to have a global catalog server.

However, this approach is not compulsory. If you want to limit the replication of Active Directory across the sites, for any particular reason, then you should place the domain controllers in the same site. Above all, you must bear in mind that a domain controller must be able to answer client queries with an acceptable response time.

D. Updating domain controllers

Before you upgrade your domain controllers you must plan the deployment of Active Directory. Consequently, before you carry out this upgrade, you must ask yourself a number of questions:
- How will you organize your domains (for example you may choose to have a single domain, or a root domain and several child domains, or another configuration)?
- Is there a DNS server that will allow you to install Active Directory?
- Will you keep your backup domain, or do you intend to migrate all your domain controllers into Windows 2000 domain controllers (in other words, are you going to change to native mode)?
- Do you have slow links that mean that you will need to create sites?

1. Primary domain controller

You must upgrade the **Primary Domain Controller** first. This is important because the first domain controller that you upgrade will create the forest. This server will play the role of global catalog server, and it will also play the role of schema master. The server then, will need to be powerful enough so as to support both of these roles.

When you upgrade your domain controllers, then their SAM databases will be migrated to Active Directory. You will lose no information relating to your user, group or computer accounts.
- User accounts and local and global group accounts will be migrated to the **Users** OU.
- Computer accounts will be migrated to the **Computers** OU.
- System predefined groups will be migrated to the **Builtin** OU.
- When you install Active Directory, the server computer account will be migrated to the **Domain Controllers** OU.

Before you upgrade your network to Windows 2000, you must choose the DNS name(s) of your domain(s) carefully. If you have a DNS name space already, then you can keep it as your domain name. However, it is the DNS that must agree with Active Directory, and not the Active Directory that must agree with the DNS. In view of this, you can keep your domain name, and create a new zone in order to manage your DNS name space. Your DNS server must be able to handle the dynamic records and SRV resource records.

If this is not the case than you will not be able to install Active Directory. The Windows 2000 DNS Server handles these types of records.

You must create a root zone if you are not connected to the Internet, or if you use a proxy server in order to access the Internet.

☞ *With all the model types, you must have at least two domain controllers in the root domain. If you have only one domain controller, and this machine breaks down, then you would not be able to replace it and you would have completely to re-install your forest (this would involve destroying all the child domains).*

➢ In order to upgrade your domain controllers, run **Winnt32** from the Windows 2000 CD-ROM.

➢ Select **Upgrade to Windows 2000 (Recommended)**, and then click the **Next** button.

➢ Accept the terms of the License Agreement and click the **Next** button.

➢ The upgrade program will then inspect your hardware and your software so as to check that your computer is suitable for upgrading.

➢ The installation program copies necessary files and then restarts your computer, so as to continue the upgrade, first in text mode, and then in graphic mode. You need supply no further information.

➢ When it has finished the upgrade procedure, Windows 2000 automatically logs on using the administrator account, and then launches the installation of Active Directory.

➢ You must then configure your server, either so that it will join an existing domain, or so that it will create a new domain (Cf. Chapter 6 - Active Directory).

2. Backup domain controllers

You must keep a backup domain controller, as long as you are not sure that all your users will be able to log on, and that all your policies and scripts have been successfully migrated, and that they function correctly. Thereby, if a problem occurs you will be able to promote your BDC to PDC.

Then, you must upgrade your Windows NT domain controllers to Windows 2000 domain controllers as quickly as possible. Thereby, you will be able to change your domain to native mode, and make full use of the features that are offered by Active Directory.

You can upgrade your Backup Domain Controllers in exactly the same way as you upgraded your Primary Domain

Controller. When the system runs the **dcpromo.exe** program, you must choose the **Additional domain controller for an existing domain** option.

☞ *The upgrade program will not allow you to upgrade a Backup Domain Controller before you have upgraded your Primary Domain Controller.*

E. Changing from mixed mode to native mode

When you upgrade your Windows NT domain to a Windows 2000 domain, you will go into mixed mode by default. This mode is designed in order to allow Windows NT machines and Windows 2000 machines to work together. However, with mixed mode Active Directory is limited to a size of 40 MB. This limit is imposed in order to accommodate Windows NT domain controllers.

When you upgrade a Windows NT domain controller to a Windows 2000 domain controller, the system policies are copied from the NETLOGON directory (%systemroot% \system32\repl\import\scripts\) to the directory %systemroot %\SYSVOL\sysvol*name_of_your_ domain*\scripts.

When the domain controllers have been upgraded, they will no longer be able to apply these system policies to the Windows NT clients. On the other hand, they will apply group strategies for Windows 2000 clients. However, group policies provide a setting that allows domain controllers that have been upgraded, to continue to apply system policies to Windows NT clients.

You must be careful with this approach though, because if there is a conflict between a group policy and a Windows NT policy, then it is the Windows NT policy that will be applied.

☞ *During the upgrade procedure, the system migrates the contents of the **Netlogon** directory to the directory **%systemroot%SYSVOL%sysvol%name_of_your_ domain/scripts**. As the sysvol directory is replicated on all the Windows 2000 domain controllers, then the Windows NT clients will still be able to find a .pol system policies file*

In addition, when you are in mixed mode with Windows NT Backup Domain Controllers, when a Windows 2000 client tries to log on, it will first seek authentication with a Windows 2000 domain controller, with the help of the DNS server. However, if no Windows 2000 server is available on the site then the client will seek authentication by the NTLM protocol that the Windows NT domain controllers use. In this case the group policies and the logon scripts will not be run. Consequently, you must have at least one Windows 2000 domain controller on each site on which there is a Windows NT Backup Domain Controller.

When you have upgraded all your domain controllers, and you do not envisage upgrading any other Windows NT domain controllers, and you have checked that your network runs as you want it to run, then you can change to native mode.

Open the **Active Directory Domains and Trusts** console, or the **Active Directory Users and Computers** console.

➢ Right-click the name of your domain, and then select **Properties**.

➢ Under the **General** tab, click the **Change Mode** button.

☞ *Important note: the change to native mode is irreversible.*

➢ Click the **Yes** button, followed by the **OK** button.

Labs

To be absolutely sure that you have assimilated this chapter, work through the corresponding labs. These are set out from page 698 to page 699.

☒ Upgrading from Windows NT 4 to Windows 2000.

Assessing your skills

Try the following questions if you think you know this chapter well enough.

Upgrading to Windows 2000

1   What must you ensure before you upgrade a server or a workstation to Windows 2000?

....
....
....

2   Which utility can you run before you upgrade to Windows 2000 so as to ensure that the hardware and the software that is installed on your computer will be compatible with Windows 2000?

....

3 An error occurs when you upgrade to Windows 2000. How can you find out what is causing the problem? ❑

....
....
....

4 Is it essential to upgrade to Windows 2000, all your Windows NT 4 servers before you upgrade your Windows NT 4 client workstations? ❑

....
....
....

5 Which command will you use in order to upgrade your Windows NT 4 domain controllers to Windows 2000 domain controllers? ❑

....

6 What happens to system policies that are situated in the NETLOGON directory on Windows NT domain controllers when you upgrade these machines to Windows 2000? ❑

....
....
....

7 Is it possible to upgrade Windows 95 client workstations to Windows 2000 domain controllers? ❑

....

8 Is it possible to upgrade Windows 3.x workstations to Windows 2000 Professional workstations? ❑

....
....
....

9 You do not want to upgrade your Windows 95/98 clients to Windows 2000 Professional machines for the moment, even though all your servers run Windows 2000 Advanced Server. Will these clients still be able to search in Active Directory? ❑

....
....
....
....

10 What will happen to the user accounts of your Windows NT domain when you upgrade your Windows NT domain controllers to Windows 2000 domain controllers? ❑

....
....
....

11 Is it possible to upgrade your backup domain controllers before you upgrade your PDC? ☐

....

....

....

12 When you upgrade all your Windows NT domain controllers, will the Windows NT system policies still be applied to your Windows NT 4 Workstation clients? ☐

....

....

13 When you upgrade all your Windows NT domain controllers, is there a way of ensuring that the Windows NT system policies will still be applied to your Windows NT 4 Workstation clients? ☐

....

....

....

....

14 What happens when you have only one Windows NT domain controller on a site in your Windows 2000 domain that runs in mixed mode, and the Windows 2000 clients of this site want to connect to the domain? ☐

....

....

....

....

....

15 When must you change from mixed mode to native mode? ☐

....

....

....

Results

Check your answers on pages 610 to 612. Count one point for each correct answer.

Number of points ┌─────┐ /15 └─────┘

For this chapter you need to have scored at least 11 out of 15.

Look at the list of key points that follows. Pick out the ones with which you have had difficulty and work through them again in this chapter before moving on to the next.

Key points of the chapter

☐ Upgrading to Windows 2000.

Solutions

Upgrading to Windows 2000

1 What must you ensure before you upgrade a server or a workstation to Windows 2000?

You must ensure that the hardware that is contained in the computers that you want to upgrade is included in the Windows 2000 Hardware Compatibility List.

2 Which utility can you run before you upgrade to Windows 2000 so as to ensure that the hardware and the software that is installed on your computer will be compatible with Windows 2000?

You must run the command Winnt32 /checkupgradeonly from the Windows 2000 CD-ROM.

3 An error occurs when you upgrade to Windows 2000. How can you find out what is causing the problem?

*You can try to start up an operating system in order to consult the **winnt32.log** file that is situated in the %systemroot% directory.*

4 Is it essential to upgrade to Windows 2000, all your Windows NT 4 servers before you upgrade your Windows NT 4 client workstations?

No, you can upgrade your Windows 2000 Professional clients without having a Windows 2000 domain.

5 Which command will you use in order to upgrade your Windows NT 4 domain controllers to Windows 2000 domain controllers?

Winnt32.exe.

6 What happens to system policies that are situated in the NETLOGON directory on Windows NT domain controllers when you upgrade these machines to Windows 2000

System policies are copied to the directory %systemroot%\SYSVOL\sysvol\name_of_your_domain\ scripts.

7 Is it possible to upgrade Windows 95 client workstations to Windows 2000 domain controllers?

No.

8 Is it possible to upgrade Windows 3.x workstations to Windows 2000 Professional workstations?

Yes, but you must first upgrade to Windows NT 3.51 or Windows NT 4.0 as an intermediate step.

9 You do not want to upgrade your Windows 95/98 clients to Windows 2000 Professional machines for the moment, even though all your servers run Windows 2000 Advanced Server. Will these clients still be able to search in Active Directory?

Windows 95/98 clients will be able to use the search features of Active Directory and they will also be able to navigate in the DFS topology, provided that you install on these clients, the Active Directory client software that is situated on the Windows 2000 CD-ROM.

10 What will happen to the user accounts of your Windows NT domain when you upgrade your Windows NT domain controllers to Windows 2000 domain controllers?

The system will copy the Windows NT (SAM) accounts database into Active Directory. This migration will cause no loss of account or group information.

11 Is it possible to upgrade your backup domain controllers before you upgrade your PDC?

No. The upgrade program will refuse to upgrade Windows NT backup domain controllers whilst you have not upgraded the PDC.

12 When you upgrade all your Windows NT domain controllers, will the Windows NT system policies still be applied to your Windows NT 4 Workstation clients?

No, the new domain controllers will apply only Windows 2000 group policies.

13 When you upgrade all your Windows NT domain controllers, is there a way of ensuring that the Windows NT system policies will still be applied to your Windows NT 4 Workstation clients?

Yes. You can use a group policy to ensure that the Windows NT domain controllers will still apply system policies, when they are upgraded.

14 What happens when you have only one Windows NT domain controller on a site in your Windows 2000 domain that runs in mixed mode, and the Windows 2000 clients of this site want to connect to the domain?

Windows 2000 clients will try to find a domain controller on the same site, using a DNS server. If there are only Windows NT backup domain controllers, then the Windows 2000 clients will seek authentication with these BDCs using the NTLM protocol. Consequently, the group policies will not be applied.

Upgrading a network to Windows 2000

15 When must you change from mixed mode to native mode?

When you have upgraded all your domain controllers to Windows 2000, and you are sure that your domain is working properly.

2.1   Prerequisites for installing Windows 2000

In this lab you must create a small primary partition in order to install the network client on MS DOS. Then, you must install Windows 2000 in the extended partition.
Partitioning the hard disk

1. Go into MS DOS and select the A: drive.

2. Using FDISK, create a primary MS DOS partition of 20 MB. Activate this partition.

3. Create an extended partition that occupies almost all of the remaining space on the disk (leave 20 MB free so that it can be used later). In this partition, create a logical drive of at least 1 GB. Leave at least 10 MB of free space in this extended partition so that you will be able to crate an NTFS logical drive later.

4. Install MS DOS (during this installation you must format the MS DOS partition).

5. Format the D: drive at the same time.

2.2   Installing and configuring the MS DOS 3.0 network client

Before installing Windows 2000 Advanced Server, you must first set up a network connection on MS DOS, using the MS DOS 3.0 network client (Windows 3.11 version, without graphical interface).
Start up MS DOS on the hard disk and then insert the MS DOS client diskette.
Then, you must configure a domain connection using the NetBEUI protocol.

Starting the installation

1. Specify the install directory. Choose **C:\NET**, the default option.

2. Select your network interface card from the list that the system displays after it has examined the system files.

3. Enter the username LAMBDA. This user is authorized to logon to the domain, so as to be able to connect to the shared directory on the server.

☞ *You need enter no password.*

The following three menus then appear: **Change Names, Change Setup Options** and **Change Network Configuration**.

Choosing the names

1. In the first menu, specify the name of your computer and modify the name of the domain as follows:

   User Name   LAMBDA **(no Password)**

   Computer Name   MACHINEx
   where x is the computer number that the course monitor must assign.

   Workgroup Name   WORKGROUP

   Domain Name   MICROSOFT

2. Click the **The listed names are correct** option.

Logging on to the domain

1. In the **Change Setup Options** menu, validate the session by clicking **Logon to domain**.

2. Click **The listed options are correct**.

Protocol and configuration of the network interface card

1. In the final menu, **Change Network Configuration**, select the **NetBeui** protocol alone, by removing all the other choices, such as **NWLink IPX**, using the **Remove** option. Press the tab key in order to switch to the Installed Network Adapter(s) and Protocol(s) pane. Select **NWLink**, press ⇄ in order to switch back to the Options pane, select **Remove**, and then press Enter. Select **Microsoft NetBEUI** in the new windows and then validate you choice by pressing Enter.

2. Select the network interface card, and then click **Change Settings**, if you wish to change the settings of the network interface card.

☞ *Configure the network interface card options according to the real settings (such as IRQ and I/O addr).*

3. When you return to the three main menus, click **The listed options are correct**.

Updating the system files

1. The system updates the protocol.ini file and the system.ini file (in the C:\NET directory by default).

2. The system updates the config.sys file and the autoexec.bat file, accordingly.

3. In config.sys, the system adds the following lines:

```
DEVICE=C:\NET\IFSHLP.SYS
LASTDRIVE=Z
```

4. The IFSHLP device is the Installable File System HeLPer. This is the MS DOS real mode network component that provides a link between the executable part and the MS DOS client (which was Windows 3.11 originally).

5. The final line (LASTDRIVE...) allows you to associate all the letters of the alphabet (up to Z), with shared directories or local disk units.

```
AUTOEXEC.BAT
```

```
C:\NET\net start
```

This command initializes the network.

Rebooting the machine

1. Restart the machine, specify a username (by default, the system proposes the username that you entered previously), a local password (this is inherited from Windows 3.11), a domain name, and another password for the domain (this password is empty here).

2. Agree for the system to create a file that contains the list of passwords.

☞ *The system creates the files that contain password lists with the filename extension PWL (PassWord List). If you allow the system to create a password list, then the system will no longer ask you to enter any passwords.*

2.3 Connecting to the distribution files shared directory of Windows 2000 Advanced Server

After connecting to the directory that contains the Windows 2000 distribution files, you must launch the machine installation via the network.

Connecting to a shared directory

1. Connect to the server shared directory for the class concerned.
   You can view the resources that are available on the server using the following command:
   NET VIEW \\servername
   In order to connect from the F: drive of your local machine, to the shared resource that is called W2K, on the Servername server, then you must enter:
   NET USE F: \\servername\W2K

2. You can save time by running the cache manager on MS DOS. In order to do this, simply enter **SMARTDRV**.

☞ *The system does not display any messages. In order to receive more information, you can re-enter the same command.*

Launching the installation

1. Start the first phase of the installation by copying all the distribution files locally.

2. Select the network drive F:
   F:

3. Then, launch the installation:
   winnt

In this first phase, the system copies all the files into the directory WIN_NT.~LS. Then, the system restarts the machine.

2.4   Configuring the Windows 2000 installation

In this phase, you must install the Windows 2000 machines.

First restart

1. The system checks the location of the installation source files (**F:\I386**), and copies all the files to a local directory. Then the system restarts the machine.

Second restart

1. The system examines the configuration, and loads the drivers into memory.
2. Then, you must choose whether you want to make a repair, a clean installation, or an upgrade (from an existing installation). Select **Installation** and validate your choice by pressing ⌷Enter⌷ .
3. The system displays the **License set up Windows 2000 now**. When you have read it, you must accept it using the ⌷F 8⌷ key.
4. The system displays a menu that allows you to modify your **Partitions schema** before you install.
5. You must install the Windows 2000 system files in the **WINNT** directory on an extended partition on the logical drive **D:**.
   Convert the partition that you will use for your installation, to NTFS.
6. The system offers to make an exhaustive examination of your hard disk. You must accept this proposal.
7. Then, Windows 2000 copies the necessary files, and then it restarts the computer.

Third restart

1. The system displays the *Windows 2000 Server setup* menu.

   Enter your regional settings, as necessary, and then click **Next**.

Entering information concerning your computer

1. Enter your **Name** and that of your **Organization**.
2. Specify **Per server** licensing mode, for **20** concurrent connections.
3. Enter the name of your computer (**SERVERx**).

☞ *Important note: this name must be unique on your internetwork. Choose SERVERx, where x is a number that your course monitor must define.*

4. Specify a password for the **Administrator** account: enter **passx** (where x is your machine number) and then confirm your password.

5. You can then specify a **component selection**. Do not select any extra components.

Installing Windows NT network management

1. Activate the **Custom settings** option.

2. Note that the TCP/IP protocol is installed automatically.

3. In order to make your server a stand-alone server, you must select **No, this computer is not on a network, or is on a network without a domain.**

2.5 Creating an answer file for automized installation of a Windows 2000 Professional workstation

1. Install the Windows 2000 resource kit.

2. Using this kit, run the **Setup manager** program.

3. Select **Create a new answer file**, and click **Next**.

4. Select **Windows 2000 Professional** and click **Next**.

5. Select **Fully automized** and click **Next**.

6. Follow the steps of the Wizard so as to specify all the information that must be used during the installation process.

Use the batch that the system creates automatically when it creates the .txt file (by default this batch file is called unattend.bat) in order to start the unattended installation process. Alternatively you can run the following command on the machine on which you must install Windows 2000 Professional:

F:\winnt32 /s:F: /unattend:unattend.txt

where F: corresponds to the letter of the drive that points to the Windows 2000 Professional source files.

7. When you have finished the installation, you can consult the Event Viewer in order to check that no problem occurred. In addition, you can consult the **Computer Management** console in order to check that there was no hardware conflict.

2.6 Preparing a disk in order to create an image for replication

1. Install Windows 2000 Professional onto a machine that you want to use as your reference machine.

2. Configure the environment (for example, set up the network connections, and install the applications that will be needed).

3. If you install applications, copy the user profile that you used for the installation into the **default user** profile.

4. Create a directory called **sysprep** on the system partition. Copy the **sysprep.exe** file and the **setupcl.exe** file into this directory. If you created an answer file for disk replication using the **Setup Manager** utility, then you must place this file (**sysprep.inf**) in the sysprep directory.

5. Select this directory and execute the command: **sysprep.exe**.

6. When this command has run your computer stops. The final step is to create the image using a replication utility of a third-party vendor.

3.1 Exploring the registry

In this lab you will explore the Windows 2000 registry. First, you will use the Windows NT/2000 registry editor. Then you will use the Windows 95 registry editor, which offers advanced features.

Starting the Windows NT/2000 registry editor

1. Open the Start menu, select Run and enter **regedt32**.

Locking data in order to prevent any modification

1. Open the Options menu and select Read Only Mode.

   Minimize all the windows to icons by clicking their minimize buttons, except for the **HKEY_LOCAL_MACHINE** window.

Using the Find Key command

1. Select HKEY_LOCAL_MACHINE.

2. Select View – Find Key...

3. Disable the Match whole word only checkbox and search for: tcp in order to find your IP configuration. Use the Find Next button in order to continue your search.

Searching for values using the Windows 95 registry editor

1. Select Start - Run, and enter **regedit**.

2. Open the Edit menu and select the Find... option.

3. Disable the Keys checkbox and the Data checkbox.

4. Enable the Match whole string only option, and search for the specific values that are listed below, and that are under **HKEY_LOCAL_MACHINE**.

Information sought	Associated value	Contents
Local IP Address	IPAddress	
Subnet mask	SubnetMask	
TCP/IP hostname	Hostname	

3.2   Driver Signing option

In this section you will set up your Windows 2000 Advanced Server machine so that it will not accept unsigned drivers.

1. Open the **Control Panel**, and double-click the **System** icon.

2. Activate the **Hardware** tab and click the **Driver Signing** button.

3. Select **Block – Prevent installation of unsigned files.**

4. Click the **OK** button in order to apply this option.

5. Close the **System Properties** dialog box, followed by the **Control Panel** window.

3.3   Hardware Profiles

In this section, you will create two hardware profiles for a computer. In the first hardware profile, the computer must communicate with a modem via its COM1 port. This profile must allow the user to connect to the company's network from home. In the second hardware profile, the same computer must communicate with a scanner via the same COM1 port. This profile is to be used when the user works in the company.

Creating profiles

1. Open the **Control Panel**, and double-click the **Add/Remove Hardware** icon.

2. Click the **Next** button and select **Add/Troubleshoot a device**. Click the **Next** button.

3. Select **Add a new device** and then click the **Next** button.

4. Enable the **No, I want to select the hardware from a list** option, and then click **Next**.

5. Under **Hardware Types**, select **Modems**, and then click the **Next** button.

6. Enable the **Don't detect my modem ; I will select it from a list** checkbox, and then click the **Next** button.

7. Select the modem that you want to add, and then click the **Next** button.

8. Select the port on which your modem must be installed (COM1) and then click the **Next** button.

9. Click the **Finish** button in order to complete the operation.

10. In the **Control Panel**, double click the **System** icon.

11. Select the **Hardware** tab, and click the **Hardware Profiles** button.

12. Select the default profile, **Profile 1 (Current)** and then click the **Copy** button.

13. Enter a meaningful name for your profile. This is the name that the users will see when they log on to the system. For example, you could call your profile "Modem". Click the **OK** button.

14. Carry out the same operation in order to create the second profile. You could call this second profile "Scanner", for example.

15. Click the **OK** button twice.

16. Restart the system. When you are prompted to choose a profile, select **Scanner**.

17. Log on as the administrator.

18. Right-click **My Computer** and select **Manage**.

19. Click **Device Manager**.

20. Right-click your modem and select **Properties**.

21. Under **Device usage**, select **Do not use this device in the current hardware profile (disable)**.

22. Click the **OK** button.

23. Go into the **Control Panel**.

24. Double click the **Scanners and Cameras** icon.

25. Click the **Add** button, and then click **Next.**

26. Select the **COM1** port and then click the **Next** button.

27. Finish the installation.

28. Restart the computer and select the **Modem** profile.

29. Log on as the administrator.

30. Open the **Computer Management** console and disable the scanner for this profile.

Testing profiles

1. Start the computer and choose the **scanner** profile.

2. Open the **Computer Management** console and check that the modem is disabled.

3. Repeat the above steps, choosing the **modem** profile, and checking that the scanner is disabled.

3.4 Updating device drivers and troubleshooting hardware problems

In this section you will see how to troubleshoot any hardware problems, and how to update device drivers.

1. Open the **Computer Management** console.
2. Click **Device Manager**.
3. If any of the devices are marked with a black exclamation point on a yellow background, right-click the device and select **Properties**.
   The dialog box displays a description that indicates the cause of the problem under **Device status**.
4. Select the **Driver** tab and click the **Update Driver** tab.
5. The **Upgrade Device Driver Wizard** will then help you to install the right driver.

   If any of the devices is disabled then it will be marked with a white exclamation point on a red background. In order to enable such a device, right-click it and select **Enable**.

3.5 Managing services and processes

In this section you will see how to stop, how to start, and how to set up services and processes.

1. Open the **Administrative Tools** menu and select the **Services** console.
2. Right-click the **Telnet** service and then click **Properties**.
3. In the **Startup Type** drop-down list, select **Automatic**.
4. Click the **OK** button, and then close the **Services** console.
5. Restart the computer.
6. Log on as the administrator.
7. Go into the **Services** console, and check that the **Telnet** service is **Started**.

☞ *The automatic startup type specifies that the service must be started automatically when the system is started.*

8. Open the **Properties** of the **Telnet** service.

9. Select the **Dependencies** tab, and notice that this service depends on the **Remote Procedure Call (RPC)** service, and that no service depends on **Telnet**.

10. In the **Log On** tab, notice that you can enable or disable a service according to a hardware profile.

11. Under the **General** tab, click the **Stop** button in order to stop the **Telnet** service.

12. Reset the **Startup Type** to **Manual**.

13. Click the **OK** button.

14. Right-click the **Telnet** service and select **Start**.

15. Press the shortcut key sequence `Ctrl` `Alt` `Del` and click the **Task Manager** button.

16. Under the **Processes** tab, the **Windows Task Manager** dialog box lists all the processes that are currently running on your computer. Notice the process that corresponds to the **Telnet** service : tlntsrv.exe.

17. Stop the **Telnet** service, and in the **Windows Task Manager** dialog box, notice that the process is automatically killed.

18. You can kill a process (that has failed for example) by right-clicking it and then selecting **End Process**.

19. Test this operation on the **taskmgr.exe** process.

3.6 Optimizing system performance

In this section you will adjust the paging file and you will check that your system is configured in order to promote network services.

1. Right-click **My Computer** and then select **Properties**.

2. Select the **Advanced** tab, and click the **Performance Options** button.

3. Check that the **Background services** option is selected, so that the system will favor network services.

4. Click the **Change** button, in order to display the **Virtual Memory** dialog box.

5. If you have several physical hard disks, then select the letter of a partition that is situated on a separate disk from that on which the system partition is located.

6. Enter values for the **Initial size (MB)**, and for the **Maximum size (MB)**. You are recommended to set the initial size equal to the RAM size, plus 50%, and to set the maximum size equal to twice the RAM size. If you notice that you do not have enough virtual memory, then you must increase the maximum size.

7. Click the **Set** button so as to apply the values that you have entered.

8. Still in the **Virtual Memory** dialog box, check that the **Current registry size** is less than the **Maximum registry size**. If this is not the case, then increase the **Maximum registry size (MB)** in order to avoid any loss of configuration information.

3.7 Configuring TCP/IP

In this section you will set up a static IP configuration on your Windows 2000 server.

Configuring a static IP address

1. On your desktop, right-click the **My Network Places** icon and then select **Properties**.

2. In the **Network and Dial-up Connections** window, right-click the **Local Area Connection** icon and then select **Properties**.

3. Select **Internet Protocol (TCP/IP)** and then click the **Properties** button.

4. Enable the **Use the following IP address** option and, in the **IP address** text box, enter your IP address. This address should correspond to your machine number. For example, 10.0.0.1 corresponds to a network number of 10 and a machine address of 0.0.1.

5. In the **Subnet mask** text box, enter the subnet mask that corresponds to your address. For example, for the address 10.0.0.1, you can use the Class A standard mask of 255.0.0.0.

6. Enter a **Default gateway**, only if you wish to go outside of your network. Unlike those of the **IP address** and the **Subnet mask**, the **Default gateway** field is not obligatory.

☞ *Note that you can manually enter the IP address of a DNS server. Alternatively, you can automatically obtain this IP address via a DHCP server.*

7. Click the **OK** button in order to terminate the operation.

8. Close the **Local Area Connection Properties** dialog box and the **Network and Dial-up Connections** window.

Viewing the TCP/IP configuration from a command prompt

1. Start up a command prompt, either using the **Start - Programs - Accessories** menu, or by selecting **Start - Run** and entering **cmd**.

2. Enter **ipconfig/all**, in order to display your IP configuration.

Testing connectivity

1. In order to check that your network interface card and your TCP/IP stack are working properly, go into a command prompt and enter the command **ping 127.0.0.1**.
   What message appears?
   ....

2. Run the ping command using your own IP address.
   What message appears?
   ....

3. Run the ping command using your an address that is not in your network.
   What message appears?
   ....

3.8 Configuring and viewing IPX/SPX settings

In this section, you will install the Novell transport protocol, and you will see how to find out which type of frame is circulating on the physical network, and with which IPX number.

Installing Novell transport protocol

1. Go into the **Properties** of your **Local Area Connection**, and then click the **Install** button.

2. Select **Protocol** and click the **Add** button.

3. Select **NWLink IPX/SPX/NetBIOS Compatible Transport Protocol** and then click the **OK** button.

4. Close the **Local Area Connection Properties** dialog box.

Viewing the IPX/SPX settings

1. Go into a command prompt.

2. Enter the following command, and note the information that the system returns:

   Ipxroute config

   ....

   ....

3.9 IP Routing

In this section, you will see how to implement IP routing on a Windows 2000 server.

Adding a second network interface card

1. So as to act as a router, your server must have at least two network interface cards. In order to add a new network interface card, open the **Control Panel** and double-click the **Add/Remove Hardware** icon. Click the **Next** button.

2. Select **Add/Troubleshoot a device** and click the **Next** button.

3. Select **Add a new device** and click the **Next** button.

4. Click the **Next** button again, so that Windows 2000 will detect your hardware.

5. If the system cannot find your network interface card, then click the **Next** button, and then select **Network adapters** in the **Hardware types** list. Click the **Next** button.

6. Select your network interface card from the lists. Alternatively, click the **Have Disk** button if your network interface card did not appear in the lists.

7. Once you have installed your network interface card, then you will have two **Local Area Connection** icons in the **Properties** of **My Network Places**.

8. Open the **Administrative Tools** menu and select **Routing and Remote Access**.

9. Right-click the name of your server, and select **Configure and Enable Routing and Remote Access**.

10. Click the **Next** button and select **Network router**. Click the **Next** button.

11. Click the **Next** button twice and then click the **Finish** button.

Labs relating to chapter 3

Viewing the routing table of your server

1. Open a command prompt and then enter the command **route print**.

2. Alternatively, you can use the **Routing and Remote Access** console. For this purpose, expand **IP Routing** and right-click **Static Routes**. Then, select **Show IP routing Table**.

4.1 Installing administrative tools

In this section, you will install the administrative tools onto your Windows 2000 Server.

1. Open the **Control Panel**.

2. Double-click the **Add/Remove Programs** icon.

3. Click the **Add New Programs** button.

4. Click the **CD or Floppy** button.

5. Open the **adminpack.msi** program that is located in the i386 directory of your Windows 2000 Advanced Server CDROM.

4.2 Customizing administrative tools

In this section you will create a console that will allow you to manage the DNS, DHCP and WINS services, using a single administrative interface.

Creating a new console

1. Click the **Start** button, and then select **Run**.

2. In the **Open:** textbox, enter **mmc.exe**.

3. Open the **Console** menu, and select **Add/Remove Snap-in**.

4. Click the **Add** button, so as to display the list of snap-ins that are available.

5. Add the snap-ins **DHCP**, **DNS** and **WINS**.

Console mode

Now that you have created the console, you must save it in such a way that the users who will use the console will not be able to modify it.

1. Open the **Console** menu in the mmc, and select **Options**.

2. Select **User mode - limited access, single window**.

3. Enable the **Do not save changes to this console** checkbox and then click the **OK** button.

4. Open the **Console** menu, and select **Save As** in order to give a meaningful name to your console, so that you can place it in the profile of each user who must use this console.

Testing the console

1. Open the console that you created above.

2. Try to add new snap-in components. Are you able to do this?

   ....

3. Rename the **Console Root** folder, by right-clicking it and selecting **Rename**. Give a new name to this folder and the close the console.

4. Re-open the console that you have just closed and note that the system did not save your name modification.

4.3 Second logon

In this section you will test the feature that allows you to run an application, with privileges that are different from those of the account that you used in order to log on.

1. Create a user called **test**.

2. Check that your user is a member only of the **Domain User** group.

3. Log on as the **test** user.

4. Open the **Administrative Tools** menu and select the **Computer Management** console.

5. Select the **Disk Defragmenter**, and then click the **Analyze** button in the right-hand pane. A message appears to tell you that you need Administrator privileges in order to defragment a volume.

6. Click **OK** and close the **Computer Management** console.

7. Open the **Start - Administrative Tools** menu, and right-click **Computer management**.

8. Select **Run as**, and then enter the administrator's name and password.

9. Select the **Disk Defragmenter** again, and click the **Analyze** button in the right-hand pane.

10. You will now be able to defragment your disks.

The objective of this lab is to install and to configure the DNS service of Windows 2000.

Try to carry out these operations by reading only the sections of this book that deal with the exercises concerned. However, if you have difficulty, you can consult the operation descriptions that are set out below.

5.1 Installing the DNS service

Installing the service

Objective:

To install the DNS service.

Operations:

1. On your Windows 2000 server, go into the **Control Panel**.
2. Double-click the **Add/Remove Programs** icon.
3. Click the **Add/Remove Windows Components** icon, followed by the **Components** button.
4. In the **Windows Components Wizard** dialog box, select **Networking Services** and then click the **Details** button.
5. Enable the **Domain Name System (DNS)** checkbox, and click the **OK** button, followed by **Next**.
6. Click the **Finish** button in order to complete the operation.

5.2 Configuring the DNS service

Creating zones

Objective:

You must configure a primary zone, and a secondary zone with the name *my_company.com*.

Creating a primary zone

Operations:

1. Go into the **Administrative Tools** menu and open the **DNS** console.
2. Right-click the name of your server, and then select **Configure the server**.

3. Click the **Next** button in order to allow Windows 2000 to examine your configuration.

4. Select **This is the first DNS server on this network**, and then click the **Next** button.

5. Select **Yes, create a forward lookup zone**, and then click the **Next** button.

6. Select **Standard primary** and then click the **Next** button.

7. Enter the name of the zone that you will manage. For example, *my_company.com*.
Click the **Next** button.

8. Windows 2000 automatically proposes a name for your zone file by adding the extension .dns to the name of your zone. Click the **Next** button in order to accept this choice.

9. Select **Yes, create a reverse lookup zone** and then click the **Next** button.

10. Select **Standard primary** and then click the **Next** button.

11. Under **Network ID**, enter the IP address of your network (for example 10.x.x).

12. Click the **Next** button twice.

13. Finally, click the **Finish** button.

14. Display the **Properties of My Computer**. Then select the **Network Identification** tab, and click the **Properties** button.

15. Click the **More** button and under **Primary DNS suffix of this computer** enter the name of your DNS domain (*my_company.com*).

Creating a secondary zone

Operations:

1. Install the DNS service on another server, which will accommodate the secondary zone.

2. On this other server, start the **DNS** console.

3. Expand the server name and right-click **Forward Lookup Zones**.

4. Select **New Zone** and then click the **Next** button.

5. Select **Standard secondary** and then click the **Next** button.

6. Enter the name of the primary zone and then click **Next**.

7. Indicate the IP address of the server that accommodates the primary zone and the click the **Add** button, followed by the **Next** button.

8. Click the **Finish** button, in order to complete the operation.

9. Repeat this operation so as to add a secondary reverse lookup zone. In order to do this, right-click **Reverse Lookup Zones** and then select **New Zone**.

10. Select **Standard secondary** and then follow the **New Zone Wizard**.

Configuring zones for dynamic updating

Objective:

To configure the primary zone so that it will accept dynamic updates.

Operations:

1. Go into the **DNS** console, right-click the name of your zone and then select **Properties**.

2. Under the **General** tab, open the **Allow dynamic updates?** Drop down list and select **Yes**.

3. Click the **OK** button so as to complete the operation.

When the primary zone is ready to accept dynamic updates, configure your clients and servers so that they are DNS clients of the server that manages the primary zone, in order that your machines will register with the DNS server.

The objective of this lab is to install Active Directory. You will create a new forest, and add a second domain controller into the domain. You will see how to change your domain from mixed mode into native mode. Then you will add a second global catalog server into the domain. Following this, you will create a new site in order to manage replication traffic, and you will set up inter-site traffic. Finally, you will downgrade a domain controller to a member server.

Try to carry out these operations by reading only the sections of this book that deal with the exercises concerned. However, if you have difficulty, you can consult the operation descriptions that are set out below.

6.1 Installing Active Directory

Before you carry out this lab, make sure you have carried out the previous lab that dealt with installing and configuring a DNS server. In fact, in order to install Active Directory, you need a DNS server that supports dynamic updates and resource type records.

Creating a new forest

Objective:

You must install a domain controller in a new forest.

Operations:

1. On your stand-alone server, select **Start - Run**.

2. Enter **dcpromo.exe**.

3. Click the **Next** button, and then select **Domain controller for a new domain** and then click the **Next** button.

4. Select **Create a new domain tree** and then click the **Next** button.

5. Select **Create a new forest of domain trees**, and then click the **Next** button.

6. Enter the name of the DNS domain that will be used for the name of the Windows 2000 domain (for example *my_company.com*). Then click the **Next** button.

7. By default, Windows 2000 offers a NetBIOS domain name in order to stay compatible with previous versions. Click the **Next** button.

8. Choose the database location and the log location. Then click the **Next** button.

9. Indicate a path that points to an NTFS 5 partition that must be used to store the SYSVOL shared system folder. Then click the **Next** button.

10. Select **Permissions compatible only with Windows 2000 servers**, and then click the **Next** button.

11. Enter the password for the administrator account that will be used when the server is started in Active Directory restore mode.

12. Click the **Next** button.

Adding a domain controller in an existing domain

Objective:

You must install a domain controller in an existing domain.

Operations:

1. Before you start this procedure, make sure that the server concerned will be able to access a domain controller and a DNS server.

2. On the member or stand-alone server that you want to promote into a domain controller, select **Start - Run** and start the **dcpromo.exe** program.

3. Click the **Next** button.

4. Select **Additional domain controller for an existing domain** and then click the **Next** button.

5. Enter the user name, the password and the domain, for a user that will have enough permission in order to add a domain controller into a domain. Then click the **Next** button.

6. Indicate the name of the domain to which you want to add a controller, and then click the **Next** button.

7. Choose the database location and the log location. Then click the **Next** button.

8. Indicate a path that points to an NTFS 5 partition that must be used to store the SYSVOL shared system folder. Then click the **Next** button.

9. Enter the password for the administrator account that will be used when the server is started in Active Directory restore mode. Then click the **Next** button.

6.2 Changing a domain from mixed mode to native mode

Objective:

If all your pre-Windows 2000 domain controllers have been upgraded to Windows 2000, then you can take full advantage of the Windows 2000 directory database by changing your domain from mixed mode to native mode.

Operations:

1. Start the **Active Directory Users and Computers** console.

2. Right-click the name of your domain, and then select **Properties**.

3. Under the **General** tab of the domain properties dialog box, click the **Change Mode** button.

4. Answer **Yes** in order to confirm that you wish to change your domain to native mode.

6.3 Adding a global catalog server

Objective:

The objective of this section is to add a global catalog server to a domain in order to provide fault tolerance concerning the roles that such a server plays.

Operations:

1. Open the **Active Directory Sites and Services** console

2. Expand
   Sites / name_of_the_site_to_which_the_server_belongs (for example: Default-First-Site-Name) / **Servers / name_ of_ the_server_that_will_become_the_global_catalog_ server**.

3. Right-click **NTDS Settings** and then select **Properties**.

4. Enable the **Global Catalog** check box.

6.4 Creating a new site

Objective:

In order to handle the traffic that is created when you replicate information across a slow link, you must create a new site into which you must move a server from the default site.

Operations:

1. Open the **Active Directory Sites and services** console.
2. Right-click **Sites**, and then select **New Site**.
3. Enter a meaningful name for you site (for example, one that indicates where it is located).
4. Select a site link that must be associated with your site, and then click the **OK** button.
5. In order to move the server(s) from the default site to your new site, right click the server(s) concerned under **Default-First-Site-Name - Servers**, and then click **Move**.
6. Select the site to which you want to move the server(s), and then click the **OK** button.

Creating subnets

1. Now that you have created your new site, you must associate it with one or more subnets. In order to do this, right-click **Subnets**, and then select **New Subnet**.
2. Enter the IP address and the mask that must be associated with your subnet and then select the site that must be associated with your subnet.
3. Click the **OK** button.

Managing intersite replication

1. When you created your new site, you associated a link with it. By default, there is only one link, which is called **defaultipsitelink**. You can create a new link in order to connect your sites together. In order to do this, expand **Sites - Inter Site Transport** and right-click **IP** or **SMTP** according to the protocol that you wish to use for the replication. Then select **New Site Link**.
2. Enter a name for your link. Then, in the left-hand pane select at least two sites that must be joined by this link, and click **Add**.
3. Click the **OK** button.
4. Double-click the link that you want to set up.

5. Assign a value in the **Replicate every** text box in order to specify the frequency with which replication must take place within the schedule.

6. In order to change a schedule within which replication information will be replicated, click the **Change Schedule** button.

6.5 Uninstalling Active Directory

Objective:

In this section you must downgrade a domain controller into a member server.

Operations:

1. Run the **dcpromo.exe** command on the server that you wish to downgrade.

2. If the server is the last controller in the domain, then enable the **This server is the last domain controller in the domain** checkbox. If this is not the case, then make sure that you still have a global catalog server in the domain. Click the **Next** button.

3. Enter the user name and the password for a user account that is a member of the Administrators group, and click the **Next** button.

4. Then, enter the password for the local administrator account.

5. Click **Next** twice.

The objective of this lab is to use group policies in order to configure the user environments, and to deploy applications and service packs.

Try to carry out these operations by reading only the sections of this book that deal with the exercises concerned. However, if you have difficulty, you can consult the operation descriptions that are set out below.

7.1   Managing user environments

Creating a group strategy

Objective:

You must create a group policy in order to configure the environment of specific users. Here are the settings for this group policy:
- Remove the **Start** menu:
  users must not have access to network connections or to dial-up connections. In addition, they must not have access to the **Run** utility.
- Control Panel:
  users must not have access to the **Control Panel**.
- My Network Places:
  Users must not have access to the **Entire Network** icon.
- General:
  You must disable the registry editing tools, and you must prevent users from modifying the display configuration.

Operations:

1. Create an OU in which you must place all the users to whom these settings must apply.

2. Right-click this OU and select **Properties**.

3. Select the **Group Policy** tab and click the **New** button.

4. Enter a meaningful name for your policy.

5. Click the **Edit** button.

6. Under User Configuration, expand **Administrative Templates**.

7. Click **Start Menu & Taskbar**, and then double-click the **Remove Run menu from Start Menu** policy. Select **Enabled** and then click the **OK** button.

8. Carry out the same operation on the **Remove Network & Dial-up Connections from Start Menu** policy.

9. Under **Administrative Templates**, select **Control Panel**.

10. Enable the **Disable Control Panel** policy.

11. Under **Administrative Templates**, expand **Windows Components**, select **Windows Explorer** and enable the **No Entire Network in My Network Places** policy.

12. Under **Administrative Templates**, select **System** and enable the **Disable registry editing tools** policy.

13. Under **Administrative Templates**, expand **Control Panel**, select **Display** and activate the **Disable Display in Control Panel** policy.

Optimizing policy application

1. Close the **Group Policy** dialog box. Select your policy and then click the **Properties** button.

2. Enable the **Disable Computer Configuration settings** checkbox. Answer **Yes** to the confirmation request.

3. Click the **OK** button, followed by the **Close** button.

4. Close the **Active Directory Users and Computers** console.

☞ *As you defined policy settings only for users in this case, then you could disable the part of the policy that concerns computers, in order to speed up the logon process.*

Testing the policy

1. After you have replicated the Active Directory using the **Active Directory Sites and Services** console, then log on with a user account that is contained in the OU for which you have applied your policy.

2. Check that your settings have been applied.

Modifying a policy

Objective:

In this section, you must ensure that your policy will not be applied to one of the users that is contained in the OU that you created. In addition, you must ensure that the users in an OU that is a child of the OU that you created will not inherit the parent policies.

Operations:

1. Create an OU as a child OU of the container that you created previously.

2. Add into this child OU, users to whom parent policies must not be applied.

3. Right-click the child container and select **Properties**.

4. Select the **Group Policy** tab. Click the **New** button and enter a name for this new policy.

5. Click the **Edit** button and enable only the **Remove Search menu from Start Menu** policy. Then close the **Group Policy** console.

6. Enable the **Block Policy inheritance** checkbox, and click the **Close** button.

7. Right-click the parent container and then select **Properties**.

8. Select the **Group Policy** tab. Click the **Properties** button and select the **Security** tab.

9. Click the **Add** button in order to add a user to whom the group policy must not be applied. Click the **OK** button.

10. Select this user. Then, in addition to the **Read** checkbox that is enabled in the **Allow** list, enable the **Apply Group Policy** checkbox in the **Deny** column.

11. Click the **OK** button twice and close the **Active Directory Users and Computers** console.

Testing the policy

1. After you have replicated the Active Directory using the **Active Directory Sites and Services** console, then log on with a user account that is contained in the parent OU and to which your policy must be applied.

2. Note that the system continues to apply the settings that were defined in the previous section.

3. Close this session and log on again with the user account for which you specified a **Deny** for **Apply Group Policy**.

4. Note that the system does not apply the policy that you defined to this user.

5. Log on with a user account that is contained in the child OU.

6. Note that the system does not apply to this user, the policy that you defined in the previous section, but that the system does apply to this user, the policy that you defined for this child OU (**Remove Search menu from Start Menu**).

7.2 Deploying applications using group policies

Objective:

In this section you must publish an application. Then you will see how to assign an application. Finally, you will see how to apply services packs for applications that were installed using group policies.

Publishing

Operations:

1. Go into Windows Explorer and create a share that can be accessed by the users for whom you must deploy applications.

2. In this share, place the source in MSI format, of the application that you want to deploy.

3. Open the **Active Directory Users and Computers** console.

4. Right-click the container that holds the users who must access the published applications.

5. Select **Properties** and then select the **Group Policy** tab.

6. Create a new group policy, or edit an existing group policy.

7. Expand **User Configuration - Software Settings**.

8. Right-click **Software installation**, and then select **New** followed by **Package**.

9. Select the MSI file of the package that you want to deploy.

10. Select **Published** and then click the **OK** button.

Checking the publication

1. Replicate the Active Directory database.

2. Log on with a user account to which you have applied the group policy.

3. Open **Control Panel** then double-click the **Add/Remove Programs** icon.

4. Click the **Add New Programs** button.

5. This dialog box should then display the application that you published. In order to install it, click the **Add** button.

Assigning

Operations:

1. Go into Windows Explorer and create a share that can be accessed by the users for whom you must deploy applications.

2. In this share, place the source in MSI format, of the application that you want to deploy.

3. Open the **Active Directory Users and Computers** console.

4. Right-click the container that holds the users or the computers that must access the published applications.

5. Select **Properties** and then select the **Group Policy** tab.

6. Create a new group policy, or edit an existing group policy.

7. Expand either **User Configuration - Software Settings** or **Computer Configuration - Software Settings**. If you choose **Computer Configuration - Software Settings** then you will assign the package to the computers, irrespective of the users who log on. If you choose **User Configuration - Software Settings** then you will assign the package to the user, irrespective of the computers onto which they log.

8. Right-click **Software installation**, and then select **New**, followed by **Package**.

9. Select the MSI file of the package that you want to deploy.

10. Select **Assigned** and then click the **OK** button.

Checking the assign

1. Replicate the Active Directory database.

2. Log on, either with a user account to which you have applied the group policy, or to a computer to which you have applied the group policy.

3. Open the **Start - Programs** menu.

4. This menu should contain the application that you assigned. In order to install this application, select the application shortcut that appears in the **Start** menu. Windows Installer will install the application and when it has finished, Windows 2000 will start the application.

Deploying a service pack for deployed applications using group policies

Objective:

You have received a service pack for an application that you deployed using group policies. In this section, you must deploy this service pack in the same way as you deployed the application to which it applies.

Operation:

1. Place the service pack files in MSI format in the directory that contains the software distribution files.

2. Go into the **Group Policy** window and right-click the package for which you want to apply the service pack.

3. Select **All Tasks**, and then select **Redeploy application**.

4. Click **Yes**.

8.1 Managing user accounts in Active Directory

Objective:

In this section you will create a user account in the Windows 2000 Directory database and will attribute account settings and personal settings.

Operations:

1. Open the **Active Directory Users and Computers** console.

2. Right-click an organizational unit in which you will create a new user.

3. Select **New** and then **User**.

4. Enter the **First name** and the **Last name**. Note that the system fills the **Full name** field automatically.

5. Under **User logon name**, enter the name that the user must use in order to log on. This name must conform to a naming convention (for example, you can prefix the last name with the first letter of the first name). The **User logon name (pre-Windows 2000)** is for the use of any clients that are running a pre-Windows 2000 system. This name can be different from that which will be used from Windows 2000 machines. You cannot enter more than 20 characters in this field.

6. Click the **Next** button.

7. Enable the **User must change password at next logon** checkbox.

8. Click the **Next** button, and then click the **Finish** button.

9. Log on with this user account.
   What question does the system ask?
   ....

10. Log on as administrator.

11. Right-click the user account that you created, and select **Properties**.

12. Select the **Account** tab and click the **Logon Hours...** tab.

13. Do not allow round-the-clock logon.

14. Log off, and then log on again with the user account that you created.
    What message does the system display?
    ....

15. Log on again as the administrator.

16. Go into the properties of the user account and select the **Address** tab.

17. Enter a full address for this user account.

18. In the **Active Directory Users and Computers** console, select the name of your domain, open the **Action** menu, and select **Find**.

19. Select the **Advanced** tab and click the **Field** button.

20. In the drop down list, select **User** and then **City**.

21. In the **Value** field, enter the name of the town or city that you entered for the user that you created and then click the **Add** button.

22. Click the **Find Now** button.

23. The system then displays all the user accounts that correspond to your search criteria.

8.2 Managing groups

Objective:

First, you must consult the initial members of certain predefined groups. Then you must create your own groups and then add users into them.

Operations:

Determining the members of predefined local groups

1. Go into the **Active Directory Users and Computers** console.

2. Select the **Builtin** container.
   What are the default members of the Administrators group?
   ....
   What are the default members of the different Operators groups?
   ....
   What are the default members of the Guests group?
   ....

Determining the members of predefined global groups

1. Go into the **Active Directory Users and Computers** console.

2. Select the **Users** container.

   What are the default members of the Enterprise Admins group?

   ....

   What are the default members of the Domain Admins group?

   ....

   What are the default members of the Domain Guests group?

   ....

Creating a group

1. Right-click a container in which you want to create a new group.

2. Select **New** followed by **Group**.

3. Enter a name for your group.

4. Select a **Group scope**. You must choose from **Domain local**, **Global** and **Universal** (provided that your domain is in native mode).

5. Select the **Group type**. You must choose from **Security** and **Distribution**.

6. Click the **OK** button.

Adding a member into a group

1. Right-click your group, and select **Properties**.

2. Select the **Members** tab, and click the **Add** button.

3. Select all the accounts (user accounts or computer accounts) that you want to include in your group, and then click the **Add** button.

☞ *You can also add several users to a group by clicking them in the right-hand frame of the Active Directory Users and Computers console, whilst pressing the* `⇧ Shift` *key, or the* `Ctrl` *key. Then you can right-click your selection and choose the Add members to a group option.*

4. The **Member of** tab allows you to add your group into another group.

8.3 Personal roaming user profiles

Objective:

In this section you must implement a roaming profile for a test user that you can call *Rover*.

This profile will be stored in the *profiles* share on the server that is called MERLIN.

Then you must download this profile from another machine.

Operations:

Viewing existing profiles on the test machine (MERLIN)

1. Right-click **My Computer**.

2. Select **Properties** and then select the **User Profiles** tab.

   Which user profiles have been created locally?

   ....

Creating a share in order to store roaming profiles on the MERLIN computer

1. Open Windows Explorer.

2. Create a new folder, call your folder **Profiles**, and share it for the **Everyone** group.

Creating the Rover user

1. Log on as the administrator.

2. Go into the **Active Directory Computers and Users** console, create a user, and call your user *Rover*.

3. Go into the properties of your new user, select the **Profile** tab and specify the **Profile path** as \\MERLIN\Profiles\ %username%.

Testing the profile

1. Log on as *Rover*, so as to create a profile for this user in the directory \\MERLIN\Profiles\vagabond.

2. Change the background color of the screen, and then change the positions of the icons on the desktop and the task bar.

3. Log off in order to save your modifications.

4. Log on as the *Rover* user on another machine.

5. Note that your desktop is in the state in which you left it.

8.4 Mandatory user profiles

Objective:

In this section, you must create a profile and then apply it to all the users. These users must not be able to modify their profile.

Operations:

1. Create a test user.
2. Log on as this user.
3. Set up the desktop so that it will meet the common needs of the users.
4. Log off so as to save the profile.
5. Log on as the administrator.
6. Open Windows Explorer and create a shared directory so that you can store the profile in it. For example, on the MERLIN computer, you can create the directory c:\profile\common. Share this new directory.
7. Right-click **My Computer** and select **Properties**.
8. Select the **User Profiles** tab and select the profile that corresponds to the test user.
9. Click the **Copy To** button and enter the path that leads to the directory c:\profile\common.
10. Under **Permitted to use**, click the **Change...** button and select the **Everyone** group.
11. Select the **ntuser.dat** file that is located in the directory c:\profile\common and rename it as **ntuser.man**, in order to make the profile a mandatory profile. If you cannot find this file, then select **Tools - Folder Options** in Windows Explorer so as to display hidden files.
12. In the **Properties** of the user accounts that must use this profile, select the **Profile** tab and enter the **Profile path:** \\MERLIN\profile\Common.

Testing the mandatory profile

1. Log on with the user account to which you applied the profile.
2. Make some changes.
3. Log off and log on again with the same user account.

    Note that your changes were not saved.

8.5 Implementing a user home directory

Objective:

In this section, you must ensure that a user has a home directory, and that only the user can access this directory. The letter P: will represent the home directory.

Operations:

1. Log on as the administrator.

2. Open Windows Explorer, create a directory on an NTFS partition, call your directory *users* and share it under the same name.

3. Open the **Active Directory Users and Computers** console, and go into the **Properties** of the user accounts that must have home directories.

4. Select the **Profile** tab. Under **Home folder**, select **Connect** and choose the letter P: from the drop down list. In the **To:** checkbox, enter the UNC path that leads to the user home directory. Use the **%username%** variable in order automatically to create the personal home database of each user, and assign the **Full Control** permission only for the user. For example, the path could be \\merlin\users\%username%.

5. Click the **OK** button so as to close the properties of the user account.

☞ *The %username% variable is particularly useful in order to create an account template to which you can assign a set of properties (such as the home directory, the profile, and group membership). Then, you can copy this account in order to create all your users.*

Testing the connection to the home directory

1. Log on with a user account that has a home directory.

2. Double-click the **My Computer** icon.

   Note that the **My Computer** console displays a P: drive that corresponds to the user's home directory.

☞ *You must note that this drive letter leads directly to the home directory, and not to the root of this folder that contains all the home directories, as it did with Windows NT 4. However, if you so desire, you use a group policy in order to make this letter correspond to the user directories' root.*

3. Open a command prompt.

   The command prompt will indicate that you are in P:, the user's home directory.

9.1 Printers

The objective of this lab is to create a printer and to adjust the permissions and the priorities that are associated with a printer.
Try to carry out these operations by reading only the sections of this book that deal with the exercises concerned. However, if you have difficulty, you can consult the operation descriptions that are set out below.

Creating a printer pool

Objective:

You must create a printer pool.

Operations:

1. Select **Start - Settings - Printers**, and double-click **Add Printer**.

2. Install a local printer and share it.

3. When you have shared your printer, the system represents it by an icon in the Printers window.

4. Right-click this icon and select **Properties**.

5. Select the **Ports** tab and activate the **Enable printer pooling** check box.

6. Select all the ports to which your printer is connected.

7. Click **OK** in order to confirm your changes.

8. Double click the printer icon in order to open it.

9. Open the **Printer** menu and select **Pause Printing**.

Adding other drivers

Objectives:

Add other extra drivers to your printer so that users that have different Windows versions can download them automatically when they connect to the printer.

Operations:

1. Go into the **Properties** of the printer.

2. Select the **Sharing** tab, and click the **Additional Drivers** button.

3. Enable the check boxes that correspond to the drivers that you want to install so that users that have different Windows versions can download them automatically when they connect to the printer.

Searching in Active Directory

1. Go into the **Properties** of the printer, select the **Sharing** tab and ensure that the **List in the Directory** check box is enabled.

2. Select the **General** tab and enter **print room** in the **Location** text box.

3. On any client machine that has Active Directory client software, select **Start - Search - For Printers**.

4. Check that **Entire Directory** is selected in the **In** box.

5. In the **Location** text box enter **print room** and then click the **Find Now** button.

6. The system should display your printer in the results pane at the bottom of the dialog box. If your printer does not appear in this list, then replicate Active Directory manually in order to force the replication process.

Managing priorities and creating two printer queues

FIRST PRINTER

1. Create a new type of printer, for example a Canon LBP-8 III. Use a different model that that which you used previously.

2. Install your printer on the LPT1 port.

3. Share this printer under the name of *Canon LBP-8 III*.

SECOND PRINTER

1. Create a second printer of the same type as the first printer.

2. Define the same printer port for this printer as you did for the first printer (LPT1).

3. Share this printer under the name of *Canon LBP-8 III 2*.

Labs relating to chapter 9

Configuring each printer queue

1. Create the group that is called **Managers**, and authorize only this group to use the first printer queue. In order to do this, go into the **Properties** of the first printer, select the **Security** tab, remove the **Everyone** group and add the **Managers** group. Allow only **Print** permissions to the **Managers** group.

2. Select the **Advanced** tab, and attribute a **Priority** of **20** for this printer.

3. Authorize the **Office Staff** group to use the second printer with **Print** permission.

   Attribute a priority of **1** to this second printer.

Testing the connections to the printers

1. Log on as a member of the **Office Staff** group, and then log on as a member of the **Managers** group, so as to test the permissions that you attributed.

2. Try connecting to both printers in both cases.

10.1 Shared resources

Objective:

In this lab you must create shares on a server, locally and remotely. You must attribute permissions to the shared folders, you must test them, and then you will see how to access these administrative shares.

Operations:

1. Open a session as Administrator.

2. Create a directory and call it **c:\public**. Give this directory a share name of PUBLIC, and enter **Public directory** into the Comment field.

3. What are the share permissions by default?

   ....

4. Create a new shared-folder and call it **Managers**.

5. Go into the properties of this folder, select the Sharing tab and click the Permissions button.

6. Add the **Managers** group and attribute Change permission for this group (if the **Managers** group does not exist then you must create it).

7. Remove the **Everyone** group from the Share Permissions list.

Accessing a shared resource

1. Log on as a member of the **Managers** group.

2. Right-click the My Network Places icon. Then, select Map Network Drive.

3. Choose the drive H: then enter in the Folder box, the path leading to the **Managers** directory that you have just created. This path must have the format: \\name_of_remote_computer\managers.

4. Enable the Reconnect at logon checkbox.

5. Carry out the same operation with the **public** directory.

6. Log off and log on again with a user account that is a member only of the **Domain Users** group.

7. Double-click the My Network Places icon, double-click Entire Network and then click the entire contents link.

8. Double-click **Microsoft Windows Network**. Then double click the name of the domain or the workgroup, followed by the computer, which stores the shared resource. Can you access the **Public** directory? Can you access the **Managers** directory?

....

9. Go into the properties of the **Managers** directory, select the **Sharing** tab and in the **Permissions** of this folder, add a user that is a member of the **Managers** group. Attribute a **Deny** for the **Full Control** permission.

10. Log on using this user account.

11. Try to access this **Managers** shared directory. Are you able to do this? Why not?

....
....

Connecting to an administrative share

1. Log on as the administrator.

Select **Start** – **Run** and then enter *remote_server_name*\c$.
Where does this lead you?

....

2. Select **Start** – **Run** and then enter *remote_server_name*\admin$.
Where does this lead you?

....

3. Select **Start** – **Run** and then enter *remote_server_name*\print$.
Where does this lead you?

....

Creating a share remotely

1. Log on as the administrator.

2. Open the **Computer Management** console.

3. Right-click **Computer Management (Local)** and then select **Connect to another computer**.

4. Double-click the computer that you want to manage.

5. Expand **System Tools - Shared Folders**, and right-click **Shares**. Select **New File Share**.

6. Then indicate the path that leads to the folder that you want to share. This path can be an existing path. Alternatively, it can be a path that you wish to create, for example: c:\new folder\ new subfolder.

7. Enter a share name and a share description, and then click the **Next** button.

8. If the folder to share does not yet exist, then answer **Yes** in order to confirm the creation of the new folder.

9. Then select the type of share folder permissions that you want to attribute to this share. Then click the **Finish** button.

10.2 NTFS permissions

Objective:

The objective of this section is to adjust NTFS permissions.

Operations:

1. Log on as administrator.

2. Go into Windows Explorer, create a directory on an NTFS partition, and call this directory **Data**.

3. Create a text file in this directory.

4. Right-click this file, and then select **Properties**.

5. Select the **Security** tab and click the **Add...** button in order to attribute **Full Control** permission to the **Managers** group, and to the **Domain Admins** group.

6. Under the **Security** tab, disable the **Allow inheritable permissions from parent to propagate to this object** checkbox.

7. Then, click the **Remove** button, in order to withdraw the **Full Control** permission for the **Everyone** group.

8. Click the **OK** button.

9. Log off from the computer that stores this resource and log on again with a user account that is a member of neither the **Domain Admins** group nor the **Managers** group.

10. Try to access this Data folder locally using Windows Explorer. Are you able to do this? Why?

   ....
   ....

11. Try to access the file that is contained in this folder? Are you able to do this? Why? What message does the system display?

   ....
   ....

12. Log on as a user that is a member of the **Managers** group and repeat steps 10 and 11.

Inheriting

1. Log on as the administrator.

2. Create a folder on an NTFS partition.

3. Go into the **Properties** of this folder and select the **Security** tab.

   Note that the **Everyone** group has **Allow – Full Control** permission. The checkboxes that are in the **Allow** column are grayed out and you cannot change them. This is because these permissions are inherited from the parent directory (c:).

4. Disable the **Allow inheritable permissions from parent to propagate to this object** checkbox, and then click the **Remove** button.

5. Assign the following permissions:
   - **Allow - Full Control** for the **Domain Admins** group.
   - **Deny - Full Control** for the **Guests** group.
   - **Allow - Modify** for the **Managers** group.

6. Click the **OK** button.

7. Create a subfolder in the folder above.
   Which permissions does the system assign to this subfolder?
   ....

8. Disable the **Allow inheritable permissions from parent to propagate to this object** checkbox, and then click the **Copy** button.

   The permission checkboxes are no longer grayed out and you can now change them.

9. Click the **Advanced** button.

10. Select the **Permission Entry** that concerns the **Managers** group.

11. Click the **View/Edit** button.

    Which of the NTFS attributes do not belong to the standard **Modify** permission?
    ....

12. Go back to the **Security** tab of the parent folder **Properties** dialog box. Click the **Add** button.

13. Add a user that is neither a member of the **Domain Admins** group, nor of the **Manager** group, nor of the **Guests** group.

14. Click the **Advanced** button, select the user in the **Permission Entries** and click the **View/Edit** button.

15. Disable all the checkboxes that are attributed to this user and assign only the special **Take Ownership** permission.

16. Click the **OK** button three times.

17. Log on as the Administrator.

Go into Windows Explorer and try to access this directory. What message does the system display?

....

19. Right-click this folder and then select **Properties**.

20. Select the **Security** tab.

21. Click the **OK** button in order to indicate that you do not have the necessary permissions in order to display the permission settings for this folder.
Notice that the list is empty.

22. Click the **Advanced** button, and then select the **Owner** tab.
Under **Change owner to**, you should see the user account with which you logged on.

23. Select this account, and then click the **OK** button.

24. Close the **Properties** dialog box

25. Go back into the **Properties** of this folder and select the **Security** tab. As you are the new owner, you can modify the permissions on this folder. Grant yourself **Full Control** permission and then click the **OK** button. Not that you can access the folder.

10.3 Combining shared folder permissions and NTFS permissions

Objective:

In this section you will see which permission effectively apply when a folder has shared folder permissions and NTFS permissions.

Operations:

1. Create a directory and share it under the name **Share**.

2. Assign for this folder **Full Control** shared folder permissions to the **Everyone** group.

3. Apply for the same folder, the **Read** NTFS permission to a user. Remove all the other NTFS permissions.

4. On another computer, log on with this user account.

5. Access the shared folder via the network.
Are you able to do this?

....

6. Try to create a subfolder in this share. Are you able to do this? Why?

....

7. Repeat this operation, assigning the **Read** shared folder permission for the user, and the **Full Control** NTFS permission for the **Everyone** group.
What is the result of this operation?

....

8. What conclusions can you draw from these two operations in which you combined shared folder permissions and NTFS permissions?

....

....

10.4 Distributed file systems (Dfs)

Objective:

In this section, you must implement a stand-alone Dfs topology and a fault-tolerant Dfs topology. Not only must the root node support fault tolerance, but the child nodes must also support fault tolerance.

Operations:

Stand-alone Dfs topology

1. Log on as the administrator.

2. Go into the **Administrative Tools** menu and open **Distributed File System** console.

3. Right-click **Distributed File System** and select **New Dfs Root**.

4. Click the **Next** button and then enable the **Create a standalone Dfs root** option.

5. Indicate the FQDN name of the host server for this Dfs root (for example merlin.enipub.com). Then click the **Next** button.

6. Select **Create a new share**. In the **Path to share** text box, enter **c:\My standalone Dfs topology**, and in the **Share name** text box, enter **My standalone Dfs topology**. Then click the **Next** button.

7. Click **Yes** in order to confirm the creation of the new folder. Then click the **Next** button, followed by the **Finish** button.

8. Right-click *your_domain_name*\my stand-alone Dfs topology, and then select **New Dfs Link**.

9. Enter a name for the new link. Windows 2000 will display this name to the users who connect to the Dfs topology. Under **Send the user to this shared folder**, enter a UNC path that leads to a remote share. Enter any **Comment** that you may wish to add, and then click the **OK** button.

10. Repeat this procedure as necessary, in order to group together all the shared folders that you wish to access via the Dfs topology.

Fault-tolerant topology

1. Log on as the administrator.

2. Go into the **Administrative Tools** menu and open **Distributed File System** console.

3. Right-click **Distributed File System** and select **New Dfs Root…**

4. Click the **Next** button and then enable the **Create a domain Dfs root** option.

5. Click the **Next** button and then indicate the domain into which the system must replicate the Dfs root. Click the **Next** button.

6. Indicate the FQDN name of the host server for this Dfs root (for example merlin.enipub.com). Then click the **Next** button.

7. Select **Create a new share**. In the **Path to share** text box, enter « c:\My Dfs topology », and in the **Share name** text box, enter « My Dfs topology ». Then click the **Next** button.

8. Click **Yes** in order to confirm the creation of the new folder. Then click the **Next** button, followed by the **Finish** button.

9. Right-click *your_domain_name*\my Dfs topology, and then select **New Dfs Link**.

10. Enter a name for the new link. Windows 2000 will display this name to the users who connect to the Dfs topology. Under **Send the user to this shared folder**, enter a UNC path that leads to a remote share. Enter any **Comment** that you may wish to add, and then click the **OK** button.

11. Repeat this procedure as necessary, in order to group together all the shared folders that you wish to access via the Dfs topology.

Implementing the fault tolerance

1. Even though Windows 2000 will replicate this topology as an Active Directory object, if the server that hosts this topology fails, then, as the administrator, you will have to carry an operation in order to make this Dfs topology available on another server. So as to ensure that the users will automatically be redirected to another server when the server breaks down, then you must create replicas. In order to do this, right-click *your_domain_name**my Dfs topology,* and select **New Root Replica**.
    Then enter the FQDN name of a backup server (for example « galahad.enipub.com ». Click the **Next** button.

2. Select **Create a new share**. In the **Path to share** text box, enter « c:\My Dfs topology », and in the **Share name** text box, enter « My Dfs topology ». Then click the **Next** button.

3. Click **Yes** in order to confirm the creation of the new folder. Then click the **Next** button, followed by the **Finish** button.

Checking the fault tolerance

1. On the desktop of a client machine, create a shortcut that points to the Dfs topology.

2. Check that you can access the different directories of this topology, and consequently that the system redirects you automatically to the resources that are located on the remote machines.

3. Shut down the computer on which you created the topology.

4. On your client machine, double-click the shortcut that points to the Dfs topology hosted by the computer that you have shut down.
    Note that you can still access this data, transparently.

Fault tolerance for the child nodes

1. Go into the **Distributed File System** console, and right-click the child nodes for which you want to create a replica. Select **New Replica**.

2. Indicate the path to which the users must be redirected if the child node is unavailable.

3. Select **Automatic replication**, and then click the **OK** button.

4. In the **Replication Policy**, dialog box, select the child node and click the **Set Master** button. Then, select all the replicas of the child node and click the **Enable** button. This will mean that the information that is contained in the initial directory will be replicated to all the replicas so that users will still be able to access this data when the child node is unavailable.

5. Click the **OK** button.

Recovering a Dfs topology

1. If the server that hosts the Dfs topology fails, and you have not created a replica, then you will have to make this topology available on another server. In order to do this, log on as the administrator on the other server, open the **Distributed File System** console, and right-click **Distributed File System** and select **Display an Exisiting Dfs Root**.

2. Then select the Dfs root and then click the **OK** button.

10.5 Managing individual compression

Objective:

In this section, you must compress and decompress files and folders that are located on an NTFS partition.

Operations:

1. Copy the contents of the I386 directory from your Windows 2000 Advanced Server CDROM, to an NTFS partition.

2. Right-click this directory on your NTFS partition, select **Properties**, and under the **General** tab, note the **Size** value and the **Size on disk** value.

   ....

3. Click the **Advanced** button.

4. Enable the **Compress contents to save disk space** checkbox.

5. Click the **OK** button twice. In the **Confirm Attribute Changes** dialog box, select **Apply changes to this folder, subfolders and files**. Click the **OK** button.

6. When the compression has finished, go back into the **Properties** of this folder and compare the **Size** value and the **Size on disk** value, with those that you noted previously.

How much disk space did you save?

....

Visual recognition of compressed files and folders

1. Go into Windows Explorer, open the **Tools** menu and then select **Folder Options...**

2. Select the **View** tab, and enable the **Display compressed files and folders with alternate color** check box.

3. Click the **OK** button.

In which color does the system display files and folders that have been compressed?

....

10.6 Managing disk quotas

Objective:

In this section, you must apply disk quotas for a set of users.

Operations:

1. Log on as administrator.

2. Go into Windows Explorer, right-click the drive for which you want to apply the quotas. The partition or volume must be formatted in NTFS 5. Select **Properties**.

3. Click the **Quota** tab.

4. Click the **Quota Entries** button.

5. Open the **Quota** menu, and select **New Quota Entry**.

6. Select the users to whom you wish to apply the quotas (you can use the Ctrl key so as to select several users). Then, click the **Add** button, followed by the **OK** button.

7. In the **Add New Quota Entry** dialog box, select **Limit disk space to**, and then indicate the values for the disk space limit and for the warning level. Then click the **OK** button.

8. Open the **Quota** menu, and then select **Close**.

9. Under the **Quota** tab, activate the **Enable quota management** checkbox, and then click the **Apply** button. The status traffic lights change from red, to amber and then to green as the system enables the quotas.

10. Stay under the **Quota** tab and define a disk space limit and a warning level for the users for whom you have not defined a quota entry. Alternatively, enable the **Do not limit disk usage** option.

11. Enable the **Deny disk space to users exceeding quota limit** checkbox and then click the **OK** button.

12. Using a client machine, log on with a user account for which you have defined a quota entry.

13. Select a drive letter that points to a shared directory on the server on which you applied the quotas.

14. Copy documents into this directory until you reach the space limit that you defined for this user.

    What message appears on the screen when the user reaches the space limit?

    ....

15. Log on as the administrator on the server on which you implemented disk quotas. Right-click the disk concerned by the quotas, and select **Properties** followed by the **Quota** tab.

16. Click the **Quota Entries** button.

17. Right-click the quota corresponding to the user who has reached his/her limit and then select **Delete**.

18. Click the **Yes** button.

19. Windows 2000 then displays all the documents on the disk that the user owns. You can free disk space by deleting the user's documents (be careful however, as you will delete the documents from the disk). Alternatively, you can take ownership of the files. You can also increase the quota for a user by right-clicking the user's quota entry and selecting **Properties** in order to increase the disk space that the user can occupy.

11.1 Upgrading basic disks to dynamic disks

Objective:

In this section you will upgrade basic disks to dynamic disks. This will allow you to replace you partitions with volumes, and implement fault tolerance using RAID 1 and RAID 5.

Operations:

1. Log on as the administrator.
2. Go into the **Computer Management** console.
3. Select **Disk Management**.
4. In the right-hand pane, right-click the disk that you want to upgrade.
5. Select **Upgrade to Dynamic Disk**.
6. Then, in the **Upgrade to Dynamic Disk** dialog box, select the disk(s) that you want to upgrade, and click the **OK** button.
7. Click the **Upgrade** button.

11.2 Implementing fault tolerance

Objective:

In this section you must implement a RAID 1 (mirroring) solution, and you will see how to recover information in the event of a disk failing. Then you must implement RAID 5 (disk striping with parity) and you will see how to recover a volume that has failed.

Operations:

RAID 1

1. Right-click the volume that you want to mirror.

2. Select **Add Mirror**. If this option appears grayed out then you do not have a dynamic disk that has enough free space in order to create the mirror.

3. Select the disk that you want to use for your mirror, and then click the **Add Mirror** button.
The system will then regenerate the data that is situated on the initial disk, onto the mirror disk.

Booting on a secondary mirror disk

1. The advantage of mirroring is that you cover the system partition. You must be able to boot on the secondary mirror disk if the primary mirror disk fails. In order to do this, you must format a Windows 2000 diskette. Then, for an INTEL type machine, you must copy the following files:
- NTLDR
- NTDETECT.COM
- NTBOOTDD.SYS (in the case where the BIOS of the SCSI controller is disabled
- BOOT.INI

2. Modify the boot.ini file so that one entry in this file will point to one mirror member, and a second entry in this file will point to the other mirror member.
Here is an example of the boot.ini file with these two entries:
```
[boot loader]
timeout=1
default=multi(0)disk(0)rdisk(0)partition(1)\WINNT
[operating systems]
multi(0)disk(0)rdisk(0)partition(1)\WINNT="Microsoft
Windows  2000  Advanced  Server  (mirror  member  1)"
/fastdetect
multi(0)disk(0)rdisk(1)partition(1)\WINNT="Microsoft
Windows  2000  Advanced  Server  (mirror  member  2)"
/fastdetect
```

3. Using your diskette, try to boot on both of these mirror members.

Repairing an original system disk

1. If an error occurs on one of the volumes that make up the mirror, then right-click this volume, and select the **Reactivate Volume** option.
If this technique is ineffective, then you must remove the mirror, and then re-create it.

2. Boot your machine using your bootable diskette and select the mirror volume on the disk that is still intact.

3. Start-up the **Disk Management** program.

4. Select the mirrored volume on the disk that is missing or defective and then select **Remove Mirror**.

5. Check that you have selected the defective disk, and then click the **Remove Mirror** button.

6. Then, you must replace the defective disk and then recreate the new mirror so that you can maintain the fault tolerance.

Creating a stripe set with parity

1. Right-click an unallocated space.

2. Select **Create Volume**.

3. Select **RAID-5 volume**, and then click the **Next** button.

4. Select at least three disks in order to set up your RAID 5, and then click the **Next** button.

5. Select the drive letter that must be allocated to your disk stripe with parity and then choose the file system that you wish to use.

Repairing a defective RAID-5 volume

1. Replace the defective disk. If the disk concerned has either an **Offline** or **Missing** status, then right-click it and select the **Reactivate Disk** option.

2. If the disk status is **Online (Errors)**, then try this same procedure. However, if the operation is ineffective, then you must replace the defective disk. In order to do this, right-click the RAID 5 volume that is on the defective disk, and then select **Repair RAID-5 volume**. A dialog box than asks you to select the disk that must replace the defective disk.

The objective of this lab is to configure the security of your Windows 2000 servers. First you must encrypt sensitive data. Then you must implement IPSec security in order to secure IP traffic. When you have done this, you must protect user accounts and passwords using security templates that you can analyze in order to ensure that the security policies that the system is applying are those that you wanted the system to apply. Finally, you must implement an audit policy. Try to carry out these operations by reading only the sections of this book that deal with the exercises concerned. However, if you have difficulty, you can consult the operation descriptions that are set out below.

12.1 EFS encryption

Objective:

In this section, you must encrypt a directory that is called **confidential**. This directory contains data in two files, secret1.txt and secret2.txt, to which only the director must have access. The director has a user account that is called **director**.

Operations:

1. Create a user account called **director**.
2. Log on as **director**.
3. Open Windows Explorer, and right-click the **confidential** directory that is situated on an NTFS partition.
4. Select **Properties**.
5. Click the **Advanced** button.
6. Enable the **Encrypt contents to secure data** check box.
7. Click the **OK** button twice.
8. In the **Confirm Attribute Changes** dialog box, select **Apply changes to this folder, subfolder and files** and click the **OK** button.
9. In the **confidential** directory, display the properties of the secret1.txt file.
10. Click the **Advanced** button in order to check that it is encrypted.
11. The secret2.txt file must also be encrypted. You must decrypt this file. In order to do this, go into the **Properties** of this file and click the **Advanced** button.
12. Disable the **Encrypt contents to secure data** check box and then click the **OK** button twice.

Checking

1. Log off and then log on again with another user account (Guest for example).

2. Open Windows Explorer and select the **confidential** folder.

3. Double-click the secret1.txt file.

4. You should receive an **Access denied** message because the file is encrypted.

5. Click the **OK** button and close **Notepad**.

6. Double-click the secret2.txt file.

7. The Notepad program starts and displays the contents of the file.

Decrypting files and folders

1. Log on as **director**.

2. Open Windows Explorer and right-click the confidential folder.

3. Select **Properties** and click the **Advanced** button.

4. Disable the **Encrypt contents to secure data** check box and then click the **OK** button twice.

5. Select **Apply changes to this folder, subfolder and files.**

   Click the **OK** button.

12.2 IPSec

Objective:

You must secure IP traffic on your local network. However, before you do this, you must check that the IP traffic is circulating as clear data. In order to do this you must capture frames from a Telnet session. Then, you must enable IP security so as to secure the traffic.

Operations:

1. Install the Network Monitor on the server that will act as the telnet client.

2. On the other server, use the **Services** console in order to start the **Telnet** service.

3. On the server that will act as the telnet client, start-up the Network Monitor in order to capture frames. Then, open a command prompt and enter the command **telnet** *ip_address_of_the_telnet_server*.

4. Select the **confidential** directory and then enter the command **edit secret1.txt**.

5. When the file contents appear on the screen, stop the Network Monitor.

6. Find the frames that have the telnet protocol. In one of these you must see the contents of the secret1.txt file as clear text.

7. On the Telnet client, and on the Telnet server, go into the TCP/IP properties of the local area connection.

8. Click the **Advanced** button.

9. Select the **Options** tab, and then select **IP security**.

10. Click the **Properties** button and select **Use this IP security policy**.

11. In the drop-down list, select **Secure Server (Require)** and then click the **OK** button, four times, in order to close all the dialog boxes.

12. Repeat steps 3 to 5.
Note that the file contents no longer appear as clear text in Network Monitor.

12.3 Account policies

Objective:

In this section you must implement a password and account policy using security templates. Then you will see how to modify user rights.

Password policy

1. Open the **Start** menu and select **Run**.

2. Enter **mmc.exe** in order to create a new console.

3. Add the **Security Templates** snap-in.

4. In the console, right-click **%Systemroot%\Security\ Templates** and then select **New Template**.

5. Under **Template name**, input **accounts policy** and click the **OK** button.

6. Expand your template - **Accounts Policies** - **Password Policy**.

7. Define the following settings:
- **Minimum password length**: 10 characters
- **Enforce password history**: 5 passwords remembered
- **Maximum password age**: 30 days
- **Minimum password age**: 29 days

Account Lockout Policy

1. Select **Account Lockout Policy**.

2. Define the following settings:
- **Account lockout duration**: 0 (an administrator must lockout the account)
- **Account lockout threshold**: 3 invalid logon attempts
- **Reset account lockout counter after**: 2 minutes

Applying the template

1. Close the console. When the system asks you if you want to save your console, answer **Yes**.

2. Go into the **Active Directory Users and Computers** console, right-click the name of your domain, select **Properties** and then activate the **Group Policy** tab.

3. Add a new policy or edit an existing policy.

4. Expand **Computer Configuration - Windows Settings** and right-click **Security Settings**.

5. Select **Import Policy**.

6. Select your policy (accounts policy) and then click the **Open**.

7. Close the **Group Policy** dialog box and the domain properties dialog box.

8. Close the **Active Directory Users and Computers** console.

Testing the template

1. Use the **Active Directory Sites and Services** console so as to synchronize your domain controllers.

2. Go into the **Active Directory Users and Computers** console, and create a new user.

3. Assign the password "secret" and then click **Next** followed by **Finish**.
Were you able to do this?
....

4. Change the password so that it corresponds to the security template (your password must contain at least 10 characters).

5. Close the administrator session and log on again with the account that you have just created (if you are carrying out this operation on a domain controller, make sure that the account has the permission to **Log on locally**).

6. Enter an invalid password, three times.
What happens to this user account?
....

7. In order to unlock the account, log on as the administrator, open the **Active Directory Users and Computers** console, and edit the properties of the account. Select the **Account** tab and disable the **Account is locked out** checkbox.

8. When you have unlocked the account, close the administrator session.

9. Try to log on with the user account twice, with erroneous passwords. Wait two minutes (this is the value that is defined for the **Reset account lockout counter after** setting).

10. Try again to log on with the user account twice, with erroneous passwords. Then on the third attempt, enter the correct password.

11. When you have logged on, change your password, using the shortcut key sequence Ctrl Alt Del.
Were you able to do this?

....

As passwords have a minimum age of 29 days, you should not be able to change your password.

User rights

Objective:

The objective of this section is to assign to a user who is neither a member of the administrator group nor of one of the operator groups, the permission locally to log on to a domain controller so as to change the device drivers.

Operations:

1. Open the **Active Directory Users and Computers** console.

2. Right-click the Domain Controllers container.

3. Select **Properties**.

4. Select the **Group Policy** tab.

5. Add a new policy, or edit an existing policy.

6. Expand **Computer Configuration – Windows Settings – Security Settings – Local Policies** and select **User Rights Assignment**.

7. Double-click the **Log on locally** setting.

8. Click the **Add** button in order to add the user and thus allow the user to log on to the domain controllers.

9. In order to allow this user to change device controllers, double-click the **Load and unload device drivers** setting.

12.4 Analyzing security

1. Create a new console and add the **Security Configuration and Analysis** snap-in.

2. In the console, right-click **Security Configuration and Analysis** and select **Open database**.

3. Enter a **File name** for your database that must store the results of the analysis and then click the **Open** button.

4. Then, select the security template that you want to analyze (for example accounts policy) and then click the **Open** button.

5. In order to start the analysis, right-click **Security Configuration and Analysis** and select **Analyze Computer Now**.

6. Once the analysis is finished, expand each part of the policy in order to check that the value in the **Database Setting** column corresponds to that in the **Computer Setting** column.

7. If you notice any differences, then right-click **Security Configuration and Analysis** and select **Configure Computer Now**.

12.5 Audit policy

Objective:

In this section, you must implement an audit policy that will allow you, to record all unsuccessful logon attempts, to audit certain Active Directory modifications, and to record the deletion of data in the **confidential** directory.

Operations:

1. Open the **Active Directory Users and Computers** console.

2. Right-click the container that represents your domain, and select **Properties**.

3. Select the **Group Policy** tab.

4. Create a new policy or edit an existing policy.

5. Expand **Computer Configuration - Windows Settings - Security Settings - Local Policies - Audit Policy**.

6. Define the following settings:
    - **Audit account logon events**: failed attempts.
    - **Audit object access**: successful and failed attempts.
    - **Audit directory service access**: failed attempts.

7. Close all windows and open Windows Explorer.

8. Right-click the **confidential** folder and select **Properties**.

9. Select the Security tab, and click the Advanced button.

10. Select the Auditing tab and then click the Add button.

11. Add the Everyone group.

12. Enable the Delete permission, in both Allow and Deny columns.

13. Click OK in order to close all the windows.

14. For the **confidential** folder, assign the NTFS permission so that the **Everyone** group will not be allowed any access, except for the administrator and the director, which must have Full Control permissions.

Testing the audit policy

1. Synchronize Active Directory.

2. Log on as the user that you created in the **Testing the template** section.

3. Go into Windows Explorer and right-click the **confidential** folder. Select Delete.

   The system displays a message that indicates that you do not have the necessary permissions in order to delete this folder.

4. Log off.

5. Try to log on as the Director account using an erroneous password. Keep trying with an erroneous password until the account locks out.

6. Log on again with the account that you used when you tried to delete the **confidential** folder.

7. Open the Active Directory Users and Computers console.

8. Try to delete the administrator account.

Consulting the security log

1. Log on as the administrator.

2. Go into the Administrative Tools menu and open the Event Viewer console.

3. Select the Security Log.

   In this log you should find entries for all the actions that you have just carried out (failed logon attempts, failed attempts to delete an account, and failed attempts to delete the **confidential** folder).

13.1 DHCP

Objective:

In this lab you must install the DHCP service on a Windows 2000 server. Then you will see how to authorize the server to attribute IP configurations, and you will also see how to create scopes. Finally, you must check that your server is working correctly by adding a DHCP client.

Operations:

Installing the DHCP service

1. Log on as the administrator.

2. Open the **Control Panel**, and double-click the **Add/Remove Programs** icon.

3. Click the **Add/Remove Windows Components** button.

4. Select **Networking Services** and then click the **Details** button.

5. Enable the **Dynamic Host Configuration Protocol (DHCP)** checkbox and then click the **OK** button, followed by the **Next** button.

Authorizing DHCP

1. Log on as a member of the **Enterprise Admins** group.

2. Go into the **Administrative Tools** menu and open the **DHCP** console.

3. In this console, right-click **DHCP** and then select **Manage authorized servers**.

4. Click the **Authorize** button and enter the name or the IP address of the DHCP server, and click the **OK** button.

5. Click the **Yes** button in order to confirm your entry and then click the **Close** button.

Creating a scope

1. In the **DHCP** console, right-click the name of your server and then select **New Scope**.

2. Click the **Next** button and enter the name of your scope. You can also enter a description for your scope. Then click the **Next** button.

3. Specify the start IP address and the end IP address. For example you can specify 10.0.0.5 and 10.0.1.20 respectively for these addresses.

4. Leave the default class A mask of 255.0.0.0 and then click the **Next** button.

5. Enter any exclusion address or any exclusion address range and then click the **Next**.

6. Leave the scope lease at its default value and then click the **Next** button.

7. Select **No, I will configure these options later** and click the **Next** button.

8. Click the **Finish** button.

9. Activate your scope, expand the **Scope** folder and then right-click the **Scope Options** folder.

10. Select **Configure Options**.

11. Under **Available options**, enable the **006 DNS Servers** checkbox and then, under **String value**, indicate the IP address of the DNS server.

12. Enable the **015 DNS Domain Name** check box, and enter the name of the domain that must be assigned to the client (for example enipub.com).

13. Activate the **033 Static Route Option** and then under **IP address** enter a first address that corresponds to a network address (192.145.1.0 for example), and then, as the second address, enter the interface via which you can reach this network (the IP address of a router that is situated on your subnet, for example 10.0.0.1).

14. Click the **OK** button so as to go back into the **DHCP** console.

Activating the scope

1. Right-click the scope that you want to activate.

2. Click **Activate**.

Configuring a client to use the DHCP server

You must test the automatic IP address attribution on a machine other than the DHCP server.

1. Edit the TCP/IP Properties.

2. Select the **Obtain an IP address automatically** option and the **Obtain DNS server address automatically** option (for Windows 2000 machines).

3. Click the **OK** button.

4. Go into a command prompt and enter the command **ipconfig /all**.

Which IP address did your client obtain? Which mask did your client obtain?

....

....

Which DNS domain name did the system attribute to your client?

....

5. Enter in the command prompt, the command **route print**. Check that there is an entry in the client routing table that specifies a static route leading to the 192.145.1.0 network that you can access by the gateway 10.0.0.1.

13.2 WINS

Objective:

In this section you must install the WINS service on a Windows 2000 server, and then you must use the DHCP server that you installed previously in order that it will specify to its client the address of the WINS server.

Operations:

Installing the WINS service

1. Log on as the administrator.

2. Open the **Control Panel**, and double-click the **Add/Remove Programs** icon.

3. Click the **Add/Remove Windows Components** button.

4. Select **Networking Services** and then click the **Details.** button.

5. Enable the **Windows Internet Name Service (WINS)** check box, and then click the **OK** button, followed by the **Next** button.

6. Click the **Finish** button when the system has finished copying the files.

Configuring clients

Configuring manually

1. Go into the TCP/IP **Properties** on the computers that do not obtain their IP configuration from a DHCP server, and click the **Advanced** button.

2. Enable the **WINS** tab, click the **Add** button and enter the IP address of the WINS server.

☞ *You must carry out this operation on the WINS server, so that it will become its own client. This will allow this server to resolve its own name.*

Configuring automatically via DHCP

1. Go into the **DHCP** console, expand your scope, and right-click the **Scope Options** folder.

2. Select **Configure Options**.

3. Under **Available Options**, enable the **044 WINS/NBNS Servers** checkbox, and indicate the IP address of the WINS server.

4. Select the **046 WINS/NBT Node Type** checkbox, and under Byte, enter **0x8** in order to specify a hybrid node type.

Renewing the configuration

1. On the client that you used previously, enter the command **ipconfig /all**.

2. Identify the node type and the IP address of the WINS server.

3. Enter the command **ipconfig /renew**.

4. Enter the command **ipconfig /all** again, and identify the node type and the IP address of the WINS server.

Consulting the WINS database

1. On the WINS server, go into the **Administrative Tools** menu and open the WINS console.

2. Right-click the **Active Registrations** folder that is situated under the name of your WINS server.

3. Select **Find by Owner**. Select the IP address of your WINS server and then click the **Find Now** button.

   The system then displays the list of registered WINS clients.

Labs relating to Chapter 13

13.3 IIS 5

Objective:

In this section you must install Internet Services on a Windows 2000 server in order to create Web sites and FTP sites.

Operations:

Installing Internet services

1. Log on as the administrator.

2. Go into the **Control Panel**, and double-click the **Add/Remove Programs** icon.

3. Click the **Add/Remove Windows Components** button.

4. Enable the **Internet Information Services (IIS)** checkbox and then click the **Next** button.

5. Click the **Finish** button when the system has finished copying the files.

Creating a Web site

1. Open the **Administrative Tools** menu and open the **Internet Services Manager** console.

2. Right-click the name of your Internet server and then select **New - Web Site**.

3. Enter a description of your site and then click the **Next** button.

4. Indicate the IP address that will be used in order to connect to this site and then click the **Next** button.

5. Click the **Browse** button in order allow the system to help you to find where the files that make up the web site are located. Leave the **Allow anonymous access to this Web site** checkbox in its enabled state, and then click the **Next** button.

6. Leave the permissions by default and then click the **Next** button followed by **Finish**.

7. In the **Internet Information Services** console, right-click the name of your site and then select **Properties**.

8. Select the **Documents** tab and indicate the name of the file that will be displayed when users connect to your site.

9. In order to test the access to your site, go into a browser and enter the URL address http://*ip_address_of_your_ web_site*.

Creating an FTP site

1. Go into the **Internet Information Services** console, right-click the name of your server, and then select **New – FTP Site**.

2. Enter a description of your site and then click the **Next** button.

3. Indicate the IP address that will be used in order to connect to your FTP site. Leave the TCP port set to **21**. Click the **Next** button.

4. Indicate the path that leads to the directory that acts as the root of the FTP site, and then click the **Next** button.

5. Assign the **Read** permission. You can also assign the **Write** permission, if you so desire.

6. Click the **Next** button followed by the **Finish** button.

7. Go into Windows Explorer, and add the documents and the programs that you want to make available to the users who will access your FTP site.

8. Go into the **Internet Information Services** console, and edit the **Properties** of your FTP site.

9. Select the **Messages** tab. Under **Welcome** enter a message that will welcome the users who connect to your FTP site, and under **Exit** enter a message to bid farewell to these users when they disconnect.

10. Activate the **Home Directory** tab, and select **UNIX**.

Accessing the FTP site

1. Using a client machine, open a command prompt and enter **FTP://** *ip_address_of_the_ftp_site*.

2. When the authentication prompt appears, enter **anonymous** without a password.

    The system then displays the welcome message.

3. Enter the **dir** command or the **ls** command.

    Note that you are viewing the documents that you placed on your FTP site.

4. Start up your browser and enter the address **FTP://** *ip_address_of_the_ftp_site*.

    You will now access your FTP site via a graphic interface.

13.4 Remote access

Objective:

In this section, you must configure the remote access service. You will see how to set up the incoming connections and the outgoing connections, and how to define remote access policies.

In order to simulate the long distance connections, you can use a null modem cable so as to link the remote access client to the remote access server. In order to ensure that the traffic is circulating properly on the WAN link, you can disconnect the network cable from the client interface.

Operations:

Installing the null modem cable

1. On the remote access server, and on the remote access client, you must use the **Phone and Modem Options** icon from the **Control Panel**.
   If this is the first time that you have run this program, then you will create a new site.

2. Select the **Modems** tab, and click the **Add** button.

3. Select the **Don't detect my modem; I will select it from a list** checkbox, and click the **Next** button.

4. Under **Manufacturers** select **(Standard Modem Types)** and under **Models**, select **Communications cable between two computers**, and then click the **Next** button.

5. Indicate the port to which you have connected your cable, and click the **Next** button, followed by **Finish**.

Configuring the remote access server

1. Using a domain member server, or a domain controller, log on as the administrator, go into the **Administrative Tools** menu and open the **Routing and Remote Access** console.

2. If you have already used this console in order to activate the routing, then right-click the name of your server and select **Properties**.

3. Under the **General** tab, enable the **Remote access server** checkbox, and click the **OK** button.

4. Then, click the **Yes** button in order to restart the service.

5. If you are using this console for the first time, then you must activate the Routing and Remote Access service. In order to do this, right-click your server, and then select **Configure and Enable Routing and Remote Access**.

6. Click the **Next** button and select **Remote access server**. Then click the **Next** button.

7. Indicate whether or not you want to add new protocols that are not listed and then click the **Next** button.

8. Select **From a specified range of addresses** and then click the **Next** button.

9. Click the **New** button and enter an address range that your server will use in order to communicate with the remote access clients. For example, you can enter 193.156.1.15 to 193.156.1.60. Then click the **OK** button, followed by the **Next** button

10. Select **No, I don't want to set up this server to use RADIUS now** and then click the **Next** button, followed by the **Finish** button.

Configuring remote access clients

1. On the remote access client, right-click **My Network Places** and select **Properties**.

2. Double click the **Make New Connection** icon, and then click the **Next** button.

3. Select **Connect directly to another computer** and then click the **Next** button.

4. Select **Guest** and then click the **Next** button.

5. Indicate the device with which your client is connected and then click the **Next** button.

6. Select **For all users** and then click the **Next** button.

7. Click the **Finish** button.

8. Try to connect as the administrator.
    Are you able to do this? Why?
    ....

Configuring a remote access policy

1. On the remote access server, open the **Routing and Remote Access** console.

2. Select the **Remote Access Policies** folder.

3. Double-click the policy that is called **Allow access if dial-in permission is enabled** so as to modify this policy.

4. Double-click the **Day-and-Time-Restriction** condition.

5. Check that users will have round-the-clock remote access, seven days a week.

6. Under **If a user matches the conditions**, select **Grant remote access permission** and then click the **OK** button.

7. Open the **Active Directory Users and Computers** console. Edit the **Properties** of a user account that you will use in order to try to connect.

8. Select the **Dial-in** tab, and enable **Control access through Remote Access Policy**, and then click the **OK** button.

9. From the remote access client, try to connect with the user account above, using the outgoing connection that you created above.

   Note that you are able to do this, because, on the one hand you conform to the conditions (in this case, the schedule), and on the other hand, you have specified that the user level permissions must refer to the permissions that you have defined in the policy.

10. Go back into the remote access policy and apply the **Deny remote access permission** option.

11. Try again to connect with a user account that has the **Control access through Remote Access Policy** permission.

    Note that you are unable to connect.

12. Without changing the policy, go into the properties of a user, select the **Dial-in** tab and enable the **Allow access** permission.

    Note that you are able to connect.

13. Go into the remote access policy and click the **Edit Profile** button.

14. Enable the **Disconnect if idle for** checkbox and enter **1 min**.

15. Click the **OK** twice in order to confirm your entry.

16. From the client machine, connect to the remote access server and wait 1 minute without doing anything on this computer.

    Note that you are automatically disconnected.

13.5 Virtual private network

Objective:

In this section, you must create VPN connections, using the remote access service that you have just configured.

Operations:

1. You have configured your server as a remote access server. You server is also acting as a VPN server. In order to verify this, open the **Routing and Remote Access** and select the **Ports** folder.

   Note that you have 10 VPN ports by default (5 ports for PPTP, and 5 ports for L2TP).

2. On your client machine, select **Start – Settings – Network and Dial-up Connections – Make New Connection**.

3. Click the **Next** button, select **Connect to a private network through the Internet** and click the **Next** button.

4. Enter the IP address of the destination (this is the IP address of the remote network interface card, and not the IP address of the PPP connection). Then click the **Next** button.

5. In order to share your connection with other users who connect to your machine, select **For all users**. Then click the **Next** button.

6. So that other computers that are located on your local area network will be able to use your VPN in order to access remote resources, you must select the **Enable Internet Connection Sharing for this connection**. If you select the **Enable on-demand dialing** checkbox, then the physical link will be set up as soon as a user uses your VPN. Click the **Next** button.

7. Enter a name for your VPN and then click the **Finish** button.

The objective of this lab is to install **Terminal Services** in application server mode. When you have installed Terminal Services, you must configure the connections and the user settings. You must install Office 97 in such a way that it can be used in a multiple user environment. You must also install the Terminal Services Client. Finally you will see how to convert your Terminal Server from application server mode to remote administration mode.

Try to carry out these operations by reading only the sections of this book that deal with the exercises concerned. However, if you have difficulty, you can consult the operation descriptions that are set out below.

14.1 Installing Terminal Services

Objective:

You must install Terminal Services in applications server mode.

Operations:

1. Select **Control Panel - Add/Remove Programs**, and click the **Add/Remove Windows Components** button.

2. In the **Windows Components Wizard**, enable the **Terminal Services** checkbox, and then click the **Next** button.

3. Select the **Application server mode** option, and then click **Next**.

4. Restart the server when the system asks you to do so.

14.2 Installing Office 97

Objective:

You must install Office 97 in such a way that all the users will be able to access Word simultaneously.

Operations:

1. Check that no users are currently logged on using Terminal Services. For this purpose, you must use the **Terminal Service Manager** console.

2. In order to install Office 97, go into **Control Panel** and activate the **Add/Remove Programs** icon.

3. When the installation has finished, close **Add/Remove Programs** window, and then open a command prompt.

4. Go to the path %systemroot%\Application Compatibility Scripts\Install, and then enter **office97.cmd**.

5. The Notepad utility runs and asks you to enter a drive letter followed by a ":" (for example P :). The system will associate this drive letter with the home directory of each user. Terminal Services must not already use this drive letter.

6. Close the Notepad in order to allow the system to continue applying the script.

14.3 Configuring connections

Objective:

In this section, you must configure the RDP connection, such that the system will disconnect all the users that have been idle for 10 minutes, and such that the administrator can monitor and remotely take control without warning the users.

Operations:

1. Go into the **Administrative Tools** menu, and open the **Terminal Services Configuration** console.

2. Double-click the name of your connection (by default this is RDP-Tcp).

3. In order to set to 10 minutes the idle time that the system will allow before it disconnects the user, select the **Sessions** tab.

4. Enable the first **Override user settings** check box, so that all the users who use this connection will be subject to the same rules.

5. In the **Idle session limit** drop-down list, select 10 minutes.

6. Enable the second **Override user settings** check box (under **Idle session limit**) and select the **Disconnect from session** option. This will mean that when the session limit is reached, then the users will not lose their current data.

7. Select the **Remote Control** tab.

8. Select **Use remote control with the following settings** and then disable the **Require user's permission** check box.

9. Under **Level of control**, select **Interact with the session**.

10. Click the **OK** button, so as to confirm the set up of your connection.

Configuring client settings

Objective:

Of the 20 users that Terminal Services will support, only two of them must have access to the Windows 2000 Terminal Server desktop. When the remaining 18 users connect to Terminal Services, they must have access only to Word.exe.

Operations:

1. Open either the **Active Directory Users and Computers** console, or the **Computer Management** console, according to whether your machine is a domain controller or not.
2. In the properties of the 18 user accounts that must use only Word, select the **Environment** tab.
3. Enable the **Start the following program at logon** checkbox.
4. Under **Program file name**, enter the path that leads to the Word.exe application.

14.4 Installing Terminal Services Client

Objective:

The objective of this section is to install the Terminal Services Client software, on the client machines.

Operations:

Via the network:

1. On the Terminal Server, open Windows Explorer.
2. Expand %systemroot%\system32\clients.
3. Share the **tsclient** subfolder.
4. On the client machine, connect to the **tsclient** directory that is situated on the Terminal Server.
5. Then access the **net** directory, followed by either the **win16** subfolder, or the **win32** subfolder, according to the type of platform on which you installed your client.
6. Run the **setup.exe** program.
7. Follow the instructions.

Using diskettes:

1. On the Terminal Server, go into the **Administrative Tools** menu, and open the **Terminal Services Client Creator** console.

2. In the list under **Network client or service**, select the platform of the client concerned (Intel 16 or 32 bits).

3. Insert the first formatted diskette into the floppy-disk drive, and then click the **OK** button.

4. When you have created all the diskettes, then you can use them in order to install the client machines.

14.5 Switching from application server mode to remote administration mode

Objective:

You have installed Terminal Services because some of your computers cannot support Windows 2000. However, after you have upgraded the computers in your network, you note that no one is using Terminal Services. Nevertheless, you still wish to use these services so that you can remotely administer your servers.

Operations:

1. Go into the **Administrative Tools** menu, and open the **Terminal Services Configuration** console.

2. Select the **Server Settings** folder and double-click the **Terminal server mode** setting.

3. Click the **Add/Remove Programs** link.

4. In the **Windows Components Windows**, click the **Next** button.

5. Select **Remote administration mode** and then click **Next**.

6. Restart the server when the system asks you to do so.

The objective of this lab is to use the Backup utility in order to backup and to restore data and Active Directory objects. The, you must install the **Recovery** console, and finally you must analyze a few counters using the Performance Monitor. Try to carry out these operations by reading only the sections of this book that deal with the exercises concerned. However, if you have difficulty, you can consult the operation descriptions that are set out below.

15.1 Backing up data

Objective:

The objective of this section is to use the Backup utility in order to schedule data backup.

Operations:

1. Go into the **Start - Programs - Accessories - System Tools** menu, and then select **Backup**.

2. Click the **Schedule Jobs** tab.

3. Click the **Add Job** button.

4. Then, click the **Next** button.

5. Select **Back up selected files, drives, or network data**, so as to specify the data that you want to back up.

6. Then, select the data that you want to back up, and click the **Next** button.

7. Indicate the media type that you want to use for the backup, along with the name of the backup file.

8. Then, select the backup type and click the **Next** button.

9. Enable the **Verify data after backup** checkbox, and click the **Next** button.

10. Indicate whether you want to append your backup to your media, or whether you want to replace any data that may have already been backed up to this media. Then, click the **Next** button.

11. Enter a name for the backup set, and click the **Next** button.

12. Indicate the user account that you wish to use for the back up process.

13. Enable the Later option, and under **Schedule entry**, click the **Set Schedule** button so as to specify the backup frequency.

14. In the **Job name** text box, enter a name for your job, and then click the **Next** button.

15. Click the **Finish** button.

15.2 Restoring data

Objective:

In this section, you must restore the data that you have just backed-up.

Operations:

1. Start the **Backup** utility.

2. Click the **Restore** tab.

3. Select the file(s) that you want to restore.

4. Under **Restore files to**, indicate the location to which you want to restore your files.

5. Click the **Start Restore** button.

6. Click the **OK** button.

15.3 Backing up the system state

Objective:

The objective of this section is to backup the directory database, the registry, the SYSVOL folder, the startup files and the COM+ Class Registration database.

Operations:

1. Run the **Backup** utility.

2. Select the **Backup** tab.

3. Enable the **System State** checkbox.

4. Under **Backup media or file name**, enter *media_drive_letter:\system.bkf*.

   Click the **Start Backup** button, and then click the **Start Backup** button in the **Backup Job Information** dialog box.

15.4 Restoring an object to the Active Directory

Objective:

In this section, you must simulate the loss of an object in the Active Directory by deleting the object concerned. Then, you must restore this object using the system state backup that you made previously.

Operations:

1. Open the **Active Directory Users and Computers** console.
2. Delete a user account.
3. Restart the domain controller.
4. During the restart, press the ⌨F8 key, when the system prompts you to do so.
5. In the menu, select **Directory Services Restore Mode (Windows 2000 domain controllers only)**.
6. Log on as the administrator, with the password that you entered when you installed Active Directory.
7. Run the **Backup** program.
8. Click the **Restore** tab.
9. Select your system state backup, and then click the **Start Restore** button.
10. When the restore has finished, close the Restore utility and open a command prompt.
11. Enter ntdsutil.exe, and when the prompt returns, enter authoritative restore.

    Then, enter restore subtree *full_object_name*.
12. Quit **ntdsutil** by entering the **Quit** command, twice.

15.5 Installing the recovery console

Objective:

The objective of this section is to install the recovery console, so that you can use it to boot your computer, and thereby rapidly to solve any startup problem that you may have.

Operations:

1. Open a command prompt.
2. Go to the **I386** directory of the Windows 2000 CDROM.
3. Enter the command **winnt32 /cmdcons**.
4. Click the **Yes** button.
5. Restart the computer.
6. In the startup menu, select the **Microsoft Windows 2000 Recovery Console** option.
7. Choose the installation onto which you want to log. If you have only one Windows 2000 installation, then press **1**.
8. Enter the administrator's password.
9. You are now in recovery console mode. In this mode, you can solve any problems that are preventing you from starting your system correctly. Enter the **Help** command in order to display the list of available commands.

15.6 Using the Performance utility

Objective:

In this section you must use the Performance utility.

Creating a real-time graph with activity generation

Creating a graph

1. Go into the **Administrative Tools** menu and select the Performance utility.
2. Click the icon that shows a plus sign.
3. Select **All counters** and then click the **Add** button, followed by the **Close** button.

Generating activities

1. Agitate the mouse for a few seconds, and watch the graph.

2. Go into Windows Explorer, start up a number of applications, and then observe the effects in the Performance utility.

3. Under the real-time graph, select **% Processor Time** and press the shortcut key Ctrl+H so as to superimpose the development of this counter on your graph.

4. Minimize the Performance utility.

5. Start up Windows Explorer, and the **Active Directory Users and Computers** console.

6. Go back into the Performance utility and observe the effect of this action.

Recording the activity in a log and using this information

1. Go into the Performance utility, expand **Console Root – Performance Logs and Alerts**, right-click **Counter Logs** and select **New Log Settings**.

2. Enter a name for your log file and then click the **OK** button.

3. Click the **Add** button, so that you can add counters.

4. Select the counters that you want to add, click the **Add** button after each of them, and then click the **Close** button.

5. Define a sampling interval.

6. Select the **Log Files** tab in order to set up the log (for example you can specify the size of this log).

7. Select the **Schedule** tab in order to specify when the log must start. Click the **OK** button, so as to return to the main window of the **Performance** utility.

8. In order to analyze the results, go back into graphic mode by clicking **System Monitor**.

9. Right-click the graph and select **Properties**. Select the **Source** tab, and specify the log file path. Then, define a Time Range for your log file.

Alert mode

1. In the Performance utility, right-click **Alerts**.

2. Select **New Alert Settings**.

3. Enter a name for this alert.

4. Add the counters that you wish to monitor, and for each of them, define the value that must trigger the alert.

5. Select the **Action** tab and the actions that the system must carry out when the alert is triggered.

6. Select the **Schedule** tab, and specify how and when the scan must be started, and how and when the scan must be stopped.

7. Click the **OK** button in order to complete the operation.

Labs relating to Chapter 15

16.1 Upgrading from Windows NT 4 to Windows 2000

The objective of this lab is to upgrade a Windows NT 4, Primary Domain Controller (PDC) to a Windows 2000 domain controller. On the Windows NT PDC, you must create user accounts, computers and groups in the SAM database, in order to see how the migration takes place.

Operations:

1. On your Windows NT 4, PDC, go into the **User Manager for Domains** and create user accounts, and local and global groups.

2. Go into the **Server Manager**, and add workstations and domain controllers.

3. Insert the Windows 2000 Advanced Server CDROM. When the system displays a message asking if you want to upgrade to Windows 2000. Click the **Yes** button.

4. Select **Upgrade to Windows 2000 (Recommended)** and then click the **Next** button.

5. Accept the terms of the License Agreement and click the **Next** button.

6. Note any information that is supplied by the system accounting report and then click the **Next** button.
   ....
   ....

7. The installation program then copies necessary files and restarts your computer so as to continue the upgrade.

8. When the upgrade operation is finished, Windows 2000 restarts. Log on as the administrator and start installing Active Directory.

9. In the Active Directory installation Wizard, click the **Next** button.

10. Select **Create a new domain tree**, and then click the **Next** button.

11. Select **No, I will install and configure DNS myself** and then click the **Next** button.

12. Enter a DNS name for your domain, and click the **Next** button.

13. Indicate the location of the database and the location of the log, and click the **Next** button.

14. Indicate the location of your shared system folder and then click the **Next** button.

15. Select **Permissions compatible only with Windows 2000 servers** and then click the **Next** button.

16. Indicate a password for the administrator account that the system will use when you start the computer in Directory Services Restore Mode, and then click the **Next** button.

17. Click the **Next** button in order to allow the system to start installing Active Directory.

Checking the upgrade

1. Open the **Active Directory Users and Computers** console.

2. Select **Domain Controller** folder, and check the presence of the computer accounts that you created for the domain controllers.

3. Select the **Computers** folder, and check the presence of all the computer accounts of your workstations.

4. Select the **Users** folder, and check the presence of your local and global groups, and also that of your user accounts.

Objectives of exam 70-215 Microsoft® Windows 2000 Server	Chapter	Pages	Labs	Pages
Installing Windows 2000 Server				
Perform an attended installation of Windows 2000 Server	II - B	24	2.3 and 2.4	618
Perform an unattended installation of Windows 2000 Server:				
Create unattended installation files by using Setup Manager to automate the installation of Windows 2000 Server	II - B - 6 b	34	2.5	620
Create and configure automated methods for installation of Windows 2000	II - B - 7	40	2.6	621
Upgrade a server from Microsoft Windows NT4.0	XVI - D	604	16.1	698
Deploy service packs	VII - F - 2	235	7.2	644
Troubleshoot failed installations	II - B - 9	44	2.1 to 2.6	615
Installing, Configuring and Troubleshooting Access to resources				
Install and configure network services for interoperability	VI	171	6.1 to 6.5	636
	XIII	447	13.1 to 13.5	678
	V	135	5.1 to 5.2	633
Monitor, configure, troubleshoot, and control access to printers	IX	291	9.1	654
Monitor, configure, troubleshoot, and control access to files, folders, and shared folders:				
a stand-alone DFS	X - D - b	353	10.4	662
a domain-based DFS	X - D - c	355	10.4	662
local security on files and folders	X - C	343	10.2	659
access to files and folders in a share	X - B	331	10.1	657
access to files and folders via WEB Services	XIII - C	483	13.3	682
Monitor, configure, troubleshoot and control access via Web sites	XIII - C	483	13.3	682
Configuring and Troubleshooting Hardware Devices and Drivers				
Configure hardware devices	III - B -1 to B - 4	63	3.3	623
	B - 6 to 7	68	3.9	629
	B - 10 to B - 14	79	9.1	654
	IX - B	291		
Configure driver signing options	III - B - 8b	69	3.2	623
Update device drivers	III	57	3.1 to 3.9	622

Objectives of exam Microsoft® Windows 2000 Server	Chapter	Pages	Labs	Pages
Troubleshoot problems with hardware	III - B -13 XV - C 1 XV - C - 3 XV - C - 4 XV - C - 5 XV - C - 6 XV - C - 7	81 570 573 573 574 574 575	3.4 15.5	625 695
Managing, Monitoring and Optimizing System Performance, Reliability and Availability				
Monitor and optimize usage of system resources	III - B - 8c XV - C - 9 XV - D XV - E	72 579 581 587	3.6 15.6	626 695
Manage processes, set priorities and start and stop processes	XV - C - 8	577	3.5	625
Optimize disk performance	XI - B	383	11.1 and 11.2	668
Manage and optimize availability of system state data and user data	XI - C	390	11.2	668
Recover systems and user data:				
Recover systems and user data by using Windows Backup	XV - A to B	563	15.1 to 15.4	692
Troubleshoot system restoration by using Safe Mode	XV - C - 6	574	15.4	694
Recover systems and user data by using the Recovery Console	XV - C - 7	575	15.5	695
Managing, Configuring and Troubleshooting Storage Use				
Configure and manage user profiles	VIII - B - 3a	274	8.3 and 8.4	650
Monitor, configure and troubleshoot disks and volumes	XI	377	11.1 and 11.2	668
Configure data compression	X - F	364	10.5	665
Monitor and configure disk quotas	X - E	360	10.6	666
Recover from disk failures	XI - C - 5 XI - C - 7b	395 399	11.2	668
Configuring and Troubleshooting Windows 2000 Network Connections				
Install, configure and troubleshoot shared access	XIII - D - 2b	502	13.5	687
Install, configure and troubleshoot a virtual private network (VPN)	XIII - D - 2b	503	13.5	687
Install, configure and troubleshoot network protocols	III - C to H	85	3.7 and 3.8	627
Install and configure network services	XIII	447	13.1 to 13.5	678
Configure, monitor and troubleshoot remote access:				
Configure inbound connections	XIII - D - 2a	496	13.4	684
Create a remote access policy	XIII - D - 5	511	13.4	684
Configure a remote access profile	XIII - D - 5c	515	13.4	684

Objectives of exam 70-215

Objectives of exam Microsoft® Windows 2000 Server	Chapter	Pages	Labs	Pages
Install, configure, monitor and troubleshoot Terminal Services				
Remotely administer servers by using Terminal Services	XIV - F	553	14.5	691
Configure Terminal Services for application sharing	XIV - A to E	534	14.1 to 14.4	688
Configure applications for use with Terminal Services	XIV - C	543	14.2	688
Configure the properties of a connection	XIV - D	545	14.3	689
Install, configure, and troubleshoot network adapters and drivers	III - B - 14	82	3.7 to 3.9	627
Troubleshooting Windows 2000 network connections	III - B - 13 III - D - 2 to D - 5 III - E	81 90 102	3.9 3.7 3.8	629 627 628
Implementing, Monitoring and Troubleshooting Security				
Encrypt data on a hard disk by using Encrypting File System (EFS)	XII - A	413	12.1	671
Security IP Sec	XII - B	417	12.2	672
Implement, configure, manage and troubleshoot policies in a Windows 2000 environment				
Implement, configure, manage and troubleshoot Local Policy in a Windows 2000 environment	XII - E and F	436	12.3	673
Implement, configure, manage and troubleshoot System Policy in a Windows 2000 environment	XII - C	422	12.3	673
Implement, configure, manage and troubleshoot auditing	XII - D	429	12.5	676
Implement, configure, manage and troubleshoot local accounts	VIII - A - 1	248	8.1 to 8.5	647
Implement, configure, manage and troubleshoot Account Policy	XII - E	436	12.3	673
Implement, configure, manage and troubleshoot security by using the Security Configuration Tool Set	XII - G	437	12.4	676

Index

Index

Index

Multitasking
  co-operative, 8
  pre-emptive, 8
Multithreading, 9
My Computer, 23, 40

Native mode, 185, 514
  changing from mixed mode, 606
NBNS (NetBIOS name server), 472
NCP (Network Control Protocol), 506
NDIS 5.0, 85
NET, 142
Net send command, 420
Net use command, 473
Net view command, 473
NetBEUI (NetBIOS Extended User Interface),
85, 105, 460, 493, 582
NetBIOS, 26, 94, 138
NETLOGON directory, 606
Netscape Communicator, 544
Netscape Navigator, 544
Netware connections, 297
Network
  domain models, 601, 603
  planning the logical structure, 600
  planning the physical structure, 603
Network and dial-up connections, 496
Network Connection Wizard, 502
Network group, 256
Network interface cards, 82, 91
Network monitor, 16, 419, 464
Network Neighborhood, 458, 474
Network printer
  connecting via the Web, 298
Networking Connection Wizard, 12
NFS (Network File System), 137
NIC (Network Information Center), 90
NNTP servers, 455
Novell network, 103
Nslookup, 158
NTBOOTDD.SYS, 394
Ntdetect.com, 60, 394, 572
NTDS.DIT, 175
Ntdsutil, 569
NTFS, 25, 29, 178, 279, 329, 343, 364,
380, 382, 399, 400, 403, 487, 535, 563,
571, 575
NTFS file systems, 25
NTLDR, 24, 394, 571
NTLM protocol, 13, 607

NTP Network time protocol, 171
Ntuser.dat, 274, 278
Ntuser.man, 278
NWlink, 102, 103
Nwlink IPX/SPX/Netbios, 85, 460, 494

Oemsetup.inf, 460
Oemtcpip.inf, 460
OnNow/ACPI technology, 10
Open View, 139
Operations masters, 186
Optimizing bindings, 105
Options classes, 467
ORG, 142
OS/2, 85
OSI model, 136, 139
OSPF, 99
OU (Organizational Unit), 172, 173, 219,
221, 266, 604
Outgoing connections, 502
Outlook, 544

Package, 231
Page Faults/sec, 588
Pages/sec, 588
Paging file, 73
PAP (Password Authentication Protocol),
507
Partition
  boot, 24
  extended, 378, 381
  primary, 378
  system, 24
Password policy
  enforce password history, 427
  password age, 427, 428
PCI (Peripheral Component Interconnect),
64
PCL mode, 307
Peer-to-peer network, 27
Performance utility (counters, graphs), 581,
582
Performances console, 581
Permission
  advanced, 346
  file, 345
  folder, 344

S